LIMITS

A
SEARCH
FOR NEW
VALUES

LIMITS

A
SEARCH
FOR NEW
VALUES

$\longleftarrow \underline{\hspace{3cm}} \quad \underline{\hspace{3cm}} \longrightarrow$

MAXINE SCHNALL

CLARKSON N. POTTER, Inc./Publishers
New York
Distributed by Crown Publishers, Inc.

BOOKS BY MAXINE SCHNALL

My Husband, the Doctor
The Broadbelters
The Wives Self-Help Program

Printed in the United States of America

Published simultaneously in Canada by
General Publishing Company Limited

Library of Congress Cataloging in Publication Data

Schnall, Maxine.
    Limits: A search for new values

    Includes index.
    1. Social values.   2. Social control.   3. United
States—Social conditions.   4. United States—Moral
conditions.   I. Title.
HM216.S278 1981   303.3′72   80-25709
ISBN: 0-517-541432

10 9 8 7 6 5 4 3 2 1

First Edition

TO GAIL SAHL
Friendship is love without his wings.
LORD BYRON

CONTENTS

CONTENTS

FOUR: FINDING OUR WAY

PROLOGUE

The idea for this book took shape gradually during the latter half of the Seventies, the so-called Me Decade, when I found myself leading a life I never would have envisioned in the Square Fifties. Like millions of others in the over-thirty-five generation, I had grown up in the grip of traditional values incorporated from my parents and the "establishment"—and I had rejected them. I had, in fact, fashioned a career out of my apostasy by founding a hotline and counseling agency for victims of postliberation culture shock (Wives Self-Help) and by becoming an interpreter and advocate for cultural change in my magazine articles and daily radio broadcasts.

Yet, as much as I reveled in the exercise of my new independence and authority, I was troubled by a feeling of alienation. I sensed that in the renunciation of past traditions, we had, as a society, plunged ourselves into a "values vacuum." We had left ourselves without a coherent system of beliefs to guide the decisions each of us must make in our daily lives—decisions about relationships, sexual behavior, marriage, divorce, lifestyles, education, job or career goals, having and rearing children.

This predicament, I discovered, was not confined to my generation alone. Many in the younger generation, who came of age after the social upheavals of the Sixties and were thus spared the constrictiveness of my upbringing, confided that they were no more at ease in the "values vacuum" than I was. The problem, I began to realize, was not a matter of adaptation to freedom but the illusory nature of freedom when there are no *limits*—no guideposts to help us define the parameters of desirable behavior.

Originally, I had intended to focus on the individual's search for limits in a confusing and hazardous world. But the more I delved into the problem, the more apparent it became that I could not separate the individual from the broader context of our cultural life cycle. As I talked to psychiatrists, psychologists, sociologists, educators, and other specialists; studied the works of Erik Erikson, Erich Fromm, David Riesman, Herbert Hendin, Christopher Lasch, and other leading psychosocial historians; and became deeply immersed in the lives of the subjects I had singled out as representatives of the different generations, I realized with excitement that I was onto a much bigger story.

It occurred to me that by emphasizing the self as the center of each person's psychological universe, popular psychologies have fostered the impression that each of us can overcome our anxieties and conflicts through our inner powers alone. What psychologists have overlooked is the social reality of our existence. The developing ego in each of us is surrounded throughout life by an ever-changing set of environmental conditions—cultural, economic, political, and social—that may influence our lives even more profoundly than genetic factors or the experiences of early childhood.

Although much has been written about the psychological stages of development all of us go through as human beings, scant attention has been paid to the stages of the *cultural* life cycle that have such a crucial bearing on our lives. Having not been made aware of how our personal problems—and their solutions—are intimately related to the forces at work in the larger culture, many of us today are overwhelmed by feelings of sorrow and hopelessness. That is why I have written this book. In *Limits* I have traced the patterns of our cultural life cycle as we have shaped it and been shaped by it over the past five decades, and, surprisingly, I find cause for reassurance rather than despair. Despite the terrifying uncertainty of our age, we are not a social order in decline but one that may be moving *upward*.

The shifts that have occurred in the formation of the American social character throughout these last five decades indicate to me that we are progressing slowly, painfully, but perhaps inexorably, toward a higher and more personally fulfilling stage of social and moral growth. While each generation has been thrown considerably off course by the deprivations or excesses of the previous one, we are nonetheless evolving into a society in which choice rather than compliance is the predominant way of life. But in the absence of a supportive public value system—boundaries to help people build a stable inner structure of life goals and standards of behavior—the movement toward self-direction bogged down in the Seventies in alienated self-preoccupation or cultural narcissism.

Now we have entered the Eighties with our vital resources depleted, our economy exhausted, our environment polluted, our government stretched beyond its means. Historians have already named this decade the Age of Limits, conjuring up visions of gasoline rationing, fuel shortages, unending inflation, cutbacks, layoffs, and the end of the American Dream. We are being told that we must set limits on our greed and competitiveness or face disaster. But that is like trying to plug the dike after the deluge. As this book shows, without a fundamental change in our internal value system and a restructuring of our institutions to support this change, our greed and envy will remain uncontrollable—and our goal of personal fulfillment forever elusive. On the other hand, if we can create a system of transcending values—purposes or aims in life that transcend ordinary self-interest— then the need for economic survival will unite rather than destroy us. And the Age of Limits may well become a more expansive time for all of us: the "Concerned Eighties."

The purpose of this book, therefore, is to help us learn not simply how to cope with our culture but how to control it. In *Limits* I try to show how the deep, unconscious roots of our greed and envy, along with our basic distrust of the self, have been exacerbated by cultural trends from one generation to the next, from the Thirties until today. By understanding how we have all been victimized by certain very powerful, very persuasive cultural myths, we can begin to replace these myths with new values that are more consistent with our goal of personal fulfillment.

With this end in mind, I present some broad new concepts for redefining love, work, and morality in our society. I also show the struggles, by turns sad, funny, touching, mystifying, shocking, heroic, that real people (only their names and identifying details have been changed) have gone through as the cultural life cycle has meshed with their lives. I tell my own story, too, only to share with the reader my personal struggle to reclaim the self from cultural conformity and to *live*, not merely survive, according to limits that are uniquely and genuinely one's own.

As much as I have tried to be original in my insights and interpretations of fact and theory, I could not have written this book without the help of many talented experts who generously shared their knowledge, time, and concern. I acknowledge their contribution here with deepest gratitude: Herbert M. Adler, M.D., clinical professor of psychiatry and family medicine at Jefferson Medical College in Philadelphia; Ann Beuf, Ph.D., director of women's studies at the University of Pennsylvania; Selma Kramer, M.D., professor and head of the Child Psychiatry Department at Medical College of Pennsylvania; Joan Enoch, M.D., psychiatrist, Paoli Psychiatric Associates; Harold Graff, M.D., clinical professor of psychiatry and human behavior, Thomas Jefferson University and chief of psychiatry at St. Francis Hospital, Wilmington, Delaware; Donald Kaplan, Ph.D., psychoanalyst, New York City and associate clinical professor of psychology at New York University; Deborah Shain, MSS, ACSW, director of Jewish family life education, Jewish Family Service of Philadelphia; Sydney Pulver, M.D., psychoanalyst in private practice in Philadelphia; Geraldine Spark, clinical assistant professor, Department of Psychiatry, Thomas Jefferson University and former associate director of the Family Therapy Department at Eastern Pennsylvania Psychiatric Institute; William A. Sadler, Jr., Ph.D., professor of sociology at Bloomfield College, New Jersey.

I am also profoundly grateful to the people, including my mother, who poured out their stories to me and gave me access to the interior of their private world, making *Limits* come alive with the searing and undeniable reality of their words and experiences.

I offer a special word of thanks to my agent, Meredith Bernstein, for her unflagging confidence and compassion, and to my editor, Carol Southern, who added immeasurably to the book with her gift for clarity and insistence on integrity of thought.

And finally, to my daughters Ilene Schnall and Rona Schnall, I extend appreciation beyond words—not only for their forbearance and sensitivity but also for their helpful perceptions that put me in touch with the outlook of the current generation.

In the end, I have come to view this book as one that I have lived rather than written. My only hope is that it will enlarge the reader as much as it has enlarged my own mind and heart in its creation.

MAXINE SCHNALL
Cheltenham, Pennsylvania
November 1980

ONE

THE
CULTURAL
PENDULUM

$\longleftarrow$ ————————— $\longrightarrow$

*This freedom should not be seen as a metaphysical
power of human "nature," nor as the right
to do whatever one pleases. . . . We do not do what we
want and yet we are responsible for what we
are—that is the fact.*

JEAN-PAUL SARTRE

THE GENERATIONAL VIRUS

Where did we go wrong? I hear that question from everyone these days, as if we are all victims of a massive shipwreck. Awash in the debris of our cultural values, the survivors struggle to keep from drowning in a limitless sea of options.

Desperately lonely people in bars and discos search hungrily for intimacy and find only another dreary one-night connection. Joyless pleasure-seekers and self-improvers obsessively take courses, quaaludes, cocaine, est, Life Spring, silicone injections, and trips to Club Med in a vain attempt to dispel their inner emptiness. Parents anguish over model children, honor students, who have vanished into cults and are panhandling in the streets. Sexually liberated career women, disgusted with the fragility of commitment, lie alone night after night rather than risk another abortive affair. Husbands who have moved out of spacious suburban homes are living a rootless existence in tiny one-bedroom apartments while the middle-aged women they have left behind are running households by themselves, working full-time, and going to school at night to stay off the welfare rolls. Anxiety-ridden students who grew up in a culture that shattered their ideals but not their aspirations are hiding out in graduate schools, afraid they'll find no place in an uninviting world. And psychiatrists are sounding a cry of alarm over the increasing number of nine- and ten-year-olds they see who are so depressed that they want to die.

In sadness, if not in judgment, the older generation surveys the chaotic, alienated lifestyle of their children and grandchildren and asks with injured perplexity: "Why is it that we had nothing and we were happy, and they have everything and they're miserable?"

How happy *they* really were does not concern us for the moment. What we want to know now is, where did *we* go wrong? The question hounds us at every turn. We didn't go wrong, we insist. Quickly we marshal all the reassuring bromides we keep for our darkest moments. The old order was too repressive—it crippled autonomy and fulfillment. Transitional times are always painful, but pain is an opportunity for growth. Loneliness and isolation are no worse than the suffocating trap we were in before.

It's clear that we were headed in the right direction, but we didn't know when to stop. We didn't know *how* to stop. Somewhere past the straits of Victorianism on our way to the brave new world, we went out of control. We disregarded the navigator in our heads yelling "No! Don't! You can't!" because some of us were sick of hearing those words all our lives, and the rest of us, having never heard them, didn't know what they meant. So we crashed through the boundaries of freedom and sailed into chaos.

The crash had been coming for a long time. As our quest for personal and sexual freedom gathered momentum in the Sixties, it set us on a blind collision course between rising permissiveness and collapsing values. Our biggest mistake, other than our gross misapplication of Freudian concepts, was in thinking of human freedom as a thing apart from our connectedness to a world order. In our headlong rush to free ourselves from all traditional bonds, we overlooked the vital link pointed out by Erich Fromm between "freedom from" and "freedom to." Separation from our primary ties gives each of us the *freedom to* develop and express our own individual self, but at the same time there is the danger of becoming *free from* a world that gave us security and reassurance.

In a competitive society like ours, where the individual self has been a mere blip on the curve of a marketing graph, the lag between the process of establishing a separate identity and the lack of opportunities to invest this separate identity satisfiably in love and work can make freedom an intolerable burden. To save ourselves from total isolation, we need to cherish our connectedness with others. There is only so far we can go flying out in space with no supports.

Our relatedness to social patterns, values, or symbols is the safety catch that prevents a feeling of utter *moral aloneness* that can lead, at its worst, to mental disintegration, just as physical starvation leads to death. Says Fromm: "*The limits* of the growth of individuation

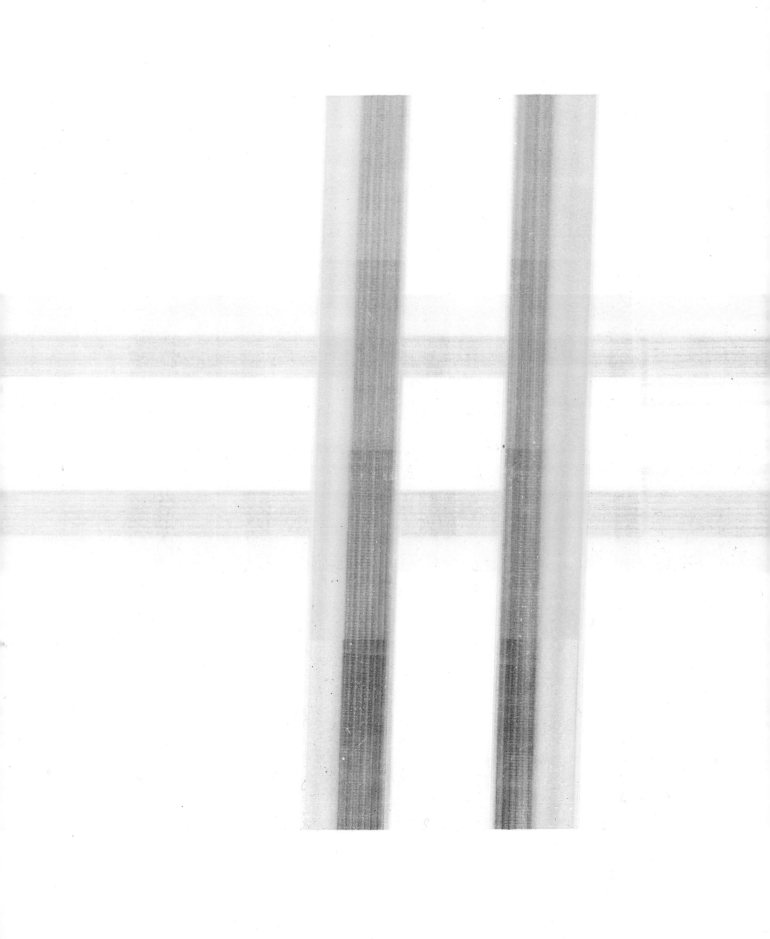

and the self are set, partly by individual conditions, but essentially by *social conditions*. For although the differences between individuals in this respect appear to be great, every society is characterized by a certain level of individuation beyond which the normal individual cannot go."

This is the dilemma of our day. Over the past five decades an interlocking pattern of cultural change has encouraged us to go beyond these limits, indeed to deny their very existence. The result is that the moral aloneness Fromm wrote about in the early 1940s in *Escape from Freedom* (explaining the psychological basis for the rise of Nazism) has erupted in America today as a national disease. In a world where there is nothing that is *not* a matter of choice, freedom of choice has become the new tyranny.

Denied a sense of structure and cohesiveness in life—the kind of stability provided by a clearly defined system of meanings—we are overwhelmed by anxiety, insecurity, and self-doubt. Like the tortured heroine of the Judith Rossner novel *Attachments,* a product of the 1950s silent generation reared in affluent Beverly Hills by well-meaning parents who were overprotective yet couldn't say no, we yearn to hear again the magic words *"It just isn't done."* We want a way of looking at things that will make the world seem reasonable "if not in its actions then in its possibilities." As Nadine says:

If I understood the world's order I would know its limits, and understanding the limits of the world I might find my own. I had been raised by parents who were fearful of everything but forbade me nothing, in a place that was at once parochial, restrictive and utterly permissive. I wanted not simply to know right and wrong as abstractions but to *experience* them in such a way that my disorderly impulses would be controlled by my knowledge.

FREEDOM WITHOUT PROTECTION: THE NEW TYRANNY

In the rebellion of the Sixties we threw away the old book of rules that governed our parents' lives, the rules they tried, however inappropriately, to pass along to us—duty before pleasure, hard work pays off, sex outside marriage is wrong, people in authority know best—because we saw how those arbitrary rules thwarted people's lives and led to the deterioration of human relationships. But in throwing that book away, we got rid of the best part of the arbitrary: the *protection* we all need from our own and others' aggression. Without that protection, the sexual and personal freedom we attain turns out to be an empty illusion.

Cut loose from social controls, we are unable to control ourselves. We have no faith in our own inner sense of limits—our internalized knowledge of right and wrong and the ideals that normally guide our behavior in love and work—and under the guise of self-fulfillment we accept standards that lead not to fulfillment but to a sense of alienation and loss. With gratification as our only guide, the sexual revolution fails to promote greater intimacy but separates people from genuine contact and becomes a revelation in mutual masturbation. And the women's movement, misinterpreted on both sides, releases women from the infantilizing protection of men but at the same time strips away *their belief in their right to protect themselves*, and thus liberates women to be exploited now with their own consent.

Michelle Triola Marvin's experience is a case in point. In 1964 Michelle at thirty-one abandoned her career as a singer and dancer and became the live-in lover of actor Lee Marvin. Michelle's father, a Sicilian-born restaurant owner, did not approve of her decision to move in with Lee without marrying him, and, by her own account, she herself was ambivalent. "I was brought up in the Forties in a strict home. My father was a real patriarch. I couldn't date as a teenager. Everything my father said (and I adored him) we'd do with no questions asked. But when I met Lee . . . I was like any young girl. Here was this man, bigger than life, who just swept me along. Lee and I were very attracted to each other. Admittedly, I was not wet behind the ears. I had been married, but I was confused. I had a set of rules, a set of morals, and I had never lived with a man before without being married." (Michelle in fact had her last name legally changed to Triola Marvin, perhaps to obviate the embarrassment of being unmarried.)

After six years, during which Michelle allegedly endured abortions, Lee's infidelity, and his abusive behavior during drinking bouts, Lee threw her out. In 1979, when Michelle was forty-six, California Superior Court Judge Arthur K. Marshall rejected her claim that she was entitled to half the $3.6 million that Lee earned during the period they had lived together—a property settlement comparable to that of a wife at the dissolution of a marriage—and instead ordered Lee to pay Michelle $104,000 for "rehabilitation" purposes. (Michelle's legal fees alone were $500,000.)

Michelle's plight shattered romantic notions about the living-together arrangement as an enlightened alternative to marriage and showed it to be a perfect example of the lag between freedom from and freedom to in our society today. The facts revealed in the precedent-setting property settlement suit—as ugly, tawdry, and scandalous as any bona fide divorce trial in Hollywood history—gave evidence that the living-together arrangement is not a fail-safe guarantee of keeping spontaneity alive in a relationship or of avoiding the classic traps of traditional marriage. Michelle's freedom from the bonds of matrimony was nothing more than freedom to become a fulltime homemaker with no rights.

In the aftermath of the trial, lawyers reported an upsurge in requests for living-together contracts, spelling out provisions for property rights and support, among the more than 1.1 million unmarried couples estimated to be cohabitating in the United States today. Earlier, these couples would have considered the mere idea of a written contract antithetical to the whole principle of laissez-faire romanticism and emotional closeness. But now, having glimpsed the pitfalls of social change without any safeguards, these same liberated couples suddenly began to look at the old rules in a different light. They saw that underneath those ossified layers of patriarchal authoritarianism or neurotic fearfulness lay values worth preserving by law in the event of love's demise. The death of permanence, they realized, does not mean that honor and responsibility should not be kept alive.

In pursuing liberation without understanding the need for limits, we wind up with *less* freedom than we had before. By undoing all the old patterns of intimacy in friendships, love affairs, and marriage and also discarding as too restrictive of our "human potential" many of those traditional values espoused by our parents—duty, honor, responsibility—what have we gained?

We've gained the right to live our lives solely on the basis of personal choice but have cut out from under us any supports to give those choices meaning and direction. We have set ourselves free to do virtually anything we choose, but we have no way of judging the validity, morality, or even sanity of our choices in a culture where everything is right and nothing is wrong. When the traditional symbols of family, religion, government, and authority have all been discounted or taken over by what social historian Christopher Lasch calls the "therapeutic ethic" with its insistence that sin is only sickness, the freedom to choose becomes illusory. What is to stop us from jettisoning time-honored commitments that conflict with new priorities, deceptively exploiting others to satisfy our own needs, or gratifying whatever impulses we may have at the moment, however base or bizarre?

Nothing, except the knowledge that everyone else is operating on the same pleasure principle as we are. Isolation, therefore, often becomes preferable to the current form of kamikaze social contact with its inherent risks of exploitation and disillusionment. Rather than endanger the self in such a rash and ruthless world, many of us are retreating into our own shelters and drawing the self over us like a bell jar. Liberation, we have discovered with bitter irony, is just another word for self-imprisonment.

THE SEARCH FOR UNCONDITIONAL LOVE

It is my contention that regardless of the particular external conditions and pressures that each generation has had to face in the past five decades and must face now—the Depression in the Thirties, the aftermath of World War II in the Forties, the cold war in the Fifties, the Vietnam War in the Sixties, Watergate in the Seventies, economic and environmental scarcity in the Eighties—our public value system has not been sufficiently supportive of our personal ego strengths. Our swing from too much structure to too little has dealt us all a collective "ego bruise." Consequently, our progress toward a higher social and moral order, one based on self-direction rather than automatic compliance with authority, has been erratic. Each generation has been forced into unproductive detours by the creation of some social fad that would supposedly correct the mistakes of the past and assuage present feelings of anxiety and self-doubt.

For the current generation, men as well as women, the cult of permissiveness has become the new problem rather than the old answer. The guilt conflicts that were the root of our social neurosis in the repressive Victorian era have been replaced, by virtue of overchoice, with depression and alienation.

As psychoanalyst Heinz Kohut has explained it, we have shifted from Freud's era of the Guilty Man to today's age of the Tragic Man. In Freud's time, children were reared in such close family units that they were overstimulated emotionally and developed neurotic conflicts when they had to inhibit the intensely erotic feelings aroused by their parents. Since the culture aggravated these conflicts in adulthood with its excessive emphasis on moral restraint, guilt came to be seen as the villain that needed to be exorcised if people were to lead more spontaneous and fulfilling lives.

Now, however, the tables have turned. Today people are flocking to psychotherapists' offices or running after the latest pop psychology movement because family life in our culture has not been nurturant *enough*. As children, many of us were emotionally *under*stimulated by our parents, who, we felt, were preoccupied with their own concerns and did not love or accept us for ourselves. They did not "mirror" us as we needed to be mirrored to gain a feeling of the validity of our real self. Whether the parents were cold, critical and rejecting, or manipulative and overprotective, we never felt sufficiently accepted for what we *were*, as separate individuals, but rather as vehicles to gratify their needs. The parents were acting only as might be expected in a culture that values the outer symbols of success—money and status—over the inner qualities of the human being.

How has this lack of confirmation of the self affected people in our society? It has made us vulnerable to our own unconscious greed and envy and has set up a need for constant recognition by others. As a defense against our deep sense of worthlessness and rejection and as a buffer against our inner feelings of loneliness and depression, we developed childhood fantasies that were intensely erotic or inflated with grandiose, exhibitionistic ambition. We would grow up and show everybody by becoming a *star*. We would be rich, famous, and powerful, recognized by strangers on the street, fawned over by headwaiters, chauffeur-driven in our Rolls-Royce limousines, and chased by beautiful young bodies who would drive us to new sexual heights. As adults, if our romantic ideals haven't been bent to our service in healthy relationships and productive work, our eroticized, excitedly pursued activities reflect our incessant hunger for response, our yearning for reassurance, and are only one step removed from our underlying depression.

The culture of today, emphasizing as it does the total lack of restraint and the gratification of impulse, only feeds the fever. Our tragedy is that our society has robbed us of guiding ideals and has discouraged us from setting those inner controls that would make us genuinely free. Instead, under the rubric of self-fulfillment we are encouraged to act out our *unfulfillable* fantasies in a never-ending odyssey that keeps us perpetually lonely and depressed.

In tracking the cause and cure of this malady I have uncovered one dominant unfulfillable fantasy at the root of our problem today. Carried down the line like a generational virus—our *Bacillus neuroticus*—it has been transmitted from our grandparents to our parents, from our parents to us, from us to our own children. The fantasy has always been there, but what makes it particularly virulent now is that, whereas in the past it was either buried or denied, today our culture has given the search for it legitimacy. It's the search for *unconditional love.*

Each generation has conducted the search in its own way, hoping to escape the tensions and pressures of life in our competitive society by attaining a state of perfect bliss. For each generation, bliss was defined differently, according to the special circumstances of the time. The determined status-seeker in the Fifties believed that material paradise in suburbia constituted bliss; the wealthy sophisticate of today is hoping to find it by "freebasing" cocaine. But no matter what the form of the search, the goal is the same—to achieve unabated ecstasy, to live out that fantasy harbored from our very earliest days.

In the collection of images that make up our fantasy life, according to psychiatrists, each of us retains an imprint of that very early state of mother/child bliss we experienced shortly after our emergence from the womb. It is an imprint of the eternal breast—that state of psychological oneness with the holding mother, who instantly gratifies our every demand—always there when we are cold or hungry, creating an impression of boundless perfection, well-being, and magical omnipotence.

But as child psychoanalyst Margaret Mahler and other leaders in the field of developmental psychology have shown, an unavoidable crisis occurs around the age of eighteen months when we struggle to emancipate ourselves from mother and build up an autonomous, individual self in the face of our waning sense of power. Ideally, over the next year and a half, there should be a very *gradual* letting go in a series of small steps, with mother remaining a reliable home base for us to return to after each hard knock in the real world. Then the frustration of giving up our omnipotent fantasies, while still painful, is at least tolerable, and we can gain a more realistic view of the world while still maintaining a basically positive feeling toward mother and ourselves.

But if mother fails to set limits for us or sets them in an inappropriate way, either by deflating our omnipotent fantasies too harshly and abruptly or by being emotionally unavailable for support, we become filled with rage. It is the impotent, global rage of a self that feels unloved and unwanted, and it is so intolerable that we defend against it vehemently.

Chief among our defenses is what psychoanalysts call the "splitting of objects," whereby our images of loved ones and our self-representations are separated out into all good or all bad. Unable to accept the bad aspect of ourselves, we frequently project it onto the outside world, which is then viewed as attacking, criticizing, or hostile. Normally, by the age of three, splitting should no longer be psychologically necessary. By then we should be capable of amalgamating love and hate feelings toward the same person and have an integrated picture of ourselves, warts and all, leading to a positive feeling toward ourselves and others. But if splitting has never been replaced with the healthy resolution of our intense early rage, we may go through life looking for the all-giving perfect partner who will sustain the fiction of our own perfection with an endless fount of unconditional love.

The search for unconditional love used to be considered neurotic, but not anymore. Today we've created a climate in which manifestations of it are seen as "viable options" rather than symptoms of an incapacity to give and to love in a sustained committed relationship. It can be argued that the culture's previous support of monogamous marriage kept some couples welded together in wretched forty-five-year marriages that damaged their children more than a divorce. And while an unprecedented 38 percent of all first marriages now end in divorce, couples used to "leave" each other before in other ways that were just as effective as physical leave-taking. Says Philadelphia psychoanalyst Sydney E. Pulver: "What couples did before was to get divorced *emotionally*—they had affairs, became totally immersed in other interests, or got into a constantly attacking relationship. The abandonment was as real then as today, it's just that the culture now makes it easier for men and women to actually do it."

But it was not the concepts of duty, loyalty, and obligation that caused the problems previously but rather the partners' own parasitic dependence. Today, it's the *defense* against that dependence that has forced the search for unconditional love into a new but equally unsatisfying pattern of superficial brief encounters, guarded open-ended relationships, and the revolving-door cycle of divorce-re-marriage-divorce. And now that we no longer have the restraints of religion, family ties, or conscience to stop us from taking up with any desirable person who drifts into our line of vision, it has become that much harder to give up the hope of having our childhood fantasies of eternally perfect love fulfilled. People who might otherwise have gotten past the rocky phase of marriage and gone on to a deeper level of intimacy as they worked through their own personal developmental crisis, now simply divorce.

Says Dr. Pulver: "In romantic love, when the idealization of the other person breaks down and we see that our fantasy of very early perfect love is not going to be fulfilled, we then have to go through a very important period of adjusting to what we see as defects in the other person—accepting the other person's individuality, really. If we've already gone through an experience with mother in which we were gradually disillusioned and the love was maintained, we will go through the same experience again. We'll develop a love that is much more enduring than passion, and this is the affectionate love that people have who've been married a long time. But someone with a real narcissistic problem, who did not have a mother who *gradually* disillusioned him, will find himself so intensely furious at the disappointment that he will be unable to accept the other person. He will maintain the fiction that there's someone out there who is ideal."

BARRY: THE CULTURAL NARCISSIST

On a wintry Sunday afternoon I pay a visit to Barry Golden, a good-natured, successful thirty-two-year-old attorney on the brink of separating from his second wife. Unshaven, Barry is still in his bathrobe after a wild night of boogieing at Second Story, Philadelphia's version of New York's Studio 54. He sits in the kitchen of his opulent suburban home, sipping coffee with me and discussing why, after three years of an idyllic relationship with his wife, Linda, he has decided to move out and on. He still loves Linda, he says, but he's not *in* love with her anymore, using that ancient classic statement that describes the inevitable breakdown of the idealization of the other in romantic love. He says that Linda is too possessive and that he doesn't desire her sexually now—the excitement is gone. A lust for freedom, a need for passion, an insatiable hunger for experience— these seem to be his demons. But as he speaks of them he reveals himself to be a grown-up adolescent, still doing battle with his parents, both now dead, and struggling with childhood furies that are only now beginning to surface.

"Running away when I feel crowded is a pattern in my life. If somebody starts telling me what to do, I don't say, 'Hey, look, I can't be crowded'—I get crazy and split. That's what happened when I had my girl friend living with me in my room at home after high school. My parents were embarrassed because the neighbors had started talking about it, and they didn't want me to reflect badly on them to their friends. They said the girl had to leave, so *I* left for college in Wisconsin. My parents were never really interested in where I was going or coming from, only in what the community thought of *them*. It was always, you shouldn't do this or you shouldn't do that because Martha next door, what is she going to think?"

Barry says that because his parents were influenced so strongly by the opinions of others, he has gone completely in the opposite direction and does what he wants to do without giving the slightest heed to what other people think. As proof, he offers two sadly revealing examples of what passes for iconoclasm today: his full-length fur coat and his handbag. I sense that behind his facade of not caring what others think, he is a man desperately crying out to be noticed.

"My mother and father were wonderful with each other but lousy parents," he says. "They were very frustrated people who gave off frustration, and their children picked it up. At one time my parents had money, but they lost everything and were down. They couldn't take trips, always gave to the kids, and I think they wanted more from their children emotionally, more understanding of their problems, but didn't know how to ask. It was a different time and age [the late Fifties]. You weren't allowed to express your feelings or confront them. My sisters and I were close with my parents, we could kiss and hug, but we weren't allowed to talk about our upsets in our family. If things weren't running smoothly, you just kept it inside and got depressed. I developed a terrible temper, and when I got angry I punched the wall. I knew somebody would notice, and all I wanted them to say was, 'What's wrong?' But that never happened. They just shrugged it off and said, 'Well, he's crazy,' or 'He's wild.' I don't put my fist through the wall anymore, but I'm still angry inside and constantly depressed. That's one of the biggest problems in my life—I always feel like something is missing."

Typical of the zeitgeist of many of his contemporaries, Barry's world view is a strange alloy of cynicism, hedonism, and pessimism. His generation, or at least the segment of it that he represents, seems to be surviving on sex and drugs the way his parents' generation once survived on the work ethic.

"All of the married guys I know, some of them from very good Catholic backgrounds, married for eight to ten years to very nice, good-looking women they say they have a great relationship with, are out almost every night cheating on their wives. Cheating is just keeping up with the times, like getting your weekly update. It keeps you abreast of what's happening in the world, makes you feel part of it, makes you feel you're a big man, that you can screw anything and still be married. I never liked to cheat, but I understand the psychology of it. Our society was led into sex by drugs, and it has become a way of life, a career almost. Everybody wants to be with the prettiest girl and if they sleep with the prettiest girl, that's even better. Our big problem is that we have so much leisure time today, and people can't be contented with themselves. They need something external so everybody can say, 'Look at the chick he's with, he's cool,' or 'Look at his clothes.' I'm guilty of the same thing."

His explanation of the widespread use of drugs is unsparingly bleak. "You take a Quaalude and you're spaced. You can barely stand, you're swaying and slurring your words, but you feel very relaxed and that's the gist of the whole thing. If people get to feel relaxed, they think everything is okay. Of course it's an illusion, but you know what Tennyson said: 'Tis better to have loved and lost than never to have loved at all.' So the feeling is that even if it only lasts for the moment, it's better to have had this illusion that you're okay and everything is fine than not to have had it."

For someone who is so much a part of the new order, Barry seems thoroughly disenchanted. He has done est and has his fur coat and his pocketbook and his quaaludes and his nightly sex and his new black Alfa Romeo nestled in the driveway—and what does it all mean? "Twenty years from now I may move to Russia because things are really going to be bad," he tells me. "Our society is so loose that people are doing almost anything today. There are no values anymore. But how do you get values if not from a parent figure?" he asks recriminatingly. "What if you had parents you couldn't identify with because they weren't happy themselves?"

To be happy is the one thing Barry wants more than anything in the world. He thought he was happy with his wife, Linda, these past three years, but she disappointed him: She became real. She's insecure, she's not a good listener, she's too passive sexually, and, worst of all, she's always *there*. Try as he will, there is nothing Barry can do to regenerate the feeling of excitement and passion he once had with Linda before time blew her cover and exposed her to be human. And what does he see as the answer? "I need to fall in love again," he says, "with someone who will love me as much as she loves herself."

Barry is by no means a pathological narcissist, but he is a good example of the American social character of narcissism today. Our relentless search for unconditional love with the inevitable problems it poses in handling commitment, our excessive centering of interest on the self, our need to validate the self through sexual conquest, our superficial way of seeking acceptance and admiration through the exhibitionistic accumulation of material goods, and our abiding feeling of loneliness manifested by the ever-flashing signal coming from inside that something is *still* missing in our lives—all of these traits have become so much a part of the American character structure today that the leading social critics of our time have defined ours as the culture of narcissism.

Although cultural narcissism is not to be confused with the severe pathology of clinical narcissism, the comparison is valid. Competitiveness, the myth of romantic love, the impermanence and impersonality of modern life, and the loss of reliable traditions combine to produce personality traits similar to those that we find in people who are seriously disturbed. There exist a grandiose sense of self-importance; the need for constant recognition and admiration; a supersensitivity to criticism; exploitativeness in personal relationships; an inability to invest totally in a relationship; a lack of empathy; en-

titlement or the expectation of special favors without assuming reciprocal responsibilities; a wild oscillation from overidealizing to
devaluing a loved one; and, most of all, a preoccupation with fantasies of unlimited success, money, power, brilliance, beauty, or ideal
sexual love, which I call the search for unconditional love.

Like the pathological narcissist who does not really love himself
but actually holds himself in low esteem, the cultural narcissist appears to be an autonomous free spirit but is really a conformist in
disguise. He has freed himself from the duty-oriented, self-sacrificing,
security-minded value system of his grandparents and parents only to
lock himself into the equally constrictive pleasure-oriented, self-indulgent, live-for-the-moment value system of his peers. They are
both merely two different faces of the same "escape from freedom."
Each is characterized by automatic or compulsive activities and the
surrender of the individuality and integrity of the self. And neither
leads to happiness and positive freedom because neither solves the
underlying problem: how to move from slavish *dependence* on outside authority, whether parents or peers, to healthy *inter*dependence.

"The narcissistic trend today is the competitive ethic displaced
onto *experience* rather than just material goods," says New York
psychoanalyst Donald Kaplan, Ph.D., associate clinical professor of
psychology at New York University. "To the observer, narcissistic
pleasure-seekers look as if they're in a state of unbridled freedom—at
Plato's Retreat, for example—but they are conforming to certain
standards set by others, not by themselves. The compulsive submission is what is empty and unhealthy about it. When you have no
internal standards to form some kind of conflict with the outside
world, you have no sense of purpose. If you're compelled to have
unending sex, it's no less a burdensome tyranny than the overly strict
control of libidinal instincts by a punitive superego."

Since the cultural narcissist, like Barry Golden, has broken away
from his parents' standards, he often thinks of himself as "independent" and has no idea of how compulsively submissive he really is.
Barry's biggest complaint about Linda is that "we're too much
alike," but how could it be otherwise when they are simply mirror
images of each other, two marionettes on strings pulled by the same
puppeteer?

Cultural narcissism is similar to the pathological variety in that
its roots go back to faulty mirroring in childhood. Severely disturbed

personalities are usually people whose early fantasies of omnipotence were too harshly deflated by a chronically cold, self-centered mother who might even have been spitefully aggressive toward her child. But the opposite—too much attention by the overprotective mother who gratifies the child's every wish without regard for his maturing, changing self—can have the same effect. Says Dr. Kaplan: "Overprotectiveness is not a *seeming* deprivation, but there is deprivation in too much. Too much protection, too much opportunity, too much indulgence produces an expectation that the world will never fulfill. The overprotective mother who represents herself as constantly available won't permit a conflict of interests between herself and her child. Since a self and other can occur only through an awareness of differences—optimal frustrations—the child can't separate, and life becomes a quest for the perfect mother."

If the mother is limitless, the child has no way of testing out what his own limits are. He then grows up saddled with two psychological defects. First, he has no sense of a discrete self apart from the important others in his life; and, second, he has a belief in perfection that makes it impossible for him to tolerate the tension that exists universally in human beings between our own little corner of reality and our unattainable ideal—the fantasy of being Number One or of finding unconditional love.

HEDONISM WITHOUT HAPPINESS

In my generation, reared in the post-Depression era, happiness was an irrelevant issue. If it was to be found at all, it would be in doing your duty—earning a good living if you were a man and marrying and raising children in suburbia if you were a woman. Our parents' value system emphasized responsibility above personal freedom and dictated strict child-rearing techniques that wrung compliance from us at the price of our maturity and earned us the name the Silent Generation.

After World War II, when we ourselves became parents in the late 1940s and 1950s, we discovered, or invented, permissiveness. Well-intentioned, wanting the best for our children emotionally as well as materially, we read into Freudian psychoanalytic concepts and other psychologies a need for sparing the child *any* frustration. As so often happens in this country, we counterreacted to an extreme by seizing on a corrective, standing it on its head, and creating a new extreme that in turn has led to its inevitable counterreaction.

Scarred by our own repressive upbringing, we went overboard in the direction of permissiveness and produced an overindulged generation with an enfeebled sense of self and grandiose illusions about perfection. After the people of this generation came of age in the rebellious Sixties and tore the old order apart for all of us, it became imperative in the Seventies to establish a new order that would incorporate the psychological problems of injured narcissism into our social character. As Dr. Kaplan explains: "The social order in any given decade will produce any kind of structure that will normalize the development that has taken place in the previous decade. In a decade where people are trained not to have to cope with frustration and to have whatever they want, a structure will be created to allow people to pass this behavior off as normal to themselves and others."

The structure we created was the culture of narcissism, and we created it not only for our children but for ourselves as well. With the crumbling of the traditional value system, we discovered that we were as greedy for experience as the younger generation and had as little sense of self. In a way, the college youth of the Sixties had been acting out a prolonged postadolescence for those of us in our thirties and forties who never really had a chance for a full adolescence in our own youth. But with a calling of a moratorium on all the traditional restraints, we became free in middle age to have an adolescence of our own. So the code we crafted for the Seventies said that people should do whatever they feel like doing regardless of who gets hurt.

In personal relationships, we took this to mean that we could indulge our own desires without assuming reciprocal responsibilities. If someone had problems with a husband or wife and said, "I want a new partner," the culture gave its support for divorce. Happiness, once a function of doing the right thing, was now said to be something that could be grasped moment to moment by constantly pursuing it. What we did, in effect, was to declare that the psychological phenomenon of "narcissistic entitlement," described by Harvard psychiatrist Robert Coles, was perfectly normal. According to Coles, the grandiose expectation that the world will provide more, more, and yet more, accompanied by "apprehension and gloom and, not least, a strain of gnawing worthlessness," came to be regarded by everyone, psychiatrists included, "as a 'character trait' rather than a 'symptom' that prompts a visit to a doctor."

We can call any behavior normal if enough people do it, but if it fails to bring them happiness over the long run, they will begin casting about for a new answer. And that is precisely what great numbers of people, from their twenties to their sixties, are doing today. The hundreds of people who come through the doors of my counseling agency year after year are beginning to say, in one way or another, the same thing. They are disillusioned with narcissistic pleasure-seeking, fragmented relationships. They have found this extreme to be no less frustrating in its own way than the opposite extreme of dutifully fulfilling socially established role requirements in the all-consuming, locked-in relationships that the nuclear family represented thirty years ago.

The old way bred inhibition and resentment, and the new has left a residue of cynicism, bitterness, and a feeling of having been cheated. At least the sustaining bonds of a committed relationship provided a hedge against catastrophe, but today's pattern of constant change, while it offers possibilities for novelty and excitement, robs people of any safety in their position. Alan Ross, Subaru of America vice-president who gained a national reputation as a male sex symbol when he became *Cosmopolitan* magazine's Bachelor of the Month, summed it all up in an interview given shortly after he announced his plans, at the age of thirty-nine, to be married for the second time: "How many times can you share the same things in your life with different people only to have them disappear in the dark of the night? Then you start the whole thing over again with someone else. Each time you are involved, you give of yourself. What's a relationship about? Sharing. How many times can you go through that, until there isn't a lot left?"

It was sociologist David Riesman who foresaw the trouble ahead when he wrote *The Lonely Crowd* in 1950, observing the transformation of the American character from "inner-directed" to "other-directed." The inner-directed person, Riesman noted, operates on a "psychological gyroscope," an instrument set early in life through identification with the values and goals of internalized parent figures and other adult authorities. Once set, the mechanism keeps the individual "on course" toward generalized but inescapably destined goals—marriage, a career—and helps the person maintain a delicate balance between the demands of his life goals and the buffetings of his external environment. "He can receive and utilize certain signals from outside," Riesman wrote, "provided they can be reconciled with the limited maneuverability that his gyroscope permits him. His pilot is not quite automatic."

In contrast to an internal code of behavior with guilt and shame controls, the psychological lever of the other-directed person, who takes his direction from his peers, is a diffuse anxiety that Riesman likened to radar. The dependence on outside authority, whether actual friends or the anonymous voice of the mass media, is "internalized" early and remains constant throughout life. But the goals toward which the other-directed person strives fluctuate with our rapidly shifting fashions and provide no secure footing.

Like Erich Fromm, upon whose concepts he principally relied, Riesman saw that the central issue both for the inner- and other-directed person was how to be "autonomous" rather than "adjusted." Whether our stiving for goals comes from dependence on internalized parents or dependence on contemporary authorities in the outside world, if that dependence violates the integrity of the self, we will never achieve "freedom to." We will never separate psychologically, resolve the crises along the developmental pathway toward growth, and fully realize our capabilities. We may be adjusted in the sense of conforming to whatever our culture demands of us, but that conformity will always be irrational and compulsive.

With remarkable accuracy, Riesman predicted that the struggle for autonomy in an increasingly other-directed, consumer-crazed society would be played out in the arena of leisure time. Sex, he felt, was the "last frontier," the one remaining bastion of privacy where acquisition could be carried on safe from public scrutiny and pressure to keep up with the couple next door. The element of privacy made sex the only avenue open to the other-directed person where he could express his individuality and seek some genuine emotional response. "He looks to it," wrote Riesman, "for reassurance that he is alive."

But thirty years have passed since Riesman wrote his book, and the last frontier has vanished. The consumption of sex, like dining out, has been opened to the full view of other gourmets in such emporiums as Plato's Retreat in New York and the Sandstone Ranch in Los Angeles. Promising "personal growth" and "personal free-dom," the commercialization of sex has reduced the other-directed person to a mere pod out of the *Invasion of the Body Snatchers*.

Marcia Seligson, describing her second trip to Sandstone with her "mate" and another couple, observes this phenomenon in her book *Options*: "Men at Sandstone, I have noticed, tend to become fo-cused on other men's penises; comparing and inevitably finding themselves wanting, they become sure they will never be able to get an erection, and even if they do, it's so much tinier than that stud's across the room, who will notice or care or desire, anyway?" Of Larry, the other man in her party, she writes:

Larry's fantasies are directly tied to high school. He is still thinking
tonight, "How do you get the beautiful girls? I want the prom
queen but she doesn't know I'm alive." What ancient but still-
nagging sting in that one, that early bruise from which we never
seem to completely recover. Larry, thus burdened, has no intention
of partaking tonight.

Larry does *not* partake, and later, when the two couples are driv-ing home and comparing notes in the car, he acts gloomy, as if "he has failed an important exam."

I keep thinking of Barry Golden's cryptic reply when I asked him what all the runners racing compulsively around the sexual track were seeking: "Security," he said. Probably that was his own way of saying the "reassurance of being alive." Other-directed people have so little sense of self that they need experience to prove they exist. The Cartesian syllogism "I think, therefore I am" becomes "I *feel*, therefore I am." But in today's era of superconsumerism, when the concept of "fun morality" has been applied to sex and has turned it into work, the cultural narcissist withdraws from even that proof of his existence. So what is left to him?

Jogging. What more exquisitely apt metaphor for our times than the loneliness of the long-distance runner? For the other-directed person, jogging represents the final refuge. It is his private gym where he can work off the anxiety aroused by always having to be attuned to outside signals. Even more important, it is a place where he can practice the art of self-consciousness necessary to disentangle himself from the adjusted others, as Riesman puts it, and move toward autonomy. To do this, he must come to recognize and respect, rather than deny or disguise, his own feelings, his own possibilities, and his own limits. And so we have the Ultimate Option: a pair of Addidas.

But alas, even jogging has been co-opted by the media and turned into the latest mandatory fad. The solitary runner may be huffing and sweating his way toward self-discovery and a personal statement, but he is as likely to be no more than another fashionable other-directed automaton compulsively doing *their* own thing.

TWO

←———————— · ————————→

OUR
INNER
COMPASS

Is there no way that we can be autonomous in today's culture without retreating into isolation? I think there is. I am convinced that positive freedom is possible only for the person who is neither exclusively inner-directed nor exclusively other-directed but a combination of the two—a self-steerer, if you will, whose compass is a set of *freely chosen* internal personal standards shaped by both parents and peers. The magnetic north is the individual's own particular sense of *purpose*—what Rollo May defines as "an assertive response of the person to the structure of his world."

When this is the reference point against which we constantly test the values tempered into us by our parents as they cross with the current winds of change, we are never adrift. We can take our social bearings without feeling the helpless rage of the child who accepts or rejects his parents' values unthinkingly and *in toto*. And we can withstand the frequent and constant bombardment of contemporaries who transmit different notions about the world and themselves through the mass media. By using our compass, we can find those standards we can depend on and feel comfortable with—the ones that fit in with parts of ourselves that *we just can't change.* It is our compass that allows us to relate to our parents on an *adult* level and to come really close to our peers without the mindless conformity that makes us, as Riesman has said, "a lonely member of the crowd."

I call this inner compass our *limits,* and I use the term "limits" to convey our gut sense of what is personally right or wrong for us and of what we would like to do in life. Our inner compass incorporates both our internalized parents and the influence of our peers but holds up the core of our identity as the ultimate authority.

This concept of limits corresponds to a form of what psychoanalysts call the *ego ideal,* the set of mental images we have of what we *should* or *would like* to be. These are our moral standards or ideals and the goals we aspire to, and they come from two different sources. What we feel we *should* be is a picture of the ideals that our parents have (or had) for us. What we *would like* to be are our grandiose fantasies or our own strivings that we pick up from those we identify with or observe. Failure to live up to either of these can cause unhappiness. But our personal sense of what is most important and satisfying in life must be brought to bear on these goals so that they ultimately become *self*-chosen. Otherwise we live in rigid compliance with our internalized parents and remain dependent children forever. Or we become narcissists, defending against feelings of worthlessness by compulsively striving to live up to unattainable ideals of perfection.

It was only with therapy, divorce, or both, and certainly with a lot of stress and conflict, that many people in the over-thirty-five generation today have been able to overcome their repressive upbringing and rescue their lost sense of self with a more liberating set of limits. Few in that generation had the fierce allegiance to the self to do the kind of separation in their youth that novelist John Irving attributes to his mythic Jenny Fields in *The World According to Garp.*

The daughter of a wealthy Boston shoe manufacturer, Jenny drops out of Wellesley in the late 1930s "when she suspected that the chief purpose of her parents' sending her to Wellesley had been to have her dated by and eventually mated to some well-bred man." Jenny sets her own limits—she wants to be a nurse and a single mother. Basically asexual, she impregnates herself with a dying patient, a wounded ball turret gunner, and remains celibate thereafter. As a wonderfully giving mother and nurse, Jenny lives up to her ideals, and her autobiography earns her fame as a kind of feminist Florence Nightingale. But her break with her family, who assumed after Wellesley that Jenny's sexual activity was "considerable and irresponsible," was not accomplished without loss:

She felt detached from her family, and thought it strange how they had lavished so much attention on her, as a child, and then at some appointed, prearranged time they seemed to stop the flow of affection and begin the expectations—as if, for a brief phase, you were expected to absorb love (and get enough), and then, for a much longer and more serious phase, you were expected to fulfill certain obligations. When Jenny had broken the chain, had left Wellesley for something as common as nursing, she had dropped her family—and they, as if they couldn't help themselves, were in the process of dropping her. In the Fields family, for example, it would have been more appropriate if Jenny had become a doctor, or if she'd stayed in college and *married* one. Each time she saw her brothers, her mother and her father, they were more uncomfortable in one another's presence. They were involved in that awkward procedure of getting to unknow each other.

Hard as it was, the struggle for autonomy for Jenny Fields and others in her day was a clear-cut battle. At least there was something to fight *against*. If you broke with tradition, you gained freedom but you had your limits nonetheless. You chose a different *role*, perhaps, but you still had prosocial values and internal personal standards that were not *so* grandiose that you couldn't live up to them and achieve self-esteem.

But what does today's under-thirty generation have? There is nothing to rebel against because everything is acceptable. Reared in the Fifties and Sixties by permissive parents who "couldn't let you get near any cliffs," as one thirty-two-year-old woman put it, they tend to look upon frustration as failure, and disappointment as annihilation. Instead of ego ideals they can live up to, they are forever seeking the unattainable fantasy of perfection. The competitive ethos—"If you're not Number One, you're nothing"—reinforces their perfectionistic strivings and their unhealthy narcissism as a defense against feeling worthless merely because they do not have (or may not get) it all. And the "anything goes" relativism of their peers breeds anxiety and depression because it gives them no sense of the world's limits or of their own.

The swing generation, those of us who traded in our "gyroscopes" for "radar," found we made a bad bargain. We bought the new morality in our bedrooms but not inside ourselves. We soon discovered that promiscuity did not address the problem of dependence and, if anything, only underscored it. We began to see that it was not unrepressed lust that was causing us to lie down with perfect strangers, but terror. We felt so empty and lost in a world that had suddenly turned into a void that we frantically had to simulate closeness in fleeting moments of sexual contact. And when we found, afterward, that we had no one reliable to call on in *any* of the ways intimacy used to ensure, we felt as cheated and deprived as we had earlier by the hidden costs of idealized suburban bliss.

After a decade of experimenting with a loose, guilt-free system and immediate, transient, pleasure-oriented relationships, the mounting casualties are beginning to cause alarm. Twenty million depressed Americans . . . the rise of the suicide rate among our young by more than 250 percent in the past twenty years . . . the horror of mass suicide in Guyana. . . . These are all indications that something is dreadfully wrong.

We cannot return to the old extreme of strict compliance with traditional, authoritarian norms because the old way didn't work. But it's a mistake to believe that our only viable alternatives are either all or nothing. "If all were variation," Yale Professors William G. Sumner and Albert G. Keller have said, "life would be an unrelated chaos, just as, if all were tradition, it would take on the immobility of death."

Somewhere between the two extremes is a sane middle ground that provides support and protection for our identity without stifling its growth. We need to accept that there *are* limits and learn how to internalize them and pass them on in such a way that we can set our own controls and our own ideals and be autonomous without being isolated. As a culture we need to give support to the "closet traditionalists" among us, those of us who have been shamed out of a personal set of standards by a hedonistic ethic that has made us feel old-fashioned and out of place. But we must take care not to initiate yet another counterreaction that will knock us back into overcontrol. And we can do this by establishing a public value system that supports personal and social responsibility without smothering individual initiative under a juggernaut of rules.

It is time that we stop "reeling like a drunk from a ditch on one side of the road to a ditch on the other," as a psychiatrist friend put it, and begin to find our balance. Our culture, as a whole, seems to be going through the wretched confusion of early adolescence when the biological, social, and psychological elements are stirred up to the maximum. By this time the message of Gail Sheehy's *Passages* has become common knowledge: that adults go through "predictable" crises of growth and development just as children do, when their external wants and needs collide with internal changes and throw adults into a state of upheaval. But I believe that the feeling of crisis during adult transitions could be greatly reduced if our culture provided us, as good parents provide their children, with a matrix of positive social values wherein personal ego strengths could be nurtured. *The mere predictability of adult crises is not enough to ease our passage through them.* Adults going through a personal growth crisis need the same kinds of concrete, well-defined goals and values that children in transition need, which they can either accept or rebel against, but which nonetheless help them chart a negotiable course through the chaos of boundless freedom.

Although the "sins of the parents" are always a fashionable scapegoat for the problems of the children, the narcissistic quality of the American social character today cannot be blamed on the inadequacies of the parents alone. Nor can it be blamed on faulty child-rearing practices as an isolated phenomenon apart from the culture that bred such practices. How could we expect "good enough" mothering from our mothers if the cultural mandate of their time forced them to become parents when they were themselves still emotionally children? How ready were *we* for child-rearing when we took up the task? How ambivalent are we about it today? What kinds of parents can we be when we are just now, in our thirties and forties, resolving the identity crises we were never *allowed* to resolve at sixteen?

In my middle forties now, looking back over the course my life has taken—a course that so closely parallels the tortured path of a whole generation—I realize that by far the greatest influence on my identity has been the culture. It was the culture that determined, very largely, what kind of parental role models I would have. And as I passed through each developmental stage, it was the cultural input that determined more than any other factor how, when, or indeed *if*, each crisis would be resolved.

When we look beyond the narrow confines of our family life, we see that each generation is parent to the next and that we are all children of our culture, determined by our social norms even as we determine them. We also see that a whole generation can suffer severe narcissistic injury, even as a child does in infancy, when our cultural parents—the authorities, our institutions, our public values—fail to set appropriate limits for us, both with respect to our need for independence and our need for continuing support.

The lesson of Guyana has shown us the dreadful lengths to which people will go in their escape from freedom without limits. To learn from that horror, we must take our problem with autonomy, individually and as a society, out of the context of blame and cast it in a historical perspective. Our purpose is not to hurl accusations of generational failings but to understand why they have occurred, and with that understanding guide the cultural pendulum and create a more stable and nurturant structure of traditions for ourselves and succeeding generations. "For if there is any responsibility in the cycle of life," wrote Erik Erikson, "it must be that one generation owes to the next that strength by which it can come to face ultimate concerns in its own way—unmarred by debilitating poverty or by the neurotic concerns caused by emotional exploitation."

THE DECADES: THE THIRTIES TO THE EIGHTIES

←————————————————————→

To hold, as t'were, this mirror up to nature;
to show virtue her own feature, scorn her own image,
and the very age and body of the time
his form and pressure.

WILLIAM SHAKESPEARE
Hamlet, III, ii, 25

THREE

THE DEPRESSING THIRTIES

It was typical of my father that in the worst year of the Great Depression, when other men were throwing themselves off the tops of tall buildings, he set sail with my mother on a luxury liner for a month-long tour of Europe. My mother has pictures of them dining in the stateroom, seated at a table laden with food and flowers, flanked by prosperous German industrialists dressed in tuxedos and patent leather pumps. To look at my father, with his party hat askew, his handsome, mustached face lit with a roguish smile, a wineglass raised jauntily in one hand and a cigarette held lightly in the other, you would never guess he was on this cruise because his doctor had advised a long ocean voyage to avert a nervous breakdown.

The pressures of making a living never rested easily on my father's shoulders. Bright but anxiety-ridden, he'd been forced by his tyrannical father to quit school after the eighth grade and join the family men's wear manufacturing business. He married my mother in 1926, and in 1928, when the Depression started, she recalls: "Daddy started having a nervous breakdown. He was worried about paying the creditors, going out of business, the banks failing. Over his father's objection, he took forty thousand dollars out of the bank, and the next day the bank closed. After that, Daddy was afraid to go out of the house during the day. He sat around in his bare feet, and at night he walked outside, crying. I had to call the police once to bring him home. I put him in Fairmount Farms [a psychiatric hospital], but he only stayed overnight. His sister Rosie pulled him out because she thought those places took rich people over for their money. Finally, the doctor suggested the trip to Europe."

They set sail in 1931, when my older sister was three and a half and my middle sister was three months old. I wouldn't be born for another three years. As long as he was removed from all that bothered him, my father was in high spirits, but when he returned home he plummeted into despair again over his business worries. He left his father's firm and started his own company. The tension of the clothing business was unbearable for him, yet as irritable and explosively short-tempered as he was at home, he was unfailingly fun-loving and charming with others. That was my father's pattern. He rode out the rest of the Depression by drawing a salary from the business but not going into work. "He took his mind off his worriment," my mother says, "by running around all day long looking at cars in showrooms and watching buildings go up."

Throughout the rest of his life until he died of a massive coronary at the age of sixty-one, when I was twenty-four, my father was preoccupied with providing for his family financially to the point of an obsession. His other major concern was guarding his daughters' virginity until we got married. Puritanical, to say the least, his notion of a "harlot"—his favorite term for an immoral woman—was any daughter of his who came home from a date much after midnight. To discourage illicit conduct in the home, he had a disconcerting habit of pacing the upstairs hallway in his white nightshirt and noisily flushing the toilet at frequent intervals whenever one of us was sitting with a suitor on the living-room sofa after a date.

The son of a dictatorial father who ruled his children's lives even to the point of choosing their marital partners or breaking up their marriage plans if he thought the partners were unsuitable, my father was similarly inclined. His approach to the transmission of values was purely negative. As my mother puts it: "None of you kids ever heard the word 'yes.' It was always 'No!' When you were babies, he never picked you up or held you. He wouldn't let me go into your bedroom even if you cried and cried and cried. You could bust your lungs. He thought it would spoil children if you held them after they went to bed."

A traditionalist in every respect, my father was of the opinion that a son was infinitely more desirable than a daughter. My mother recalls that he didn't look at my older sister for ten months after she was born because she wasn't a boy. As the "baby" of the family, I was my father's favorite, and that may account in part for my yearning to be the son he never had. Nicknamed "Mike," I became a raging tomboy, climbing lampposts, playing ball in the streets with the neighborhood boys, and identifying with the "masculine" role of the competitive achiever rather than the "feminine" role of the passive nurturer.

Although I was never consciously aware of "penis envy" as such, I was never *not* aware that being a girl in my time meant a foreclosure of options that was a serious deprivation. In homes where there is not even a subtle preference for boys, according to Margaret Mahler, girls feel a very early sense of lack and anger. In the toddler stage, many blame the mother for their fantasied shortcoming, expect reparations, and cling to the mother in a hostile dependency, getting stickier and more underfoot. If the mother needs the daughter for her own purposes and won't give her the "gentle push" away, as Mahler describes it, this can be the basis of extreme dependency in adult life.

In my case, encouraged by my father's blatant preference for boys, I reacted against my dependent feminine wishes and became the softball champion of Arlington Street. I was luckier than some girls but not as lucky as others. In preadolescence I never accepted the rigid limits on what a girl could or should do in our culture, and I gained some faith in my own abilities and individual initiative. But when I reached my teens, society's expectations of me as interpreted by our family code suddenly came down on my dreams like a guillotine. Any fantasies I had of making my mark in the world through independent achievement were given short shrift. What did it matter that I always got the highest marks in school, was elected class president, voted the one "Most Likely to Succeed"? My goals were laid out for me in the form of an unwritten law that wasn't even open for question.

THE CLOSED FAMILY

In those Depression-haunted days, when we lived a barnaclelike existence on the row-house fringe of a well-to-do middle-class Jewish community in Philadelphia, the supreme value drilled into our heads in countless daily exchanges was *security*. For a girl, no matter how ambitious or gifted, that meant an early marriage to a professional and as a backup earning a college degree in education. It meant, in short, such narrowly defined limits that the thrust of our own stand toward the world had no room at all.

Why, I wonder now, did so many of us—and that includes all the compliant *boys* of my generation as well as the girls programmed to marry them—yield up our identities without a fight? Why did we follow orders as docilely as the thousands of systematically brainwashed young American Moonies of today or the more than nine hundred Peoples Temple victims who submissively downed their Kool-Aid laced with cyanide? Why did we not stand up to our parents at a certain point and say: "No, you can't make me do this."

Each of us differs constitutionally in our basic ability to handle aggression. But looking at the phenomenon generationally, I think we can see the same social forces at work in the nuclear family of yesterday and the cults of today. Many of us growing up in the post-Depression era were, with respect to our extraordinary obedience to adult authority, not so very different from prisoners of totalistic socializing systems like the cults. We followed orders out of a similar suspension of will, paralyzed in our resistance by the same combination of "manipulation from above and idealism from below" that Dr. Robert Jay Lifton describes as the technique used to instill obedience in cult members.

In the restrictively closed system that our parents created to provide for our welfare, the idealism from below was the image projected to the outside world of a television family like the Waltons—a caring, close-knit group who weathered the calamitous struggle for survival intact, psychologically unbruised and harmoniously bound together through unbreakable ties of love, loyalty, and devotion. The manipulation from above was through guilt. How could we dare go against our parents' wishes when we saw our mother wearing the same coat for ten years so we could have piano lessons and ride bicycles and go to summer camps like the other children on the block?

The unconscious mind control of their children by super-sacrificing Jewish immigrant parents, martyrs who had devotion in their blood and transmitted guilt to their children like an errant gene, found its ultimate literary expression in Philip Roth's *Portnoy's Complaint.* Who can forget Roth's vivid metaphor of the guilt ship, "the biggest troop ship afloat," stacked to the bulkheads with "sad and watery-eyed sons of Jewish parents, sick to the gills from rolling through these heavy seas of guilt . . . still in steerage, like our forebears," crying out intermittently, " 'Poppa, how could you?' 'Momma, why did you?' "

Jewish immigrant parents were certainly not the only ones to wring compliance out of their children through guilt. On the contrary, it was a universal child-rearing technique of the Thirties and Forties, as evidenced by Germaine Greer recalling her convent girlhood in Australia in *The Female Eunuch:*

We could see that our mothers blackmailed us with self-sacrifice, even if we did not know whether or not they might have been great opera stars or the toasts of the town if they had not borne us. In our intractable moments we pointed out that we had not asked to be born, or even to go to an expensive school. We knew that they must have had motives of their own for what they did with and to us. The notion of our parents' self-sacrifice filled us not with gratitude, but with confusion and guilt. We wanted them to be happy yet they were sad and deprived, and it was our fault.

My own mother used a far more subtle technique. Although their trip to Europe was the last vacation she and my father ever took together, she never complained. She never said: "Look at what we've done for you. We gave up everything so you could have all the things the other children had." It was never her own sacrifice she pointed out, only my father's—how hard he worked, how he never took anything for himself, how he struggled with his insecurity about money —and then she belittled him for not doing better.

My mother's anxieties took a different form from my father's. Although he was monstrously insecure, as a native-born American from a family of means he at least had a sense of belonging, a pride of place. My mother, on the other hand, came here from Russia at the age of four. She was the youngest of eleven children of a driving, ambitious mother and a kindhearted father who had a tailor shop on the first floor of their three-story house in an area comparable to New York's Lower East Side. Extremely traumatized by her immigrant status, my mother was an outsider in this country and felt like an outsider all her life. She still has, in her seventies, the "What-will-the-neighbors-think?" folk attitude of a transplanted Eastern European child coming to a strange land, wearing strange clothes, eating strange foods, and growing up poor. Her mother wanted her to go to college, but her father wouldn't let her, so marriage became a momentous choice that would either make or break her for life. But she was not acquisitive for herself. Basically, it was her other-directedness that made her ridicule my father for failing to live up to her expectations. "I was always angry at Daddy because he didn't do as well financially as the others," she admits now, explaining: "Wexler [our next-door neighbor] always laughed at him because the other fellows were doing better."

But there was something deeper at work in my mother's negativism, her need to attack my father, to tear him down constantly even though she was utterly devoted to him. I doubt that her dissatisfaction would have been any different even if he had been a millionaire. She would have found some other shortcoming, some other vulnerability, to justify her frustration. Granted, my father was far from perfect, but my mother's frustration was not with him—it was the frustration of her masked and denied hunger for unconditional love.

"Grandmom was mean to everyone. She was a selfish woman who was only interested in those who could get ahead and make something of themselves," my mother says of her mother, whose own mother abandoned her in Europe when she was only one year old (the genealogy of early narcissistic injury reads like a psychoanalytic *Roots*). Jack and Harry, my mother's two older brothers who went on to become respectively an orthodontist and a surgeon, were always my grandmother's favorites. Lena, an older sister of my mother's, ran the house, and Elka, another sister, did all the sewing.

"I always worked and turned over all my money," my mother says. "If I spent fourteen dollars for a pair of shoes, grandmom yelled at me. Anyone she could push down, she did. I had to sleep on the dining-room floor at night, and my older sisters brought their boyfriends in while I was there. Grandmom didn't care about what other people thought. She could defy them all. Her main concern was making her business successful. She ran a food market in Russia, and she had a record store here as a sideline to my father's tailor shop. She wasn't a good mother. She never told me about menstruating. I learned about it from kids on the school line." My mother stops herself and laughs. "Where did *you* learn about it?" she asks.

I can see now how the curious contradiction in my mother's aspirations for her husband and children, through whom she lived, was anchored in her own maternal deprivation. If you didn't achieve, according to whatever the accepted standards of achievement were, she was critical. But if you did achieve, no matter how far above the norm, it was never enough.

These boundless limits imposed on their surrogates signify the unconscious greed and envy of parents who endured too much frustration of their own needs in childhood. As they grow older, their demands on their children to achieve a forever-elusive goal may soften, but they never entirely disappear. Recently, when I called my mother and told her that I would be hosting a weekly three-hour radio show on the CBS station in Philadelphia, she seemed pleased but still *dis*pleased—her acceptance, like her own self-acceptance, always equivocal. She congratulated me, then asked: "But it's only radio, not television?"

Since my mother never received the validation she needed from her own mother, how could she be expected to give it to me? She admits that she, along with my father, never gave my sisters and me compliments or praise when we were little and, at first, explains: "We thought everyone's kids were good in school and that you were just supposed to accept it matter-of-factly. We thought children *had* to do well—we didn't think it could be different. Daddy could never say a nice word to your face, but behind your back he raved. We got praise from others because of you, *we* were lauded, but we didn't see why we had to give praise or compliments or encouragement to children." On reflection she adds: "I never got it from my mother. I can't remember her ever saying, 'Oh, you got a nice job. You're doing well.' Kind words, affectionate names embarrassed me because I never heard them at home."

THE INTERNAL JUDGMENT MACHINE

The withholding of love and nurturance and the scarcity of praise and approval were effective power tactics that induced children to accept unquestioningly the values, attitudes, and moral orientation of their self-sacrificing parents. Holding out love and praise as rare commodities, hard-won rewards to be earned by behaving in certain established ways, played upon the normal dependency needs all children have and kept children in line. There was always the hope, like a carrot on a stick, that if only one were *good enough,* the rewards would be forthcoming.

Like the contemporary cults described by Dr. Lifton, some authoritarian traditional families perpetuated control over individual guilt by stressing criticism and self-criticism. A fifty-year-old woman whose Viennese immigrant family in Kansas City scraped together enough money after the Depression to send her to a private boarding school remembers constantly outdoing herself in a futile attempt to gain recognition from her hypercritical parents. The capstone of her school years came in the eighth grade when she had the lead in the school play, won the dramatic award, and gave a two-hour recital. "My mother was sick and didn't come. She never came to anything," she recalls. "The best compliment I ever got from her was when I gave the welcoming speech to our new pastor. She said: 'Aunt Kate said you did a marvelous job on your speech. It's a shame your dress was too short.' "

Similarly, a fifty-eight-year-old man who grew up in the Depression years in Princeton, New Jersey, and has subsequently become a psychoanalyst, remembers: "When I came home from school with good work that I'd done, my mother's response to me was 'Oh, that's nice, Tom,' followed by a fifteen- to twenty-minute dissertation on what *she* had done in a similar situation that was better."

And a hard-driving forty-year-old editor at a New York publishing house, the product of an immigrant home where the father was under constant attack from her deeply traumatized, faultfinding mother for not earning enough after losing everything in the Depression, says: "The battle that I now face is to take that internal judgment machine I have and turn it off. It's the judgment that I got throughout my whole growing-up years and it's now internalized. I don't realize that it's actually my mother's voice talking to me. It says: 'You're no good. You're a failure. You didn't marry well enough. You should be farther ahead. You don't know how to get along with people.' Whatever frustration occurs, I use the machine to attack myself."

As effective as this negativistic method was for the intense incorporation of family ideals, the indoctrination was accomplished at the expense of the child's own social and moral growth. When disciplining a child was like "training a wild horse, breaking the horse in the way you wanted him to be," as an eighty-year-old retired police captain explained his child-rearing technique to me, the child's spirit often got broken along with his wild ways. In a culture that emphasized the duty and responsibility children owed their parents but denied them uncritical love and approval, dependency gained an intractable foothold.

For many of us, this dependency took the form of a doomed quest to regain our parents' unconditional love by forfeiting our identities to repay their sacrifice for us, living not for ourselves, but for them. We attempted to placate mother by becoming a goody-goody and following her dictates. We wanted to make her happy by being what she was not, or if she berated father for not living up to her expectations, we were determined to do better. But the limits we accepted for ourselves were inauthentic and bound to cause us trouble. Either we would rebel against them when their falsity became intolerable or we would succumb to depression when we realized that we could never live up to our exalted ideals and had no alternative goals to substitute for them.

Psychiatrist Silvano Arieti, coauthor of *Severe and Mild Depression*, feels that trying to recover what children perceive as a "sudden" loss of parental love through lifelong subservience to a "Dominant Other" or a "Dominant Goal" is a key factor in depression. In the 1930s and early 1940s, children were generally expected to grow up fast and be on their own at an early age. Older brothers and sisters were expected to take care of their younger siblings and assume some of the responsibility for the family's welfare. My older sister Phoebe for example, was pressed into "mothering" my sister Arlene and me when my mother had to go to work in my father's business. My ex-husband's brother, Sol, the oldest of seven children, gave up a scholarship to college so that the others could get an education.

Of course, for these children, this kind of responsibility meant a change in family status and a loss of freedom. Some adjusted well in making sacrifices for younger brothers and sisters. But for others, this experience is akin to what Arieti calls "Paradise Lost": To regain paradise, the child reacts in one of two ways. He can become entirely dependent on others for the gratification of his needs, later finding substitutes for the depriving mother or father—a spouse, a companion, the firm where the person works, or a social institution to which he belongs—whose love, affection, or approval is essential to his well-being. Or he becomes a compliant person, imbued with a strong sense of duty, who believes that love is not available now but will be if he can live up to the expectations of others. "When he does not succeed in obtaining what he wants," says Arieti, "he tends to blame himself. He feels he has not done enough. He could do more."

The potentiality for depression and conflict that people have when they try to live up to ideals and standards out of a compulsive need arising from an early narcissistic wound was graphically illustrated by the case of Richard Nixon. The former president's childhood history of an impoverished family life and maternal deprivation is well known. Says psychoanalyst Dr. Sydney Pulver: "Nixon's achievement of the presidency rescued his self-esteem, but there was always a fragility to his esteem, making him vulnerable to disaster, that would not have existed had he not been a victim of early narcissistic injury."

Haunted by a fear of the future and the stark terror that everything would be pulled out from under them again, Depression parents tended to create a paradoxical situation for their children. They wanted to spare their children hard times, yet they gave their children a hard time by living through them too much. The children's personal goals often became subverted by parental hopes, frustrations, and anxieties so that the children's sense of limits kept pulling them in opposite directions—their own and their parents'.

In Freudian terms, with the resolution of the Oedipus complex between the ages of three and six, the child's goals and aspirations shift from unrealistic, sexual goals to neutralized, attainable ones in the realm of achievement and in the acceptance of moral values and standards. The superego, a product of the individual's internalized images of the parents, contains two subsystems: the conscience and the ego ideal. The latter sets the goals aspired to and the moral standards or ideals, while the conscience judges and regulates the person's behavior, punishing transgressions through guilt and suppressing or redirecting instinctual drives that, if acted on, would violate the moral code internalized by the child.

When the child feels unaccepted by a constantly critical parent, the parent resides in the child's ego ideal and conscience like an "internal judgment machine." Through insight and gratification in other relationships, some of us overcome the fear of abandonment that could keep us enmeshed in a competitive struggle to fulfill unrealizable parental needs. We detach ourselves from the internalized parent's crippling demands for perfection by consciously structuring healthier limits for ourselves based on our own needs and the external demands of reality.

When I read *The Managerial Woman*, the book by two Harvard Business School graduates documenting how twenty-five women who reached college age during the Great Depression went on to gain top management positions in the United States, the thing that impressed me most was the pivotal role their *fathers* played in the women's lives. To these fathers, their daughters were not lesser human beings than boys but "special" in their own right. By confirming their freedom to be more than tradition and society prescribed, the fathers encouraged their daughters to be autonomous and to act out of positive feelings about themselves rather than defenses against self-doubt.

The closeness in these families was not based on the emotional blackmail of narcissistic love that says: "I'll love you as long as you give me something to brag about to my friends." It was based, as this recollection by one of the subjects in *The Managerial Woman* shows, on the parents' *non*-self-centered love and shared values that encouraged their children to develop personal responsibility and initiative:

From my earliest recollections my parents and I were friends. Of course we like each other, but we loved each other very much. I always wanted to be just like my mother and just like my father. . . . Yet in spite of this I think my parents really encouraged me to be myself. They always encouraged me to think through things very carefully and to venture my own opinion, even when I was very very young. I think they really trusted me and I them. It was as if we all dared venture out on our own, because no matter what happened, we would all come together again and we all preferred each other anyway. . . . I think, perhaps in my early years they were more protective of my feelings than of my physical safety. I don't mean they would let me kill myself, but the idea of a cut or even a broken bone didn't panic them. I remember wanting to climb a very tall tree when I was about five. My dad said it was too tall for me but I could try if I insisted. My mother said that I would fall. My dad said that if I fell I would learn a good lesson about where my limits were but if I made it I'd learn not to always let others set limitations for me. I climbed that tall tree right straight to the top and I never forgot the lesson.

I must confess that when I read this account and others in the book, I was jealous of these women who had such caring and supportive fathers, friends rather than autocrats, who helped their daughters become all they could be. I remembered how my own father wanted to slap you in the face if you disagreed with him, how conventional his attitude was toward girls, how consumed he was with his own insecurities.

And remembering this, I was overwhelmed with pangs of remorse at my disloyalty. As surely as the men who leaped out of the windows of skyscrapers so that their survivors could live off their insurance, my father forfeited his life in order that his family would never have to worry about money the way he did. For all his natural gaiety and wit, I don't think he ever conceived of himself as someone with a right to enjoy life. Hemmed in by the narrow limits of his time, inhibited by his upbringing, he thought of himself solely as a provider. An innocent patriot in those days when romanticized, idealistic illusions about our cultural institutions still flourished, he blamed himself entirely for his financial problems. He saw them strictly in terms of his own humiliating personal failure and could not make the connection between the Depression and a social order that had neglected to curb greed at the top with proper controls. Instinctively, even when I was too young to understand it all, I sensed my father's vulnerability underneath his Clarence Day exterior and knew how scared he was of life. Sometimes, at the dinner table when I listened to him boast about how he got all A's in arithmetic and was always the first one to hand in his paper, I couldn't help wondering what he might have achieved with his skills if his father hadn't cut short his education.

Eventually my father prospered. He got out of the clothing business, became a real estate developer, and bought an apartment building. After he saw his three daughters married, their safety assured in his eyes, he seemed more relaxed, less pressured, but the strain of providing for us all those years had taken its toll. The last time I saw him alive was through the window of an airplane. He was smiling and waving good-bye as my husband and I, still in the newlywed phase, took off for a trip to Nassau. Two days later, while visiting my sister Phoebe and her family in New York, my father died of a heart attack on Jones Beach.

I flew home for the funeral in shock. When I walked into the old row house on Arlington Street, the house I grew up in, and saw my mother lying on the sofa weeping like a lost, abandoned child—utterly alone in spite of all the people around her—I felt a lurch of love and pity for her as strong as pain.

At the funeral, after the others had filed out, I stood in front of the open casket and told my father I loved him. I spoke to him with a desperate, crazy kind of urgency, wanting to believe that he could hear me because it was so terribly important that he know. When I bent toward him, my hand grazed the sleeve of his jacket, and the feel of death frightened me. I pulled back and stared at my father, all dressed up in his unworn best suit—had he been saving it to be buried in?—and I began to cry. I wept for all the things he'd never done, the places he'd never been, the pleasures he'd never known. I wept for the passing of an unfinished man.

HARD TIMES AND HIGH HOPES

In Studs Terkel's *Hard Times,* his remarkable "Oral History of the Great Depression" based on interviews done in the 1960s, psychiatrist Nathan Ackerman describes how the men who came to him were suffering from depression because their wives belittled and emasculated them for not "bringing home the bacon," and the men felt despised and ashamed of themselves. Then he makes this comparison between the 1930s and the 1960s, a comparison that still holds true today:

Many complaints today are pitched to the level of social actions. We have a great deal of acting out. Instead of patients coming with a constrained neurosis, today they are less prone to choke up their distress. They live out their emotions in conflict. They get into difficulty with other people. They create social tensions. They act out: drinking, drug-taking, stealing, promiscuity. . . . In place of complaining, they explode. They live out some of their urges. They don't contain the disturbance within their own skin.

Thirty, forty years ago, people felt burdened by an excess of conscience. An excess of guilt and wrongdoing. Today there's no such guilt. In those days, regardless of impoverishment, there was more constraint of behavior. I cannot imagine looting thirty-five years ago. Despite want, the patterns of authority prevailed. Today, those standards have exploded. Looting and rioting have become sanctioned behavior in many communities.

Dr. Ackerman goes on to say that despite deprivations, there was predictability and more continuity in the way of life during the Depression. People could make long-term plans, knowing that if they worked hard they could look forward to their reward ten years down the road. "Today there's no such conviction," says Ackerman. "People can't predict five years hence."

Although there was hardship during the Depression, the greater degree of structure in people's lives at least gave them the security of knowing where they stood. As that structure came undone in the Sixties, people began to voice a new complaint. Calling it "anguish in their aloneness," Dr. Ackerman describes it: "They don't know where they belong. . . . They complain of feelings of disorientation. They are afraid of close relationships. They are not happy with their wives. They fail utterly in controlling their children. They are bewildered, they are lost."

This lost feeling of middle-class people today is similar to the rootlessness that the unemployed miners felt in the Thirties. There is the same feeling of loneliness and alienation that comes from being "outside society," as Dr. Ackerman put it, except that the middle-class loneliness of today stems not from the lack of money but from the breakdown of the social community.

Dr. Ackerman's observation in *Hard Times* that another Great Depression might have the beneficial effect of bringing people closer together in mutual consideration and concern—"something like the quality of caring in London during the blitz"—struck me with a peculiar shock of recognition. I recalled how Barry Golden, the young attorney I interviewed when he was preparing to leave his second wife, had remarked glumly, "The only thing that can save this country is a Depression."

This kind of catastrophical thinking, dubbed "hardship therapies" by David Riesman, presupposes that only the iron rod of hardship can stiffen the spine of individual character and force us into group cohesiveness. It represents both a yearning to break out of the bell jar of amoral privatism, and at the same time, a refusal to take personal responsibility for becoming less selfish. In its childlike dependency, catastrophical thinking reminds me of the "rescue fantasies" infantilized people entertain of a messiah swooping down out of heaven and lifting them out of trouble. The pull of this particular fantasy is probably what accounts for the phenomenal success of the rash of disaster movies in the Seventies: the myriad *Airports, Earthquakes,* and *Swarms.* We know we are out of control, but we have no faith in our power to control our wayward impulses except in the face of impending doom.

Yet when impending doom became a reality with the threat of a radioactive explosion caused by a reactor failure at the Three Mile Island nuclear power plant near Harrisburg, Pennsylvania, on March 28, 1979, the public's reaction was strangely subdued. Inured to the thought of the Apocalypse by so many dress rehearsals in the movies, people felt as if they had already lived through the nuclear accident in *The China Syndrome.* A disaster movie with a nuclear fuel "meltdown" theme, *The China Syndrome* had been released, uncannily, shortly before the Harrisburg incident occurred, prompting cynical sophisticates at cocktail parties to speculate that the malfunction at the Three Mile Island plant had been staged by Hollywood to hype the movie.

This response of cynicism mixed with a stoical "business-as-usual" attitude represents a widespread feeling of futility and apathy today. Unlike the naïve idealists in the Thirties, the public has lost confidence in the ability or desire of government to protect the people from the venality of commercial interests. Having tired of protest, we lose ourselves in escapist pursuits and prepare for doomsday by going to apocalyptic movies.

Our doomsday obsession indicates that as much as we hated the constrictiveness and guilt-production of the moralistic Thirties, we would like to revive the idealism and social concern of that time. People were suffering then, but they drew together in a common dedication to a better way of life. They were sustained by the belief that things *could* be better. Today we believe they *can't,* and this disillusionment with society's most cherished ideals, particularly the ideal of fidelity and permanence in marriage, has caused a regression to uncompromisingly self-seeking behavior.

"Getting yours" has become the new moral code because people feel that the old moral code of restraint and ethicality was a hypocritical lie. Many of those who were schooled to obey stern prohibitions against sex outside of marriage feel that they were duped—first by their parents, who cheated them out of the healthy enjoyment of their developing sexuality, and later by their partners, who broke their commitments and betrayed them. Both the "good" boys and the "nice" girls indoctrinated with moral restraint in a more repressive age harbor resentment. What was the purpose, they wonder, of having been made to masturbate shamefully in the bathroom or wear their virginity like a straitjacket during their courtship years, when their marriages didn't last anyway?

Most of the men and women I interviewed who were reared in the pre-sexual-revolution era reported experiences similar to mine. Their parents used the disgrace of an illegitimate child as the *deus ex machina* to enforce rigid sexual taboos that had more to do with the parents' own conflicts about sex and their possessiveness of their children than they did with bastardy.

"GUILT WORK"

Those of us who later rebelled against the harsh moral restraints of our parents and became sexually "free" learned that freedom is *more* than just another word for nothing left to lose. The mere fact of breaking the rules and being able to bed down a dizzying array of partners—or any partner indiscriminately—without feeling conscious guilt is no proof of autonomy. It is merely proof that we have, for the moment, *repressed* our responsible social impulses and the internalized guilt controls that guide them. But it does not mean that we have done the necessary "guilt work" to liberate those controls from domination by outside authority—parental or peer—and formulate limits of our own.

Our sense of guilt arises out of our ability to tolerate coexisting feelings of love and hate as infants, and it is the basis for our growth into socially mature and personally fulfilled adults. During the first years of life, if the nurturant mother is emotionally available to receive affection from us as "reparation" for our sadistic fantasies, our guilt sense is transformed from anxiety into concern. This concern later leads to the gratifying investment of the self in love and work. If an opportunity for "reparation" is denied, or our infant life is marred by the intrusion of a very powerful authoritarian influence, we may grow up with an oppressive sense of guilt that hampers our full enjoyment of life. But competent therapy, in most cases, will not cause us to lose the capacity for a sense of guilt—it will only lessen it. Once relieved of irrational fears of abandonment or reprisal for harboring early feelings of rage, we can tolerate ambivalence—hate as well as love—and our guilt is no longer a Damoclesian sword but an ethical guide leading us toward autonomy and personal fulfillment.

As Rollo May points out in *The Meaning of Anxiety* (1950), genuine autonomy is not possible without corresponding responsibility. When the attempt to reduce guilt repudiates a person's constructive moral urgings and concern for others, the result is often neurotic anxiety instead of the hoped-for happiness. By the same token, excessive guilt will not magically disappear merely by acting out the conflicts underlying it. These conflicts between our sexual or aggressive urges and our opposite and, perhaps, even more primal needs for constructive social ties must be confronted and worked through before we can achieve moral autonomy.

It is simplistic to believe that sexual self-expression in and of itself will free us from unhealthy symbiotic ties to parental love objects. What if, in our fantasy life, our sexual partner is actually our mother or father? Or what if the partner is *not* the parent we need that person to be? The clinical literature is filled with the histories of people who have sexual affairs and are still deeply tied on an infantile level to their mothers and fathers. Sexuality is an expression of *something* because in the sex act we are saying "I *am*"—but that does not make us an adult.

Ada, one of two black young women in Rollo May's study of unmarried mothers in *The Meaning of Anxiety*, is a case in point. Her dilemma represents the failure to achieve liberation through sexuality when our moral standards are devoid of *individual* content and are nothing more than the parent internalized. A compliant, acquiescent nineteen-year-old, Ada was reared in the days of the old moral order and had a strong superego in the conventional sense. Although she started having sexual relations while still in high school and became pregnant without guilt, she was not free to follow her own desires without anxiety:

Ada . . . had a "great need to measure up *but no self-chosen goals or
feelings of what she wanted to measure up to.*" As a consequence,
her spontaneity and inner instinctual promptings were almost
entirely repressed. Her responsiveness to others gave her anxiety
because she could not respond in ways that fitted her high standards.
When she felt she had not lived up to her internalized expectations,
a profound disorientation occurred and much neurotic anxiety
ensued.

The "bind" in which she was caught consisted of the fact that she had learned to comply with authority, and when the young man by whom she was pregnant insisted on his wishes, she could not say no to *his* authority. She was not guilty because of the sex or pregnancy as such, but rather because she responded to an authority other than her mother.

Much of the "instant intimacy" and socially irresponsible behavior that passes for freedom today is nothing more than the flip side of the self-sacrificing moral code of the Thirties and early Forties. People reared under the sword of threatened rejection for not living up to parental expectations may be acting out their sexual or aggressive conflicts, but they are not coming to terms with them. Guilt is only a bit player in the piece, not the villain. We need to feel guilt when we have disregarded or violated our moral standards, but they must be *our* standards, not imposters masquerading as our own.

Final Payments, Mary Gordon's novel about an Irish Catholic woman's emancipation from a self-destructive burden of guilt, traces the source of this masochistic guilt to the fear of loss of the earliest love objects or their withdrawal of love. Isabel Moore, whose mother died when Isabel was two, is the only child of the "neighborhood intellectual" of Queens, a professor of medieval literature at the local Catholic college. Unyielding in his orthodoxy, Isabel's father is enraged when he finds her in bed, at the age of nineteen, with David Lowe, his most devoted student and the first and only boy Isabel had ever dated. Weeping with shame, David cries out: "I'll marry her, Professor. It will be all right; I'll marry her." But Isabel's father, in pure hatred, forbids David ever to see Isabel again.

Less than three weeks later, Isabel's father has an incapacitating stroke. Feeling responsible for his illness, Isabel makes the decision to give up her life for her father, caring for him alone in their one-family house in Queens for the next eleven years, until his death. She lives through the Sixties like a nineteenth-century anachronism of familial devotion, leading a sterile life with "the balletic attraction of routine." In this rumination on her motives for getting caught in bed with David Lowe, Isabel hints at the oedipal overtones of her deep love relationship with her father:

Was I trying to punish my father for something; for his lack of attention to my obvious adulthood, for his lack of jealousy at the intrusion of so clear a rival? He didn't even tease me about David. Perhaps I was outraged at his lack of outrage at what could so obviously have separated us. Would it be so easy for him to let me go? Perhaps the prospect so deeply appalled me that I had to construct the scene that would forbid me marriage during my father's lifetime, that would make impossible the one match he might have approved.

After her father's death, with the loving help of two childhood friends, Isabel cuts a path through "the sickening expanse of potential" toward an autonomous adult life. She lands a political job and becomes heavily involved in an affair with Hugh, a married man who has been cheating on his hostilely clinging wife for years. Hugh wants to leave his wife for Isabel, but the wife confronts Isabel at a party and again at work. Nastily playing on Isabel's vulnerabilities, she asks: "What would your father say if he knew what kind of life you lead?" She flails away. "You couldn't wait for your father to die so you could get a man between your legs." Then she hits Isabel where it hurts the most. "You want to be a good person," she says judgmentally. "I know you are a good person at heart."

The confrontation triggers profound feelings of repressed fear and guilt in Isabel, and she sinks into depression. She abandons Hugh and attempts to win back her dead father's approval, as she had when he was alive, by once again sacrificing her life to become a caretaker. This time she goes to live with Margaret Casey, the mean, arthritic former housekeeper whose plans to marry Isabel's father had been dashed when Isabel, at the age of nine, became jealous and sent her packing.

At Margaret's, Isabel regresses to infantile submission. She humbly endures one indignity after another at the malicious old woman's hands, growing fat as she comforts herself with food, all for the certitude of saintliness as opposed to life and its inevitable risk of loss. Hugh writes to tell her that he has left his wife and is waiting for her. Her friends stay in touch. Finally, after a particularly vicious insult from Margaret, Isabel makes up her mind to renounce martyrdom and rejoin the living. She settles her debt to Margaret with a twenty-thousand-dollar check from the sale of her house—"you could change lives without giving up your own life," she realizes—and has her two faithful friends come pick her up.

Only when Isabel reclaims her standards from her father's domination is she free to live. By overcoming the terror of his loss, she is able to risk losing the others she loves. Released from struggling to win her father's approval, she can replace the ascetic ideal of being "a good person" with more realizable limits that are genuinely her own:

It came to me that life was monstrous: what you loved you were always in danger of losing. The greatest love meant only, finally, the greatest danger. That was life; life was monstrous.

But it was life I wanted. Not Margaret. Margaret's unlovableness rendered her incapable of inflicting permanent pain. She could decay the soul, but she could not destroy it. Only love could do that, and the accidents of love. So that at Margaret's death I would feel nothing: only relief. But it was life I wanted. Life and loss.

If I wanted I could have, perhaps, everything—love, work, friends. If I wanted, perhaps I could give reasonably without giving my life. And perhaps I would get, for my pains, refreshment, sustenance, and the rewards of a reasonable life.

Regardless of our ethnic background, all of us reared to behave obediently and to respect authority or tradition in the Thirties and early Forties can relate to Isabel Moore's struggle to achieve moral maturity. We can appreciate the degree to which òur fear of the withdrawal of parental or social approval shaped our moral values and behavior and how our maturity, like Isabel's, suffered for it.

Trained to be "good" and to live *for* our parents as they had lived *through* us, our generation accepted the mission assigned us by our families as readily as Isabel gave up her life for her father. In his fascinating analysis of the family system, German psychoanalyst Helm Stierlin traced out the way in which certain children are selected to fulfill distinct missions for their parents.

The "superego children" are the goal-oriented ones who are expected to bring acclaim and distinction to the family, like my mother's two older brothers, for example, or daughters who are supposed to take the place of sons. Many narcissists, incidentally, are these "superego children" of unusual ability or attractiveness whose exploitation by a hostile parent seeking admiration through them has set them off on a search for compensatory attention and gratification. Narcissistic patients, according to psychoanalyst Otto Kernberg, "often occupy a pivotal point in their family structure, such as being the only child or the only brilliant child, or the one who is supposed to fulfill the family's aspirations. A good number of them have a history of having played the role of genius in their families during childhood."

The "ego children" are the ones chosen to bring home to the parents the reality of the outside world and their know-how in getting along with the people in it. In immigrant families, these were the children who brought the American language and customs into the home, and in the Sixties and early Seventies they brought in blue jeans, long hair, and marijuana.

The "id children" have been assigned the mission of living out their parents' pleasure-seeking impulses. They are too much of a burden for the parents who are so emotionally depleted themselves that they can't even use the children to feed their narcissistic needs on the ego or superego level. Since the parents feel that the "id kids" must be gotten rid of somehow, the unconscious message to them is to get lost somewhere or to go off into space or to go off and not come back. These children then become the runaways or they disappear into the drug culture ("Bohemia," in the Thirties) or, in the extreme, they commit suicide.

Viewed from Stierlin's perspective, a whole generation of us—the over-thirty-five generation reared by self-sacrificing, overcommitted parents scarred by the Depression—were "superego children." Our mission was to fulfill our parents' vicarious aspirations: to have all the material things they never had, to be respected and secure, to be pampered by life, to be happy in a way they longed to be but wouldn't admit they weren't, to find unconditional love. Because we believed that our parents' approval was as necessary for life as oxygen, we had to create a stereotypical social order that would rectify the ills of the past and guarantee a perfect future. And so, in the heat of our innocent passion to please, we conceived a shimmering new fantasy of perfection that would utterly consume us for the next two decades—the myth of Suburban Togetherness.

FOUR

$\longleftarrow$ ⎯⎯⎯⎯⎯ $\longrightarrow$

THE
PATRIOTIC
FORTIES

No matter how casual the times, there is always a certain amount of pretense that civility demands of us. But in the days before "letting it all hang out" became fashionable, much of the energy that should have gone into the development of our individual strengths and skills went instead into the creation of a likable, socially acceptable persona. In the 1940s, when World War II gave rise to a new wave of nationalism and ushered in a new era of prosperity, unequivocal conformity to the status quo became a dominant theme in our culture. The discovery of the atom bomb and the onset of the cold war with Russia produced a pervasive jitteriness about loyalty to "the American way" that reached its fanatical extreme in McCarthyism. In an atmosphere charged with the persecutorial fervor of the witch hunt, with practices like blacklisting and the signing of loyalty oaths designed to sniff out "Pinkos," "Commies," and "Leftists" in influential positions or professions, compliance with accepted values became the watchword. The pressure to conform was of such magnitude that many of us became, at least to some degree, what psychoanalysts call "as if" personalities: We ignored our own creative, original responses to life and assumed the role of the all-American boy or girl as if that imitation represented how we felt ourselves to be.

The bobby-soxers of the Forties, O.D.ing on milkshakes and jumping to zany jukebox hits like "Mairzy Doats" in the local soda shop on Saturday night, petting but not going "all the way" at parties, hero-worshiping wholesome idols like Joe Di Maggio and Doris Day, seem incredibly innocent by today's standards. They *were* innocent, but theirs was the innocence of compulsion, not informed choice.

The mere fact that fewer teen-agers in previous generations became pregnant, abused drugs, ran away, or committed acts of violence is no indication of the moral superiority of American youth in earlier times. Although young people in the Forties remained responsive to traditional parental discipline, their good manners should not be confused with goodness of heart arrived at by self-chosen ethical principles. They were polite, well-behaved, and respectful to their elders, but their interests were no less narcissistic than those of the younger generation today. A Purdue University survey defining the major concerns of teen-agers in the late Forties, after World War II had ended, revealed that 33 percent felt there was nothing they, personally, could or should do to prevent wars; 50 percent of all girls regarded their own figures as their major preoccupation; 37 percent of all boys were primarily concerned with having "a good build"; and one third of the two thousand respondents agreed that the most serious problem facing the American teen-ager was acne.

As a teen-ager in the late Forties, I know how totally dependent high school students were on external authority or tradition. We were good because we were afraid to be bad, not because we had genuine charity or concern for others in our hearts. In our baggy, rolled-up blue jeans, sloppy shirttails, and loafers with pennies in them, we rigidly conformed to peer codes of dress and conduct. Our clonelike appearance was outwardly symbolic of the relatively immature level of our moral reasoning. We conformed to standards without making the free choices necessary for a truly moral act. We stayed out of trouble to please others or because that was the law rather than out of any firmly held convictions about how we should behave.

On those occasions when we exhibited concern for others or acted in the supposed interest of a higher good, there was usually a selfish motive lurking beneath the mask of altruism. Most of the time we were worried about getting good grades or being popular, and the feelings and viewpoints of others were of no consequence to us unless they served either of these two purposes. We took an interest in world problems, for example, only to the extent that we could expound on them knowledgeably in history class. Socially, we avoided any topics that might tease out a serious or profound thought and result in ostracism from the crowd for being "different." The impassioned essays I wrote in class preaching tolerance and understanding and service to others were a reflection not so much of the values I had incorporated as they were a shrewd assessment of what the teacher would reward with a good mark.

I cringed when I recently came across this reprint of a "Letter to the Editor" of a 1946 issue of *Seventeen* magazine, but most teenagers at that time, if pressed, would probably have admitted to the same sentiments:

"I think you should have more articles on dates and shyness and put in some more about movie stars, too. Stories like those on atomic energy are very boring."

As young people in the Forties we said and did the "right" thing, but the fact is that our "goodness" was almost unfailingly motivated by a self-orientation. What's worse, it was not even our *true* self that we were promoting, but only a *false* self that we had erected as a protective façade.

FALSE SELF VS. TRUE SELF

In his elaboration of the False Self/True Self concept, British pediatrician and psychoanalyst D. W. Winnicott has given us a valuable insight into the havoc compliance plays with the growth of identity. Since coming of age in the Forties was very much a matter of strict conformity to authoritative codes, Winnicott's description of the role of the False Self sharply recalls the bogus personality many of us felt obliged to develop in order to win approval. Says Winnicott:

A principle governing human life could be formulated in the following words: only the True Self can feel real, but the True Self . must never comply. When the False Self becomes exploited and treated as real there is a growing sense in the individual of futility and despair. Naturally in individual life there are all degrees in this state of affairs so that commonly the True Self is protected but has some life and the False Self is the social attitude. At the extreme of abnormality the False Self can easily get mistaken for real, so that the Real Self is under threat of annihilation; suicide can then be a reassertion of the True Self.

To some extent, all of us conceal from public scrutiny those aspects of ourselves that we are ashamed of or that we think aren't "normal"—our secret fantasies, fears, hates, lusts, idiosyncrasies. We "launder" ourselves to conform to the images we have of majority or "natural" behavior. In the psychologically healthy person, says Winnicott, "the False Self is represented by the whole organization of the polite and mannered social attitude, a 'not wearing the heart on the sleeve.'" The individual has had to forgo some spontaneity, he says, but the gain is "the place in society which can never be attained or maintained by the True Self alone."

Winnicott explains how the defense of the True Self arises in early infancy, like the splitting defense, as a result of the mother's inability to sense her infant's needs. Instead of adapting to the infant's gestures and affirming the primary illusion of omnipotence, she reverses the process and substitutes gestures of her own that the infant makes sense of through compliance or imitation. The infant "gets seduced into a compliance," as Winnicott puts it, and a compliant False Self grows up, continually reacting to others' demands while conveying the appearance of accepting them:

Through this False Self the infant builds up a false set of
relationships, and by means of introjections even attains a show of
being real, so that the child may grow to be just like mother, nurse,
aunt, brother, or whoever at the time dominates the scene. The
False Self has one positive and very important function: to hide the
True Self, which it does by compliance with environmental
demands.

In the healthy person, the compliant aspect of the personality is only a social manner, representing an admirable compromise—but an expendable one. When the issues become crucial, the compromise can no longer be allowed, and the True Self is able to override the False Self through an assertion of will, determination, or courage. If we lack the strength to expose the True Self to rejection or anger when it really matters, then we run the risk of our "nice guy" or "good girl" False Self splitting off from the True Self and being mistaken for the whole person.

This is exactly what happened to many of us growing up in a

tradition-bound era like the Forties when the serious testing of social values by adolescents was not permitted. If we hadn't feared the annihilation of the True Self, we would have questioned the standardized roles we were expected to assume as adults in society. But we had been taught to believe that we lived in the best of all possible worlds, and we saw no alternatives to the existing social structure that weren't considered deviant. Since we were denied legitimate opportunities to test the values we had learned as children, our youthful "rebellion"—sorority and fraternity pranks, hot rodding, surreptitiously smoking cigarettes, drinking and "messing around" at parties—was merely a precocious parody of our parents' behavior. In a rush to "grow up," we succumbed to our assumed roles with the appearance of an embrace. Men didn't *enter* the professions or women marriage—we *invaded* them, running hard. But inside ourselves we had the uneasy feeling of acting out a charade, miming a part with convincing sincerity but somehow never quite bringing it to life.

The irony about the False Self is that the more successful the defense is, the greater social success the person may enjoy while feeling more and more unreal and futile:

The world may observe academic success of a high degree, and may find it hard to believe in the very real distress of the individual concerned, who feels 'phoney' the more he or she is successful. When such individuals destroy themselves in one way or another, instead of fulfilling promise, this invariably produces a sense of shock in those who have developed high hopes of the individual.

In show business, where the astute manipulation and merchandising of False Selves earns talented people a fortune, this phenomenon is not uncommon. The suicide of comedian Freddie Prinze at the age of twenty-one is a contemporary example. The son of a Hungarian tool-and-die maker and a Puerto Rican mother, Freddie Pruetzel, as he was then called, was remembered in the mostly black and Puerto Rican tenement neighborhood where he grew up as "the chubby little white kid that everyone beat up on." Overweight and asthmatic, Prinze learned early on that he could deflect aggression away from himself and win acceptance by turning the hardship of his life and the anguish connected with it into a joke. He amused his schoolmates with his antics to the point where he was expelled from school for being disruptive. After three months of enforced absence, he was accepted into the School of Performing Arts.

In his junior year, Freddie landed a part in the school production of *Barefoot in the Park*. He was supposed to be a Jewish telephone repairman, Harry Clark, but he changed the name to Jose Perez and played the role as a Puerto Rican. He was a smash, and from then on Freddie Pruetzel became Freddie Prinze.

Regaling audiences with his transfigured recollections of his childhood, Prinze molded his False Self into a successful comedy act by the time he reached eighteen. In the next four years he earned well over two million dollars and appeared to be on his way to earning millions more. But in the last months of his life, Prinze suffered increasingly from feelings of dissociation and meaninglessness. The applause, the press clippings, and the other external acknowledgments of his existence were not enough to sustain his sense of being real. He came to rely heavily on drugs and complained of feeling like a lifeless commodity in a world built on sham and pretense.

Actress Gene Tierney is another example of a person who was able to use the False Self defense as a basis for career success as a performer but suffered deeply from a loss of inner reality. Her autobiography *Self-Portrait* juxtaposes reminiscences of her starring roles in films like *Laura* and *Tobacco Road* with harrowing accounts of her seven years in mental hospitals. "I had no trouble playing any kind of role," Tierney says in the book. "My problems began when I had to be myself."

Whether famous or obscure, severely or mildly troubled, people with a successful False Self often spend a lifetime looking for a way of getting to their True Self. This, in fact, was a major concern of the Seventies: the finding of the "real me" by people brought up to hide and protect it with a False Self. Although legitimate, the quest was misdirected. Indulgence in drugs, sexual promiscuity, and superficial pop psychologies fail to produce a sustained feeling of inner reality because the way to the True Self is not through the id but through the ego.

As Winnicott explains it, people with successful False Selves have become alienated from the True Self by always *reacting* to life instead of *existing*. Their instinctual id demands, particularly their sexual desires and aggression, are threatening to them and are felt to be alien, as much external as "a clap of thunder or a hit." It is up to the ego, the rational part of the personality that copes with reality and protects the individual against the dangers of the external world, to recognize sexual and aggressive urgings as part of the True Self. As long as the ego is afraid to bear the risks and frustrations involved in satisfying these instincts, the beneficial effect of gratification will be lost. The person will either reject these inner needs out of fear of annihilating the True Self or act on them with the automatic compliance that only the False Self augments. Gratification of id demands might give the appearance of "free" or even wildly liberated behavior, but lacking spontaneity and resonance, it will have a detached, unreal quality—as if it were happening to somebody else. It is *principled choice* that makes experience authentic—and choosing gratification requires a knowledge of personal power as well as of personal limits.

In the Forties, the younger generation complied with the rigid moral and social code of the day and chose frustration as a way of preventing the feared destruction of the True Self. The fear in the Forties was that if we chose gratification, we would be annihilated by parental and social rejection. Our reluctance to break the rules caused us to break with the True Self and become actors and actresses instead of real people. It is only when the ego believes in the power of the True Self to survive the satisfaction or frustration of the instinctual drives that love and work can be experienced as deeply genuine.

THE MARRIAGE RUSH

Replacing fantasies of annihilation with a belief in the ability to survive is not easily done in a culture that makes the individual feel helpless and insignificant. Both the excessive structure in the Forties and the lack of structure in the Seventies have had the effect of reducing people to humanoids—the one by browbeating us into conformity and the other by exposing us to terminally high levels of exploitation that have rendered us incapable of feeling. In terms of spontaneous behavior, there is not much difference between the mass-produced, synthetically sweet young innocents who poured out of our high schools and colleges in the Forties and the burned-out, sexually experienced automatons in their teens and twenties today who, as one thirty-year-old man put it, "would rather get stoned and jerk you off than have an emotionally intimate relationship."

What is different about these youth is their ideology. Constricted as they were, young people in the Forties had social values that guided their identity and gave them the impetus to shoulder the obligations that went along with entrance into the adult world. Today those values are in disarray. The young have lost confidence in our leaders and in parental support and harmony. Because they have no assurance that excellence will get them to the top in the adult world or that relationships entered into will endure, they have succumbed to cynicism and apathy.

If the youth of today are old before their time, they are never old enough, it seems, to assume the mature responsibilities of supporting themselves and raising a family. In the Forties, the opposite was true. Only by assuming mature responsibilities, often before they were ready, could adolescents be considered old enough to enjoy the freedoms young people are indulging in earlier and earlier today. Adolescents in the Forties saw no other way to escape the oppression of traditional morality than to rush off prematurely into the adult world.

For people in my generation, marriage was often seen as the only viable way to gain some semblance of personal and sexual freedom. But it was only a *semblance* of freedom that we gained. Since compliance had already done its dirty work, the typical marriage was a union of two False Selves, each rigidly adhering to socially prescribed roles and each person hoping the other would provide the unconditional love that had not been found at home. Both were stuck at the level of dependence, and neither was ready to grow up *in* the marriage through the different developmental phases—one's own phases, the partner's phases, the children's phases—while at the same time facing the responsibilities involved in commitment.

Ostensibly, the fear of commitment so prevalent today seems in sharp contrast to the rush to marriage in earlier generations. Yet when we hurried into marriage previously, it was often a *counterphobic* move, our rash haste masking our ambivalence about assuming the sex roles cut out for us. Most of the men I know who married in late adolescence and got divorced in mid-life said that they married out of a sense of duty or obligation. They had serious doubts about their readiness for marriage, but they looked upon marriage as an accomplishment, proof that they were somehow more of a man. The women said they thought they had no choice.

Until I met Milt Stevens I had always thought that it was only women in my era who gave up their more glamorous ambitions in order to become a schoolteacher, settle into an early marriage, and make it big in suburbia. But Milt, a contemporary of mine, tells me that's what happened to him. I've known Milt for almost thirty years, but I never really got to *know* him until recently when I interviewed him for this book.

For twenty-five years, until his divorce in 1976, Milt had been married to Charlotte, a high school classmate of mine, and my impressions of him were drawn from a collage of random, superficial social encounters dating from the late 1940s to the present: a blond, baby-faced Milt looking like a long-legged colt in his "Cuba Libre" jacket at our high school graduation party . . . an up-and-coming Milt proudly showing me through the plant of his new electronics company . . . Milt, the arriviste yachtsman with mustache and goatee, hosting a weekend jaunt down the Sassafras River on his plush cabin cruiser . . . the mid-life crisis Milt, candidly discussing his psychoanalysis at a New Year's Eve party while Charlotte is off in a corner drunkenly pursuing an affair with a friend's husband . . . the post-divorce Milt, a spray of wrinkles around his eyes, confiding to me over a friendly lunch about his business problems, his worries about his children, and most of all, the meaninglessness of his sexual diversions with the "tennis bunnies," some of whom Milt had romanced while he was married—scheming suburban dilettantes, all out to shake down their once-but-not-future husbands for a six-figure divorce settlement.

To me, Milt had always seemed like the quintessential cultural narcissist—charming, ambitious, materialistic, fiercely competitive, and a promiscuous womanizer incapable of real intimacy. At our luncheon meeting prior to the interview, everything he said confirmed this image, particularly his description of his relationships. In a tone of jaded frustration he spoke of mechanically juggling them the way someone shuffles a deck of cards, and his parting words were the standard refrain of the unconditional love song: "I know the perfect woman is out there somewhere, and I'm going to keep looking until I find her."

But several months later, driving out to Milt's mile-long factory to interview him, I was in for a surprise. During the long hours we spent with the tape recorder, an entirely different picture of Milt emerged, and I realized that all along I had been taken in by Milt's False Self. He, too, had been railroaded into being someone other than the person he was or wanted to be. He'd played the game, then broken the rules, and now, like so many others, had tired of raiding the "candy store." He was enjoying a committed relationship for the first time in years—no, she wasn't perfect; he was just ready—and his biggest concern was how to take a firmer hand with his children without being coercive.

A self-made millionaire by the time he was forty, Milt remembers growing up in the humble "mom and pop" grocery store with the apartment above where his parents moved after having lost everything in the Depression. "I saw my mother and father," he says, "each working and co-parenting in a dual role—two people on the same track doing the same things and both reacting to me almost simultaneously. They were there together, and I got them both on the scene within seconds of each other. I was an only child, and my relationship with my parents was very warm, very very close. There was more of a real affection rather than the bubbly, overbearing kind, and there was a subtle awareness of values and goals instead of a direct confrontation."

But there was also the incredibly effective manipulation by guilt. Although Milt worked in the store as he grew up, his parents constantly made him aware of their sacrifice. "My dad always reminded me how hard he was working," Milt says. "I got five dollars to go out on a date, and he told me how long it took to get those five dollars and that I should spend it wisely—and have a good time. Five dollars!"

Milt speaks of the Forties and early Fifties in terms of "cycles" and "plateaus"—periods where he was borne along by outside influences and had very little control over his life. "It was always what *they* wanted, what *they* felt was best," he recalls. "I was a musician. I belonged to the union, and having never been away from home, was looking for independence. When I finished high school I had a job offer in Miami Beach playing in an orchestra making two hundred dollars a week. And I was going to take it—in those days that was good money. But my father said: 'What you should do is become a music *teacher*. Go to school for four years and if you lose your job, then you'll have security.' I knew where he was coming from. Here was a man who'd been riding around in Pierce Arrows before and all of a sudden had zero, to the point where he had to become a working partner in a grocery store. With the Crash, my parents' generation became ultraconservative and saw the professions as the answer to my generation, a way to overcome the restrictiveness of an organization and become an independent operator—a doctor; lawyer; in my case, a teacher. I didn't really want to be a teacher, but I had no brothers or sisters I could relate to or learn from or ask, 'What do I do about this?' The friends I had were very limited; I had one close friend who lived a block and a half away, and we did talk and socialize together—we were double dating—but basically we didn't delve into the depths of our inner feelings as you might do today. So after all this time, all this preparation, all these years of taking music lessons—violin lessons, clarinet lessons, saxophone lessons—I switched to secondary education and went off to Glassboro State College to begin a new life."

In college, Milt started dating Charlotte, a pleasant, conventional girl from a wealthy family, who was described in our high school yearbook this way: " 'Char' wants to teach in a high school that has a tall science teacher . . . pastime is driving to Glassboro on Friday nights . . . likes 'M's' new car and knitting sweaters for 'M' . . . thinks well of 'M' himself, too."

Milt was twenty-one when he married Charlotte, and she was eighteen. They "thought well" of each other, but it was social and family pressure that drew them into marriage rather than the irresistible pull of attachment. "I remember walking up and down the street in Glassboro for four hours," Milt said, "with a buddy of mine who had just gotten married. It was a week before my wedding, and I was trying to figure out what this was all about. Why was I going to get married just because everyone else seemed to be getting married? Charlotte was very nice. We had gone together for three years. It was about time, I guess—and her mother wanted her out of the house."

In terms of social experience with women, Milt was a neophyte prior to marriage. Charlotte was the only woman he'd ever really dated. He had never taken anybody else out to dinner. "Like the commitment to a profession," he says, "marriage at a very early age was the start of another cycle that created a series of goals for me—created them *for* me as opposed to my creating them." Becoming a family man was a spur to growth for Milt in the business world, where he used his background as a science teacher to develop a phenomenally successful line of electronic equipment. But in the world of relationships, as Milt discovered a number of years down the pike, his marriage to a compliant surrogate like Charlotte had been, in his words, "a kind of left turn for growth."

Eventually, we'll follow Milt into suburbia, where both splendor in the crabgrass and the serpent of lost innocence await him, but for the moment, let us retrace our steps and consider some important factors. By his own account, Milt came from a poor but loving home where his mother and father participated equally in parenting and family responsibilities. His was not the classic "arrested development" case so often described in psychoanalytic literature of the narcissistically self-centered or overprotective mother out of sync with her child's needs and unaided by the absent father. The fact that Milt was an only child may account for his becoming an overachiever, but it does not explain why he became a member of what psychologist J. E. Marcia named the "identity-foreclosed" group—people whose passive acceptance of goals their parents have laid out for them spares them the struggle of giving precedence to the True Self, but also results in taking a "left turn for growth."

To explain that peculiar growth-evading acquiescence so typical of Milt's generation—*even in homes where parenting was close to ideal*—we have to look to the cultural values of Milt's time. Riffling through my high school yearbook again, I am appalled at the awful duet the pages sing. Bellowing out of the boys' side of the book is a loud basso profundo of blatant materialism, and arising from the girls' is a dulcet counterpoint of cloying, and often equally materialistic, domesticity:

"Al" aims to graduate Penn as a lawyer and become a millionaire	"Candy's" favorite pastime is loving Sonny to death
"Ace" hopes to be a millionaire or a president	"Cece's" ambition is to get married and have twins

"Dick" wonders if he'll ever become a millionaire as he wishes

"Buddy" aims to be a millionaire and drive a Cadillac

"Harv" hopes to play for the Warriors and make a million dollars

"Dorrie's" ambition is to have a house with a swimming pool

"L" wants to marry "him," make a million, wear a mink

"Lottie" hopes to march down the aisle with a rich hubby

If adolescence is the time of idealism, of searching for causes and heroes greater than ourselves to inspire the definition of our identify, what in the world was wrong with us? Why were we such greedy little monsters who had no interest in any social values other than making a million dollars or marrying it?

Our aspirations for monied togetherness were merely a mirror of the distorted outlook of a postwar society. Again, in a counterreaction to the extreme of discipline and sacrifice demanded by the war, we abandoned ourselves, as we had in the Twenties, to an orgy of self-serving consumerism. The whole country was now engaged in a kind of tribal celebration of our victory abroad. Having discharged our duty to others by making the world "safe for democracy," we now felt free to devote ourselves unabashedly to the pursuit of the good life. Joseph Adelson captured that quixotic dream in this wistful reminiscence:

We had as a nation emerged from a great war, itself following upon a long and protracted Depression. We thought, all of us, men and women alike, to replenish ourselves in goods and spirt, to undo, by an exercise of collective will, the psychic disruptions of the immediate past. We would achieve the serenity that had eluded the lives of our parents; the men would be secure in stable careers, the women in comfortable homes, and together they would raise perfect children. Time would come to a stop. Call it what you will—a mystique, an illusion, a myth—it was an ideology of sorts, often unspoken but, perhaps for that very reason, most deeply felt.

It is not hard to understand why the Charlottes of that era, those legions of argyle-knitting Madame Defarges, conspired to bring about the suburban revolution even though it often meant that their own heads would roll at some future time. As girls, they were nothing more to their parents than marriage fodder, and the law of upward mobility, so deeply entrenched in our culture, mandated that their sole purpose in life was to marry better than their mothers. What else *could* they do but join the mass exodus into the suburban split levels that symbolized success?

While Milt remembers a "subtle awareness of values and goals instead of a direct confrontation," most of his female counterparts whose aspirations for themselves differed from their parents' were often forced into submission by what amounted to emotional strong-arm tactics. They did not fall in love, they were pushed. For all the element of choice they had in selecting an emotionally (rather than financially) compatible partner, their "love matches" were indistinguishable from arranged marriages between two strangers. Later they would say they "outgrew" one another when, in fact, many were mismated from the very beginning or, in some instances, were not fit to be mated with anyone at all.

It was the tragedy of women like Vivian Brooks that they were forced into marriages with men who gave the appearance of being highly eligible prospects but were actually so immature and emotionally unstable as to be unmarriageable. In 1945, Vivian was in her freshman year at the University of Pennsylvania, a bright, beautiful young woman who thought she had world enough and time for a career in psychology and marriage when she met the right man. She recalls: "I was an honor student on the Dean's List, on the varsity swimming team, and that year had just finished being the most exciting year of my life. Every night I would come home and say, 'I don't want this day to end, I don't want this week to end, I don't want this year to end.' I was having a ball. I never believed that overnight all of this would be wiped out."

The private atomic explosion that wiped out Vivian's dreams occurred on her eighteenth birthday. For several months she'd been dating Martin, a precocious twenty-two-year-old dental student from New York who was completing his education in the army. On a summer weekend, Martin's family drove down to Philadelphia from Brooklyn to celebrate Vivian's birthday, and they came bearing a birthday cake that was an innocent-looking Trojan horse. When Vivian sliced through the fluffy mounds of white icing into the delicate center, the knife struck something hard. It was a gleaming two-carat diamond engagement ring. For Vivian, it was as if she'd plunged the knife into her own heart.

"I had no intention of getting married then," she says. "It was the farthest thing from my mind, becoming engaged. I didn't even know Martin. Dating at that time was a very formal situation where he came out to the house a dozen times or so. I felt very much nipped in the bud. Basically, my mother made this decision. It wasn't out of malice aforethought, but out of what she thought was my inability to know what was good for me."

Vivian wanted to break the engagement, but her mother wouldn't let her. "She felt that this was an opportunity that might pass me by," Vivian explains. "I was the oldest of three daughters, and daughters certainly weren't considered prize packages in that generation. They were to be gotten rid of as quickly as possible. It was one down, two to go; two down, three to go. In our community it was an accomplishment to marry your daughters off early to what were considered to be good marriage partners, especially professional men. I'm sure my mother felt that she was doing me a great favor."

In 1946, a year after the war's end, Martin received orders to report to Menlo Park, California, where he was to be stationed. It was a time of decision for Vivian. "The dean of the university told my mother, I think it's so very, very wrong to take this girl out of school. This boy is not going into the army to get killed. He's going into the dental corps. Let her finish school, and when the right time comes along, she'll settle down and get married.' I felt that the dean was as close to being a father who could look at this objectively as I could find. My own father was very weak in that respect. He left child-rearing entirely to my mother. And to her, finishing school, having a profession—those were not worthwhile values. My goal in life was to marry."

Why did Vivian not stand up to her mother? "You didn't have the support of your peer group or of the media in those days," she says. "You didn't have the alternatives that are offered to young people today—communes, living together. At the age of seventeen I came into an environment where I certainly wouldn't have been able to pitch for myself. Running away from home would have been devastation." She makes this further comparison between growing up in the Forties and coming of age today. "The war years were like being a little girl and playing at being an older girl. Today I notice that the kids revel in their youth and in their extended childhood. Women of thirty speak of themselves as girls and act like girls, dressed in their blue jeans. In our generation, when you got to be sixteen years old, you borrowed a dress from your mother and put on her high heels and you went to a USO dance (where she met Martin). You wanted to grow up, mainly because the privileges of adulthood were reserved for adults. Sex was in the service of marriage. There was no such thing as sexual experience outside of marriage, at least not for middle-class, aspiring, upwardly mobile kids. You had to look forward to getting married in order to be treated as an adult, to be liked as an adult, to escape from the authority of your parents. In order to have any fun out of life, you were forced to grow up very fast."

Vivian's description of her mother's mind control through guilt-production is both comical and harrowing. "Many of the things she said made no sense at all, and I knew that they made no sense, but I wasn't strong enough to counter her or take the alternative to make my own decision and not follow hers. My mother would say, 'You're eighteen, and in another year nobody will want you.' I knew it wasn't true—I wasn't that stupid—but I had second thoughts: Maybe no one else will like me, or show up. You have that feeling that maybe you're not okay, maybe this is it, what if she's right? I would hear my mother talking to my father downstairs, discussing how they would face the disgrace of a broken engagement: 'If she doesn't marry him, you'll give up your business, we'll move away from Philadelphia, you'll buy a small farm.' I knew they weren't going to do this, and yet I also knew that I was making life unbearable for them. When I pleaded with my mother not to make me go through with it, she said: 'What will we tell your Uncle Fred? Your Aunt Helen will say that the boy left you because he got you pregnant.' They made it so unpleasant at home that the situation became overwhelming. Finally, I chose between two evils. I think you become very neurotic at that point. You don't trust yourself. You don't have any confidence in your own judgment anymore, and that's the turning point. Now they begin to make your decisions for you."

In California, within two weeks after the wedding, Vivian recognized that there was something terribly wrong with Martin. He was emotionally unstable, given to wild mood swings and violent, uncontrollable temper tantrums. "I called the airport and tried to get a plane back, not knowing where I was going," she recalls. "I knew I wasn't going home because they weren't going to let me back in—and where do you go at eighteen, without a college education, without a dime in your pocket? Today, maybe young people would have more confidence. I felt very, very trapped. It was a matter of jumping out of the frying pan back into the fire, and I was going to do it. But I couldn't get a plane. The next day I discovered that Martin had hepatitis, and my rationalization was, 'Well, he's sick.' That was to be the beginning of a long series of rationalizations."

As Vivian later affords us a glimpse of her life through the child-rearing years until her divorce from Martin in 1972, we'll see how she was able to survive for so long in an untenable marriage by immersing herself in the suburban ideology. Yet to most casual observers, her divorce at the age of forty-four was simply another statistic in the annals of "mid-life crisis" casualties, another tiny nail in the coffin of the case for permanency in marriage. Vivian herself sees it differently: "Now as I look back, I think that somebody like Martin, in this generation today, would not get married. He was twenty-two years old. He had been pressured to achieve, and that was one thing he *could* do. He was driven, too. He was driven to marry a girl from a comfortable family so they could help him. This was his 'opportunity.' He wasn't ready for marriage either, nor was he ready to assume not only his own care in the world but the care of another human being and of children. This was certainly going to be a tremendous amount of stress for him, and by the time he got to middle age he couldn't cope with it at all. It was my misfortune that he was sick, very unstable. There are some people who married in my generation at seventeen or eighteen under those same circumstances, and they're still happily married."

"FUN MORALITY"

To people like Milt Stevens and Vivian Brooks, the onetime traditionalists who became parents in the late Forties and Fifties, the original doctrine of permissiveness in child-rearing was as much a reflection of the national social character then as narcissism is today. A dogma that preached the evils of repression and encouraged parents to give their children a free rein was enormously attractive to

young newlyweds who had escaped or been released for good behavior from the parental jailhouse in an immediately postwar era.
Historically, it was a time when we've always gone a little wild in
letting loose our pent-up emotions, and this new generation of parents was determined not to make the same mistakes in the Eden of
suburbia that their parents had made with them. These enlightened
parents were going to cater to their children, lavish abundant affection on them (whether they felt it or not), and above all, *enjoy* them.

The young parents of that time were still smarting from an infancy where "you could bust your lungs" crying, as my mother put it,
because no one would dare pick you up a moment before your regi-
mented feeding schedule. In the Thirties tradition of Puritanism, it
was believed that you could destroy a child for life if you didn't curb
this bundle of dangerous impulses from the very beginning. The
impact of Freud, or rather of a misreading of his conflict theory of
neurosis to fit the growing counterreaction to repression, can be seen
in Martha Wolfenstein's celebrated article "The Emergence of Fun
Morality" that appeared in the *Journal of Social Issues* in 1951.

In her comparison of the various editions of the *Infant Care*
booklet published between 1914 and 1945 by the Children's Bureau
of the U.S. Department of Labor—over 28 million copies had been
distributed by 1952—Wolfenstein showed the steady swing away
from behaviorism toward permissiveness. From the obedience school
policies of John B. Watson and structure of Arnold Gesell in the
early period, child-training writers increasingly reflected a more pleasure-oriented view. The old moralistic belief that the pleasant and
the good were mutually exclusive was replaced by a new "fun morality" that held the pleasant and the good to be not only synonymous
but obligatory for parents and children alike. Wrote Wolfenstein:

Mothers are told that "a mother usually enjoys entering into her
baby's play. Both of them enjoy the little games that mothers and
babies have always played from time immemorial." (This harping
back to time immemorial is a way of skipping over the more recent
past.) "Daily tasks can be done with a little play and singing thrown
in." Thus it is now not adequate for the mother to perform
efficiently the routines for her baby; she must also see that these are
fun for both of them. It seems difficult here for anything to become
permissible without becoming compulsory. Play, having ceased to be
wicked, having become harmless and good, now becomes a new duty.

Exiled to suburbia to enjoy producing perfect children while they were still little more than children themselves, parents understandably fell upon Dr. Spock's *Baby and Child Care*, initially published in 1946, as their Bible. It is equally easy to see why they misinterpreted Spock's writings in the same way that they misinterpreted Freud's. As Freud's exploration of neurotic conflict because of excessive frustration was taken to mean that children should not be frustrated *at all*, Spock's advice was similarly misapplied.

On the subject of feeding schedules, for example, parents misquoted Spock as saying, "Feed your baby on demand." Spock's explicit advice in his book, however, was to feed the baby on demand the *first week* and to lengthen the waiting period gradually, accustoming the baby to frustration in small doses, until an approximate four-hour feeding schedule was reached. When Spock told parents to trust themselves to help their children unfold naturally, he meant to restore to mothers and fathers the confidence in their own judgment that had been squelched by their constrictive upbringing. But Spock's reassurance that what the parents instinctively felt like doing for their children was usually right was construed to mean that the child, if left alone, could do no wrong.

The fact is that the parents did not have any instinctive sense of what to do for their children. They knew only what they did *not* want to do. They did not want to say "no" to their children as their parents had done to them. They did not want to stifle their children's initiative nor truncate their emotional growth, but neither were they prepared to set limits for their children that would wean them away from dependence. Intending to give their children unconditional love yet still searching for it themselves, the parents pushed on beyond the city limits to where the grass was greener. They were lured away by the sweet-sounding madrigal of suburban bliss, not knowing that this melodic tune was only a prelude to the mournful wail of the barbecue blues.

FIVE

THE
SQUARE
FIFTIES

In the fall of 1952, I entered the University of Pennsylvania on a Mayor's Scholarship and spent four years collecting strings of A's the way a beachcomber walks along the shore gathering shells for a necklace. I had no idea why I wanted all those A's or what they were *for* except that they looked good, and I was a collector of excellence.

I commuted to college the whole four years, riding to and from school every day on the trolley. My junior year was particularly bad for me. The tall, lanky air force veteran I'd gone with for two years—a psychology major—had left for graduate school brokenhearted after he'd asked me to marry him and I'd turned him down. I was brokenhearted, too, but my parents told me that he would never make a living. They suggested a doctor instead.

I met the doctor at a resort in New Hampshire shortly before I was to begin my career as a high school English teacher. He came to me like a reprieve from a death sentence. We were married in 1957, lived in a center-city apartment for two years, and settled into suburbia in 1959 to begin the slow process of luxurious stagnation that passed for happiness in those days.

Among the more memorable moments of our courtship in 1956, were our long, sometimes heated debates on the telephone arguing the respective merits of Eisenhower versus Adlai Stevenson. My husband-to-be, who was ten years older than I and had served in both World War II and the Korean War, was a great apologist for Eisenhower. I idolized Stevenson.

It seemed to me that Stevenson, when he spoke of "burning idealism" and issued lofty injunctions against thinking of freedom as a "soft option," understood how flabby the moral fiber of the country had become. I was ashamed of myself for wasting my four years of college and studiously avoiding any byway that might lead me off my programmed course toward a "good" marriage and a "good" life. (One of my English professors consistently inscribed invitations to see him privately about becoming a writer, but I refused to go.) I thought Stevenson really had us pegged when he said:

The softness which has crept into our educational system is a reflection of something much broader, of a national complacency, of a confusion of priorities. . . . We have lacked, I fear, the deep inner conviction that education in its broadest sense unlocks the door of our future, and that it gives us the tools without which "the pursuit of happiness" becomes a hollow chasing after triviality, a mindless boredom relieved only by the stimulus of sensationalism or quenched with a tranquilizer pill.

I cast the first vote of my adult life for Stevenson, but that was a way of paying hush money to my conscience to keep it quiet. Although Eisenhower's milky blandness was singularly unappealing to me, like a custard diet for invalids, I shared this much in common with the great majority of the country who voted for him and soundly defeated Stevenson both times: I, too, under my thin veneer of idealism, wanted the "soft option," the easy way out of doing something for anyone else except me.

GETTING AND SPENDING

The smug, optimistic privatism of the Fifties (as opposed to the nihilistic variety of privatism today) had a kind of Alice in Wonderland quality about it. We were in the world, but not really of it. The cold war that had begun in 1945 and would not end until 1963 created a sinister twilight zone between war and peace that drove us into paranoid insularity. As we erected our dream houses in suburbia, filled them with gadgets and babies, barbecued hamburgers in the backyard, chauffeured the children, commuted on clogged expressways, wriggled inside hula hoops, reveled in togetherness, and took advantage of the continuing business boom by indulging in one long orgiastic spending spree, we were only dimly aware of what was going on in the rest of the world—and we preferred it that way.

The cold war produced both the mass dread of an atomic holocaust and the prosperity enabling us to escape from our paranoia. As much as the flight to the suburbs was the realization of the capitalist American Dream, it was also a way of retreating from the fear of worldwide Communist aggression. While Secretary of State John Foster Dulles played brinkmanship abroad and Senator Joseph Mc-Carthy played on our anxieties at home, the rest of us busied ourselves in what author Harvey Swados called "the great commodity scramble."

In 1956 Americans—only 6.6 percent of the world's population—consumed more than half of all the goods made and sold on earth. We bought 3.7 million vacuum cleaners; 8.3 million electric irons; 1.9 million electric blankets; 5.4 million portable and clock radios; 3.6 million stoves; 3.9 million toasters; 590,000 garbage disposal units; and 975,000 home freezers. By that year two out of every three Americans owned and occupied their own home, and 90 percent of these homeowners had bought refrigerators, 87 percent had automatic washing machines, 76 percent had television sets, and 60 percent had telephones—most of them newly acquired. They also owned 8.2 million power mowers; 23 million electric shavers; and 18.4 million electric coffee makers. In the same year Americans purchased 582 million pairs of shoes; 24 million men's and boy's suits; 60 million men's and boy's separate trousers; 1.75 billion pairs of stockings for men, women, and children; 528 billion cigarettes; 6.6 billion cigars; 88 million bottles of catsup; 648 million cans of peaches; and—was Adlai Stevenson ever right—over a *billion* tranquilizers!

This insatiable getting and spending was the main preoccupation of the 14 million of us who moved into the vast tracts of housing developments that sprang up in suburbia during the Eisenhower years. We found in this obsessive consumerism both an answer to the economic insecurity that had plagued our parents and a distraction from the atomic age of anxiety. Gobbling up goods also satisfied the pangs of loneliness and alienation we felt at having forced our True Selves into hiding when we prematurely assumed our culturally prescribed roles. Our fixation on material growth helped blind us to the stunting of our own emotional and moral growth. The acquisition of "things" replaced developing a sense of our own identity as well as a capacity to care deeply for others.

But this blocking our of inner poverty with the acquisition of material wealth masked what had begun to be an ever-widening chasm between inner and other directedness. As historian Carl Solberg writes in *Riding High*, his perceptive book about America in the cold-war era:

The basic virtues that Eisenhower and Dulles extolled out of their nineteenth-century, small-town past, the old Progressive values of self-reliance, hard work and self-denying thrift got in the way of the galloping rush to cash in on the greatest consumer buying spree that had ever been seen. . . . There was a loosening of the sense of a social responsibility, a falling away of the spirit of public community as instant gratification shouldered away not only forbearance and frugality but the citizenly habit of looking to the common weal.

To Solberg, the split-level house spawned in the Fifties was a mirror of the deep schism in the society as people turned away from the traditional beliefs of their self-sacrificing parents and grandparents toward the new norm of private indulgence. "The split-level was a half-step house, a dwelling in which the open gave way to the secret, the face became a façade, and aspiration was separated from style, a half-story apart," he notes, and it reflected "a heightened discrepancy between what people were and what they seemed, between what they did and what they said."

It was an era when a whole array of new products was available to provide the False Self with a suitable ambience of phony glamour: plastic flowers; wigs; toupees; matching bags, shoes, and gloves; false eyelashes; rented Cadillacs; catered parties. Managing the appearance of success in the eyes of their peers became the all-consuming purpose of the upwardly mobile couple. Both the "glad-handing" husband and the "happy homemaker" wife quickly shed their inner code of personal limits—the traditional values drummed into them by their parents, their schoolteachers, the church, the government—in order to gain the approval of their group. And to the group, nothing else mattered except how well you decorated your home, how lavishly you entertained, how expensively you dressed, which exotic vacation spot you visited, what fancy new restaurant you went to on Saturday night. Success was measured strictly in terms of popularity, and popularity derived from a "marketing orientation" toward life that stressed *selling* your personality instead of *molding* it.

The tragic consequences of relying on the commercialism of the

American business creed to provide a value system for the whole of life were dramatized in Arthur Miller's *Death of a Salesman.* Willy Loman, portrayed on Broadway by Lee J. Cobb, was a sixty-three-year-old salesman who had worshiped material success all of his life and believed that the only way to achieve that success was to be popular and well-liked. He tried to get through life by "riding on a smile and a shoeshine," guided by beliefs like "personality always wins the day" and "start big and you'll end big." But when he realized that he was a washed-up failure carrying a suitcase full of samples and empty slogans and that he had reared his two sons, whom he loved, to be failures, too, he killed himself. Willy Loman had looked to his peers to supply his sense of identity, and when they rejected him, he felt he had no significance. In Miller's words, "He never knew who he was." *Death of a Salesman* opened on February 10, 1949, and didn't close until the end of 1950, after having won both the Pulitzer Prize and the Drama Critics' Circle Award. Despite this wide acclaim, there were some on whom the play's message was totally lost, like the salesman who was heard to remark as he was leaving the theater, "Well, that New England territory always was tough."

In place of the Willy Lomans plodding along toward oblivion with their outdated dreams of Horatio Alger success, a new breed arose in the corporate ranks—the organization man. Supremely aware of the importance of "packaging" in an age dominated by status-seeking and style, Willy Loman's successor dressed in a gray flannel suit and carried an expensive attaché case. He succeeded where Willy Loman had failed because he learned how to manipulate the system as deftly as it manipulated him. Whereas Willy Loman was freighted down with the baggage of traditional beliefs in sacrifice, hard work, and self-restraint, the light-footed organization man had no such impediment. Ruthlessly competitive beneath his affable manner, he jettisoned any values that were in conflict with the profit motive, turned his False Self loose, and developed a winning style by working smart instead of hard.

This prostitution of the old values in the Fifties did not change the fact that men in our culture still defined themselves in terms of their work role and business success. The organization man had no identity apart from his work any more than did the older casualties of the competitive struggle, like Willy Loman, who, if they didn't commit suicide, sustained themselves on the soothing gospel offered by Dr. Norman Vincent Peale in the *Power of Positive Thinking.* What had changed for the organization man was that the signals for his direction were now coming from his contemporary social milieu rather than from his forebears.

Most people remember the Fifties as a national do-nothing period of sterile complacency. But it was a time when the *wrong* kind of growth was taking place. In our single-minded preoccupation with consumerism we were growing farther and farther away from the center of ourselves, both as a nation and as individuals. With the shade drawn over our picture windows, we neglected social issues fermenting around us that would later rage out of control, and in our private lives we were so involved in creating an "image" that we completely lost touch with our inner reality. Like marijuana abuse among young "burn-outs" today, our stupefying absorption in make-believe diverted us from the important tasks of growing into psychological adulthood.

MILT: THE "ABSENT FATHER"

Although an "independent operator" rather than an organization man, Milt Stevens (of the previous chapter) conformed perfectly to the Fifties norm of upward mobility and suburban togetherness. He remembers the first nine years of his marriage to Charlotte as "relatively happy," but it was a deceptive illusion of happiness achieved by looking through those peculiar bifocal glasses we all wore then. By concentrating on our private sphere of gratification at close range, we were able to keep the less satisfying areas of our lives out of our line of vision where they remained, for the most part, out of mind.

Milt thinks of it as having divided his world into two separate environments: "In the early Fifties I had just started a business," he recalls, "and it was exciting to be creating something new. I jumped into my work so completely and with such fervor that achieving financial success became the main focus of my whole life. In my marriage I set up what you might call a 'separation of church and state.' I had this concept that the woman's job was to run the house and the man's job was to run the business and that the two of you got as much togetherness as you could by eating together and sleeping together and occasionally doing things together with the children. But I never did that much with the children," he adds,

"because I was always preoccupied with my work. I was hardly involved with the kids at all."

For the first year of their marriage, Milt and Charlotte lived in
his in-laws' house. When that became "difficult," as Milt puts it,
they moved in 1953 to a small split-level in Broomall, a respectable
middle-class suburb outside of Philadelphia, where they remained for
the next six years. "I was so intent on leaving my in-laws' house,"
Milt remembers, "that we moved into our new house two or three
weeks before the refrigerator was scheduled to be delivered. It was
wintertime, and I left food outside overnight so it wouldn't spoil.
One Saturday night the neighborhood dogs came by and ate the
sausages for Sunday breakfast. The refrigerator came, finally, and
little by little we furnished the house in Early Bare."

When I asked him to describe "Early Bare" for me, Milt says,
"We started from pretty much of a zero base—nothing but chairs in
the living room, dining room, and kitchen. If you had six chairs, two
in each room, it was a big thing because it made the house look
somewhat furnished. Then we bought a bedroom set, and we got a
circular sofa as a gift—from either Charlotte's parents or mine, I
think—but basically, it was just chairs."

Despite the austerity of these early years, Milt claims that they
were happy. It was a time filled with the pride and satisfaction of
starting a family—Milt and Charlotte had three sons, one every three
years. Charlotte's father, a wealthy real estate developer, staked Milt
to his start in business, but Milt was determined to make it on his
own. "I was drawing thirty-five dollars a week in the beginning," he
says, "because the business couldn't afford to pay me much more
than that. Even in those days that wasn't a lot—it was subsistence—
but we managed to get through. The cold war and the space race
with Russsia spurred the demand for the kind of electrical equipment I'd developed, and my company kept doing better and better
—it was almost an evolutionary experience. At one point my father-
in-law said to me, 'If you stick to it, Milt, some day you'll be making
ten thousand dollars a year.' And I remember sitting in the car with
him that afternoon, saying to myself, 'Good God, if only it would
come true.' "

Five years later Milt was making thirty thousand dollars a year
and, in his modest phrase, was considered to be "moving along very
nicely" for a man in his late twenties. But somehow he never seemed

to be earning enough. "I was always behind the eight ball," he says, "because I always seemed to buy something before I could afford it. Charlotte wanted us to be ahead of ourselves. She'd see something that she liked and I'd get it for her, and then I'd figure out a way to juggle all of the other costs in order to swing that. Furniture, furs, jewelry, cars, a boat—whatever we'd get, it was better than we actually could afford but we'd end up affording it, always." A big project in Milt's life was designing something special for Charlotte and saving up for it. "I bought her a chinchilla jacket that I designed," he recalls, "and as the business did better, I was constantly at the jeweler's, having something made up for her—I liked that. For myself, I enjoyed cars and good clothes, but mostly it was getting the mortgage and the bills paid—that was my big achievement. Work achievement. When I had a new product accepted, I was really high."

Milt describes his social life as one of total insulation from the larger world. Except for a year-long stint as the president of a fraternal lodge in his community, his life revolved around work, family, and the usual Saturday night outings or Sunday afternoon barbecues with friends in the neighborhood. "Our social life was very limited because there were always kids and work," he says. "Our friends were mostly neighbors, and we'd go out to dinner or the movies with them, have parties in each other's homes, or visit with them on a Sunday while the kids would play together. There was this group of us—three couples—and I called it the 'Six-Sided Triangle' because the six people, the three guys and three wives, did everything together. Charlotte and I were one side of the triangle, and Marilyn and Dave and Alan and Sandy were the other two." Milt explains that he never felt hemmed in by his limited social life or found it dull and boring because of his overriding interest in his work. "The business gave me all the excitement I needed," he says. "I enjoyed every minute of it."

And that was his downfall. Milt was so engrossed in reaching his goal of financial success, so busy juggling accounts to catch up with Charlotte's runaway aspirations, that he was completely unaware of the affair Charlotte was having with his best friend in the "Six-Sided Triangle." "It was a total shock, like going from night to day—that's how extreme it was," Milt says about the revelation of Charlotte's infidelity in their seventh year of marriage.

Milt was home baby-sitting one night, as he often did, never suspecting that Charlotte was out with her lover, when Marilyn dropped in to keep him company. "Marilyn and I gravitated naturally toward each other," Milt reveals, "because her husband was out a lot at night, too, and she didn't know what to do with herself. She was attractive, and we flirted and teased when she would come over, but that's as far as it went. On this particular night, she was very aggressive. She sat next to me on the couch, played around with me a little, and said, 'Look, why don't we go upstairs?' I thought that was kind of crazy. I told her, 'But Charlotte could come back any minute. The kids are sleeping upstairs. How can we do something *here?*"

Whether out of anger or digust—Milt doesn't know which—Marilyn told him. Dave, her husband, was having an affair with Sandy, Alan's wife; and Charlotte had been having an affair with Alan for at least a year.

"I was so naïve," Milt says, "that I didn't believe Marilyn. I had to find out for myself. I waited until Charlotte came home, and then I went over to Alan's. Sandy hadn't gotten in yet, and Alan was upstairs, lying in bed. I walked up, went into the bedroom, and said, 'Alan, what's going on?' He looked at me as if I'd asked a stupid question. He said, 'What's going on? Charlotte is sitting on the fence. In the next day or two she's going to decide whether to stay with you or go away and live with me.' I almost fell off the chair!"

The discovery of Charotte's involvement with another man rocked Milt to his very core. He'd been faithful to Charlotte during those first seven years of marriage and intended to continue to be, and he had assiduously done what he was supposed to do as a husband and father. Her affair was not simply a personal betrayal of their commitment, but a negation of Milt's whole being. Everything that he had worked for, stood for, believed in, had now been exposed to him as a sham. The experience was a turning point that caused Milt to challenge the traditional role he had accepted so compliantly in the Forties and Fifties, the mental straitjacket that constricted his view of himself to that of a money machine.

"I realized at that time the fragile nature of life," Milt says, "and I decided that never again was I going to be that blind. There were things I didn't see because I probably chose not to see them, and that's where the mistake was made." Milt went into therapy and learned that the fulfillment of his life in the business world was not necessarily as all-encompassing as he thought it might have been. "It was very comfortable to lose myself in business," he says, "and believe that life would follow suit—would take care of itself—but it's not that way in marriage. You can't put your head in the sand and say, 'My rear end is warm because the sun is on it—it'll stay that way,' and think you'll never have to worry about it. You can't eliminate the negative, restrictive elements in your life by blocking them out or running away from them as my generation did. Hindsight is the worst sight—it's like waking up."

When I asked Milt what the "negative" or "restrictive" elements were that he tried to eliminate, he replied: "I thought I had a reasonably happy marriage with Charlotte, but looking back, near the end of those first seven years, I began to see that they were less than what I would call terrific. My marriage wasn't satisfying to me because all Charlotte did was hang on me to be fed—and there's nothing worse than someone constantly demanding of you, 'Fill me up, fill me up, fill me up.' "

Like the rest of his generation, Milt thought it was his *duty* to fulfill someone else, and he had never stopped to think what purpose or goals in life he might personally choose for himself. "I was so controlled by conscience and guilt," he says, "that I couldn't balance where I wanted to go with where I'd been. You can't achieve an honest balance, either by coping or growing, without being aware—aware of yourself, aware of the world around you. And I wasn't, prior to that point."

Milt's reaction to the discovery of Charlotte's affair with Alan was immediate. He wanted to move out of the house and file for a divorce. The notice of the divorce action was already in the newspapers when their family lawyer talked Milt into going back to Charlotte and the children. "In my mind the marriage had already ended," Milt says, "because I refused to expose myself emotionally to Charlotte. She wasn't an equal partner nor was she a giver, and I couldn't see how that would change. Yet I felt obligated, for the family's sake, to give the marriage a fresh start."

The "fresh start" involved getting out of the old neighborhood, severing all ties with the "Six-Sided Triangle," and moving into an impressive fifty-five-thousand-dollar home in an elite upper-middle-class neighborhood where the average yearly income was in the six-figure range. In his usual style, Milt bought the house first and figured out how to pay for it later. He spotted it during a Sunday afternoon automobile drive with Charlotte and the children after the reconciliation. "I liked the house, saw a For Sale sign on the lawn, and began negotiating to buy it," Milt says. "The man living in it was very sick and wanted to get out in a hurry, so I made a deal right away. We moved in even before we sold our old house, and we lived with furniture in only a couple of rooms for a while."

Despite this auspicious (and familar) new beginning, Milt knew that the divorce he'd filed for in 1959 would happen inevitably some day. His postponement for seventeen years is an indication of how powerfully the two major cultural influences of the Forties and Fifties—financial insecurity and guilt—shaped people's lives. Says Milt: "Time didn't matter. I wanted the monetary security to be able to do anything for the children and for myself that I saw fit, and I didn't want to be guilty about hurting the children at an early age."

Although he appeared to be zestfully starting over with Charlotte in the house of their upwardly mobile dreams, Milt Stevens was only marking time.

THE LEGENDARY FIFTIES MOTHER

From the very beginning the Silent Generation had trouble denying their children anything. They had come to suburbia like refugees from internment camps where they had been in bondage to their parents' orthodoxies. They were ready to begin a new life—the opposite of what they had known. As domineering, insensitive, and constrictive as their parents had been with them, they would be devoted, perceptive, and indulgent with children of their own. The repression they had endured convinced them of the need to be totally permissive. Reared by parents who had always said "no" to their children, they couldn't bring themselves ever to say "no" to theirs. What they wanted was to give their children a.taste of freedom, but they succeeded only in making them helplessly—and hostilely—dependent. Like any blueprint for living that is not an integration of past experience and future hopes but only a counterreaction to a previous extreme, the excessive doctrine of permissiveness carried within it the seeds of its own destruction.

The legend of the Fifties suburban housewife and mother, as told by male psychosociologists and cultural historians, is a witch's tale with a disturbingly unsympathetic heroine. Two of the most popular of these writers—Herbert Hendin and Christopher Lasch—

have delineated the Fifties mother in the harshest possible light, accurately rendering her flaws but showing a remarkable lack of compassion. Without mitigating empathy, she is portrayed as a selfish, materialistic, possessive yet uncaring child-woman whose permissiveness was a cover-up for emotional abandonment. The suburban princess, we are told, was permissive only out of slavish dependence on the external child-rearing authorities of the time and, at bottom, sought to control her children and set goals for them without any regard for their interests, pleasures, or wishes.

In *The Age of Sensation,* Herbert Hendin's psychoanalytic exploration of college youth in the 1970s, the author gives us a chilling view through the disaffected students' eyes of the woman who became a mother in the 1950s. Her children describe her as "overprotective without any real warmth" . . . a woman "who just ignores anything you say and talks right on past you" . . . "an efficient machine" who had "more feeling for her cocker spaniel than for anyone else" . . . "determined to love (him) as her son who has gone to college and done well there" . . . a mother of four who "hated having children and was never around them" . . . "somebody who feels a child must be exactly what she wants it to be" . . . "a chronically unhappy person who took out her dissatisfaction with (his) father and her life on her children."

Drawing on interviews with four hundred Columbia University students, Hendin reveals the 1950s mother to be a woman who was embittered toward her husband and either had been totally unavailable to her children or had attempted to control every aspect of their lives. Her relationship with her daughter, if not one of perpetually rejecting her, involved choosing everything for the daughter from her ideal weight to her ideal future, and an insistence that the daughter fulfill the fantasy the mother had for *herself.* With her son, the mother was, again, incapable of involvement because of personal depression or her need to belittle or control, or she had a devouring concern for her son's professional success but almost no concern for his happiness. Her husband, whom she never forgave for defaulting on her emotionally and abandoning his children to her so that he could retain his freedom, escaped from her unhappiness into work or the company of friends.

According to Hendin, mothers in the Fifties so engulfed their children and subordinated them to their own needs that the children's whole lives have become a desperate flight from emotion. They are obsessed with control—with setting limits to protect their autonomy—and fear commitment as a deadly trap that must be avoided at all costs if one is not to be devoured by another. For the young men, "brothers in mistrust of women," the demand for sexual pleasure becomes bound up with the desire to hurt. As for the young women, just as they could set almost no limits on their mothers' control over their lives, so they are unable to set limits with their boyfriends, friends, or husbands, and increasingly see life as "fatal to the woman who is not impenetrably cool." A Hendin puts it: "Certainly the revolution begun in the fifties against the work and ambition ethic has become a revolution against intimacy."

How did it happen that the suburban mother of the 1950s, who wanted so much to *prevent* the constriction of her child's True Self, brought about the very thing she feared? How was it possible that this generation of well-educated, middle-class women, who were more psychologically sophisticated than any other generation of mothers before them, could have been so grossly out of touch with their children's needs in infancy and the early years? Hendin suggests that women in the postwar culture expected to be totally fulfilled through marriage and child-rearing, and when that fulfillment proved elusive in the isolation of suburbia, they vented their anger, frustration, and disappointment on their children as the scapegoats for their discontent. Caught in "an unavoidable existential conflict" between their two great expectations—their hopes for personal growth and their desire to be good mothers—they were torn by concern for their children's welfare and their own happiness.

Hendin admits that "finding a balance between a child's needs and a woman's aspirations" was a particularly painful dilemma for this generation of women. More of them than in any previous generation had been college-educated—or had been exposed to a tantalizing year or two of college before dropping out to get married. Their expectation of an intellectually stimulating life was due for sharp disillusionment in provincial Fifties suburbia.

Women who had given up or postponed career aspirations sometimes felt engulfed in resentment of their children and self-hatred for letting themselves down as well. At the same time they often found their husbands without much sympathy or understanding for their position and escaping from them by burying themselves in work. *Women in the past had been able to bury their frustration with their husbands and with their own lives in devotion to their children.* But this was virtually impossible for women who felt they had had other, larger alternatives and had hopes for personal fulfillment.

The real answer to what went wrong in the Fifties lies in this traditional cultural encouragement of women to bury their frustration in "devotion" to their children. This narcissistic use of children to bridge the gaps in their mothers' identities practically guaranteed that women in the 1950s, despite their best intentions, would repeat the same mistake with their children—only in a different way. Pushed into the overwhelming responsibility of child-rearing before they had been fully born psychologically themselves, these conformity-minded young women simply did not have a strong enough separate identity to love their children unselfishly or even—in more instances than anyone would like to admit—to love them at all.

As Erich Fromm pointed out in *The Art of Loving:* ". . . the ability to love as an act of giving depends on the character development of the person. It presupposes . . . [that] the person has overcome dependency, narcissistic omnipotence, the wish to exploit others, or to hoard, and has acquired faith in his own human powers, courage to rely on his powers in the attainment of his goals. To the degree that these qualities are lacking, he is afraid of giving himself—hence of loving."

Not very many of us who became parents in the 1950s were ready to love as an act of giving. We had been trained to get, not to give. Having been treated as commodities by our parents, who were themselves victims of the culture's "marketing orientation," we had never overcome our dependency on others' approval or our need to exploit others to make up for our feelings of inner worthlessness. We lacked the courage to rely on our own powers to attain our goals because our goals were rarely self-chosen. Most of us who married young in the 1950s were no more ready to give ourselves to our *partners,* as two lovingly autonomous but interdependent human beings, than Eisenhower was ready to kiss and make up with Khrushchev at the height of the cold war. Much less were we ready to give ourselves to young children, with their enormous emotional needs and demands, in an altruistic, unconflicted way.

In *The Culture of Narcissism*, Christopher Lasch portrays the 1950s woman who became "the American mother" in even more unflattering and less compassionate terms than Hendin. Charging that she conceals her indifference to her children beneath an appearance of continual concern and gives them "suffocating yet emotionally distant care," he writes: "Outside experts have taken over many of her practical functions, and she often discharges those that remain in a mechanical manner that conforms not to the child's needs but to a preconceived ideal of motherhood."

According to Lasch, the self-centered, impulse-dominated, falsely solicitous mother of the late 1940s and 1950s was a willing collaborator in the collapse of parental authority and the disastrous take-over of the family by industry, the media, and the health and welfare professions. Pictured by Lasch as devoid of any authentic "maternal feelings," the "narcissistic American mother" was only too happy to be relieved of familial functions by outside authorities while she anxiously pretended to make her child the center of her world. Under enormous cultural pressure to produce a perfect child, she hungrily sought out the advice of experts on child-rearing like the nervous owner of a new automobile trying to learn how to drive it from a mechanic's manual.

Though Lasch's argument is well taken, his faulting of insecure young mothers in the 1950s for lacking an authentic "maternal instinct" is unfair. He assumes that such an instinct immediately puts a mother in tune with her baby's needs, and he concludes that "the American mother's" reliance on outside authorities would have been unnecessary were she not so narcissistic. We have, however, no conclusive evidence to support the existence of a "maternal instinct" in human beings, so we must assume that Fromm is right: The ability to nurture—in women and men alike—is a function of character development and as such reflects not only our cultural values but our identification with early love objects. Our industrial society with its competitive creed has not, as Lasch so rightly points out, fostered the kind of character development that makes good nurturers of us all. But by the 1950s the damage had already been done. The paucity of good role models provided by the family in our culture—

mothers and fathers who loved each other and their children un-self-centeredly—made it *mandatory* for women in the Fifties to look elsewhere to learn the art of loving and caring for another.

THE SILENT GENERATION *CAN'T* SAY "NO"

Our mistake in the Fifties was that women looked for child care training *too late.* Did we expect men to tumble into work and automatically make money without any preparation? The perfunctory yet suffocating love that was thought to be so unnatural in "the American mother" of the Fifties was only to be expected, given her lack of readiness. Had the Fifties mother been allowed to wait to have children until she really *wanted* them, instead of having them because she thought she *should,* she might have had what her critics have accused her of lacking—that "easy, almost unconscious, self-assurance of the mother of more patterned societies, who is following ways she knows unquestioningly to be right."

Like everyone else whose children were young two decades ago, I rationalized my inability to say "no" to their demands, even if it was clearly in their best interests to oppose them, on the grounds of enlightenment. I thought I was promoting the full flowering of their initiative and creativity. Yet I was aware that, in my older daughter's case, there were times when I was handing her a power over me that she neither wanted nor was ready to handle. To divest herself of that power, she would occasionally behave so abominably that I was provoked into a tempestuous clash of wills from which I would emerge a shaken, remorseful victor while she seemed curiously relieved at having lost. She reminded me of Dostoevski's Raskolnikov, relentlessly driven to give clues to the investigators of his crime so that he could be caught and punished. She, too, was asking to be punished in order to make sense of the spontaneous guilt feelings her aggression aroused and to reassure her that there were limits beyond which she could not go.

In spite of what I recognized as sometimes desperate signals sent out by my two daughters to apply the brakes to their runaway impulses and help them achieve self-control, I found it almost impossible to tolerate their being frustrated or deprived, even momentarily. The sight of one of them as a preschooler folding in on herself like a wilted flower when she was denied her way filled me with pain. But I realize now, having learned a thing or two about symbiosis, that it was not my children's frustration that I couldn't tolerate—it was my own. I couldn't bear for them to be unhappy or angry or made to do something they didn't want to do because I was *too* empathetic to their discomfort to provide the discipline they needed. My own sense of self was so shaky that I couldn't stand *their* withdrawal of love. Fear was a major factor. I was afraid that if I made my children angry, that would alienate them from me. Although I often felt overwhelmed and helpless in the face of their demands in infancy and sometimes ran from them like a fugitive, I was unable to separate myself from my daughters. I was caught in a fierce double bind. On the one hand, I resented their terrifying need of me and yearned to be free of it so that I could pursue my own interests without always being torn and divided. And on the other hand, I was incredibly attached to them. Not being mature enough to handle the growth process—theirs and my own—I mistakenly believed that by not saying "no" to them, I could assuage my guilt, make the whole problem of loss go away, and keep my children with me forever.

It was Betty Friedan, long before Nancy Friday (*My Mother/My Self*), who exposed to the general public the terrible truth that psychoanalysts had discovered about unhealthy mother-child symbiosis. Stripping away the glossy, plastic image of the 1950s "happy housewife heroine" with such ferocious honesty that she started a revolution, Friedan revealed in *The Feminine Mystique* how the culture had manipulated suburban women into forfeiting the growth of their identities in order to continue living through their husbands and children. These educated middle-class women, myself among them, were gulled into renouncing any ambitions outside the home by a culture that sold them on piling up material possessions as a substitute for personal growth. To discourage them from becoming a serious threat to men in the job market—in 1956 women made up a third of the U.S. labor force—wives were kept "mindless and thing-hungry," as Friedan put it, and devoted almost exclusively to the "cult of the child." Consequently, symbiosis, the stage of psychological oneness between mother and child that normally precedes the formation of two separate identities in the first three years of life, became a narcissistic cocoon from which their enmeshed personalities never emerged.

Friedan rightly saw that this destructive absorption of the child's personality by the middle-class mother was a process of "progressive

dehumanization" of mother and child alike, beginning in one generation and continuing to the next. As each generation of mothers
evaded growth through the promise of magical fulfillment in marriage, they arrested their development at an infantile level, with a
weak core of self. Forced to seek more and more gratification from
the child, they kept the child in a correspondingly infantile state—
hopelessly dependent, emotionally passive, and in fearful retreat
from outward-directed activity to inward-dwelling fantasy. Later, in
the Sixties, the increasing use of drugs among middle-class children
in "the pleasant bedroom suburbs"—children who'd had all the "advantages" provided by their successful, educated parents—gave evidence that Friedan was right. Privileged as these children were, they
had as little sense of self as their undeveloped mothers and were
similarly afflicted with a weak moral sense:

The symbiotic love or permissiveness which has been the translation
of mother love during the years of the feminine mystique is not
enough to create a social conscience and strength of character in a
child. For this it takes a mature mother with a firm core of self,
whose own sexual, instinctual needs are integrated with social
conscience.

Whether one calls it "progressive dehumanization" or the neurotic search for unconditional love, each generation has chosen its
own particular method for avoiding the pain and loneliness involved
in the struggle for autonomy and the definition of healthy personal
limits. Our cultural institutions, which have always been geared to
sell rather than to save, have never failed to provide a dogma that
would make the flight from growth legitimate. In the Fifties, the
doctrine of permissiveness was made to order for women like me who
couldn't set limits for their children because they never had learned
how to set and defend authentic limits for themselves. Instead of
encouraging women in the Fifties to work through their conflict between the assertion of self and their compliance with the traditional
mother role, permissiveness gave them a way to play the role to the
hilt. It justified their inability to say "no" by making that the mark
of good mothering. Women were excused from having to deal with
their children's anger, and by not dealing with it, they could keep
their anger at their own parents repressed (or displace it onto their

husbands). A victim of the whole country's wishful vision, the Fifties woman believed that if she could just sleepwalk through her role long enough, waving the magic wand of permissiveness, her unfrustrated children would grow up to be perfect and she herself would *not* have to grow.

But the longer the impulse to grow is avoided, the greater is the accumulation of unexamined rage and the more powerful the explosion when the defenses finally crumble. It is this potentiality for violence that makes our cultural pattern of extreme and counterreaction so dangerous. If the "feminine mystique" had not urged women to disown their True Self so completely in the Forties and Fifties, their anger at everyone connected with their compliance might not have erupted with such volcanic fury in the Sixties. And if these same women had been able to tolerate their children's anger as they were developing their own identities, the children might not have had to go to such drastic lengths to separate from their parents in later years.

Counterreacting to their repression with a new extreme of permissiveness, parents in the Fifties had no way of knowing that they would be castrating their children psychologically. The "too good" mother in the Fifties, trying to anticipate her child's every need in order to spare him frustration, killed her child's autonomy with kindness. She deprived the child of the chance to experience the good things that happened to him as the result of his own doing rather than hers. Not only did she spare him frustration, but she also denied him a chance to gain a sense of self separate from hers by testing his environment in his own way. Given everything except limits—and the maturity of love and caring that the setting of limits involves— these children would become, in Marilyn French's words, "typical suburban monsters . . . expecting every luxury, expecting to be driven everywhere, terrified of independence and full of blame for their parents for this terror."

Psychoanalysts have noted that the mother who is unable to respond to the child's changing requirements and give up their "merger-enmeshment" after early infancy, when this phase is no longer appropriate, will become depressed and lonesome. The mother's seeming overcloseness obscures the fact that the child's self—the True Self—is psychologically undernourished. The failure of the "too good" mother to gain fulfillment by participating in her child's growth because she needs the child for her own narcissistic needs fills the child with rage. But since the parent has never said "no," the child has ostensibly no reason ever to get angry at the parent, so he turns the rage inward and becomes depressed. He is left with two alternatives: either remaining in a permanent state of regressive merger with the mother, or else staging a total rejection of the mother, even the seemingly good one.

These are the children who, despite the summer camps and the orthodontia and the sports cars and the trips to Europe, show up in psychiatrists' offices complaining that their parents never accepted them for themselves. They feel that their parents rejected their own career choices, talents, interests, and enthusiasms while seeming never to deny them anything. These children who were reared not to feel guilty about anything are unbearably guilty about the one thing they should *not* feel guilty about: wanting to be themselves.

Because the possessively permissive mother equates psychological separation from herself with abandonment and intolerable loss, her children perceive separation with dread. They feel that to be different from what the mother wants them to be is a rejection of her that neither the children nor the mother will be able to survive. So concerned with doing the "right thing," permissive parents committed the unpardonable sin of stifling that part of their children's identity that was different from their own. And in so doing they caused their children to become "sinners" as well. For the emerging self there is no greater immorality, as D. W. Winnicott has stressed, "than *to comply at the expense of the personal way of life* . . . as compared with which a sexual misdemeanour hardly counts." It is small wonder that so many of these children, wanting desperately to establish an independent place for themselves in the world but lacking enough sense of self to do it, have turned to drugs, religious cults, even anorexia nervosa, as a way of asserting both the existence of their true identity and their anger at its negation.

Goaded by the "cult of the child," many frightened and insecure mothers in the Fifties misunderstood their role to be that of a clairvoyant. They felt it their duty to divine what was going on inside their children's heads, the better to mold them into perfect human beings. Heinz Kohut's observations about the children of psychoanalysts and other psychoanalytically sophisticated parents, such as psychologists, social workers, psychiatrists, and others, show the harm parents can do by participating too intrusively in the child's inner life. These parents studied by Kohut claimed, often correctly, that they knew more about what their children were thinking, wishing, or feeling than the children themselves. The children eventually sought psychoanalysis because they had trouble experiencing themselves or their emotions as real, and they had an intense, yet disturbing, need to attach themselves to powerful figures in their surroundings "in order to feel that their life had meaning, indeed, in order to feel alive."

Parental intrusion interfered with the formation of the children's identity and weakened their sense of self. To protect against the threat of crumbling apart inside, the children walled themselves off against the danger of being understood by others and tried to merge with strong personalities, although they resented being engulfed by them. Whenever the feeling of inner uncertainty became overwhelming, the children engaged in a temporary, frantic increase in mental and physical activity, like a cat excitedly chasing its own tail.

Kohut maintains that analysis of these patients failed to effect significant changes in their behavior when it repeated the same mistake their parents had made: reading their minds instead of mirroring their True Self lovingly and empathetically. Real change did not occur until the growth process was worked through again correctly, and these "overanalyzed" children were induced to drop their protective shield and offer their self to be admired and confirmed and exposed to very gradual frustration. As they gained a sense of their own reality—by being allowed to exist without having their every move interpreted for them—their fantasies of unlimited greatness and merger with omnipotent others were transformed into healthy self-esteem and wholesome devotion to ideals. Their search for unconditional love had ended. As Winnicott observed in his classic essay "On Communication," although healthy persons communicate and enjoy communicating, each also has a secret, silent core of the self that is *"permanently noncommunicating, permanently unknown, in fact unfound."*

Knowing only too well how little sense of self mothers themselves had in the Fifties and how terrified they were of making a mess of their children's lives, I can see how they blundered into the quagmire of intemperate permissiveness. Some mothers, like me, hated the utter helplessness of infancy because it evoked a nameless horror: the primitive anxiety of our own preverbal state when we existed in a wilderness of needs, unspoken and often unresponded to. Our own neediness made the incessant, insatiable demands of our babies too threatening to us, and we became the remote, rejecting kind of mother always running for cover for fear of being emotionally destroyed by her children. Other contemporaries of mine adored their infants because having someone abjectly dependent on them made them feel loved—a typical confusion of devotion and dependence in our culture. They became disenchanted with motherhood when their children started to talk back. From there on in, life became a continuing struggle between the mother's narcissistic need of her children and their healthy assertion of independence. As the emotional demands of our children lessened and we ourselves became more mature, with a stronger core of identity, we began to enjoy motherhood and form loving, responsible relationships with our children—but that came later.

VIVIAN: THE "PERMISSIVE MOTHER"

Vivian Brooks, the woman we met in the previous chapter, is typical of the hordes of former "happy housewife heroines" who used their children to block out their discontent with early, often badly made marriages.

In the late 1940s, after Martin was out of the army, Vivian lived with him in a little two-room apartment over a drugstore in Brooklyn, with their two babies in the living room and Martin's dental office in the front. Vivian worked in the office, took care of the apartment, and raised the two babies in one room.

"The marriage was terrible from the very beginning," Vivian recalls, "but there was so much struggling to better ourselves—have a bigger apartment, take a vacation, get a car, move to the suburbs—that it pushed other things aside. A lot of energy went into just trying to cope with everyday life. Struggling to establish something was a way of not facing Martin's inadequacy. I was always rationalizing: 'As soon as he makes more money, he'll be happier, it'll be better. We'll have a nicer place to live, he'll be calmer, it'll be better. The kids will get a little bigger, we won't fight, it'll be better.' The days passed. I formed close friendships with counterparts of myself, other educated young marrieds whose husbands were professional men, and we shared a lot. I loved the children. I loved motherhood.

My life was filled with caring for the babies and hoping that each year would bring my husband more success, and along with it, an improvement in my marriage."

Fervently adhering to the ideology of suburban bliss, Vivian staved off the collapse of her marriage to Martin for twenty-three mostly miserable years during which she and the children endured incredible psychological, and sometimes physical, abuse. "If Martin came home from work and found hamburgers for dinner instead of steak," Vivian recalls, "he was not above smashing all of the dinner plates and glasses against the wall. He constantly belittled the children and screamed crazy curses at them. One of his favorites was, 'You should die, die, die, like a chicken with a broken neck on the street of cancer.' Once when he was baby-sitting for me, I came home and found Nancy, who was three years old then, with vicious-looking red pinch marks all over her body. Martin had gotten angry at her because she was playing in the bedroom and had accidentally spilled some perfume."

Martin also had a mania for spending money, which, even in the accumulation-happy Fifties, was wildly extravagant. When he took up photography as a hobby, he spent thousands of dollars on professional equipment that he used once or twice and then relegated to the cellar, where it lay gathering dust. He was an equally profligate stamp collector: Vivian once discovered a handful of rare and priceless stamps stuck to the inside of his shirt pocket when she retrieved the shirt from the washing machine. Martin dressed in a lavish wardrobe befitting a suburban prince, splurging on a half dozen car coats at a time and matching Tyrolean hats. And while he was constantly refurbishing his dental office with the latest gadgetry, his mismanagement of funds kept his income surprisingly low. When Vivian tried to intervene, fearful that Martin was digging the family into a financial hole and squandering the money for the children's future education, Martin furiously resisted her help.

Vivian endured the dissatisfactions and uncertainties of her life with Martin mainly by overinvesting herself in her children's lives and deluding herself with our cultural greed creed that money in itself will buy the resolution of one's problems. Swept up in the mythology of the Fifties, she believed that if only one acquired enough things, the internal loneliness and alienation would be satisfied—and she paid for this delusion with a terrible waste of life.

Reminiscing about making it to suburbia in the Fifties, Vivian conjures up what that driving dream meant to her personally and to her whole generation. "I never wanted to remain with a number on my door in an apartment house—that was just something temporary," she says. "Having your own home in suburbia was the goal that meant you were getting somewhere in the world. It was a step upward, something to look forward to and to work together for, one other way of rationalizing that *now* we will be happy. It was a whole life that was so *exciting*. Having a car and going out and watching the house being built—seeing the floor going in and the walls and the spackle, picking out the colors and comparing things with your neighbors and buying a new refrigerator—it was all such a thrill. It was yours. It was a possession, maybe your first possession in the world that was important."

Vivian sees among young couples today the same trend to get out of an apartment and buy a home in a "good neighborhood," but she remembers a special urgency about the move in the Fifties. "After the war you *had* to push out to suburbia," she explains, "because there was no place else to go. Brooklyn was overcrowded. You had all of the war babies. There were no apartments in the city except the new ones that were going up, and who could afford them? The lure of suburbia was to have somewhere large enough to raise the children and to get them off the Brooklyn sidewalks. Where we lived the neighborhood was turning bad, and you didn't want your kids to grow up in a slum. You were forced to move out. We thought of it as getting out in time—moving out to a place where the kids would be able to play, grow in a safe area, take advantage of the outdoors, have a good education."

Vivian's description of life in suburbia in the Fifties reads like one long confessional of a "happy housewife heroine": "We joined the Civic Association, mowed the lawn, pulled the crabgrass, barbecued. I was active in B'nai B'rith, I had Mah-Jongg games. We had a group going in the neighborhood where we entertained each other on a weekly basis. The neighbors were our personal friends. We were very close-knit. We had the Cub Scouts. I became a den mother. I went into it whole hog. My whole life revolved around that house and the children."

Was there ever a nagging sense that this was not enough? Did Vivian ever feel thwarted in her own growth while she was investing all this energy in the time-consuming performance of the "happy housewife role"? She admits that dropping her education as abruptly as she had in order to marry Martin bothered her, but not enough during the Fifties to do something about it. "There was a lot of pain associated with my aborted education," she says. "I couldn't go back to the U of P, even visit it, for many years. The sense of not accomplishing what I had set out to do, of leaving something unfinished, troubled me deeply for a long time and eventually spurred me to go back to school. But during those early years I was really immersed in the children and the house. I thought I was very happy. I probably was one of the most efficient people I know at finding all kinds of mental defense mechanisms by which I didn't focus on the problems of my marriage or my own frustrations. I was able to face the situation by becoming totally neurotic in that I could live in this bad marriage—very unfulfilling, very unrewarding—with a guy who added little joy to life and was not a partner in a marriage, but like a child in it himself. We had hardly any time together—he came home late at night—and what we had wasn't altogether pleasant. My strategy for survival was to throw all of my energy into being a suburban housewife."

Vivian's "strategy for survival" bought her the time she needed until she felt ready to return to school and prepare herself for financial independence from Martin. But the cost of her overinvestment in her children and in her role of suburban housewife during these very critical years was, as we'll discover, extortionately high.

BUY NOW, PAY LATER

The Milt Stevenses and Vivian Brookses of the Fifties were typical of all the other "absent fathers" and "happy housewife heroines" whose towering preoccupation with status-seeking and upward mobility protected them from unpleasantness in their own lives and in the culture around them. On a large scale, their furious concern with creating an *image* while evading real growth and their tendency to ignore problems until they exploded in their faces were also typical of a national habit. "The oldest dilemma that has afflicted American society from its founding in the New World," Carl Solberg has written, "has been the ceaseless conflict between its often unbridled individualism and its fitful and inadequate sense of community."

Like one huge colony of suburbanites drunk on backyard bliss, the whole country had been paralyzed in the Fifties by dangerously shortsighted political, economic, and social policies. Obsessed with achieving technological and military supremacy over Communist Russia, we plunged ahead with industrial expansion at home and interventionism abroad without regard for the consequences. We were motivated by short-term gain, unmindful of the long-term costs of exploitation, repression, and neglect. Did we really think that giant corporations could continue to push their production rates up endlessly; that housing developers could go on gobbling up the countryside forever; that more and more automobiles, indispensable to commuter living, could flood the highways; that the military-industrial complex could run the cold war indefinitely in Europe, Asia, and outer space; that our colleges and universities could keep churning out ever-growing numbers of graduates who would find a niche in our relentlessly upward-striving society? Did we really think we could do all of that without eventually having to pay a terrible price?

There were rumblings of trouble all around us, but we steadfastly chose to ignore them. On the domestic scene, the civil rights movement was gathering momentum. There was the boycott of the buses in Montgomery, Alabama, in 1955, led by Martin Luther King, Jr. Two years later came the ugly confrontation at Central High in Little Rock, Arkansas, between federal troops enforcing desegregation and crowds of screaming, jeering racists. Both events served notice that the blacks (then called Negroes) would not tolerate their continued disadvantaged status while the rest of the country reveled in greater material success and higher social position than ever before. We read the newspaper headlines and scanned the pictures, but most of us could not see how this local reneging on the Supreme Court's 1954 decision to end the "separate but equal" doctrine was anything more than a purely "Southern" problem. What could it possibly have to do with us?

We were glad when Senator McCarthy finally got his comeuppance in 1954, exposed by folksy, bow-tied chief army counsel Joseph M. Welch as a "cruel" and "reckless" Communist-baiting opportunist during the spellbinding McCarthy-Army hearings on TV. Yet we were deeply chagrined when Russia beat us to the punch in 1957 by launching *Sputnik 1*, the first artificial earth satellite, and our fanatical determination to get to the moon before the Russians did took precedence over all other priorities. Convinced that this international status-seeking was necessary for our survival, we were spared having to face treacherous social problems—the rotting of our cities, the depletion of our environment—problems that were harder to solve and ultimately more life-threatening than our shortage of nuclear missiles.

Nowhere did the emphasis on lockstep competitiveness as a substitute for personal growth have more far-reaching and devastating effects than it did in the realm of higher education. Our colleges and universities became factories geared to producing unthinking but highly skilled technocrats. Their rigid quality control systems—stiff grades, heavy science requirements, and uninspired, pragmatic-minded teaching—turned us into the well-known Silent Generation. Ours was not to question why, it was merely to get that degree so we could snare that high-paying job (or that husband with the high-paying job, if we were women) and push the country on to technological greatness. No one considered what the country was going to do with all the Ph.D.'s we were turning out, like so many cookies stamped by a cookie cutter. The assumption was that our economic growth would indeed be limitless, and we would somehow find room to accommodate these rigorously trained robots with advanced degrees.

Like the credit-card spending spree we started in the Fifties, launching a spiraling inflation with no end in sight except a disastrous recession, our "buy now, pay later" approach to higher education set in motion a runaway trend that would disrupt the entire country. In the first place, where we once pushed the young into adult society before they were ready, we now delayed their entrance until they began to question whether they would ever be ready to enter it or even if they wanted to anymore. When they took a look around at their parents' lives—the pretentiousness of their parents' status-seeking, their uneasiness about sex, their inability to enjoy their children as people because they were so conflicted about or overburdened by their roles—young people in the Fifties became increasingly doubtful about the value of the college and graduate school grind. They knew that society was forcing their parents to buy them the academic credentials necessary for admittance to the world of middle-class respectability, but they suspected how dearly they would have to pay later for that respectability with their personal unhappiness.

Young people growing up in the Fifties had also been led to believe that if they obeyed the rules of the "system" and achieved high academic success, society would protect them from harm. As they became aware in the Sixties that our institutions could not be relied upon to protect *anyone* from harm—by pollution of the environment, by violation of guaranteed civil rights, by involvement in an unjustifiable war—their rage became uncontrollable. Permissiveness had not trained them to cope with disillusionment, and a stagnant, paternalistic society had lost its responsiveness to the need for change. Neither having grown during the Fifties as they should have, the infantilized young and the immobilized social order around them were due for an unavoidable and violent confrontation in the coming decade.

Artists and writers, who have their antennae out to the winds of change before everyone else, signalled the explosiveness that was seething beneath the frozen calm of the Fifties. Abstract expressionists like Jackson Pollock revolutionized modern art by spilling pails of paint across the canvas to create images of suppressed energy furiously unleashed. Like the indomitable voice of existentialism that emerged from gutted and bombed-out postwar Europe, this new form of painting was another way of asserting that life was larger than rules. In a hopelessly absurd world, the only basis for living, Jean-Paul Sartre had declared when he started the existentialist movement, was existence itself. Sartre meant to convey that there is nothing *but* freedom—that it was up to each individual as a free human being to create his own authentic self, accepting responsibility for his actions and seeking personal meaning through "engagement" or direct involvement in his social and physical environment.

In America, mired as it had been in a deep rut of status-seeking conformity for over a decade, existentialism was bastardized into a justification for dropping out of the social order completely and doing one's "own thing." Self-creation became confused with an absence of self-restraint, freedom with freaking out. The "beats"—or beatniks, as they were nicknamed by the Fifties' "straights"—presaged the coming of the hippies. Taking their cue from Jack Kerouac's *On the Road,* they expressed their rebellion against the smothering conformity that had claimed their peers by drifting aimlessly along the country's highways or hanging out in coffee-houses where they listened to Allen Ginsberg's antiestablishment poetry readings.

"We love everything," Kerouac proclaimed, naming a cultural laundry list that included Eisenhower, Zen, and rock and roll. (By then, Elvis Presley's thumping version of back-country music mixed with rhythm and blues had driven out the creamy schmaltz of Patti Page and Jo Stafford). But of course, Kerouac intended a putdown. Far from loving everyone, the "beats" could tolerate no one except others like themselves: "The only people for me are the mad ones, the ones who are mad to live, mad to talk, mad to be saved . . . the ones who never yawn or say a commonplace thing, but burn, burn, burn like fabulous yellow roman candles exploding like spiders across the stars."

The explosion of the "mad ones" would not be long in coming. Disillusionment with our long spell of growth-evading materialism was already pushing us, like a derailed train speeding crazily out of control, toward the farthest reaches of the cultural pendulum. "It is paucity of ideas," observed Carl Solberg, "that makes for the cyclical in human existence." If conformity had run its course, could revolt be far behind?

SIX

←——————— • ——————————→

THE
REVOLUTIONARY
SIXTIES

On the day they buried John F. Kennedy I was in my pediatrician's office. My younger daughter had been born less than a year before, and I was there with her on November 26, 1963, for her routine monthly visit.

Someone had brought a television set into the waiting room, and we were all holding our babies in our laps and staring at the set in heartsick silence. It was nearing the end, and some of us were weeping openly. There was Jackie, veiled in high mourning, her face swollen with grief as she received the folded flag from her husband's coffin. I was caught up in the moment, but then a flash of horror overtook me. My mind skipped, and I felt that I was watching a movie about some distant banana republic where fallen leaders were a daily occurrence and nobody was safe. I held my baby close and kept asking myself over and over again: Where will it end?

The Sixties seemed to be one long series of cataclysmic events— assassinations, riots, war atrocities, demonstrations, cult murders—all so shocking as to induce a feeling that life had been taken over by a demented movie-maker with a lust for violence. It was a terrifying, sickening thriller that we were compelled to watch unfold without being able to make any sense out of it. What Dwight Macdonald said about our unintelligible intervention in Vietnam was no less true of the outrageous conflict between warring forces within our own society: "It has become a mindless, impersonal process that keeps grinding on and on at an accelerating tempo like a machine out of control."

That was the essential point—we were *out of control*. What began as a reasonable assertion of self-interest by antiwar protesters, by youth, by blacks, by women, ended in a display of uncontrollable aggression. Once begun, our long-delayed reaction in the Sixties against the rigid defense of the status quo that existed in the previous decade quickly escalated, along with the Vietnam War, past the bounds of sanity. Legitimate social movements aimed at ending the war, achieving racial equality, revitalizing our educational system, and liberating the sexes from dehumanizing roles were each subverted, at some point, by the "crazies"—those self-indulgent, self-serving revolutionaries who were not content with trying to change the system but who wanted to see it destroyed.

For a while it looked as if the rhetoric-spouting, rabble-rousing extremists would cause the whole country to go up in smoke. The colleges had their Mark Rudds and the barricades and the Weathermen; the blacks had their Eldridge Cleavers and the Black Panthers and the summer of '67; the antiwar movement had their Berrigan brothers and the draft card burnings and the blood-spillings; and the feminists had their Ti-Grace Atkinsons and their Redstockings and their man-hating polemics on the joy of masturbation as an alternative to the "institution" of sexual intercourse.

In the end, the evils that the movements sought to address outweighed the folly of the extremists. The Vietnam War *was* a case of unjustifiable "creeping genocide" made all the worse by Lyndon Johnson's betrayal of the public trust; the students *were* subjected to an educational system that was intellectually bankrupt and grossly out of date; the women *were* socialized into subservience to men and systematically excluded from access to economic, political, and social power; the blacks *were* the victims of massive, hideous oppression.

The overwhelming rightness of the cause in each case prevailed over the fury of the radicals and the angry waves of backlash they provoked. It was in the great tradition of middle-class responsibility, not in an atavistic thirst for blood, that 200,000 people, black and white, marched on Washington on that day in August 1963 when Martin Luther King, Jr. immortalized his dream. And it was in the same vein of responsible social concern that more than 250,000 Americans came to Washington on November 15, 1969, and staged the biggest demonstration in the capital's history—and a peaceful one—for ending the war in Vietnam. The sum of these movements proved to be greater than their parts, and they succeeded in effecting change in spite of the militant fringe rather than because of it, as some would have us believe.

While the social protest movements of the Sixties appealed to our highest moral urgings, they were also lightning rods for attracting free-floating narcissistic rage. Disaffected young people, blacks, and women had a lot to be angry about in the Sixties, and for many, the expression of their anger in legitimate protest was a sign of health. But there is a big difference between anger that is governable, and therefore capable of redress, and global narcissistic rage that knows no bounds. The target of this rage, however appropriate, is incidental.

"If you experience narcissistic rage and can separate it out from a feeling of anger," says psychiatrist Joan Enoch, "you can see that narcissistic rage is all-encompassing, annihilating, and very oral in a way—the kind of rage that can eat up the world. It's the helpless impotence of the furious infant, and when it hasn't worked itself out well, it can continue as an underlying theme throughout life. It will then get attached, as we repeat our patterns in each stage of the life cycle, to other people, authority figures, or institutions. If the rage is there and it gets turned on the institution that's saying you have to go to war or the college that says you have to take this course or the husband who is not being the 'good mother,' it takes this ugly form."

The distinguishing feature of this kind of rage, Dr. Enoch stresses, is the feeling of utter helplessness that goes along with the fury and causes us to strike out with a chaotic vehemence intended to burn all of our bridges behind us. At the eye of the hurricane is an impulse to destroy any possibility of a resolution of the problem. "We're not starting out from a position of being merely angry," says Dr. Enoch, "but of feeling on some deeper level, 'I will lose.' "

In the social protest movements of the Sixties, and in the way each of us responded to them, the difference between anger and narcissistic rage was always in evidence. It was in evidence during the student uprising at Columbia University in April 1968, when the protesters were not content with simply occupying the buildings they took over but found it necessary to burn Professor Ranum's papers (the product of a decade of historical research) and to defecate in President Grayson Kirk's wastebasket. It was in evidence among the idealistic young political activists who had good relations with their parents and identified with the values they had learned at home and the alienated middle-class revolutionaries who took to throwing bombs as a way of getting even. And it was in evidence among the dissatisfied homemakers who were moved by the women's movement to make constructive changes in their lives without discarding their families like squeezed lemons and the runaways who rocketed out of suburbia, gypsy silks over their jeans, and took off on a cross-country hegira to see how many men they could fall into bed with in one day.

YOUTH IN REVOLT

The tendency of those in the grip of narcissistic rage to go off the deep end pushed the Sixties antiestablishment rebellion past the point of reform to repression's opposite number—enslavement by self-indulgence. The shock of mass-movement rhetoric jolted people out of rigid compliance to the old rules and they lost the capacity to make moral distinctions. Once the crack in the picture window of middle-class values had been exposed, the youth movement and its followers assumed that the whole foundation of middle-class life was rotten to the core.

Disgusted with a culture that preached brotherhood, equality, and morality but where back-stabbing, exploitation, and chronic adultery were the norm, many young people in revolt indiscriminately rejected their legacy of middle-class values as spiritually empty. As children who had witnessed what the overstructured Forties and Fifties had done to their parents, they now saw structure of any kind as inimical to growth. If loyalty to the corporation had done their fathers in, they now reviled earning an honest living as a sell-out. If their mothers had forfeited their identities by marrying too young, they now scoffed at traditional marriage as an anachronism. In their zeal to swim out of the mainstream they became as intolerant and antipermissive as the establishment they despised.

Out of this absolute renunciation by the Sixties generation of all the values they had known as children, the counterculture was born. As the name suggests, it was to be the reverse of conventional capitalist society—communal as opposed to competitive, peace-loving as opposed to warlike, sexually permissive as opposed to puritanical. In this hippie version of utopia, there would be no room for the oppression of the success ethic or the bondage of sexual exclusivity or the phoniness of material accumulation. Jobs, schooling, respect for authority, monogamy, the nuclear family—all the pollutants that had poisoned the wellspring of middle-class life (and had also ensured its stability)—would be outlawed. Peace and love would reign supreme.

The counterculture's attempt to restructure both personal priorities and those of society along the lines of total spontaneity and "freedom" was doomed to a brief life. To a generation whose very existence was threatened by the Vietnam War, "Woodstock nation," as Abbie Hoffman dubbed it, offered an attractive escape from a world where the only alternatives seemed to be physical extinction abroad or death by alienation at home. But it was only a temporary refuge from growing up. Like the ideology of suburban bliss that had preceded it, the countercultural mystique was based on a naïvely false hope. The one led people to believe that they could acquire an identity by accumulating enough things; the other led people to believe that they could acquire an identity without concerning themselves with economic survival.

In the skyrocketing affluence of the Sixties, economic survival appeared to be a permanent given. Had it not, it is doubtful whether so many middle-class, college-educated people of the younger and older generation alike would have carried out their rebellious impulses as flamboyantly as they did. Fat allowances and rosy employment prospects made it possible for youth to engage in a protracted (and long overdue) moratorium period—questioning the 1950s materialistic ideals and exploring possibilities for other kinds of growth. When their parents caught the contagious spirit of rebellion later in the decade, they had the money to support a full-blown mid-life crisis, complete with divorce and the setting up of two households.

In the youth movement itself, money was channeled into two directions: political activism and escapist passivism. In contrast to the political activists, who expressed their dissatisfaction with the establishment in peace marches, sit-ins protesting racism, demonstrations against university policies, Freedom Rides in the South, and other forms of engagement, the passivist hippies simply dropped out of the larger culture. But the world they tried to replace it with was as illusory as an LSD trip. It was the age-old problem of "freedom from" versus "freedom to."

The hippies knew what they were *against*—the war, corporate power, the concentration of wealth, corruption in government, sexual prudery—but their notions of what they were *for* lacked specificity. They lumped their vague longings for a better world under the broad umbrella of peace and love, which generally translated down to readily available sex, an inexhaustible supply of drugs, free food in the park, rock concerts, and flowers.

In search of their dream, the hippies, or "flower children," as they liked to be called, flocked to New York's East Village or, better still, to Haight-Ashbury in San Francisco. "California, in 1967, was our Never-Never Land, the golden place where no one grows old and everyone is free," recalls psychiatric social worker Ann Braden Johnson, who was a student throughout the Sixties and has retained an empathetic feel for the times.

In her perceptive essay, "A Temple of Last Resorts: Youth and Shared Narcissisms," Johnson compares the hippie counterculture and the political protest movement of the Sixties and the fanatical religious cultism of the Seventies. She finds "a common thread of desperation and self-preoccupation" running through all these movements: "the love-feasts of 1967, the pitched battles of 1969, and the sidewalk chantings of 1974." Ultimately, she claims, these movements represent "a total rejection of the adult world and the effort to find a permanent substitute for it, or avoid it altogether by a regressive, narcissistic retreat from the world." As evidence of the element of narcissism shared by the "stoned flower-children" and the "radical bomb throwers" in the Sixties and the "pacified religious devotees" of today, Johnson cites some striking similarities:

The total self-absorption of both drug use and meditation

The belief that by arcane measures like the practice of astrology and witchcraft one can be so powerful as to predict the future or control the forces of nature

The childish effort to aggrandize the self through an unrealistic choice of one's supposed previous incarnations

The shared narcissism of a retreat into a new world of one's own making, occupied only by the chosen of one's peers.

Johnson is aware of the difference between the real hippies—the rootless drifters who panhandled and crashed in different pads at night—and the "plastic" hippies whose trendy weekend jaunts to the Haight or the East Village were financed by their affluent suburban parents. But the difference seems to be more a matter of degree than of kind. The less troubled seekers were not as deeply disillusioned with nor as alienated from the larger society and not as given to profound depression and total desperation as those attracted to hippiedom, but they were nonetheless afflicted with similar feelings of loneliness and isolation. They, too, felt left out and misunderstood. Many of those who preferred not to drop out of college still expressed that same masked rage against an overwhelmingly powerful and monumentally indifferent "establishment," an anger reducible in many cases, Johnson suggests, to anger against the parents.

At bottom, the counterculture's attempt to break away from the larger society and form communes and collectives was a vivid dramatization of the classic struggle in adolescence to separate from the family. The quasi-hippies, overwhelmed by the pressures of upward mobility, were seeking to escape their parents' suffocating expectations of achievement. The real hippies, on the other hand, although generally intelligent, college-educated, and white middle-class, often came from broken homes and chaotic backgrounds that had left them with "the sad conviction that their parents were unable to offer relevant models of competence." It was the Vietnam War that gave the Love Generation's adolescent breakaway the illusion of a politically inspired movement. But most of the flower children lacked a sufficiently consolidated sense of self to work effectively for political change or to construct a permanently feasible alternative to the system in their own lives.

While the media treatment of hippie communes in *Life* magazine picture stories or in counterculture film epics like *Easy Rider* tended to romanticize them into enclaves of perfect homespun democracy, in real life they more closely resembled refugee camps for the dispossessed. During a trip to the West Coast in 1968, I paid a visit to Haight-Ashbury and discovered a colony of sad, scruffy, vacant-eyed runaways, lost to themselves and each other in a retreat from reality. The sense of community I had expected to find was conspicuously absent. Wilted flower children, pale and malnourished, aimlessly wandered the streets or congregated in filthy, dilapidated old houses where they drifted through the day on drugs, fantasizing about becoming rock stars or sleeping with them, and "partied" continually at night until they "crashed" on mattresses without sheets. To support themselves, they dropped in on the larger society periodically and begged, stole, dealt drugs, or worked at temporary jobs. It appeared that their relationship to the larger culture was not "counter" so much as helplessly parasitical.

Although the prospect of a clean and absolute break with their parents' world seemed highly seductive to many vulnerable adolescents in the Sixties, the reality of unlimited freedom was terrifying. When children enjoy the kind of relationship with their parents that makes them want to emulate their parents' roles and internalize their values, they have a feeling of belonging that gives them a solid foundation for forming a separate identity. No matter what the impact of their contemporaries, their evolving identity has a firm underpinning of inner controls and reliable tradition. But when their parents and the social institutions fail to provide a consistent, responsive source of guidance, they go into the world psychologically naked and unarmed. It is then that the struggle to form their own identity traps them into bouncing from one dependency to another.

"IDENTITY-SHOPPING"

As idealistic as the goals of the hippie communes sounded, they were, in fact, simply the Sixties version of the search for unconditional love. The high-sounding egalitarianism espoused by the communards turns out, on closer inspection, to be a wish for symbiosis—not the old parent-child merger that was violently abjured, but a more acceptable, if no less regressive, enmeshment with one's peers. The absolute equal sharing of everything by everyone—food, money, sex, drugs, space, thoughts—was a way of blurring the boundaries between each of the members so that the group became a kind of surrogate womb.

Using the Mars-on-Earth model conjured up by science fiction novelist Robert A. Heinlein in his celebrated Sixties classic, *Stranger in a Strange Land,* many communes discouraged any expression of individuality or privacy, even down to an insistence on sharing or rotating sexual partners. This fluidity and interchangeability in living and mating patterns was intended to bind the communards to each other in eternal love and loyalty in the same way that Heinlein's "water brothers" achieved a supernatural attachment by drinking water together and practicing free love. In reality, however, the complete absence of sexual controls in hippie communes often failed to eliminate jealousy and possessiveness; and when it succeeded, it produced not the longed-for communion of eternal love but, at least among many of the women, the feeling of being "loose change."

While the leaders and rules of the larger society had deeply disillusioned them, the flower children found after a while that life without any control—external or inner—was equally disillusioning. In the first place, absolute sexual freedom and experimentation with psychedelic drugs failed to relieve their feelings of loneliness, boredom, and depression. Like the middle-aged people today who feel that they have been let loose in the "candy store" of life after the breakup of their marriages, the Love Generation confused the lifting of all restraints on their impulses with liberation. They felt that by abandoning themselves to the consumption of experience they could stir to life intense emotions that had been deadened by the "straight" world's conformity to the work ethic. But the total lack of restraint had, as gluttony always does, exactly the opposite effect. Continual "highs" led to an anesthetizing of feeling and the "*under*sensitivity to stimuli" that Philip Slater described in *The Pursuit of Loneliness*. Counterculture people, Slater noted, "seem to be more certain that desire can be gratified than that it can be aroused." Trained by their "Spockian mothers" to move toward gratification before a need became compelling, "they aren't altogether clear which need they're feeling," Slater explained. He added: "To make matters worse they're caught in the dilemma that spontaneity evaporates the moment it becomes an ideology: it's a paradox of modern life that those who oppose libidinal freedom may be more capable of achieving it."

It is also a modern paradox that those most attracted to the "free life" are the ones who have the least capacity to function well in a setting without structure. Confused and conflicted about what they thought they should or would like to be, the flower children gravitated to meccas where they presumably could be anything they wanted. But they were further disillusioned to find that the mere banding together with others in a similar situation did not give them the sense of belonging and identity they were so desperately seeking. While they talked of "sharing" and "communal" living, their unwillingness to set rules for themselves and each other—except in a few well-organized agrarian communes, like the Farm, that are still in existence today—only underscored their feelings of helplessness and fragmentation.

The anxiety associated with limitless freedom of choice led the flower children to turn to exotic forms of external control, like astrology, Eastern religious movements, and mysticism. All of the traditional sources that should have established guidelines for their behavior had bitterly disappointed them. Since their parents, teachers, ministers, and the other usual adult role models in the larger culture had failed to gain their trust, the alienated young were severely hampered in developing a moral sense, and with it, a sense of direction. Without ideal prototypes to emulate, they were unable to acheive the self-restriction that would convey which rules and behaviors felt right to them. To paraphrase Erikson, not only were there no boundaries on the horizon of the permissible, but there was also no direction toward the *possible*. Left in the grip of their unbridled early childhood dreams of perfection, they abandoned responsibility for their fate to astrology, Tarot cards, the *I Ching*, Eastern religions, and mysticism.

By embracing such exotic systems of external authority, these frightened postadolescents in the Sixties tried to shortcut the process of separating from their parents and form a unique and authentic identity of their own. Instead of deciding which aspects of their parents' lives and those of other influential figures they wanted to incorporate into their behavior and transforming and internalizing them, they completely abandoned their parents' values and looked around for someone else to tell them what to do. But the shortcut didn't work. Shifting absolute control over their lives from their parents to their gurus kept them in a state of childish, self-indulgent dependency. To break out of that, they would have to become personally accountable for their actions, a task impossible to accomplish without accepting some elements of the value system and morality of the culture at large.

To people bound up in conflict over the wish to be autonomous versus the fear of separation, the belief in exotic forms of mysticism or other "magical helpers," as Erich Fromm called them, seems like the perfect answer. It gives them the illusion of having separated from their parents and the comfort of still remaining merged. American flower children of all ages who sought out Maharishi Mahesh Yogi or took up Zen Buddhism in the Sixties appeared to be asserting their independence by embracing beliefs markedly different from anything in the larger culture. But like the cult members of today, they were simply doing what Ann Braden Johnson has called "identity-shopping." Rather than resolving the conflicts that prevented their weaning themselves away from dependency on external control and defining their own limits, they were searching for "a ready-to-wear identity that often comes complete with a new name and all."

Since the Sixties, more and more people, both young and old, have become "identity-shoppers," going from movement to movement as each one comes along—Esalen, Scientology, Transcendental Meditation, rolfing, est, Life Spring—and is popularized into a fad by the media. Ironically, most of the Eastern religions and the newer psychologies aim at the development of the autonomous self: Zen Buddhism, for example, is based on the belief that what one *is* determines what happens to one (the oneness of cause and effect); Transcendental Meditation teaches that the source of spiritual power is within us, not outside; est is predicated on transforming one's life by assuming responsibility for one's own actions. There are some Americans who have been spiritually and psychologically uplifted by these systems because they have embraced them realistically as *disciplines* for learning trust in the self and in one's ethical beliefs.

But most Americans drawn to these movements want an instant panacea for the ambiguity of life and their own inner anxiety. It is not really an identity they are searching for, but the unconditional love of the perfect mother (or father) who will forever banish their anxiety and depression. Since this is an unfulfillable fantasy, the seekers are destined for perennial disillusionment. As Edith Jacobson has observed:

Fighting their dependency trends, such persons may derogate their parents and turn away from them in adolescence, but as adults they continue to emulate and lean upon other persons and groups and unduly admire them until they again rebel, abandon them in rage and disappointment and look for the next object to be glorified and emulated.

Immediately there comes to mind a long succession of luminaries in the Sixties—Mia Farrow, the Beatles, the Beach Boys among others—who made their pilgrimage to an ashram in the Himalayas to sit at the feet of a small, thin, white-robed, bearded man who, they hoped, would free them from all spiritual pain. Photographic spreads of the celebrities in a state of euphoria after meeting with Maharishi

Mahesh Yogi soon began popping up in all of the leading magazines. Subsequently, Mia Farrow, the Beatles, *et al.*, announced their disenchantment with the meditation movement—but not before it had rolled over the ocean into America and fanned across the continent, gathering into its fold both troubled flower children helplessly stalled in an extended postadolescence and their "identity-shopping" middle-aged counterparts.

On a triumphant tour of the United States, Maharishi Mahesh Yogi filled New York's Madison Square Garden with masses of delirious followers and drew seven hundred meditators to Squaw Valley, California, for a month-long conference at the resort in August 1968 ("Tahoe," explained the Maharishi, "has the best vibrations of the West").

Long after its trend-setting "discoverers" had grown disillusioned and moved on to something else, Nehru jackets, beads, medallions, and the smell of incense filled the land. By the end of the 1960s, hundred of thousands of Americans were practicing the "TM program," meditating for twenty minutes twice a day. And in 1975, the multimillion-dollar "nonprofit" movement had some six thousand TM teachers in the country and over 380 "neighborhood centers" distributed throughout the major cities of the United States, prompting the *New York Times* to call Transcendental Meditation "1975's biggest cultural whirlwind."

But a funny thing happened on the way to the ashram. The movement that had promised spiritual enlightenment and an alternative value system to Americans who felt alienated from our ruthlessly competitive social institutions in the Sixties had been converted, by the Seventies, into a school for survival in the rat race. Instead of providing the seekers with spiritual values, the movement became a dispensary, handing out psychic tranquilizers to help the adjusted play by the old rules. With our famous gift for technology, Americans quickly siphoned the *technique* out of the Hindu religion and shucked aside its matrix of ethical principles—the very principles that the counterculture had supposedly been searching for—as a useless waste product.

The TM Book, the best-selling book-length advertisement for the "TM program" that was published in 1975, is an unintentionally tragicomic example of how the profit motive debased the counterculture's desperate search for a more spiritually satisfying alternative to the competitive ethic. Stressing over and over again that the "TM technique" is purely *scientific* and produces scientifically verifiable results—lower blood pressure, slower heart rate—the authors (two TM teachers personally trained and qualified by Maharishi Mahesh Yogi) repeatedly reassure the reader that the "TM program" involves no belief or philosophy: "There are no pleasures you must abandon, nor any new traditions you must uphold." Nothing *spiritual*, God forbid. Then there are the testimonials in the front of the book. For a movement whose earliest devotees had dropped out of the larger culture in flight from its military imperialism abroad and its competitive aggression at home, the words of praise come from two very improbable sources: "Joe Namath, Quarterback, New York Jets" and "Major General Franklin M. Davis, Commandant, U.S. Army War College."

The dependency problems of many of the seekers made them as exploitative of the Eastern religious movements as the movements were of them. Like the compulsive gambler who gets a rush of euphoria from surrendering control over his life to the roll of the dice or the turn of the roulette wheel, the seekers wanted to be free of choice. They were looking to their horoscope or the performance of a mystical ritual as a way out of having to accept responsibility for determining their own course through life rather than using Eastern religions to help them assume that responsibility. While the concept of Karma as the determinant of the seeker's future was so far removed from the image of the parents as to suggest complete separation, the helpless dependency of those who misapplied the concept was exactly the same as it had been in the symbiotic early childhood state.

Instead of providing an alternative to the consumerism and self-indulgence of upper-middle-class values, Eastern spiritualism fed into these tendencies because those who flocked to it had not developed sufficient trust in themselves to give up their fantasies of narcissistic omnipotence. By relying on magic, they could avoid "selling out" to more attainable goals that they either feared they could not achieve or believed were not monumental enough to win them unconditional love. In the same way that the "corporation man" and the "happy homemaker heroine" in the Fifties had evaded growth by losing themselves in the creed of accumulation, the flower children in the Sixties tried to block out their dread of autonomy by relying on magic and letting their instinctual life run wild. It was a trend that many restless seekers continued to follow well into the Seventies, as Eleanor Coppola revealed in this excerpt from *Notes* (published in August 1979), the diary she kept during the time her husband Francis Ford Coppola directed the filming of his Vietnam War epic, *Apocalypse Now:*

If I tell the truth, we both strayed from our marriage, probably equally, each in our own way. Francis has gone to extremes in the physical world—women, food, possessions—in an effort to feel complete. I have looked for that feeling of completeness in the nonphysical world: Zen, est, Esalen, meditation. Neither is better or worse than the other.

THE PIED PIPER OF ALIENATION

On American college campuses in the Sixties, Swiss author Hermann Hesse was idolized for novels like *Siddhartha,* the literary embodiment of this narcissistic struggle to overcome inner emptiness through the cult of experience and mystical, abstract love of *all* beings instead of a deeply committed relationship with one. Hesse's legend of Siddhartha is the story of a Brahmin's son who leaves home as a youth and sets off on a long, tortuous journey toward self-knowledge. Celebrated as an inspirational allegory, it reads, on closer inspection, like a case history of a confirmed narcissist.

Abruptly and permanently severing all ties with his parents, the young Siddhartha travels across India, desperately seeking to escape from the "torment of Self." The pattern is a familiar one. First, Siddhartha tries to gain complete mastery over his pleasure-seeking impulses by rigorous asceticism—meditation, fasting, and self-denial. He meets the Buddha but rejects his teachings just as he had earlier rejected his father's. Then Siddhartha swings away from asceticism to the opposite pole, abandoning himself through the tutelage of Kamala, a beautiful courtesan, to sensuality and material acquisition. He becomes a wealthy merchant and engages in a long and passionate affair with Kamala, his only close friend. But Siddhartha's success leaves his real self curiously untouched. Devoid of empathy for others, he goes through the motions of daily living with the detachment of a man playing a game. Coolly, Siddhartha regards the people around him with condescension—he is a "star" and they are only "falling leaves"—but at the same time he envies them because their ability to love is a secret that he and Kamala can never share:

Gradually, along with his growing riches, Siddhartha himself acquired some of the characteristics of the ordinary people, some of their childishness and some of their anxiety. And yet he envied them; the more he became like them, the more he envied them. He envied them the one thing that he lacked and that they had: the sense of importance with which they lived their lives, the depth of their pleasures and sorrows, the anxious but sweet happiness of their continual power to love.

In mid-life, deeply disillusioned with secular pleasure, Siddhartha uproots himself once again and continues his search for inner peace. On his last night with Kamala, in love play that is particularly intense, Siddhartha unknowingly impregnates the aging, world-weary courtesan and takes his leave of her, "his heart full of misery and secret fear." Wandering through the forest in despair, he stops at a river bank and sees his face reflected, Narcissuslike, in the water. A wave of self-hate engulfs Siddhartha, and he is about to plunge into the river to his death when a long-forgotten word surfaces to consciousness and stops him. It is *Om*, the ancient beginning and ending of all Brahmin prayers, meaning "the Perfect One" or "perfection."

Siddhartha sinks into a deep sleep and awakens a new man—or rather, a newborn child. Having given up the struggle to find his own limits, he has at last killed "his small, fearful and proud Self," the self that had tormented him for so many years and would not be destroyed either by the extreme of fasting and penitence or by the opposite extreme of wanton sensuality and material possession. For Siddhartha, peace from the "torment of Self" comes from the merger of self into a seamless unity with a divine universe accomplished by clinging to a belief in perfection. Unable to define his own limits through identification with his father or the Buddha, a father-surrogate, Siddhartha envisions a world where limits do not exist because he is at the center of it:

Therefore, it seems to me that everything that exists is good—death as well as life, sin as well as holiness, wisdom as well as folly. Everything is necessary, everything needs only my agreement, my assent, my loving understanding; then all is well with me and nothing can harm me.

Ordinarily, the state of transcendence—the sense of extending beyond oneself and feeling at unity with all others who have lived and loved and suffered before—is achieved in a deep relationship with another. But Siddhartha uses an intellectually formulated transcendence to keep others at a safe emotional distance. By means of this elaborate defense, he imagines himself to be at one with everyone when he is actually close to no one.

Alienation, however, begets alienation. In his later years, after Siddhartha has taken up a peaceful, introspective life as a ferryman on the same river where he contemplated suicide, he again meets Kamala. Her days as a courtesan long behind her, Kamala is traveling with Siddhartha's young son to pay her last respects to the dying Buddha. But Kamala has been bitten by a snake en route, and she dies in Siddhartha's hut. For the first time in his life Siddhartha falls madly in love—with his son. Although uplifted by this very human, very painful passion, Siddhartha values it mainly as another of his impulses that has to be lived out through experience. The son, in turn, no better able to identify with his pietist father than Siddhartha had been, runs away to learn about life from experience—the self-seeker's only teacher. Siddhartha overcomes the grief of separation—and the need for attachment—by his belief in the mystical unity of Om that gives him, finally, the omniscience and impenetrable serenity of another Buddha.

It is easy to see why Hermann Hesse, as the Pied Piper of narcissistic alienation, so enraptured America's college students in the Sixties. Like Siddhartha, they, too, felt they could learn nothing from their parents and teachers, but finding separation unbearable, masked their repressed longing for love in a hunger for experience and detached mysticism. Hesse was himself an incurable narcissist who would not go to his beloved dying mother's bedside or even attend her funeral because to have done so, according to his biographer, "would have drawn Hesse into a vortex he feared most, that palpable awareness of loss from which he tried to protect himself all his life." But there is no protection against this awareness of loss except alienation. In Siddhartha, Hesse mined the depths of his own inner loneliness and produced the perfect parable of the Love Generation's psychological malaise: the torment of the self when children have received everything from their parents except those genuinely empathetic acts of love that provide a sense of limits.

One imagines, reading this passage from *Siddhartha* reflecting Siddhartha's son's feelings toward his father, that the feelings described closely resemble those of any overprivileged but underloved son of upper-middle-class "too good" parents in America in the 1960s:

> There was nothing about this father that attracted him and nothing that he feared. This father was a good man, a kind gentle man, perhaps a pious man—but all these were not qualities which could win the boy. This father who kept him in this wretched hut bored him, and when he answered his rudeness with a smile, every insult with friendliness, every naughtiness with kindness, that was the most hateful cunning of the old fox. The boy would have much preferred him to threaten him, to ill-treat him.

This passage calls to mind the revelations of a Columbia University student revolutionary named "James," a sophomore at college in 1970, who was interviewed by psychoanalyst Herbert Hendin for *The Age of Sensation*. James, a member of SDS (Students for a Democratic Society), "wistfully" described to Hendin the mixture of fear and exhilaration evoked in him by past confrontations with the police and recounted a dream in which he was leading a dangerous and violent political confrontation. He brought it off successfully but, fleeing the scene, was caught in a barbed-wire fence. Badly mangled, he was captured and put in a preventive detention camp. When James discussed the dream, he predicted that radical activity would provoke a right-wing reaction and student revolutionaries throughout the country would be put in preventive detention camps. Discerning a veiled wish beneath James's prediction, Hendin concluded: "He almost seemed to need and want some forceful outside reaction to control his behavior."

The anguish James felt at not having this responsive outside control to prevent him from hurting himself or others was revealed in his recollection of an incident that took place during Christmas vacation when James was home visiting his parents. As Hendin tells it:

A blizzard had left a great deal of snow and ice on the ground. James wanted to drive the car. Both his parents were anxious over his taking it, but his father said nothing and let him have the car, although he had been out and he knew driving was impossible. "Fifteen times," James said furiously, "I nearly killed myself or someone else." He came home and argued with his father over why he let him use the car, knowing the conditions as he did. His father answered that he had not wanted him to take it, but that he felt James would think he was overprotective if he refused and would be angry.

Any of us who are middle-aged parents today will immediately recognize this scene as vintage 1950s permissiveness come home to roost. We can sympathize with the father's desire not to insult his son and provoke a furious battle by appearing "overprotective"— after all, how many other-directed parents in the turbulent Sixties could stand having themselves branded "square"? But we can also see how the father's fear of frustrating his child, besides involving an almost criminal risk of physical danger, is so out of touch with the son's emotional needs that it is interpreted as a lack of love and arouses his rage. And this rage is far more profound than the temporary outburst of anger that occurs when a child is frustrated but unconsciously welcomes that frustration because he is seeking a staying hand to protect him from his destructive or self-destructive impulses. This rage, blanketed by pervasive depression and loneliness, is that all-consuming narcissistic rage of a child who feels emotionally invisible because his parents, out of a wish to avoid conflict, have consistently failed to recognize or confront his actual emotions. Revolutionary students in the Sixties, Hendin maintains, were plagued by just such a lifetime of emotional invisibility.

REVOLUTIONARY RAGE

For radical students, revolutionary activity became both a vehicle for their rage and a retaliatory weapon to use against the parents. James, for example, began his sessions with Hendin claiming that his parents supported his radical aims, if not all of his violent tactics. But "he eventually admitted with a satisfied smile that he sensed his father was inwardly seething at the things he was doing, but was unable to say anything about them." In the same way that the parents' "permissiveness" toward their children had the effect of negating the separateness and authenticity of the children's needs, the children now dismissed the *parents'* real feelings as "irrelevant."

Hendin observed this turning of the tables on their parents among all of the radical students he interviewed. Whether they openly attacked their parents or claimed to have their support, they knew they had put their parents in the position of feeling obliged to go along with a situation they hated but could not control. Out of loyalty to their children—or, more accurately, symbiotic merger with them—the parents swallowed their anger, presented a surface picture of harmony with the radicals, and often steadfastly continued to support them in or out of college. The students accepted this support unhesitatingly and, like James, even seemed to derived a smug satisfaction out of manipulating the upper hand in this twisted way.

But Hendin sees these domineering student revolutionaries as more than just the violently bratty products of overpermissive parents. He also rejects the point of view, advanced by the young revolutionaries' sympathizers, that their violence was justified by the enormity of the social, cultural, and political ills of our society in the Sixties. He sees the rampaging radicals as neither *enfants terribles* nor *enfants merveilleux*, but as victims of narcissistic injury whose identification with the poor and the oppressed gives some indication of their own feelings of inner impoverishment:

To insist that they are products of over-privilege, the spoiled sons and daughters of the affluent, is to insist that the only hunger is for food and the only deprivation is economic. The fervor with which they scorn America's concern for money must be understood in the context of their lives. They themselves have suffered in families who more than provided for their material needs, but frustrated their personal needs, and continue to be blind to them as people. In rejecting the life-style of their parents as too concerned with property, wealth, and economic security, what they do not readily say but clearly feel is that their parents were too unconcerned in any meaningful way with them.

A woman news reporter I interviewed about the Sixties, a twenty-six-year-old work ethic devotee who attended boarding school in

Stockbridge, Massachusetts, from 1967 to 1970, recalls in vivid detail the emotional deprivation of the counterculture's spoiled sons and daughters. She arrived in Stockbridge, the home of the original Alice's Restaurant in Arlo Guthrie's famous twenty-minute song of that name celebrating the joys of anti-Vietnam War activities, in the very same year that Guthrie's epic was released. Having enjoyed a happy, close-knit family life in Chevy Chase, Maryland, she had come to Stockbridge—with her parents' approval—in pursuit of "independent and pure learning," as she jokingly refers to it. Her purpose was to escape the narrow, materialistic values of her snobbish peers in Chevy Chase, but she soon found that she had jumped from the frying pan into the fire.

"The kids at the school in Stockbridge were all these rich New Yorkers," she says, "mostly nouveau riche Manhattanites who came from very unhappy homes." She remembers her first Parents' Day in the fall. "The parents arrived in their pink Cadillacs, and the mothers emerged in their matching pink pants suits. We weren't allowed to have cars, so one of the fathers, a corporation president, parked a Cadillac down the road for his son when he left and had someone drive him home. The kid needed a car to get to his psychoanalyst three days a week."

According to the reporter, most of her classmates were in analysis, but it didn't seem to be doing them much good. "These kids were so out to lunch," she says, "that they had almost no awareness of reality or their ability to deal with it. They had no secure feelings of family and were searching for security among themselves. Some were buying up the farms around Stockbridge for 'free love' communes, and others were involved in very intense, mutually dependent relationships where they glommed together twenty-four hours a day. If you were still a virgin after the first year, you were an outcast." The parents knew about their children's sexual activity, she maintains, but would never talk to them about it: "When the kids went home on vacation, they would find information on V.D. that their parents left for them on their toilet seats."

Some cultural historians see a strong link between this failure of the parents to intervene directly in their children's lives and the refusal of institutional authority to respond to student protest in an open and personal manner. The deaf ear of government and university authorities exacerbated the children's feelings of emotional invisibility and rage and helped turn originally nonviolent student protest into revolutionary activity.

Like the black movement, student activism began peacefully and continued throughout the first half of the Sixties to focus on effecting change within the system. But just as disillusionment among the blacks led to the emergence in the mid-Sixties of a separatist revolutionary faction that scoffed at Martin Luther King, Jr., as an "Uncle Tom," the growing despair of student protesters over the system's implacable indifference made the youth movement ripe for radicalization, too. Partly, it was the sheer grandiosity of the student protesters' aims that defeated them and pushed them over the brink of despair into violence. As Kenneth Kenniston has pointed out, the New Left organized the Vietnam Summer of 1967 to bring about—over and above the end of the Vietnam War—the end of war itself as an eventuality ever again. Besides the frustration inherent in goals of such sweeping magnitude, the rejection encountered by the student activists at every turn made them feel increasingly that violence was the only answer. All of their efforts—to end the war, to oppose racism, to champion the working class—were ignored or rebuffed, often by the very people they were trying to help. Enraged and alienated by this unresponsiveness, a growing number of campus radicals gave up on trying to work within the system and succumbed to uncontrollable aggression.

In her firsthand remembrance of this all-encompassing rage—"rage at the War, at the draft, at LBJ, at General Hershey, and ultimately, at the Establishment or adults/powermongers/capitalists/institutions in general"—Ann Braden Johnson pinpoints the attitude of the authorities that brought student protest to such a pitch of "non-negotiable" violence:

The most awful part of student protest was the invisibility of the other side. I vividly recall a March on Washington to End the War when John Mitchell was still the much-despised attorney general; as the crowd passed the Justice Department, virtually everyone spontaneously made the classic obscene gesture—to a man who wasn't there.

Johnson claims that the violence of the SDS and other radical groups, "made up as they were of the most precariously organized (psychologically) of the activist students," was entirely predictable in view of this absolute remoteness of authorities at every level. But, like Hendin, she also sees a more personal target of that global rage:

Rejection and rage, resentment and the feeling that one is left out, unwanted by the big people, seeing one's hard work doomed to failure and ridicule, not to mention the very real possibility for males of being drafted—all this and more can easily be seen to have so depressed, frightened, and infuriated student protesters that the step towards fighting back, meeting aggression with aggression, eventually became easy to take. . . . This is an enormously more active stance than that taken by the hippies, and that it should degenerate into violence and generalized, uncontrolled aggression can be no surprise. The real object of that aggression is clear, if we are to take the word of one of three national officers elected by the SDS 1969 national convention: "Bring the revolution home, kill your parents, that's where it's really at."

This murderous rage no doubt reflects the cumulative impact of the multiple shocks of the previous year: the My Lai massacre, the abdication of Lyndon Johnson, the assassination of Martin Luther King, Jr., the Columbia takeover, the assassination of Robert F. Kennedy, and the Battle of Chicago. To the militants, this last orgy of violence must have seemed like an intimation of the terrifying yet longed-for *Gotterdammerung* that would come about if the youth movement clashed often enough with the brutality-crazed forces of law and order. But by the end of the Sixties the lust for violence had been spent. The inflammatory words of the' revolutionaries—in the black community as well as on the college campuses—failed to strike fire. Blood had been spilled, bombs thrown, lives lost, property destroyed—and there was no victory. Exhausted and lethargic, the violence junkies began to realize that uncontrolled aggression, bounding out of its cage like an untamed beast, was not the answer—either to the problems of the world or to the more basic, more compelling problem of the torment of the self.

Many in the older generation tend to think that students lost interest in violent political activity only because of obvious pragmatic reasons—the end of the Vietnam War, the refusal of society to put up with violent protest any longer, a decline in the economy that made a return to careerism of paramount concern. These were significant influences, but even more meaningful were the anxieties and fears that violent political protest aroused in the students while doing little to relieve their pervasive feelings of depression and inner emptiness. Temporarily, they got a "high" from releasing their rage in violent political activity. Yet this outlet kept them addicted to rage and unable to gain control of it because the expression of their anger in confrontations with the police diverted them from its real source. And appealing as violence was, it was also scary. Many students feared their own violence, having glimpsed the total destructiveness that can result when aggressive impulses are given free rein. It was one thing to *talk* about killing, another to do it. When the Weathermen took to throwing real bombs—and when the Ohio National Guard shot students down at Kent State in 1970 with real bullets—most of the radicals lost their taste for revolution.

Another paradox that drove students out of the radical movement was its fascistic rules in the name of freedom. Like the passivist hippies retreating into their womblike communes, the activist radicals were also seeking unconditional love through a total merger of the self with the group. Everyone was expected to be a team player, and the members rigidly discouraged any assertion of personal choice that was not directly tied to furthering the group's purposes. As one Columbia student interviewed by Hendin said of the radical movement: "They want to control every aspect of their members' lives while preaching that when they come to the power everyone will be free." Since the members derived their sense of identity from the collective identity of the group, any expression of individuality was experienced as a violation of the self—the False Self they had created through symbiosis.

YOUTH-DIRECTION

Despite the repugnance that most over-thirties felt at the fanaticism of the militants and the freakishness of the drug-wasted hippie fringe, the spirit of rebellion was contagious. For a large segment of the affluent upper middle class, against whom the revolution was directed, this was the moment they'd been waiting for. The sense of having sacrificed too much personal freedom, particularly sexual, had begun to rankle many of those who had achieved the American Dream but were still bored and dissatisfied. Some denied their dissatisfaction, barring it from themselves as inadmissible evidence of having been defrauded by the Dream, and reacted furiously against the counterculture for having the guts to question the system as they themselves had not. But many others, more oriented toward social protest—as long as it was socially approved—joined the young and took up arms against the entire value structure of the larger culture as soon as their radar picked up the signal that the revolution had begun.

The real meaning of the "revolution" in the Sixties was that the American social character, having changed from inner-direction to other-direction in the Fifties, underwent still another transformation in the following decade and changed from other-direction to what I call youth-direction: *Instead of taking their moral and social norms from their peers, the middle and upper middle class began to orient themselves by their children.* This represented not merely an alteration in our social character but a seismic reversal of the whole socialization process.

From society's earliest beginnings, the moral norms regarding sex, religion, authority, and role obligation to others had always been conveyed to children by their parents and other mentors in the larger culture. In the Fifties, there was a shift away from the normal mode of the transmission of values when the parents began to replace their internalized traditional codes with conformity to their peers. And in the Sixties, the transmission of values broke down altogether and began to flow the other way: Disgusted with the empty artificiality of their institutions, the parents passed the responsibility for shaping rules, meanings, and behaviors to the children—an unprecedented turnabout of authority that was to become the new problem rather than the answer.

With the advent of youth-direction, the narcissistic use of the young by the older generation exceeded anything we'd ever seen before. The worst offenders were influent adult authority figures who defected from the establishment and co-opted the lifestyle of the young for their own aggrandizement; people like Timothy Leary, the Harvard psychology lecturer turned Sixties LSD guru turned Seventies comic, who appeared in clubs all over the country. Like all "identity-shoppers," the symbiotic youth-worshipers were dependent on some "magic helper" outside themselves to be the source of their security and happiness. Frustrated in the spontaneous expression of their thoughts and feelings, they hoped that youth, rather than the ability to act on their own decisions, would set them free.

Nowhere was this expectation more clearly expressed than in *The Greening of America*, the highly influential best-seller by youth movement evangelist Charles A. Reich, professor of law at Yale from 1960 to 1974, who now lives and writes in San Francisco. First published in October 1970, Reich's book went through twelve hardcover printings through March 1971 and twenty paperback printings from June 1971 through September 1978.

Singing praises to college youth in the Sixties for having reached a higher level of consciousness than the older generation, Reich labeled this rarefied state "Consciousness III" and defined it as a total rejection of the Protestant work ethic and rational thought and a new emphasis on "drug-thought," the senses, mystical community, and the self. But having reached "Consciousness III" themselves was not enough. Reich insisted that "now our young people must take another step and assume responsibility for their parents, their college teachers, their younger brothers and sisters, and on outward into society, to all those who seem to be enemies but are only the deceived, the broken, and the lost."

Reich's bitter diatribe against the Corporate State for usurping our minds and turning us into the powerless pawns of technology pulsates with the sense of *betrayal* most of the Silent Generation felt by the late Sixties. All of our lives we had dutifully followed the rules, with no other explanation given us except "Do it or else," only to be hit broadside in middle age with the message in *The Graduate*. Guess what, folks—we'd been had: There was no light at the end of the swimming pool.

Now we looked around and saw the new generation reveling in the "freedom" that we never had, proclaiming that self-denial was dead (along with God, duty, honor, the family, hard work, obligations to others, love of country, money, and success). While we stood by and watched, marveling at their nerve, the young insurgents stormed the walls of organization-world, smashed its rock-bound rules, and with a shout of the new moral imperative—"If it feels right, do it!"—crowned Experience king.

We burned with envy. After all, hadn't it been our permissiveness that had given youth their birthright to this "liberated" lifestyle while we, the timid, dull "straights," were still locked inside our own cheerless institutions? We seemed to have only two alternatives: either stay in our safe, claustrophobic worlds for the rest of our lives and seethe with anger over "the fear that some pleasure is being enjoyed by others but forever denied to us," in Reich's words, or break away from our peers and follow the lead of youth.

Reich makes it very clear that in urging our "conversion" to the raised consciousness of the new youth culture, he is asking the older generation to forfeit their accustomed status in society as role models to the young—a seniority most of us felt uncomfortable with anyway—and to adopt the younger generation as our models to emulate and identify with instead. And where did the new youth culture get *its* model to copy? From the *blacks*. Says Reich:

The vital importance of having a model to emulate is revealed by the influence of the black life-style and music in changing the consciousness of nineteen-fifties white teen-agers. It was black music, in the form of rock 'n' roll, which first offered teen-agers an alternative to their own sentimental and insipid music. And it was the hip black life-style, with its contempt for white middle-class values and its affirmation of the sensual, the earthy, and the rebellious elements in man, that gave high school and college students something to copy instead of the existing pattern; as early as the middle fifties, rebellious white teen-agers were copying black language styles.

Reich concludes:

What workers and the middle class lack, then, is a model to copy. They have not been able to identify with blacks or with youth, and they have no models of their own. Unmistakably, that is the missing factor. And we can be more precise: what is lacking is a model that demonstrates new goals, new values, a new definition of what constitutes being happy.

What is Reich's answer to the values vacuum? It is not to *restore* the authority of the self—that is the real "missing factor"—but to *transfer* authority to a more exciting source of other-direction than one's immediate peers. This pattern of youth-direction emerged, Reich notes, among rebellious white teen-agers who identified with antisocial teen-agers in the the black subculture during the 1950s, and these James Dean-type "rebels without a cause" were the precursors of the revolutionary new generation in the Sixties.

THE DOCTRINE OF PERSONAL FULFILLMENT

Reich projects onto this whole emerging pattern of "hip" adolescent rebellion his own generation's need for a "magic helper" to deliver them from the self-denying constraints of the success ethic. He takes the youth culture's rejection of all of the dominant values of the larger society and fashions a new ideology of *personal fulfillment*. He envisions everything in the youth culture—"from ideals to campus demonstrations to beads and bell bottoms to the Woodstock Festival"—to be part of a "consistent philosophy."

The new philosophy of personal fulfillment declares the individual self to be "the only true reality." It would be hard to quarrel with this except that Reich makes it clear that there is only one True Self for everybody. This is the self immersed in the "liberated" lifestyle, where experience of every kind—murder and rape are mentioned as the only two possible exceptions—is regarded as "the most precious of all commodities."

While Reich stresses egalitarian concepts, he detaches the philosophy of personal fulfillment from the grass roots of social and political activism. A changed consciousness alone, he insists, is enough to correct the evils of the Corporate State. This was welcome news to the youth movement, whose zest for social protest had been beaten out of them by the early Seventies. Disillusioned with dissent, they were vulnerable to Reich's easy assurances that we need only work on ourselves to change the world. The formula acts like a chain letter. Starting with the individual and with culture, the philosophy of personal fulfillment will spread from youth to include all people in America, Reich predicts, and will change the political structure "only as its final act."

Central to the Reichian philosophy of personal fulfillment is its distorted notion of transcendence, a confusion very similar to Hermann Hesse's in *Siddhartha*. Reich mistakenly believes that transcendence is a "rising above" the existing social order to create a purely personal world of one's own, rather than a linking up with the eternal structures of family and community to achieve continuity beyond the self. He also confuses schizophrenic withdrawal with the competitive world's compulsive splitting apart of work and pleasure into two separate realms. *Real* emotional withdrawal is that "magnificent sense of detachment" Reich describes when one's raised consciousness lifts him beyond the reach of anyone else's reality but his own.

Like the rebellious youth culture he has chosen to emulate, Reich is torn between his desire to separate from traditional codes and his fear of entrapment in new ones. Breaking away arouses the same "palpable awareness of loss" that Hesse tried to protect himself against. Reich finds his protection in the "protean" aspect of personal fulfillment—the most insidious of the devices aimed at concealing the fear of autonomy under the cloak of liberation. Named after Proteus (the Greek sea god who could change his shape into any form in nature, but had trouble keeping his own), the protean approach offered the self no better alternative to locked-in traditional roles than a fugitive existence in a constant state of flux. The idea of keeping open unlimited possibilities in beliefs and relationships, "including the possibility of whatever new and spontaneous thing may come along," is supposed to be necessary for the self's "wholeness." But instead, it contributes to the diffusion of the self and provokes profound anxiety.

To an older generation hungry for experience and a younger one starved of discipline, the protean notion that "the most basic limitations in life—the job, the working day, the part one can play in life, the limits of sex, love and relationships, the limits of knowledge and experience—all vanish, leaving open a life that can be lived without the guideposts of the past" was very appealing. But we can see in Reich's propagandizing of the youth culture's protean lifestyle in the 1960s the makings of the most serious problems for both youth and the older generation in the subsequent Me Decade:

Young people today insist upon prolonging the period of youth, education, and growth. They stay uncommitted; they refuse to decide on a formal career, they do not give themselves fixed future goals to pursue. Their emphasis on the present makes possible an openness toward the future; the person who focuses on the future freezes that future in its present image. Personal relationships are entered into without commitment to the future; a marriage legally binding for the life of the couple is inconsistent with the likelihood of growth and change; if the couple grows naturally together that is fine, but change, not an unchangeable love, is the rule of life.

Here, in rebellion against the extreme of stagnation, we have the new extreme: the rootlessness of constant change. But along with the excesses and distortions of the philosophy of personal fulfillment, we inherited something even more destructive—the whole process of youth-direction. The co-optation of the youth movement by the older generation was not merely a matter of parents' imitating their children's taste in clothes and music or copying their indulgence in marijuana and recreational sex or taking up their causes and forms of social protest. If the youth-directed parents in the late Sixties and early Seventies had gone no farther than relying on their children to keep them abreast of the times—as some did—there would have been nothing particularly virulent about their conformity. Or if they had simply supported their children's idealism or tolerated their rebellion *while still being there to provide safety,* this, too, would not have exceeded the bounds of responsible parenthood.

But for many parents, permissiveness had obliterated the boundaries between themselves and their children. In desperation, the children were driven to distance themselves from the parents as far as they could. Their drugs, their music, their protest, their sexual experimentation were all a way of asserting to the parents who made them feel invisible—and to the institutions that made them feel powerless—the existence of a private self. The youth culture's assault on the institutions was intended to provoke a caring response—an end to the war, more openness, less dehumanization by technology. And from the parents, what the younger generation wanted was recognition of their emerging autonomous self. The *last* thing they wanted or needed was an invasion of it. Yet, the persuasive huckstering of the media, of the human potential movement, and of youth culture propagandists like Reich all combined to encourage the older generation to invade and claim as their own the emerging self of their rebellious adolescent children. This was different from the way parents in immigrant families in America and in other times and places have learned from or been influenced by their children. For a whole generation of parents—my generation—our conformity with the youth culture went beyond the obvious imitation of their cultural style to an assimilation of their emotions and thought.

There was, of course, nothing *personal* about the philosophy of personal fulfillment that we absorbed from the younger generation. How could it be personal when the definition of what constituted "self-fulfillment" was part of a clearly defined dogma that had been lifted in its entirety from a source external to us? For all its talk of "choice" and "freedom," the doctrine of self-fulfillment ignored the True Self, the core of each person's individual identity, as arbitrarily as had the ideology of suburban bliss. We were told, very emphatically, what the rules were, and we were expected to comply with them whether it made us uncomfortable or not. Getting rid of the discomfort was, as it had been with the competitive ethic, merely a matter of adjustment.

The "out"/"in" dichotomy so popular in the Sixties—and so indicative of the other-directedness of our standards of value—might be summarized as follows:

Out	In
commitment	keeping your options open
discipline	instant gratification
loyalty	novelty and excitement
responsibility	openness to experience
rational thought	psychedelic feeling-perceiving
structure	spontaneity
guilt	lack of moral restraint
obligations to others	self-centeredness
hard work	pleasurable activity
concern about the future	living for the moment

Anyone glancing at the "Out" column immediately sees how harsh, confining, and irredeemably bourgeois the old values seem compared to the carefree new "In" ones. The new values that purportedly make "personal fulfillment" the highest goal resonate with a feeling of childlike fun—the old "fun morality" that Martha Wolfenstein observed in the way the babies (who would grow up to be counterculturalists) were reared back in the 1940s. The doctrine of personal fulfillment holds out the ideal that one should live the whole of life like a vacation-goer on an extended holiday.

At first blush, there is something irresistibly appealing about the ideal of life-as-vacation—no worries, no troubles, no one to answer to except oneself. To an older generation of "nice girls" and "good boys" who had always lived to please others, embracing the "fun morality" code appeared to be the only way to rescue a self bound and gagged with parental rules and societal conventions. But on closer inspection, the doctrine of personal fulfillment offers only a new package of "should nots"—anti-limits—to replace the old package of "shoulds." It assumes that the injury done to the self by excessive compliance with one set of standards can be undone by compliance with a set of opposite but equal ones: You *should not* deny yourself any sexual experience; You *should not* refrain from using drugs; You *should not* make sacrifices for your family; You *should not* fully commit yourself to anything or anyone; You *should not* put another's interests above your own at any time; You *should not* expect marriage to last forever; You *should not* live in the suburbs (as if the suburbs themselves automatically breed mindless materialism and sterility).

Everything about the doctrine of personal fulfillment conveys the feeling of taking a much needed vacation from the rigidities of Fifties "togetherness." But the mandatory hedonism of the doctrine and its insistence on continual openness to new experience make it a vacation of a very circumscribed kind. There is an aura of studied decadence about it that suggests the Kit Kat Club in *Cabaret*, where an obscenely leering master of ceremonies in grotesque makeup introduces the evening's entertainment and urges us to have "a good time." Suddenly we realize that this new M.C., who will not let us escape living out our fantasies, is only our old mercilessly punitive guilt and shame controls in lurid disguise.

Even without imposing a stereotype of liberated behavior, this doctrine would still not restore the integrity of the self or lead to a feeling of inner completeness. Its "holiday" vision of life ignores the fact that man cannot live by leisure alone—not only for economic reasons but for psychological ones as well. The youth culture was justified in condemning the regimentation of the organization man and dad's definition of his identity solely through his work role. But college students in the Sixties failed to ascribe to the nine-to-five grind its value in supplying, in addition to income, some of the essentials of psychological well-being: self-respect, independence, a sense of personal effectiveness in the larger world, a set of concrete goals, a conviction that one's private goals and behavior also contribute to the welfare of others, a feeling that one's world is reasonably stable, and an overall sense of meaning and coherence in one's life.

THE NONWORK ETHIC

Observing the job market from the sheltered vantage point of college students whose parents were supporting them during a period of extraordinary affluence, the youth culture in the Sixties took a dim and narrow view of the working world. They focused only on the "meaningless" and "degrading" quality of most of the work available in our society and its inconsistency with "self-realization." Riding the crest of optimism in a booming economy, they had the complacent outlook that our abundance was inexhaustible. The ever-tightening job market of the Seventies was not yet upon them, and they felt cocky enough to extol the virtues of holding out—forever, if necessary—for work that was the perfect expression of their "fun morality."

College students in the Sixties could afford a magnificent contempt for money because it was there. And when it wasn't, the youth culture simply took what they wanted without paying for it—a form of stealing which, because it was open, did not strike them as dishonest. At the much glorified Woodstock Festival, for example, most of the 400,000 in attendance were gate-crashers. As a result of this giant swindle by the Love Generation, it took the Festival's two youthful promoters, Michael Lang and John Roberts—both under twenty-five at the time—the better part of ten years to make up their $1.6 million loss through film and record residuals. (As an ironic footnote, Warner Brothers, the epitome of the materialistic, technologized organization world that the counterculture despised, made $35 million from the festival.)

If they often displayed very little regard for other people's money, most of the counterculture people I talked to in the late 1960s seemed obsessed with making a great deal of their own—including Andy Warhol, who talked about nothing *but* money. What was important to the college students was that they make money *on their own terms*. This usually meant entering a "fun" field, like music, the theater, or the arts, where, if they achieved success, they could combine a lucrative income with the hip lifestyle. They knew that their traditional middle-class parents frowned on such chancy, "nonrespectable" callings—which made them all the more alluring—but would subsidize them anyway so that survival was not a problem.

Credit must be given to this generation for making great strides in entering nontraditional fields in which success could be measured only by their own achievements rather than by comparison with their parents' generation. In so doing, they paved the way for the emergence of a new standard in the workplace—*lateral* rather than upward mobility.

Since upward mobility had become increasingly difficult, many extended their desire to achieve into areas that were outside the established hierarchy approved by their parents but were nonetheless socially useful as well as personally satisfying. Those who had the specific talents and skills to succeed as rock musicians, lighting designers, writers, artists, craftspeople, health food entrepreneurs, et cetera, were able to carve a niche for themselves where their ambitions and the necessity to earn a living were not at odds. Many less gifted counterculturalists were also able, through a fortuitous combination of grit and chance, to find work that satisfied both their creative urgings and their needs for survival. They were the lucky ones.

Unfortunately, many others were encouraged to stay out of the workplace and join the ranks of the idle poor. They would choose not to work, preferring to beg or to scheme up ways to live on welfare and food stamps, unemployment insurance, government grants, or the earnings of relatives—the scam. Joined by their emulators in the older generation, they would form a subculture in the Seventies that would comprise some 40 percent of the unemployed. Like the hippies in the Sixties, they would justify their narcissistic entitlement on the basis of idealism. But it was their *distorted* ideals—ideals of punishing perfection—that would make the term "self-fulfillment" a code name for endless disillusionment in work and love.

At the start of the Seventies, a strange phenomenon occurred. As more and more "converted" members of the older generation began dropping out of the rat race to "find themselves," the reconverted youth culture began pouring back into the mainstream to find work. The lowering of the youth culture's consciousness while everyone else's was being raised was partly the result of our changed economy, but mostly the result of growing up.

What appeared to the impressionable older generation to be part of a "consistent philosophy" among the young was neither as consistent nor as philosophical as it seemed. Most former flower children now admit that they never expected their hippie lifestyle to last forever. They felt as coerced by their peers into their role of "rebel-with-a-cause" as we had felt coerced by our parents into our "nice girl–good boy" orientation. All throughout their protest and rebellion the young secretly hoped to achieve mobility in the work force when all the shouting died down. But they carefully concealed their bourgeois intentions from everyone because they feared, more than anything, not being socially with the trend. As one twenty-nine-year-old woman told me, recalling her first peace rally as a college freshman in 1968: "We were in the dorm getting dressed to go, and everyone was running around asking, 'What do you wear to a moratorium?' "

In a *New York Times* article (August 13, 1979) on the tenth anniversary of the Woodstock Festival, the interviewees who had attended the festival reveal the extent to which peer pressure shaped their countercultural views. One woman, now a married occupational therapist in a psychiatric clinic, once considered herself a "committed political activist" but admits: "Ten years ago I had to belong to political organizations to feel I fit in. Now I don't need other identities to express myself." Another woman, a married director of creative affairs for a film company in Los Angeles, describes how the atmosphere at Woodstock was so thick with drug-dealing and masses of the stoned that fear of a stampede forced her to leave prematurely when it started to rain: "I didn't want to see the unity smashed, but I felt a greater need to survive. It was then that I felt my personal will beginning to assert itself."

And in the same article, Lynda Sidhoum, a projects director for the Urban Development Corporation in New York City, says: "I remember thinking that when it was all over, I'd go get a job and be a success. I went to all the peace rallies, but I never thought it would be a permanent lifestyle. It was play time. Of course, I never told my friends that." She goes on: "Logic dictated you should be against the war. But I really didn't know enough about history to argue intelligently. It's a problem I think a lot of us had, and still do."

I suspect that this was true for many of us youth-directeds in the older generation, too. Although our abhorrence of the Vietnam War was genuine, our affinity with youth went beyond our politics. Like everyone else who takes what they need from a movement—the parents who took "permissiveness" out of Freudian thought, the men who selected out sexual liberation from the whole plethora of accomplishments of the women's movement—we took from youth their ability to thumb their nose at authority and "do their own thing."

Because we had reached the point where self-denial was intolerable, we selected out from the youth movement the spirit of rebellion and the "play time" philosophy of personal fulfillment. Not only did we detach these from their context of social and political activism, but we also disregarded the fact that the postadolescent role models we had chosen were in a particular stage of their life cycle. They were suspended between childhood and adulthood in a specially sanctioned state of delayed commitments—the "moratorium" period that Erikson has described as "the restless testing of the newest in possibilities and the oldest in values." Their overemphasis on instinctual gratification, openness to experience, experimentation with sex and drugs, nonreason, and the like represented only one part of the two-way process of growing up. They were turning away from their parents and identifying with their peers in order to find new aspects of their personality to add to the ones they had already incorporated. The next step was to integrate the two—sexual freedom with moral restraint, nonreason with rational thought, pleasure-seeking with achievement-orientation. But, as Erikson has explained, when personal or cultural conditions do not support a harmonious mutuality of our alternatives, we *counterpoint* rather than synthesize them and are driven "to decide definitely and totally for one side or the other."

The older generation lacked the strength of self to prevent this kind of totalistic breaking away by their children in the Sixties, and in the coming decade, by themselves. What was only *half* the answer—rebellion against the traditional roles that they had unquestioningly accepted—was crafted into a whole philosophy by which to live one's life. Divorce, the equivalent for the older generation of the youth culture's violent breaking away from the family and repudiation of the parents, was often deemed a necessary concomitant of self-growth. But those who "found" themselves after divorce discovered that it was the ability to fit the new pieces of themselves in with the valued old—at the *self's* discretion—that gave them a sense of genuine identity. The exhilaration came not from defying their parents' goals and values, but in releasing their goal-setting ideals from external domination, parental or peer. It came from the strength of rising above dependency to the exercise of *will*—free choice coupled with self-restraint. And once personal choices in love and work, no matter how traditional or nontraditional, were made, it was *commitment* to those choices, the full investment of the self in them without fear of the loss of ego or regret for the loss of options, that brought, finally, the longed-for feeling of self-fulfillment.

MY "AWAKENING"

For most of us in the middle class in the Sixties, especially women, our awareness was still at the Neanderthal level. Our idea of free choice was Aruba over St. Thomas, Saks over Bloomingdale's. My own awakening in the Sixties was slow and painfully reluctant, a jumbled mixture of inchoate yearnings and fierce resistance to change. I was like someone who had taken a barbiturate and over-slept, and now the alarm clock was ringing and it was time to get up. Part of me longed to go on sleeping, curled up, snug, comfortable, warm, and safe. But another part of me could not shut off the sound of the alarm. It hounded me with the sense of time slipping by irretrievably, of the world moving on whether I stayed in bed or not.

I remember how disturbed I felt, how angry and ambivalent, when I first read Betty Friedan's *The Feminine Mystique*. I still have my copy of the paperback edition printed in 1963—navy blue cover, title in bright red, yellowed pages dog-eared and underlined through-out. My immediate reaction was one of indignant denial. How could this woman dare to suggest that the wife-and-mother role assigned to us by society was not enough? I wasn't ready to admit to anyone, least of all myself, that I needed more than the status of suburban princess to make me feel alive. Even though I had already begun writing, and the publication of my first book (a humorous chronicle of my life as an obstetrician's wife) was less than three years away, I pretended that my compulsive scribbling was only an innocuous hobby. I was a secret behind-the-drapes writer who stuck to humor-ous fluff in the giddy suburban headache vein, writing not to make order out of chaos, but to *laugh* at the chaos so that I could shield myself from the underlying pain.

The truth was that I despised the role of "happy housewife hero-ine" but lacked the courage to purposefully pursue a serious career as a writer because I was afraid of failure and even more terrified of success. I was a victim of the mixed messages that all of us had received in childhood—messages that equated being successful with being destructive. We were expected to do well, but we also knew that if we did *too* well, others would be jealous and hate us for our success. Principally, these others were our parents. As much as they wanted us to succeed, we knew they might also feel threatened by our success because it only underscored their own unrealized ambitions and disillusionments with life. We wanted to excel to make them proud, but we feared that if we outshone them they would abandon us—or worse still, in our infantile fantasies, obliterate us completely. Unable to release our goals and standards from the grip of contradictory parental demands, we remained trapped in a limbo of frustrated potential, trying to succeed and yet always undercutting our mastery.

For me, as an achievement-oriented yet still traditional wife and mother in her late twenties, the predicament was particularly painful. If I toyed around forever at the periphery of a career as a serious writer, I would not be living up to my own standards of performance. But if I went at a career full-tilt and succeeded in it, I would not be living up to cultural standards of what a woman should be. I knew that my parents, my husband, my relatives, my friends and contemporaries wanted nothing more for me—and I mean nothing *more*—than to be doctor's wife, to play bridge and golf, to belong to the local country club, to lie around the pool and discuss gourmet dishes and good wines, to lead, in short, an elegantly parasitical life with my children wrapped in the blanket of privilege. My literary aspirations made them all uneasy. They looked askance at my writing as if it were some aberration, a bizarre eccentricity, excusable only if I achieved success of such magnitude as to justify my rejection of the traditional lifestyle. As one of my sisters-in-law put it: "If you're not going to be James Michener, why bother?"

It was the old "If you're not Number One, you're nothing" syndrome, and I succumbed to it. In the face of reactions ranging from subtle disapproval to frank hostility, I lived out my ambivalence about having career goals by affecting the "happy housewife heroine" role while playing at work without ever actually putting myself on the line for it.

But inside, the anger grew. On an unconscious level I was furious at myself for having been so dependent on parental and cultural expectations of my female role. Driven by feelings of powerlessness, I set impossibly high standards of instant stardom and would later punish myself with guilt and frustration for not living up to them. Although I wrote very little in the early Sixties, I was determined that my meager output win me the rewards of a lifetime devoted to my craft. In keeping with my grand design, I spent most of my developing years as a writer running round and round in an anxiety rut, shopping, lunching with friends, and meeting with agents, promoters, and corporate vice-presidents in charge of dreams and aspirations. Instead of focusing my energies on developing my abilities and testing them in realistic ways in the workplace, I knocked myself out maintaining the persona of the talented suburban princess who had the best of both worlds.

And then Betty Friedan came along and blew my cover. After reading *The Feminine Mystique,* I felt so threatened by the book that I immediately dashed off a wry little parody of it called "The Feminine Mistake" and sold it to the *Denver Post*'s Sunday supplement for fifty dollars. That relieved my immediate discomfort, but Friedan's message could not be so easily dismissed. The more I pondered its meaning, the more convinced I became of its essential truth. And yet, my original underlinings and annotations scrawled in angry red ink reveal more than just the defensive maneuvers of a latent feminist fighting an unsuccessful battle against her liberation. They show legitimate concern about the effect on family life and on sexual intimacy of encouraging women to leap out of their homes and go chasing after a romanticized ideal of personal fulfillment.

I knew that what Betty Friedan meant by "personal fulfillment" and what the youth culture meant by "personal fulfillment" later in the decade were two different things. But I also knew that confusion between the two was bound to occur. The women to whom Friedan's book was addressed—women like me—had been pushed into marriage and motherhood prematurely and had very often picked men out of calculation rather than desire. Many of us were hungry not only for the sense of our personal effectiveness in the larger world through a paid job or career, which is what Friedan was talking about, but were ravenous for all the things we had missed in late adolescence before committing ourselves to marriage. Besides reentry into the world of ideas, we wanted sexual encounters, travel, the experience of living away from home on our own—"the restless testing of the newest in possibilities and the oldest in values" that had been denied us in the authoritarian pre-Pill era in which we had been groomed to marry young and have babies.

It was the knowledge of this deeper hunger in women that set off warning bells inside my head when I came across an innocent passage like this in *The Feminine Mystique*: "But what happens when women try to live according to an image that makes them deny their minds? What happens when women grow up in an image that makes them deny the reality of the changing world?" Because I *knew* what happens to such women and feared where our untapped rage might lead us, I retorted at the bottom of the page in my red ink: "*And what happens when women try to live according to an image that is unrealistically glamorous and exciting? Or makes them minimize their need for stability and security? Or deny their need for commitment?*"

The warning bells went off again when, later in the book, I read:

It is time to stop exhorting mothers to "love" their children more, and face the paradox between the mystique's demand that women devote themselves completely to their home and their children, and the fact that most of the problems now being treated in child-guidance clinics are solved only when the mothers are helped to develop autonomous interests of their own, and no longer need to fill their emotional needs through their children.

I could not have agreed with Friedan more. But some dark inkling of how that inarguable statement might be misconstrued in the future prompted me to scrawl in the margin: "*But will children fare any better when mothers devote themselves completely to* themselves?"

Given such prickly forebodings of trouble to come, I shied away from any direct involvement with the women's movement in the Sixties, preferring to struggle with my growing inability to conform to the "mystique" on my own. Actually, my greatest ally and conspirator in fomenting my eventual mutiny against the traditional female role was a man. Paul, an esthetic-looking, hippie-style lawyer in his late thirties, lived around the corner from me in the suburbs but had a storefront practice in a ghetto neighborhood in North Philadelphia. He was my bridge to the wider world. We met through our children in the late Sixties, became wildly infatuated with one another, and had what I suppose might be termed an emotional affair.

It was Paul who opened up my mind to the world of ideas again, prying away the dry rot that had been deposited there from countless lunches with the women at The Bird Cage. Paul had worked his way through law school as a jazz musician and had wide-ranging interests from civil rights to esoteric jazz artists I'd never heard of before. His taste in friends was eclectic, too, running from old-time social activists forged in the New Deal days to apparent wierdos, kooks, and freaks—mostly would-be artists and writers—from the hip subculture. His wife was a beautiful, brilliant young woman of twenty-four, a tall, gentle madonna who wrote poetry, read Jung, and would later get a graduate degree in clinical psychology. What Paul found irresistibly attractive about me, I think, was that I had actually been *published.* I had written *My Husband, the Doctor,* put out by a small but legitimate firm. He secretly longed to write (but was dreadful at it), and out of all the supposed literati he knew, I, alone, had produced a book that was enshrined for all eternity in the Library of Congress.

What was there about Paul that attracted me to him? Everything. His pale face, sandy-colored hair, twinkling eyes, zany sense of humor, facile mind, sinewy body, devastating way with a story, and most of all, his aliveness. Paul's childlike enthusiasm for each new thing that caught his fancy, whether it was some op-art toy a friend of his had invented or Norman Mailer's *Armies of the Night,* was utterly contagious. Several times a week, unexpectedly and usually when my husband was out, Paul would stop by the house and mesmerize me with accounts of rallies or lectures he had attended. He woke up my mind and made me think, and our verbal fencing was a kind of exquisite foreplay. He rarely left without pressing into my trembling hands reviews of books that he thought I should read. Ours was a relationship in the historic tradition of all adoring women and their male mentors—he talked about the books, and I *read* them.

Gently, without shaming me, Paul opened my eyes to what a provincial philistine I was, and suddenly I was subscribing to the *New York Review of Books* and immersing myself in the convoluted polemics of magazines like *Commentary.* While my husband lay in bed dozing off to Johnny Carson, I sat bolt upright next to him, poring over Nathan Glazer's running argument with Noam Chomsky. Glassy-eyed, my head throbbing as I tried to cut through the fog of high-minded liberal tendentiousness and morally smug radical sloganeering, I read on and on through the night—all so that I could discourse intelligently with Paul the next day. Sometimes, I didn't have to wait that long. More than once, long past midnight, the phone would ring and it would be Paul, calling from a phone booth in a club to tell me some startling profundity he'd stumbled on while out drinking with his intellectual buddies. The phone was on my husband's side of the bed, and silently he would pass the receiver to me. Then he would lie beside me half-asleep, with the telephone cord stretched symbolically across his neck, while Paul and I talked and talked and talked the night away.

In my innocence, I thought that Paul's ever-changing parade of brief, intense enthusiasms was part of his magnificent love affair with life. It did not occur to me that he was in the throes of youth-direction, a protean man for *any* season, trying this role and that in search of a self. In his Hells Angels phase—my daughters' favorite—he would show up on his Honda motorcycle and take the children for a ride in the sidecar. In his country squire phase, he would turn up in dignified tweeds and tell me about the romantic chalet he had purchased in the Poconos. In his touchie-feelie phase, he came by in Nehru jacket and sandals and talked glowingly about the high he'd reached on a marathon weekend encounter. Whatever phase he was in, he was always appealing, bright, funny, stimulating, and Svengali-like in his hold over me. I was completely enthralled by him. Next to all the other men I knew—wheeler-dealer businessmen or bionic-brained physicians who could talk of nothing else except disease and the rising cost of medical malpractice—Paul was the only one who seemed to have any excitement, vitality, or idealism. I had no idea that he was all style and no substance. It shocked me to learn, as I later did, that he was deeply committed to nothing—not to the ghetto people he served, not even to his marriage. The shifting of his alignments could be forgiven, I suppose, but not the way he deceptively exploited them.

My husband tried to warn me. At the outset, he had declared that Paul was a phony. Possessed of what Marilyn French has aptly described as a "shit-detector," my husband unerringly smelled hypocrisy where I was intoxicated by the aroma of charm. He tolerated Paul and our adolescent infatuation with each other because he trusted me and believed that I could enjoy Paul intellectually without letting our relationship get out of bounds.

Even more to the point, my husband was incapable of depriving me of anything. There was nothing he would not do to *make* me happy, and that was the problem. He had accepted the role of fairy godfather and meant to demonstrate his love for me by indulging me without restraint. But his was the permissive love of the "too good" parent—the kind of parents that our whole generation had become, not only to our children, but to each other as well. Typical of many "magical helper" husbands of rebellious wives in the late Sixties and Seventies, mine felt guilty because I was dissatisfied with the identity he had handed me on a silver platter. When I began to break away and establish my own identity, his permissiveness, intended to bind me to him, only drove us farther and farther apart.

With Paul, though, my husband came to understand—in the nick of time—the need for setting some limits. He reached that realization on a lovely Sunday afternoon in the summer of 1968, when he was out at the country club playing golf. Paul had dropped in on me at home for one of his accustomed visits. The children were playing upstairs, and the two of us were in the den, earnestly discussing a Sunday newspaper article that just about everyone seemed to be writing those days: "Is Fidelity in Marriage Out of Style?" What could have been more indicative of how youth-directed we had become as a culture than that question? Sexual fidelity in marriage, once a principle of moral conviction that had been passed by the standard-bearers from one generation to the next, had now become nothing more than a matter of *style*. That it was an adolescent style was evident in the ludicrous situation of a grown man and woman *talking* about infidelity as a social phenomenon while they teetered on the brink of becoming lovers.

Little by little, with infinite caution and delicacy, Paul was beginning to bring the subject of infidelity out of the abstract and closer to home. My heart had begun to pound wildly. For months I had been fantasizing about sex with him, imagining our couplings in vivid, delicious detail. Now here he was in the flesh, sitting in my den, talking about, of all things, infidelity; and he wasn't talking about the newspaper anymore, but asking me—had I heard him right—What did I think about Us?

He was staring at me intently, waiting for my reply. I stared back at him, feeling very much like Molly Bloom, but unable to make poetry out of a passionate *yes*. At that very moment—and I swear that this is true—it suddenly grew dark as night outside. Lightning flashed and crackled, thunder boomed, the house shook and all the lights went out, and a torrential downpour fell from the sky. The children, frightened by the storm, began to shout and scream upstairs, but Paul and I just sat there in the dark, staring at each other, saying nothing. A moment later, the lights went on again, and my husband burst through the front door. Drenched, his shirt sticking to his chest and his dark curly hair slapped against his forehead in wet ringlets, he came into the den. He took a quick, appraising glance at Paul and me, mumbled something about the thunderstorm, and went upstairs to change his clothes.

Five days later my husband and I were on a plane bound for the Bahamas. He had decided, on the spur of the moment, that he was overworked and needed a vacation, so there we were. Since Paul's last visit I had thought about him obsessively but had not seen him. I knew the real reason for this trip. My husband had sensed where my relationship with Paul was going, and he wanted to get me away from him as quickly as possible. On the beach I would have the space to think.

By the time we returned home, I had made up my mind. I had been married eleven years and had two children, and I was bored, restless, and dissatisfied with my life. I needed change and a feeling of purpose. I was captivated by Paul because he was articulate and loved books, ideas, movies, the theater, music, art, photography, and the other joys of life the way I did. He was probably the kind of man—apart from his unreliability—that I would have liked to marry after I had grown up and learned what *I* wanted in contrast to what society and my mother thought was right for me.

But I also saw that Paul was not the answer to my present problem—Betty Friedan was. After all these years of conformity to an empty role, I could feel my True Self starting to emerge. It was Paul who had coaxed it out of hiding, but all he wanted to do was sleep with it. Friedan had the blueprint for its development. I knew then what I had to do was set new limits for myself. In work, I would have to set limits that were in line with my abilities, inhibited neither by infantile fantasies of perfection nor by the "foiling fear of punishment" for success. In love, I would have to abide by commitments already made. I decided that I believed in fidelity in marriage. I believed in it whether or not the Sunday newspaper had reached the conclusion that it was "out of style." I believed in it, not as a command, but as a condition of the way I thought I should be. This condition, because it felt *right* to my perception of myself and my relation to the world, and not a violation of it, as had been the traditional female role, was not subject to change at that time.

After I had come back from the trip and defused my relationship with Paul into a strained, short-lived friendship, it occurred to me what fragile things our beliefs are. How, I wondered, would any of our beliefs survive when we are so rarely strong enough to fight for them? This time, my belief in fidelity had been rescued by a fortuitous combination of circumstances, not the least of which was my husband's prescient intervention. But in the future, what support would my belief in fidelity find in a culture in revolt against traditional values where words like "moral relativism" and "pluralistic society" were used to justify *only* those beliefs and behaviors that were "in style"? It seemed hypocritical to me that the doctrine of personal fulfillment, so filled with talk of *self*-awareness and *self*-realization, refused to recognize the validity of any *self-decision* in favor of a traditional belief. We had liberated ourselves from blind obedience to past authority only to become a cultural police state ruled by our new peer group—the kids. As the doctrine of personal fulfillment propelled us into the Seventies, we had become a society without parents; people, in the words of German psychoanalyst Alexander Mitscherlich, "for whom to a large extent only two standards of value exist—being socially with the trend, or popular, and being forgotten, out-of-date, worthless."

Had my "emotional affair" with Paul been sexually consummated, I know only too well how drearily it would have ended. Ever the protean man, Paul divorced his wife and gave up his ghetto law practice after the funding for a Hispanic newspaper begun in his Ralph Nader phase never materialized. The last I heard, he had become a very successful management consultant and was living in a posh high-rise in town, working very hard at keeping his options open with a steady girl friend while simultaneously juggling a number of other relationships.

My desultory awakening in the Sixties finally clicked into place in 1969, with Jane O'Reilly's famous (*Click!*) of recognition, when I was watching the "David Susskind Show" on TV one night after my husband had gone upstairs to bed. There was a group of interesting women on the show whom Susskind had introduced as "radical feminists." I found them spellbinding, particularly the arrogant dark-haired one with the high forehead, sharp nose, thin mouth, and acerbic way of talking. Her aloof condescension toward Susskind reminded me of all the intimidatingly bright "grinds" I had known in college who always made the rest of us feel a little stupid. She was Kate Millett, and apparently this was before her book *Sexual Politics*, published in August 1969, had created the furor that turned her into a *Time* cover story because I knew nothing about her. Jacqueline Caballos, more maternal and soft-spoken than Millett, was also on the panel and was saying something about the sense of loss women feel when they marry and give up their own name to take their husband's. It was a minor point, but somehow it honed in on the spurious feeling I had about myself then as a married woman: I was an imposter always trading on my husband's name in the world.

Susskind, employing his usual technique of pompous incredulity, tried to infuriate the women to the point of making them look ridiculous. But for me, he did not exist. Only the women were real. The things they were saying electrified me because they were so in touch with the secret core of my self. I began silently cheering them on, nodding emphatically in agreement whenever one of them made a particularly telling point. Something was happening. Something big. I felt that I was rooting for an unknown underdog in a matter of life and death.

And then I suddenly realized—that underdog was *me*.

$\longleftarrow$ — —————————— $\longrightarrow$

THE
SELFISH
SEVENTIES

In the Seventies, the search for unconditional love moved out of the family and into the singles bars. Horrified by the way traditional marriage had reduced their parents' generation to symbiotic, role-playing automatons, the younger generation shrank from commitment in intimate relationships as if it were a contract written in blood. Simultaneously, the "liberated" older generation bounded out of their marriages and turned fear of attachment into a cultural phobia. Disguising this phobia as "openness to new experience," the formerly monogamous gravitated toward the opposite pole of total sexual freedom. Noncommitment, they thought, was the yellow brick road to an authentic identity. Chasing after a fantasy of sexual perfection replaced relationships. For both the never-married and the ever-married, the fast lane of life seemed like the only alternative to conventional patterns of intimacy in love affairs and marriage. And so the revolution that had heralded the dawning of the Age of Aquarius ended by ushering in the era of Looking for Mr. (Ms.) Goodbar.

As cultural conditions like the experience explosion and the bias against commitment fostered the growth of our *Bacillus neuroticus,* the search for unconditional love entered a deadly stage. Before casual sex for women as well as men became the norm in the post-Pill era, the only casualty to the person in search of unconditional love was continual disillusionment. But when the culture urged people away from attachment and legitimized the mutual exploitation of the sexes, the search for unconditional love became ugly, mean, and dangerous. As illustrated by Roseann Quinn's brutal murder by a singles bar pickup in New York City in 1973—the actual event on which the "Goodbar" novel and film were based—the search could even be violently fatal.

In a provocative article entitled "Who Else Is Looking for Mr. Goodbar?" (Ms. magazine, February 1978), writer Tracy Johnston ponders some of the questions that the real "Goodbar" murder raised for women about their "newly visible sexuality" in the Seventies: "Is casual sex a good substitute for finding the right man? Is it possible for women to go after sex, treat men as sex objects without taking the consequences of male hostility? Was Roseann Quinn's story proof that 'good girls' shouldn't go too far? Or can we salute her courage despite the tawdry end?"

Johnston laments the fact that neither Judith Rossner's novelization of the murder in Looking for Mr. Goodbar nor the adaptation of the novel for the screen by Richard Brooks deals with these issues of loneliness and casual sex and the place of women in our sexually liberated times. Johnston attempts to do it, but what she gives us, mostly, is a picture of her own ambivalence.

Using Lacey Fosburgh's Closing Time: The True Story of the "Goodbar" Murder (Delacorte), Johnston presents the spare facts of the short, unhappy life of Roseann Quinn, called "Katherine Cleary" in Fosburgh's book. At the time of her death, she was a twenty-eight-year-old Irish Catholic schoolteacher in an urban school where she had almost been raped in her own classroom. She had been hanging out in the singles bars, feeling and acting alternately manic and depressed, and had been seen in the company of men who looked like dope dealers and hustlers. A civil rights activist in the Sixties, she came from "an upper-middle-class home and caring parents" and was known to her many friends in her college days as "outgoing and good-humored." Toward the end of her life she had become depressed, was seeing a psychiatrist, and, says Johnston, "like many never-married women of twenty-eight, she was worried about her relationship with men, was looking for 'the right one.' "

Johnston concludes:

One thing is clear: by breaking away from her background and in her "liberation," she had practically become a nonentity to her traditional family and her Catholic religion. She was neither a child, a virgin, a wife, nor a mother.

Yet she was also an "ordinary girl." She was not particularly creative, ambitious, or determined to pursue a fulfilling career. Nor was she likely to find happiness, with or without a man, in some oddball lifestyle. And what if she had survived her last pickup? There are still too few of us who know how to survive in the "new lifestyle" or who even know how to support the "Katherine Cleary's" who are floundering, unnoticed, except by the men who sense their desperation.

Correctly, Johnston identifies the root of Cleary's problem: her break from the traditional social ties of her childhood and her inability to fill the void with self-chosen ways of relating to the world in love and satisfying work. But then Johnston reveals her own confusion about how to survive—or help someone else to survive—in the "new lifestyle." Had Johnston not been so ambivalent, she might have pointed out the obvious contradiction between what Cleary was *really* looking for and where she went to find it. By her own admission, Cleary wanted a relationship—sex *with* love—with "the right one," something she had almost no hope of finding among the hustlers, dope dealers, and instant intimacy artists who peopled the West Side singles bars she frequented. Cleary must have known how the odds were stacked against her—she had, after all, gotten through teachers' college—yet she felt compelled to go to the bars, pick up men indiscriminately, and sleep with anyone she brought home. Cleary was a closet traditionalist. She wanted a deep emotional connection with a man, the kind of exclusive relationship that was being touted as quaint and old-fashioned by the feminists and the media in the early Seventies. Without the capacity to act on the basis of her own choices, Cleary concealed her wishes (except from her psychiatrist) and systematically engaged in casual sex in order to be "liberated"; i.e., socially with the trend. In so doing, she forfeited not only the identity she was struggling to achieve, but in the end, her life.

In the nature of her conflict, Katherine Cleary was very much a woman of the 1970s, torn between the sense of her own limits and the need to belong. While Tracy Johnston means to be sympathetic to her, she unintentionally provides an insight into the kind of cultural pressure that was a significant factor in Cleary's undoing, as in her exchange with *Goodbar* movie director Richard Brooks:

"What do kids believe in these days?" Brooks asks, in a booming tone of voice one has to learn is casual. "Politics? Marriage?

Children? Church? Nothing. They are not committed to anything at all. They have the right to go out and do whatever they please." "Shouldn't they have that right?" [Johnson asks.] "Even women?"

The affirmative action stance Johnston takes toward casual sex— her defense of it as every woman's inviolable "right" as well as every man's—reflects the way sexual promiscuity became politicized into a symbol of women's liberation in the Seventies. As a result of the sexual revolution and the women's movement, there was now an unwritten law on the books—a kind of sexual Title VII—guaranteeing women equal opportunity to engage in unrestricted sexual activity with a variety of partners without being stigmatized for it. Like the right to choose an abortion, it was, of course, meant to be only an option, not a mandate. But for all the Katherine Cleary's who were trapped between their traditional values and the need to be in step with the times, helpless conformity with the new ideal of total sexual variety replaced autonomous action. In an era of noncomitment, the opportunities for a binding emotional relationship with a man had become extremely difficult. Rather than face the conflict, rejection, and loneliness involved in pursuing the desired relationship, these women repressed their desires and became the defiantly independent and isolated habituées of the singles bars. Theirs was a spurious "independence" and an even more phony "freedom": They had *not* gained the right to do as they pleased, but had simply lost the right to say "no."

THE *FEMINIST* MYSTIQUE
Inevitably, writers like Tracy Johnston are disappointed when they search the "Goodbar" story for answers to the larger questions about independent women in the Seventies and come up with nothing except "a numbing emphasis on destruction." There seems to be a stubborn refusal to make the connection between "one woman's psychologically twisted and masochistic need for sex without love" in Rossner's novel and the plight of *all* unattached women in the Seventies. This couldn't be Everywoman, the reviewer protests. And the movie is even less satisfying. Surely Brooks, "a good liberal," meant to tell us something about his "contradictory" feelings about women—"they have the right to be independent and yet they need

protection"—but remained so faithful to Rossner's story that he wound up giving us "an ancient morality play" about a woman being punished for going after cheap thrills.

Katherine Cleary makes us uncomfortable because she is so different from what we want her to be. She is an archtypical victim—helpless, fragmented, and desperate—and we want her to be a survivor. We want her to be the "new woman" we have heard so much about from the feminist writers—proud, strong, and self-confident, able to take her sex straight, like the men she meets in bars, and always, always be in control. We expect her to conform to the *feminist* mystique:

> . . . a young woman who lives alone and likes it. She has a job that
> she enjoys, and is not interested in giving it up or sharing it with
> marriage. But she likes men, enjoys their company, wants to
> maintain warm and friendly relations with them, would like a variety
> of men friends. She might even, from time to time, invite one to
> spend the night or the weekend with her if the relationship was
> especially congenial. But she does not want to assume any
> responsibility for him; she does not want him to become dependent
> on her; nor does she want to become dependent on him.

This is what the propounders of the *feminist* mystique would have liked Katherine Cleary to be—but reality speaks louder than rhetoric. In real life, the prototype envisioned above by sociologist Jessie Barnard in *The Future of Marriage* (1972), if she exists at all, is one of a very rare minority. There are heterosexual women, mostly never-married successful careerists, who have conditioned themselves to live happily without a deep or enduring relationship with a man and with no desire of ever entering into one. But Katherine Cleary was not a prototype. She was a flesh-and-blood human being; and she was, in her pathetic vulnerability, far more typical of her class than the golden girl who "lives alone and likes it." Her loneliness, confusion, alienation, and desperate search for attachment through casual sex are an acknowledged part of the folklore among the more than 56 million singles in America who make up our country's largest growing subculture—the New Displaced Persons.

Most of the women in Katherine Cleary's subculture drop out of the singles bar scene before they are destroyed by it—psychologically or otherwise. But it is not unusual for them to have taken extraordinary risks. Besides the hundreds of women I have interviewed or have come into contact with through my work with Wives' Self-Help, I personally know of many others, well-educated and well-reared, who, in trying to live up to the *feminist* mystique, could easily have come to the same end. Their survival of brief encounters with smooth-talking "Johnny Ventures," as one woman called them—*macho* pick-ups about whom they knew nothing until they went to bed with them (and scarcely any more afterward)—was purely a matter of chance. Can we presume that these women, simply because they were luckier in the outcome of their encounters, were any less "psychologically twisted" or "masochistic" than the woman in the Rossner novel?

From the time Freud identified *"lieben und arbeiten"* (to love and to work) as the foundation of a fulfilling life, a mature, genital relationship with a loved partner involving mutual trust and interdependence has always been considered one of our most basic human needs. In psychopathology, the avoidance of contacts that commit to intimacy has long been known as a disturbance that can lead to severe character problems as well as profound emotional disorders, such as alienation, loneliness, and depression.

Even as recently as 1977, a well-publicized study of divorced family members conducted over a period of two years by psychologists E. Mavis Hetherington, Martha Cox, and Roger Cox, yielded these findings:

The divorced individuals wanted sustained, meaningful relationships and weren't satisfied with a series of superficial encounters. The formation of lasting intimate relations, involving deep concern and a willingness to make sacrifices for the partner, as well as a strong attachment and desire to be near the person, was a strong factor in happiness, self-esteem, and feelings of competence in sexual relations for both divorced men and women.

The researchers made the point that in the first year following divorce, some of the men were pleased with the opportunity to date a variety of women and have diverse sexual experiences. Dating and casual social encounters at bars, clubs, cocktail parties, and other social gatherings satisfied them *for a while*. But by the end of the first year, the men wanted "longer lasting, more meaningful relationships."

As for the women, the researchers found: "The stereotyped image of the carefree, swinging single life did not hold up for the women, either. For them, casual sex brought on feelings of desperation, depression, and low self-esteem."

Knowing how profound the connection between sex and loving feelings is for normal human beings, we must conclude that the practice of recreational sex as a habitual lifestyle—the "liberated" lifestyle—is a sign of disturbed behavior. We agreed with Betty Friedan that conformity to the feminine mystique, which made us deny our minds, led to our "progressive dehumanization." Can we now say that the *feminist* mystique—this grotesque distortion of the purpose of feminism by commitmentphobes who would have us deny our feelings and treat sex like an animal appetite—is not also "progressively dehumanizing"? The question we should be asking ourselves is not how do we survive in this new lifestyle or help support others who are floundering in it, but why do we want to conform to a lifestyle that makes us emotionally sick?

In the first flush of liberation from the old sexual mores, casual sex for women was exciting and fun. For the white, upper-middle-class woman, there was something enormously adventurous in being able to go to bed with a forbidden stranger—a black, a blue-collar worker, a much younger man—purely for the erotic experience and without any concern about how he would stack up as a marriage partner. The woman felt she could be totally uninhibited with this man and not care if she ever saw him again because she had nothing at stake except physical release. But many women, even though they went into a one-night encounter saying, "It doesn't matter," were left with a terrible depression afterward precisely because it didn't matter.

A thirty-eight-year-old psychiatrist who specializes in sexual dysfunction, a divorced woman, candidly talked to me about her own encounter with a young orderly at the hospital where she was a resident, explaining that many of her patients have had a similar experience:

I went out with him and we had a very pleasant evening. We smoked grass and he seduced me. It was nice to be seduced, not to have to be the seductive one. It seemed very clear to me, even in the haste, that it was just for one night. The kid was so much younger than I as to be absurd. But what happened was, I liked it. I liked *him*. After a couple of days, I was starting to think about him. I felt an emotional pull. Unbelievably, against my rationality, against my will, against everything, came attachment.

Then he called and said, "I have to tell you—I have a girl friend. I feel so guilty about what I've done." He was twenty-four; the girl friend was nineteen. I was gracious and made all the right noises: "Don't feel so guilty. . . . It's not so terrible . . ." But it took me four days to stand up. Later, when I met the girl friend with him at a hospital party, I could see that she was a plain-looking little girl— and he was a *little* boy. Something had gotten started in me that had nothing to do with the reality of the situation at all.

The *feminist* mystique would have women shrug such experiences off and go back into the fray more guardedly, desensitizing themselves against the arrival of attachment. Originally, it was the purpose of feminism to help women achieve their own sense of self in order to interrelate with men on a mature genital level instead of clinging to them in childlike symbiotic dependency. But the mystique has come to encourage the "independent woman" to operate on the same phallic level of raw sex as the immature male. Thus in a 1978 *Ms.* magazine cover story, "Can Women Really Have It All?," subtitled "Love, Work, Guilt, and Other Trade-offs," there appears among the interviews this frighteningly brittle profile of the consummate "new woman" of the Seventies:

On the surface, Barbara Jacobs seems to be a whirlwind of a woman, professionally and personally. Now thirty-six, she's changed careers several times and been successful at all of them: as a government public relations officer, as a teacher, and as a child psychologist. After two marriages, she got pregnant five years ago— and decided to have the child anyway after the relationship broke up.

Barbara and her son live in Boston, where she holds down two jobs—one as a college teacher and one as a psychological consultant— and works on her doctoral thesis in her spare time. "I feel like the meter's always running."

Barbara feels that she's had to make certain choices: "What's been given up is leisure time. I miss it. I've given up sleep. I've given up political activism, because when I go out, it's so expensive and such a hassle that I want to have a wonderful time. I want goodies coming in, not going out."

Another sacrifice is "friendships with men. I only want them to screw around with, and if that's not what's in it for me, forget it. I like women's company better, and I don't have enough time to spend with my female friends. But it makes me feel like a 1950s high school boy. It's so calculating."

The similarity between the 1950s high school boy and the 1970s wonder woman is remarkable. For both, having it "all" is having half—*"arbeiten"* without *"lieben"*—a trade-off of love and guilt for success in work. Both are crippled by the same "scoring" mentality that confuses autonomy with egocentricity, self-reliance with self-aggrandizement. Just as the work ethic of the Fifties destroyed intimacy for men, the *feminist* mystique of the Seventies destroyed it for women.

Like Barbara Jacobs, women who followed the *feminist* mystique believed they could overcome their dependency on men by becoming *counter*dependent—avoiding men totally except for the purpose of "screwing around with them." But counterdependency is not the same as independence, any more than taking a part of a person to use for masturbation is mature genitality. Without assuming any responsibility for the people we "screw around with," we achieve only "pseudo-individuality" rather than genuine autonomy. We become one of those "defiant, aggressive types" described by psychotherapist Rollo May—isolated individuals who may be deemed a "success" in our competitive culture but whose considerable anxiety is a nagging reminder of the humanity they have repressed.

I noticed that some patients did not repress their sexual, aggressive, or "antisocial" urges (in Freud's sense) in any discernible way. Instead they repressed their needs and desires to have responsible, friendly, and charitable relations with other people. When aggressive, sexual, or other behavior in egocentric form emerged in the analysis, these patients showed no anxiety. But when opposite needs and desires emerged—i.e., to have responsible and constructive social relations—there appeared much anxiety, accompanied by the typical reactions of patients who feel a crucial psychological strategy to be threatened. Such repression of constructive social urges occurs particularly, and understandably, with defiant, aggressive types of patients.

May observes that people who can "successfully" exploit others without feeling conscious guilt rarely show up in psychoanalysts' offices because our culture supports and "cushions" them. The opposite "nonaggressive types," who repress their hostility and sexual urgings, are considered the culturally "weak" neurotics who need help. This may be the reason why most psychoanalytic theories, May speculates, have emphasized repression of sex and agression as causing anxiety.

He concludes:

Possibly if we could analyze more of the aggressive types—those "successful" people who never get into a therapist's office—we should find that the concept of anxiety as repression of responsible impulses is true on a broad scale.

While it is true that many persons have guilt and anxiety because of fear of expressing their own individual capacities and urges, sexual or otherwise, as Freud originally indicated, it is at the same time true that many have guilt and anxiety because they have become "autonomous" without becoming "responsible."

The sexual revolution had brought us to an impasse in the Seventies where we had too much freedom *from* moral restraint and, because of the reactive dread of commitment, not enough freedom *to* form new relatedness. Casual sex and transient, need-filler relationships rushed in to occupy the vacuum. With varying degrees of success, ranging from Katherine Cleary at one end of the spectrum to Barbara Jacobs at the other, the "new woman" repressed her need for genuine intimacy and chose defiant isolation. But the anxiety in such "pseudo-individuality" without responsible relatedness to others is evident in the compulsive quality of the "new woman's" life.

As the use of the word "trade-off" in the subtitle of the *Ms.* article suggests, the noncommitment of the Seventies has often been credited with releasing women from the demands of traditional relationships in order to concentrate on achievement in the larger world. But there is some evidence that this boon is greatly overrated. Research reveals that of the seventy women proposed by corporate management in New York City in 1977 for the Academy of Women

Achievers—career women aged twenty-six to fifty-five, all of whom earned as much or more than their husbands—almost 90 percent said that their marriage helped their careers.

Among the unmarried women careerists I have personally surveyed, many expressed the feeling that they could achieve *more* in their fields if they had the emotional nourishment from a stable, satisfying relationship. Others expressed regret that they did not have an intimate partner with whom they could share their success. Their comments were not unsimilar to this one from an anonymous letter-writer to *Ms.* in response to a 1978 article on the changing shape of intimacy:

> Your issue on "The New Intimacy" came, and I began reading before I took off my coat. I don't know what to say. Maybe if I knew I would not be writing this letter.
>
> The holidays are coming and this was the third year that I'd be spending them "alone." I thought I had gotten used to it, but something happened this year that made me realize that in spite of the sustaining power of friends, feminism, and modern times, some things are still hard to bear.
>
> While it is good to be alive during a time when love and independence are supposed to be able to exist in some harmonious combination, I am both amazed and appalled to realize that until the time when I manage to reach that happy state, I would be willing, at least temporarily, to chuck the independence in exchange for love.

This is not meant to suggest that women *should* chuck independence in exchange for love and rush back into symbiotic dependence on men to ward off loneliness. But it is meant to suggest that conformity to the "liberated lifestyle" of the Seventies is no more of an answer to the problem of an autonomous self than was conformity to the constricted roles of the Fifties. The super-independent woman remains above the battle, safe but stranded, in a high, dry place between her repressed desire for a new level of interrelationship and the seductive possibility of reengulfment against which she must struggle all her life. Like the heroine in Lina Wertmuller's *Swept Away,* she may lose that struggle. But endlessly avoiding intimacy through casual sex and transient demi-relationships consigns her to a lifetime of rigidly patrolling the borders of her self without ever learning how to make good contact with others and still maintain her separate integrity.

COMMITMENTPHOBIA

At first it appeared that the "cool" style of intimacy in the Seventies was merely a temporary "holding pattern" that had a basic survival and adjustment value following the upheavals of the Sixties. But when the culture began to glorify egocentricity and rejection of commitment as healthy norms, what might have been merely a transitory way of coping with change turned into a sustained regression to infantile narcissism.

Taking their cues from women in revolt, men fashioned their own concept of a "liberated lifestyle" that freed them from assuming responsibility for their actions and the effect of their actions on others. By condoning this irresponsibility of the single male, the culture gave its support to men to stay stuck at the level of indulging and indulging and indulging their most primitive instinctual urgings. Like Siddhartha in his sensuous, materialistic phase, "Disco Dan" of the Seventies was not trying to "*find* the real me," as the password went, but to *lose* it. Under even more pressure than the "liberated" woman to conform to an image that made individualism a fearsome burden, he sought escape from the "torment of the self" in compulsive hit-and-run sexual activity.

For men in our postliberation culture, the "defiantly aggressive type" was still considered the model of success in the working world although women wanted him to get in touch with the nurturing side of his nature and become sensitive and caring. The melding of strength and tenderness by the competitive male could not be so easily accomplished in one generation, and the new ideal of masculinity—Alan Bates in *An Unmarried Woman,* Jon Voight in *Coming Home*—existed largely in the movies.

It was a step forward when men were given cultural permission to talk about their feelings, even to cry, but it was still difficult for them to transcend the boundaries of self and become genuinely empathetic with the feelings of women. Their tendency to equate commitment with entrapment infuriated women who considered themselves autonomous, but the fear of engulfment by a loved one in a committed relationship was much greater for the "new man" than it was for the "new woman." Psychologically, the male was the endangered species since it was he who was being asked to give up his traditional defenses: control over the loved one and emotional detachment. Faced with the possible loss of the self in a threatening relationship of equals, the "new man" was driven into promiscuity or aloneness. His dual fears of engulfment by a woman or her abandonment of him forced him to become what pop psychologists have called a "dance-away lover." While the "new woman" indulged in promiscuity but secretly yearned for a stable, committed relationship based on mutuality, the promiscuous "new man" kept backing away from intimacy because he wanted a good, close relationship with a loved one but feared it at the same time.

In the period since 1973, various factors combined to reduce the pressure on the American male toward upward mobility on the job. The economic limits and shortages imposed by "stagnation"—high inflation coupled with high unemployment—plus the influence of the doctrine of personal fulfillment brought about an age of lowered expectations materially. But these inroads into the greed creed—"more is always better than less"—did not extend into the area of personal relationships. Perhaps *because* the upwardly striving male felt frustrated by these new limits on success and mobility, his expectations of a sexual partner became higher than ever. No matter how satisfying or desirable a man's current partner, the revolution of rising sexual expectations decreed that she couldn't be as good as the woman he might meet in the future.

Whether he was overprotected by his parents or rejected by them, the upbringing of the "new man" of the Seventies played into the exploitativeness of the greed creed and the commitmentphobia of the liberated lifestyle to produce the complete cultural narcissist. Men with a long history of alienated behavior and intimacy problems suddenly became trendy. Only in the Seventies could a distinguished middle-aged college professor airily dismiss his divorce from his spurned wife of two years with the quip "I have a short attention span" and arouse no other response among his friends and colleagues except smiles. Stories of skittish men, from their twenties through their sixties, usually bright, charming, gifted, and attractive, who lost all desire for sex with a lover when the involvement threatened to become too serious, became a staple of sex therapy case records in the 1970s.

The fragmented nature of transient relationships—at once described and extolled by Alvin Toffler in *Future Shock*—enabled us to "plug into a module" of the "disposable person" and thereby safely limit liability on both sides. In our relationships with the shoe salesman, the mailman, and other impersonal figures in our urban environment, this kind of limited engagement was probably necessary. But justifying the carry-over of transience and depersonalization into intimate relationships was a serious mistake. The repeated assessment of permanence and fidelity in marriage as old-fashioned and unrealistic—by Toffler, Slater, and nearly every other well-read social historian in the Seventies—popularized patterns of intimacy that were a haven for people with disturbed psychosexual development. As the onus was removed from instant intimacy, throwaway relationships, and extramarital sex (even the pejorative term "infidelity" fell out of use as too judgmental), it became impossible to tell the healthy "liberated" person from the pathological narcissist. By making sexual exclusivity something to escape *from* rather than work *toward*, the new lifestyle turned intimacy into a morbid game that any two (or more) could play. But the players were often forced to act in the same manner, if not out of the same motives, as the narcissists who appear in the clinical literature:

. . . sexual promiscuity of narcissistic personalities is linked with the sexual excitement for a body that "withholds itself" or for a person considered attractive or valuable by other people. Such a body or person stirs up unconscious envy and greed in narcissistic patients, the need to take possession of, and an unconscious tendency to devalue and spoil that which is envied. Insofar as sexual excitement temporarily heightens the illusion of beauty (or food or wealth or power) withheld, a temporary enthusiasm for the desired sexual object may imitate the state of falling in love.

Soon, however, sexual fulfillment gratifies the need for conquest, coinciding with the unconscious process of devaluing the desired object and resulting in a speedy disappearance of both excitement and interest . . . unconscious greed and envy tend to be projected onto the desired sexual object, and as a consequence, fear of possessive greed coming from this sexual object is a potential threat to the narcissistic patient's need to escape into "freedom." For the narcissistic patient, all relations are between exploiters and exploited, and "freedom" is simply an escape from fantasied devouring possessiveness.

It might be a leap of the imagination to say that the transient pattern of casual sex in the Seventies, stressing exploitativeness, competitiveness, and constantly shifting affections *caused* narcissistic disturbances in people. But I have no doubt that instant intimacy, predicated on noncommitment and the detached consumption of experience, stirred the primitive greed and envy that lurks in us all and exacerbated the normal sexual fears and anxieties that everyone has to some degree—fear of rejection, fear of dependency, fear of commitment, fear of the opposite sex.

Instead of freeing women from the culturally induced masochism of their traditional role, the new lifestyle exposed women to a *double* dose of masochism—victimization by the exploitative men who used them and disappeared, and secondly, victimization by their own need to possess the person considered "attractive or valuable" by others.

A male veteran of the singles world, an attractive yet unassuming businessman in his early thirties, gave me this embittered account of the phenomenon he had personally experienced among women scorched by cultural narcissism: "They all say they want to meet a nice person who is honest and down-to-earth, a good person who is going to communicate with them and care for them and do for them and let them love him in return. But that's *not* what they want because when they get it, they don't know how to deal with it. They always think there's a motive, and they'll push you away. The Don Juan, the great-looking guy everyone wants to be with—that's the one they all go after. And he'll shit all over them. He'll fuck them three or four times and tell them to get lost. Then they'll be furious at him and say he's a bastard, but they walked into it with their eyes wide open. Someone who was hitting on them and being really nice, who is a nice person, they weren't interested in—yet that's what they tell you they want."

To understand such sadomasochistic behavior, we need only remind ourselves that both sadism and masochism are opposite sides of the same symbiotic coin—attempts to *lose* the self in another's existence either by possessing someone we unconsciously envy and need to devalue or by merging ourselves with someone we think is greater and more powerful than we are. A competitive culture that promotes casual sex as a basis for forming relationships infantilizes us to the point where sadism and masochism are almost inevitable. Even the healthier among us are driven to seek out partners who conform to our adolescent fantasies—"the great-looking guy (girl) everyone wants to be with"—rather than those who can realistically meet our more mature needs for adult sexual love. And the less healthy are encouraged to stay that way. In our society, those who are unable to fall or stay in love because of their unconscious envy, fear, or hatred of the opposite sex are admired, particularly in the singles subculture, as ever-growing proteans or successful survivors. Promiscuity and transient relationships afford them an opportunity to repeat their basic conflict compulsively instead of trying to overcome it and achieve the capacity to integrate sexual feelings and tenderness.

In the Seventies, social conditions fostered resentment and hostility between the sexes to such a degree that both women and men began to believe that being alone was preferable to attempting a relationship. "Everyone wants a relationship, but nobody knows how to get one," states a newspaper article after a depressing survey of Philadelphia's sophisticated singles circuit. The women are intimidated by the sheer statistics in a city where they outnumber the men by more than 100,000 (New York City women, by comparison, are said to outnumber the men by 500,000). The reactions of the women, including a lawyer, an artist, and a librarian, all in their early thirties, range from disgust at being disadvantaged by the lopsided numbers ("You get tired of feeling the other person has the advantage," says the lawyer) to anger at the residual feeling that a woman is nothing without a man ("Even though I know that's a bunch of—, the feeling is still there," says the artist) to bitterness at the air of superiority affected by the men ("They are unwilling to make any commitment, any effort. They act as if they are doing you a big favor just by spending time with you," says the librarian).

But the article reveals that the cynicism of the men is a cover-up for their feelings of emotional inferiority to women. The men are afraid that the more interesting women will find them emotionally shallow. They want intimacy but don't know how to achieve it, says a twenty-nine-year-old divorced man who admits that "thirty" of his friends are home by themselves on a weekend. The men in bars seek out one-night encounters with the ubiquitous flashily dressed and drugged mannequins—"friskies," as one man calls them—who will perform any kind of sexual exploit in the hopes of getting a relationship started. The "prime" women—educated, attractive, independent—are the more likely candidates for a serious relationship, but they, too, have taken to their homes. According to a knowledgeable womanizer identified as "Robert," these women "stay at home and are desperate" because "they don't know where they can find a man who's not jaded, unreachable, or untouchable."

One surmises that Robert's own invincibility is the male cultural narcissist's common defense against fear of abandonment by a woman since his last serious relationship ended *seven years* ago. He claims that he can't avoid meeting desirable women everywhere—"in stores, restaurants, on the street, at the dry cleaners"—yet he does avoid *relating* to them, preferring sexual conquest to intimacy. He is quoted as saying: "After years, things become predictable, you become jaded. But at the same time, you also become more desperate to find that needle in the haystack."

Despite the numerical odds in their favor, men in the Seventies were not served any better by the sexual revolution than were women. Without cultural support for connectedness, the consumption of experience led only to endless frustration. It did nothing to help overindulged but underloved men trade in their adolescent "needle in the haystack" fantasies of sexual perfection for a mature genital relationship. Financially independent women, with their demands for emotional openness, appeared even more devouring to these commitmentphobic men than the old submissive types. By the end of "the Decade of Women," as *Ms.* magazine called the Seventies, "liberated" women found that they had outdistanced men in their social growth, but they also discovered that they had won the booby prize: isolation.

MILT: THE "ABSENT FATHER"

Milt Stevens' experience with the sexual revolution, I find when I see him again, has been typical. The years have been both kind and harsh. Since the Fifties, when his work-obsessed oblivion was rudely invaded by his wife Charlotte's infidelity, Milt, now forty-seven, has gone through many changes. His electronics firm doubled in size in the affluent Sixties and made him a millionaire when he sold it in the early Seventies, but he is now ensnared in deep financial troubles with a new business enterprise he has started. After having numerous extramarital affairs himself, he finally ended his marriage to Charlotte several years ago and has subsequently earned a reputation as an adroit juggler of multiple relationships. He lives in a posh condo, having sold the dream house he bought Charlotte after their reconciliation in 1959, and he owns a twenty-six-foot cabin cruiser called *Acting Out*—a name he borrowed from his psychiatric therapy. His three sons are almost grown (two of them are in college) and it seems that both Milt and his boys have become part of the Me Generation at the same time.

Calling awareness "the new buzz word of our time," Milt lights up a thin cigar and leans back in the chair behind his oversized desk. We are in the plush, blue-carpeted office of a newly acquired paperbox company, and he is expounding on what the Me Generation means to him: "The 'Me' world says that *me* does exist. It's not a group context, it's not a third party, it's really *you*: how you relate to the world, how the world relates to you, what it means to you, what it doesn't mean to you. We may not be just the Me Generation when we say, 'I want, I need, I must have,' but we may have arrived at the point where we're asking ourselves questions that we never dared ask before: 'Am I? Can I? Should I?' "

Explaining "me-ism" of today, Milt says: "In the Fifties we simply assumed because of parental pressure or society's dictates that we had arrived at some degree of achievement or permanence in the major areas of our lives, and all of a sudden we're into a whole series of questions. And it's a very difficult process to give yourself an answer that's not an absolute but a feeling answer, an emotional answer, which is always at the outside open-ended: 'Well, on the one hand, it could go this way; but on the other hand, it could go the other way'—and they're both right. We're more comfortable as children when we get an answer that you can or can't do something. The maturing process gives us an opportunity to take tributaries or excursions from that one yes or no. The point really is that everyone is getting these opportunities to take excursions from one ambiguity to the next one, and there is never any sort of definitive comfort. Yet there are certain definitive comforts that we can arrive at from *decisions within ourselves*."

One decision that Milt arrived at, after struggling for almost twenty years with the rupture of his well-ordered Fifties world by Charlotte's betrayal of trust, was that merely "treading water" in relationships was not enough. After years of building an impenetrable wall around his wound, both in marriage and later out of it, Milt decided that he needed to find someone whom he could trust implicitly with his vulnerability again.

Why did it take him so long? Says Milt: "Men are at a disadvantage in a relationship because we have been developed in a framework of work and profession and competition and achievement, and women are basically much more mature. Relationship has always been an important aspect of a woman's life, but men in my generation couldn't even identify what we were looking for in a woman emotionally when we got married, much less what she was looking for in us. Our responsibility to the family was all-consuming, and we expected loyalty in return."

Charlotte's disloyalty in 1959 made Milt realize that no matter how much he would do for her or give her, it would never be enough. He knew she wanted something from him—a sense of self—that he could not provide, and he sought escape in outside relationships. "It was more a matter of running from something than running toward someone," Milt says. "The affairs weren't satisfying beyond the immediate rewards. They were not looked at as a possible replacement but as a place to go—a harbor, a refuge. While they were fantasies that I lived out and they provided excitement and thrill, I'm sure they interfered with any possible improvement of my marriage."

One of his longest affairs was with an ex-nun whose brother was a priest. Another, an exclusive relationship with a married woman, lasted five years. Milt was aware that Charlotte was also very active sexually, but he pretended not to know. During the last few years of their marriage there were rumors of Charlotte's serious involvement with Ted, Milt's lawyer, an attractive but passive man who would never leave his wealthy wife. When Ted abandoned Charlotte for another of the wives in their social circle, Charlotte began drinking heavily and became depressed and increasingly promiscuous. She was seen leaving motels with strange men she'd picked up in bars. And word got around that Charlotte had a fondness for strays and lost souls. Reports were flying that she was driving down weekdays to the marina in Maryland where *Acting Out* was docked and was trysting on the cabin cruiser with the boat boy—a young navy veteran who'd had part of his face blown off in Vietnam. Shortly before separating from her prior to the divorce, Milt came home one night and found Charlotte lying in bed comatose from a combination of sleeping pills and liquor. He rushed her to a nearby hospital, had her stomach pumped, and explained to friends that she'd had food poisoning.

After his divorce, Milt's seemingly narcissistic behavior those first few years—what he calls his "playboy existence"—was a confused and frightened search for *inner* control by someone who'd spent his life living up to others' expectations of him. "I went through many, many relationships," he says, "most of them multiples because I didn't want an emotional attachment—*never* an emotional attachment—and I did not want to commit myself to an exclusive relationship and what it entails. I decided that I would have two or three girl friends, so it would be every other weekend or there would always be somebody else or I'd never commit myself that fully. As I found my female companions getting more and more deeply involved with me, I would find another person to go out with, and I'd end up going out with six women in one week. And it didn't solve my need except that this was my way of forcing my hand. By overextending myself I reached a place where I said, 'I just can't handle this—it has to stop.'

I was like a kid let loose in a candy store. Marriage had come very early, and this was a juvenile catching up. It's like whatever you didn't have, if you can remember, now's the time to get it. If you never had a chance to get to the candy store or if you don't recall what it was like and you'd like to go again, divorce gives you that opportunity. You don't have to worry about anybody else, and if you can afford to do it financially or time-wise or emotionally or commitment-wise, you go. Now the candy is out there—it's around you and it's accessible. Most people think that to have too much candy will be satisfying. Not until you're stuffed so full that you lose all pleasure and desire do you begin to understand the meaning of everybody's me-ism. They're trying to get to the point where they can say, 'This is me: I'm a person who likes candy, but I want to taste it and not just swallow it and gorge myself.' That's when you make decisions. You have to realize that you are in control of your decision-making—you're not just a consumer—before you start to get to another cycle. When I recognized that I was going nowhere with all the relationships that I had, some of which had been bouncing around for maybe four or five years, I decided that I was ready to be vulnerable again and make a commitment. But by this time I knew what I wanted: a relationship between two autonomous people, neither being so dominant that the other becomes subservient."

As with his love relationships, Milt's relationship with his chil-

dren has been a continuing struggle to find a healthy balance between the traditional values that dominated his life in the Fifties
and the social dynamics in more recent years. He admires the younger generation for questioning the work ethic, but he is not too
happy about having to support the expensive tastes his children have
acquired while endlessly expanding their minds in lieu of entering
the work force.

"My children are very strong in areas that I was very weak in,"
says Milt, "and I respect that. They grew up in the Fifties and Sixties—their generation taught the adults about a whole new world of
fun and pleasure. We were programmed to believe that the only way
to find happiness was through money, power, and prestige, and that
security comes from work. So we've worked our asses off in order to
become secure and happy. The kids look at us and say, 'Good God!
They're fighting all the time, they're unhappy, these people who said
work was the answer. I reject that.' But the kids in turn are trying to
achieve in a world that is not affording them the background to
achieve. They have nothing to hang their hook on. They may want
to achieve in emotional growth, in spirituality, in the expansion of
their minds and their horizons, and that's fine—provided they don't
have to *eat*. They're walking out into our world to compete with
those who are already there saying, 'Okay, I took courses in wine-
tasting, guitar-plucking, and photography. And I can pluck a guitar, I
know great wines, and I can take a lot of photographs. The only
problem is that I can't afford to buy the good wines, I can't afford
any film for my camera, and what am I going to do now that I have
to look for a job? And I've got a girl friend—she doesn't know that
inflation has taken over—who says we have discos to go to, concerts,
theaters, and your dad has a great boat and can we go fishing next
week?' It's that kind of world where they're into the material goodies, but they can't handle the responsibilities of their age."

On the subject of graduate school, Milt sounds even more caustic
and perplexed. He feels that as rigidly goal-oriented and security-
minded as people were in the Fifties, that's how unfocused their
children are today. "Years ago you didn't have parents supporting
their children through graduate school because they didn't have the
money," he says, "so most of us went to college to learn a trade.
When I asked my kids why they were going to college, the answer I
got was: 'To be prepared for graduate school!' Today it's not a mat-

ter of whether or not to go, it's when to stop. It's wonderful that our kids have the results of our preoccupation with the work ethic to support their extended learning period. When *do* we stop? How about the doctorate? And if we have another degree beyond the doctorate, then they'll have to go to that one, too, because they've never learned how to make a living in the context of our society's needs for food, clothing, and shelter. The biggest problem we face is that being an adult places constraints on the young after they've strived to eliminate them all. That's why we're so hung up on preparation. We've never had so many aptitude tests. They're being tested to death. One thing that bothers me about tests is that they usually lead to another test. We may get the greatest test-takers, but we don't get too many of them who are schooled for life. We're never defining anything for ourselves because to define is to limit. And to limit is counter to the new expand concept that says expand your mind, expand your life, expand your world—don't limit anything. We can expand if we expand vertically, but to expand horizontally is just to wallow in no direction. And that's what we're finding a lot of our young people doing today—expanding horizontally and expanding to chaos."

Milt tries to explain the hesitancy of parents his age. They are afraid to interfere in their children's lives, or even to guide them at all. "We're the Reluctant Generation today," says Milt, "the same as we were the Silent Generation back in the Fifties. We're reluctant to say 'Do this' to our children for fear of making a mistake or doing the same thing to our kids that we had done to us. We're also becoming very aware of ourselves and of all the inadequacies that we have, and that, in turn, makes us reluctant to offer this great advice coming from on high. But in our reluctance we're now being inundated by this glut of options on the market.

"My oldest son, after graduating from Cornell and working as a trainee in a company, wants to go back to school for an advanced degree because he sees that he doesn't have the skills for a particular profession or line of work. I can't define what he can do and neither can he. My younger two sons are headed for the same quandary. They're all part of the new youth group whose attitude is 'I want to get some skills, but I'm not sure what I want to do with them and I'm not sure what skills are necessary to do something.' That's a double negative. They're poorly prepared in two respects: background and direction. They may decide on a direction at some point but have no background. And we're reluctant to advise them as to which options to take because we're afraid to cut off their freedom. But if we don't say anything, our silence is a statement just the same. No decision is a decision. We're letting them down by our unconscious refusal to help them make responsible choices. We have to let them know that the work ethic isn't all bad—that you can have work and achievement and happiness along with it."

VIVIAN: THE "PERMISSIVE MOTHER"

Having played out her strategy for survival in the Fifties—throwing all of her energies into being a suburban "happy housewife heroine"—Vivian Brooks has become the new kind of Seventies survivor: the postmarital "head of household heroine." Divorced in 1972 at the age of forty-five, Vivian has gone through the familiar resocialization process—returning to school, completing her education, finding a job, rearing her children alone, searching for a new partner. For the past six years, she has been involved in a typical Seventies relationship with a divorce-scarred man who is unable to make a genuine commitment. Frank, her fifty-three-year-old boyfriend, is consumed with unraveling the tangled mess that his badly confused, drug-addicted twenty-year-old daughter has made. Vivian has her own problems with her sixteen-year-old son, Andy. Her two older children are married, but Andy, who still lives with Vivian in her home in Great Neck, New York, is not well motivated in school, places partying above preparation for college, and treats Frank with open, unmitigated hostility.

Like Milt Stevens, Vivian Brooks has awakened from the dream of suburban bliss to find herself in a strange place. Having made it round the bend of the enforced developmental detour of late adolescence and gotten closer to their True Selves in middle age, both Milt and Vivian are now struggling with a reversal of the whole process with their own children. Milt's children, Vivian's, Frank's, and many others, it appears, are confused and lost; suffering as much from lack of direction as their parents suffered from too much. The children are burdened with the same high expectations of achievement that the law of upward mobility requires, but they have very little in the way of constructive parental support. They have parents who, because their energies have been sapped by their own delayed growing up in mid-life, have adopted a hands-off policy with their children that is tantamount to a *permissiveness of negligence*. This is not the same permissiveness that began to develop in the late 1940s and reached the proportions of a fad in the Fifties, where the motivation was to bring up an "uninhibited" child in a pseudo-Freudian sense. In the Seventies and early Eighties, laissez-faire parents in the Milt Stevens and Vivian Brooks mold are being permissive mainly because they want to avoid the onus of being traditional parents as they know traditional parents to be. The very idea of having to supervise their children's behavior and make value judgments about it is impossible for them, so they are fudging their responsibility under the guise of giving their children maximum freedom and independence.

Vivian now feels that her two older children, Jon, thirty, and Nancy, twenty-eight, were badly undermined emotionally not so much by permissiveness as by her dread of breaking the cultural taboo against divorce in the Fifties. The children suffered because Vivian tried to make a traditional two-parent family home life out of an essentially single-parent family situation. Jon, a pharmacologist, is married to a severely handicapped woman from a working-class background, and Nancy, a schoolteacher, lived with an alcoholic construction worker after college, had his baby, and later married him when his drinking problem had been resolved.

Vivian attributes her children's obvious lack of self-esteem mainly to her husband's incompetence as a father and her reluctance to divorce Martin sooner and spare the children his psychological abuse. But she also sees how her own use of the children to compensate for the emptiness in her life contributed to their lack of sense of self. "My children had a difficult life and coped as best they could," says Vivian. "They were easy to raise. They tried to please. In the tradition of 'togetherness' I convinced the children that they had to overlook their father's violent outbursts because he couldn't help himself, which wasn't right. It was unfair."

As for being the typical overprotective yet too-permissive Fifties mother, Vivian says: "I might have been overprotective with the children in my concern for their safety and in never allowing them to be unattended, but in terms of what time they went to sleep or what they ate, I tended to be very lenient. But I don't think my permissiveness spoiled them. What I see as the product of permissiveness carried to extremes are children who have no concept of reality, who take advantage, who are demanding, who are greedy, who are exploitative of their own parents and of other people, who don't take responsibility. My children were the antithesis of that. They were very well disciplined. They went through school without even telling me how deprived they were. Nancy dropped out of college for a half year and went to work on an ice cream truck to make some money because she couldn't live like her brother on a pot of spaghetti all week. My kids didn't take advantage in any way. I made my big mistake when I sent the children out of town to college to get them away from Martin. I should have recognized that if Martin wasn't going to get help, *he* should have been the one I threw out of the house and not my children. I don't think my daughter, who was so close to me, was mature enough to handle that kind of separation. That's how she made those associations with people I never would have expected her to associate with."

Inevitably, Vivian's reference to prematurely "throwing" her daughter out of the house at eighteen calls to mind Vivian's harrowing description in the chapter on the Forties of her own forcible ejection from the nest by *her* mother when Vivian was eighteen years old and terrified of being on her own. There is also, ummistakably, the same certainty on Vivian's part that she, Vivian, always knew better than her daughter what was right for her daughter to do. It is hard to believe that this is the same Vivian who explained how her parents destroyed her confidence in her own judgment when they began to make her decisions for her. It is the very same Vivian who, summoning forgiveness from God-knows-where, said that it wasn't with malice aforethought that her mother engineered the disastrous marriage to Martin three decades ago, "but out of what she thought was my inability to know what was good for me."

We see how history repeats itself—*must* repeat itself—in the search for unconditional love. Without a cultural environment that supports a valuable period of dependence in infancy and a gradual weaning away through the *mutual* setting of limits by parent and child, both generations are arrested at the stage of needing or dreading their need of infantile merger. Despite, or rather because of, her bruising experience with parental coercion, Vivian was no more able to resist trying to stage-manage her two older children's lives than her mother had been able to resist managing hers. While a bitter disappointment to Vivian, Jon's and Nancy's choice of marital partners may indeed reflect an assertion of their True Self. As such, their marriages are probably more likely to succeed, as they seem to be doing, than Vivian's marriage.

With Andy, her younger son, Vivian feels that she has become a better mother because she has achieved some of her own goals and does not have to prove herself through him as she did with Jon and Nancy. But now she is struggling with a new conflict—striking the right balance between expectations that are too high and no expectations at all. She doesn't want to burden Andy with pressure to achieve for her benefit, yet she still has *some* aspirations for him because she knows that the world will demand performance of him even if she doesn't. Like the rest of the "Reluctant Generation," Vivian is having a hard time finding that elusive checkpoint where beneficial permissiveness crosses the line into the enemy territory of neglect.

"It wasn't until I got to the third child," says Vivian, "that I truly felt that this child owes it to himself to live his life in his own way, and I'll be perfectly adoring of him as long as he's good to himself and to others, and is happy in the world. I'm not particularly anxious for him to be anything that's going to please me or to marry someone who'll meet my approval. I did have different expectations of my other children. Yet they weren't bad values. Everything we incorporated from our parents wasn't bad, but our parents didn't have respect for children. Children were something that happened to them—a burden and a responsibility. Even though I didn't have the knowledge and background with my two older children, I still had respect for them. The trouble was, I needed them to bolster my ego, to prove that my kids were the smartest, the best. With Andy, I'm more relaxed. I trust him. When you've realized some achievements on your own, you don't have to demand perfection of your kids. The main thing I've learned is to let Andy make his own decisions rather than imposing my will on him, because I think that your children assimilate more by observing you than by anything you say to them. It's very important to like each other and to respect each other as individuals. At least I've matured about what's important. I have different priorities. It doesn't matter how the kid is dressed, but be clean. It doesn't matter *which* university, but get an education."

But Andy is not preparing for college. About to enter his senior year in high school, he spends very little time studying and is even flunking art, a subject for which he has a natural inclination. He is a likable, easygoing boy, undemanding yet assertive in stating his needs, who knows the difference, as Vivian puts it, between "a kid who parties and a kid who's a pothead, a kid who has a beer and a kid who's a potential alcoholic." Yet he seems to have fallen into the "cognitive vacuum" that parents offer their children when they say, "I don't care what you are so long as you are happy." As social scientists Caryl Rivers, Rosalind Barnett, and Grace Baruch have discovered, while too much pressure on children to achieve makes them tense and anxious, the opposite extreme—*no* parental expectations or standards—can be equally damaging:

Is it really healthy to say to a child, "I love you whatever you are, whatever you do, and I approve of you no matter what"? Parents who have too rigid or too high expectations for children can be destructive, but parents with no expectations at all, or those who are unwilling to voice any, may not be helping their children to become independent adults who can deal with the rest of the world.

The world doesn't say to people, "You're terrific no matter what." In the outside world there are standards, tasks, tests, and the child who gets no clues from parents about how to perform in that world may be in trouble.

The worst problem that Vivian has had with Andy, she claims, is that he couldn't concentrate in school during the divorce proceedings, which began when he was nine and dragged on for more than three years. With her admitted gift for rationalizing away what is too painful for her to confront, Vivian tends to focus on the effects of the divorce and Andy's relationship with his father as the chief source of his problem. Her own failure to provide direction is largely overlooked. It is hard for Vivian to admit that in veering from overinvolvement in her children's lives to noninvolvement, she has left Andy stranded in the middle of a void. She wants him to "get an education," but she refuses to bring him face to face with the reality of qualifying for college.

In one area—her pursuit of romantic love—Vivian is fully aware that her needs are antagonistic to Andy's. What to do about it, after her six-year-long relationship with Frank, is still an unanswered question. "Andy doesn't accept Frank and doesn't like him," says Vivian. "Part of it has to do with the fact that Frank is an intruder—an outsider—and there's always loyalty to the original parent. But another part of it is a personality conflict—different types of people. After twenty-three years of unhappiness, I wasn't especially looking for a father figure for my child—I was looking for a friend for *me*. Really, for the first time in my life I had a *romance*. There were others I could have chosen. The first man I met wanted to come in and cut my kid's nails and take him for a ride in the car. But I was more interested in a partner. It seemed to be very critical at that time, and it's still important. The kid is going to survive. He accepted some men more than Frank, but I don't know how it would have been if he knew they were going to be around on a permanent basis."

The frustrations Vivian is enduring in her triangular relationship with Andy and the "once-burned-twice-shy" Frank, who lives in another city and simply can't get far enough past the failure of his first marriage to chance another marital commitment, represent a universal phenomenon today. Sometimes ludicrous, more often heartbreaking, the scenario Vivian is enacting is being played out in the Seventies by legions of liberated female "single-parent-heads-of-households" who were the former dependent "happy housewife heroines" of the Fifties.

"If it hadn't been for Andy," says Vivian, "I would have put more pressure on Frank to get married. Frank has such a tremendous amount of trouble with his daughter's drug problem that I don't know whether he can cope with any more stress. He expresses it in terms of not being able to take on a 'ready-made family.' Andy wouldn't be Frank's problem—he's *my* responsibility—but Frank senses Andy as a threat, knows the kid is very hostile toward him, and doesn't go out of his way to be friendly to Andy either. I took a Parent Effectiveness Training course, but it didn't work. I tried 'active listening' with Andy. I said, 'Tell me why you don't like Frank.' And I got back answers like, 'He's a faggot.' Without getting upset, I pursued the line of questioning very receptively, the way you're supposed to. 'What do you mean he's a faggot?' I asked. 'He's a pussy,' Andy answered, and that ended the conversation."

Vivian laughs, but her laugh ends on a note of despair. "I've often been tempted to sell the house, move in with Frank, and force the issue," she confides wearily, "but that would mean uprooting Andy. There's a lot to be said for maintaining the stability of the home and family patterns. Andy has a wide circle of friends here, his father lives reasonably close and sees him sometimes, and my sister lives nearby with her two kids." She sounds increasingly grim. "I've stuck it out so far, so maybe I should stick it out for another two years until Andy's in college." Suddenly Vivian looks very old, and there's an expression on her face that says, If this is liberation, is it worth the price? "I feel that a lot of my life is slipping by," she says finally, "and it's not as satisfying as it could be. It's a sacrifice. I have to weigh one against the other."

BARRY: THE CULTURAL NARCISSIST

Whatever happened to Barry Golden, I ask myself, as I wander through the rectangular maze of an apartment complex not far from the opulent suburban home where Barry, the young attorney who was separating from his wife, Linda, used to live. I had heard that Barry, separated for almost two years now, had been sharing an apartment for over a year with his girl friend Amanda. A lissome, blond twenty-six-year-old model, pretty in a classic yet sensual way, Amanda invites me into a stylishly furnished living room where Barry is lounging on the sofa in jeans and a short-sleeved sports shirt. His expertly groomed beard and moustache are of recent vintage, as is the discreet tattoo on his forearm: "Barry," written in script.

Looking none the worse for wear, despite being in the middle of bitter, messy divorce proceedings, Barry stuns me with the news that Amanda and he are not living together anymore. "She just moved out this past week," he announces, adding quickly, "We're still seeing each other, we're still going to date—but Amanda has a lot of problems to work out."

I turn inquiringly to Amanda, who has settled into a seat opposite me and looks composed but guarded. Speaking in a measured, faintly Southern drawl, she says: "I think my moving out is the best way to save our relationship. Barry has become very frustrated with me because he thinks I'm irresponsible. I'm too carefree and tend to come and go as I please. Barry prefers a woman who has a little bit of independence, yet is dependent. He has to be shown that Amanda is not a child—Amanda can be an adult. I just need to do a lot of growing up."

When I ask what prompted this realization, Amanda explains that she has recently started therapy and has gained some understanding of her difficulties with responsibility. She describes herself as the product of a broken home where the lack of parental guidance was her undoing. "My father's absence might not have been such a focal point for me," Amanda says, "if my mother had been more aware of situations. But she more or less lived in her own world."

Amanda's parents were divorced when she was a year and a half old. Almost immediately, her father remarried and moved to the Midwest. Her mother didn't remarry until Amanda was in her late teens. Working full time and with two babies—Amanda and her older brother—to raise by herself in the Fifties, Amanda's mother became permissiveness personified. "She didn't interfere in her children's lives or guide them at all," Barry says. "Whatever Amanda wanted to do, she could do—and then her mother said, 'No, that was wrong.' All she could ever do was bail Amanda out if she got in trouble." Even after she left home, according to Barry, Amanda never learned to think or act for herself: "She always lived with different guys. They were short, temporary relationships—no deep involvements. Nobody cared enough to say, 'Hey, Amanda, this is what you should do.' She was very content with whatever happened."

Amanda makes a sudden revelation, rendered all the more startling by her quiet, matter-of-fact tone: "I had a baby who was given up for adoption. I was sixteen when I got pregnant. I had no inkling that I was going to have a baby until we moved to Houston and I had to get a physical examination for school. The doctor took one look at me and said, 'You haven't put on weight. You're pregnant.' I was shocked. I was heavily into drugs at the time and completely out of touch with reality. My mother never admonished me, never asked any questions—she just took over from there. We don't speak about it at all. It's as if it never happened."

Giving the baby up for adoption was not difficult for Amanda—"not at that time," she says. She was more psychologically disturbed by something else that happened that same year. "After we moved to Houston," Amanda recalls, "I was rummaging around in the basement one afternoon and I found a lot of letters to my mother from my father—ugly, shocking letters about the divorce. I remember feeling sick to my stomach when I read some of the things he said: 'You can take those kids and do anything you want with them' . . . 'You can all go to hell—I don't care.' That was in 1969, and I haven't spoken to my father since. *I hate him.*"

From the letters, Amanda learned that her mother had to hire a detective to go after her father to collect the two hundred dollars a month child support the court had originally ordered him to pay. "He finally got the order down to eighty dollars a month," Amanda says bitterly. "Here my mother was, out busting her tail earning a living, and she had to have a detective trailing him plus all those legal bills. By that time my brother and I were almost too old for my father to have to pay support, so all that money was down the tubes. It's a long story." Amanda sighs. "My father had responsibilities that he did *not* meet." She speaks as if she is talking to divorced fathers everywhere. "Even if you're not going to be there, give financially— do *something* for the kids so they know that 'Okay, he's not here. He and my mother can't get along, but at least he's helping her out.' Don't leave the whole thing on the woman just because she's the mother. What's she going to do—walk away from the children?"

Amanda claims that although her mother was well-meaning, she was oblivious to the fact that children need direction. "My brother and I are a product of her upbringing—hers alone—and you see what happened," she says. "My brother went through six years of college and is managing a Woolco store in Ohio. He's not dumb—it's just that nobody ever sat down and talked with him about what he should do. I coped with the lack of direction by building a fantasy world at a very early age. There was no one there to penetrate it, no one I would let penetrate it, because I felt no one cared."

Barry says: "I was the first person who ever forced Amanda into a situation where she had to think for herself or do things for herself or reveal what she felt. Take her modeling, for example. She's getting a lot of work now, mostly for Gimbels. She got an incredible break. She's in the paper every week and in the Sunday supplement—four color pages—seventy-five dollars an hour. She wants all these things, but she's afraid to do them on her own. She needs somebody there pushing her."

Amanda concurs. "I just fell into modeling by being pretty," she says, "but by not showing up, by missing bookings, and not keeping in touch with my agency, I barely worked for about two years. After meeting Barry, I got back into it again. He kept insisting, so I called my agent and she said, 'Sure I have work for you, but are you going to be there?' I said, 'Sherry, I'll be there.' And she took me back. It was just a matter of learning how to be reliable."

According to Barry, teaching Amanda how to be reliable in their personal relationship was a comparative fiasco. Although she knew she was precipitating a split-up that she didn't want, she simply could not control her infuriating habit of not calling or coming home when she said she would. Barry had decided never to see her again after the most recent episode. "The relationship was going to be over," Barry says, "until Amanda persuaded me to give her therapy a chance. I thought that she just didn't give a shit. I talked to her until I was blue in the face, and then she would do exactly the opposite of what she promised. Her therapist says that it isn't that she doesn't love me or doesn't care—it's just that she doesn't think. She doesn't consider the consequences of her actions. She's not used to doing the right thing."

When I ask Barry what *is* the "right thing," he answers: "Responsibility is the right thing, being a stable person you can rely on and count on, *dependability*. The right things—whether we're talking about sex or trading baseball cards—are the things that give you peace and give the people that you care about peace."

In the area of sex, it turns out that the "right thing" for Barry and Amanda is Amanda's bisexuality. For the last six months, about once a month, they have been involved in threesomes—Barry watches Amanda with another woman and then makes love to both—and he says that this has become important to him. "I'm a romantic," he explains, "and it's very romantic to watch two women together. It's very sensual, sensuous, beautiful—two people who really understand the needs of each other. They envelop each other—it's very passionate." He adds, perhaps providing a clue as to what his partner's bisexuality means to him on a deeper level, "With a bisexual woman, you break down a very important barrier—*womanhood*. She becomes not just a woman, but a woman who's a person—who has a distinct personality—and I think seeing her that way enables the relationship between the man and the woman to grow. It makes it so much stronger."

I wonder if Barry does not mean that he feels closer to Amanda because he can identify with her pre-oedipal longings—the infantile wish to merge with the mother and get sexual love from her. Barry contends that homosexual fantasies are universal among the women he meets and that the drug culture has given people permission to act them out. When I ask him if he thinks Amanda would be bisexual without the quaaludes they both take routinely, he responds emphatically, "No way. I don't think she's ever made love to a woman when she wasn't 'luded.' When she's high, I usually initiate it. She enjoys it, but she's not motivated to do it herself."

Amanda contradicts him. " 'Ludes' don't *make* you do things—they *let* you," she says carefully. "Loving women is something that I want to do, but it's always been forbidden, frowned upon. The more I grow and realize that I don't have to hide it—that it's all right, that Barry isn't going to leave me if something like that happens—the more free I can be. I'm not going to use the excuse that I was 'luded'—that's all it is, an excuse."

Although Amanda has enjoyed making love with women for several years, even before she knew Barry, she has always done it in the presence of men. "I love men and I love women," she says, "but the women are secondary. I need a man to be there. It turns me on to know that Barry is enjoying it and that this is basically a show."

When she tells me that she has never discussed her bisexuality with her therapist, I form my own hypothesis: Amanda has admitted being a lonely child who walled herself off into a fantasy world to escape her harried mother's emotional unavailability. Her sexual activity with women appears to be an attempt to get the emotional closeness—the "mother's warmth"—that she felt deprived of as a child. At the same time, according to the sexual scenario Amanda has described, she is playing out her childhood fantasy of bringing her absent father back. By using another woman as a foil to arouse sexual passion in a man, she is luring her father home—to her mother, but mostly to herself.

Both Amanda and Barry find my interpretation plausible, especially since they are aware that psychiatrists have linked the lack of a father figure to another sexual proclivity commonly practiced among their friends today. "Women like to be beaten," Barry says. "They like to be tied, they like to be whipped, they like to be called a slut, a whore—I can't believe how many women are that way. Guys talk about it all the time. Amanda has done S-M—she's been hit with a belt on her ass and stuff like that—and she said she had orgasms and enjoyed it. I tried it, but I was like a ninety-year-old man hitting her with a piece of spaghetti. But here's the interesting thing: She no longer fantasizes about that or has that desire. I asked her, 'Is it because you know I won't do it?' And she said, 'No, I just don't need it anymore.' Maybe I've replaced that father figure—that voice of authority that says, 'This is right, this is wrong; this is what you should do, this is what you shouldn't'—so she no longer has the desire for physical domination or discipline."

"That's what most psychiatrists say it is," Amanda tells me, "when the girl especially likes bondage. If they check into her background, they either find that she had no father figure or one who was very weak and passive. I know that's what I was looking for from it—the excitement and relief of finding a firm, strong figure who would be dominant when I needed him. A lot of my friends want just the experience of being tied down. They want to have no choice in the matter. It's like, you can't get up and with a rebellious attitude say, 'I'm leaving'—you know, you're *there*."

While I know how complex and multidetermined any sexual behavior is, I see the validity in Amanda's explanation of sadomasochistic desires among young women today as a cultural phenomenon. With the waning of parental authority and closeness in the home, guilt is no longer as much a motivation for deviant sexual behavior as is the distorted search for parental love and guidance. For many young people, the sexual revolution has dispelled the guilty feeling that one should be punished for having "dirty" sexual desires. But permissiveness has created a new need for sexual "discipline" as a substitute for the loving discipline that was missing in childhood.

It occurs to me that if Amanda's *masochistic* fantasies have been "answered," not by acting them out but by addressing the emotional needs they symbolize, then the same might be true of her *bisexuality*. If she could work through her hatred of her father in therapy, her acceptance of him might help her achieve an exclusively heterosexual relationship with Barry of much greater depth and stability. But Barry has a vested interest in keeping Amanda actively bisexual, and it has more to do with his conflicts about commitment than it does with his particular taste in eroticism. Barry believes that in his "open sex life" with Amanda—their monthly threesomes and occasional foursomes on vacations—he has found the way to have a committed relationship without cutting himself off from other options.

By involving Amanda, he thinks he has overcome the problem of jealousy and possessiveness:

"When I was married to Linda, I didn't cheat on her," he says, "but I always had the desire. I was always fantasizing about other women. Linda was very strict. I couldn't even look at another woman without her making a beeline over to me." By comparison, his relationship with Amanda sounds idyllic. "Since we've been having an open sex life," he reports, "I've had absolutely no desire for other women when we're not together. It's almost like giving a kid all the toys he wants, and he says, 'I don't want to play with them.' But I know that if I do, it's okay. It's okay for me and it's okay for Amanda as long as we're honest about it and don't deceive one another."

The extraordinary freedom he has with Amanda, Barry feels, is the key to his happiness with her. "I get along better with Amanda than I've ever gotten along with anyone," he says, "in that we are totally, totally open with each other. There is nothing I can't do in front of her, nothing I can't say to her. I'm completely committed to our relationship because of it. There's no restriction on anything. If I want to talk to another girl, I don't have to worry that Amanda's going to be jealous."

But Amanda tells a different story. It seems that she is not altogether pleased with the new sexual "openness" in general and, in fact, is not as "open" and free of jealousy as Barry would like to believe. Says Amanda: "I think women have ruined it for themselves by taking the attitude that men are just to be used—men aren't worth anything. It's a backlash. We're trying to get even with the men and treat them the way we've been treated, especially when it comes to sex. The Pill made it possible for women to be much more free and not have to worry. It's cool now to talk with your friends about your sexual escapades—ten years ago it wasn't. The sexual revolution opened up a lot of people, and it's caused a lot of *different* problems. Now we're having the problems of how to deal with this new openness: How do you get a man to respect you? How do you get a man to really care for you? How do you get a man to be committed?" She shrugs off "all these people with open marriages" and says, "It's fine for me, but I don't want Barry to do it. I *do* have jealousy. When Barry came home from a dinner meeting last Thursday night and told me he'd been sitting next to another girl, I knew in my mind that nothing happened—I know he loves me—but there was still jealousy at the thought of another woman getting close to him."

The "open sex life" Barry lauds so highly is merely an *illusion* of freedom he has created for himself by capitalizing on Amanda's bisexual tendencies. He needs this illusion in order to maintain his autonomy in the relationship, but it is the connection with Amanda that really counts. "What's the big deal with a one-night stand?" he asks. "Whether you're in the mood and you physically want someone, whether it's an ego trip or something else, it's not important. Amanda and I *enjoy* each other, not so much sexually as just being together. The sexual thing is the free lunch, so to speak—a bonus." He explains why sex with Amanda is special: "When Amanda and I make love, I know exactly what she's going to do, she knows exactly what I'm going to do; she knows what to say, I know what to say; I know when to touch her—that's something that takes a long time to build up."

But with Linda, I recall, Barry had found this sexual familiarity boring. "You said," I remind him, 'I know exactly what she's going to do, she knows exactly what I'm going to do, et cetera. It's no good anymore—the excitement is gone.' "

"*Really?*" Barry is astonished. "Well, Amanda's not selfish," he says, "whereas Linda was—and that's a big difference." He tries to explain. "I get great pleasure out of giving to a woman—I like to buy her things, turn her on, be a nice guy. If you give to a woman like Linda, who's absolutely selfish, that's all you'll be doing the rest of your life. You'll never get anything from her, and eventually you'll become bored. But I can give and give to Amanda and never tire of it because I always know I'm going to get a lot back in return. She *appreciates* things. She may not do the right thing to show her appreciation, but she *does* appreciate. And I think that's the most important thing of all—to have someone realize that you *are* being nice, you *are* trying, you *are* making an effort. Linda needed so much for herself that she never saw what she was getting, and she never saw what she had to give back."

Barry sees Linda's selfishness not simply as a personal trait but as evidence of how the competitive ethic, coupled with the loss of traditional family values, has crippled people's capacity to love in our culture today. "Today there's no depending on people because they won't tolerate anything," he says. "They're motivated purely by self-ish gain—the invisible hand that runs our economy and makes the system work. Always covering your own ass is what works in the economy because the only way to succeed in business is never to lose sight of your own fiscal needs. But in the social reality, things are not *businesslike*—supply and demand, cause and effect, black and white—because the needs you're dealing with are emotional. To succeed in relationships, you need things like caring, nurturance, sensitivity, a system of give-and-take. If you do everything just for yourself, you end up alienating the people you love. You make them feel that they can't depend on you because you're not really into helping out. So all they can do is make you live in a world by yourself."

But I point out to Barry that the opposite is equally true. When you're completely altruistic in a social relationship—*all-giving*—you often set yourself up to be taken advantage of, as he had with Linda. Where do you draw the line? How do you know *those* limits?

"It's very simple," Barry says. "It's something I never grasped until this point in my life. *You have to pick the right people*—it's that simple. If you pick people who are not selfish themselves, then you don't have that problem."

Amanda explains why she feels Barry is the right kind of person for her. "I respect Barry because he won't tolerate my irresponsibil-ity—it makes me feel that he really cares," she says. "In my other relationships I always thought I loved the guys, but I'd just walk away the moment there was any trouble, rationalizing, 'Well there's someone else who can supply me with what this person is giving me.'" But with Barry, Amanda claims that she has experienced a depth of feeling unlike anything she has ever known before. And because of that, she is willing to hang in and fight for the relation-ship rather than walk away. "I've taken verbal abuse from Barry that I wouldn't have believed," she admits, "but I've never had the same happiness with a man either. He's strong; he has his feet on the ground; he's not constantly putting me in a corner and saying, 'Don't talk—just sit there and look pretty.' He treats me like an adult and yet he's very compassionate and reassuring about my insecurities."

According to Amanda, her insecurities are not inconsiderable. "I'm totally insecure—*absolutely*," she insists. "If one person says the wrong thing to me, I immediately assume, 'They hate me,' 'I'm ugly,' 'I'm fat,' 'I'm stupid.'" Some of these thoughts are clearly incongruous in view of Amanda's flawless looks, but she says, "They're only an excuse to escape out of the real world and back into fantasy. The real world is very painful because you have to know how to deal with people, and I never learned that when I was growing up."

Drugs are the nemesis that Amanda has been confronting in her struggle to live as a responsible person in the real world. "I haven't been doing drugs to any great extent for a year," Amanda says. "Besides making me look physically bad for my work, having drugs all the time makes me undependable. The minute I slipped—the minute I got close to it—I almost killed my relationship with Barry. I smoked cocaine one night at my friend's and never came home. I knew in my head that I was supposed to go home at ten o'clock, but I'd do a couple of hits and just like that"—she snaps her fingers—"I was right back in my fantasy world." Although Amanda still smokes marijuana and takes quaaludes at what Barry refers to as their "once-a-month party," she has given up the heroin, LSD, and other hard drugs that she used in the past. She claims that she doesn't need a "drug outlet" now that she has found someone she cares about and can be happy with. "People don't know how to have a good time anymore without drugs," she muses. "They're afraid *not* to do drugs."

Barry, who refrains from taking hard drugs but smokes marijuana every night ("It replaces my evening cocktail"), believes that so many of his contemporaries habitually use cocaine, quaaludes, and marijuana because they have been deeply affected by the instability of our social institutions. "We see so many absurdities around us that we lose faith in the meaning of our own actions," he says. "There's nothing to believe in anymore. Take marriage, for example. The ultimate security-giving institution is really a joke today. There are more people getting divorced than there are getting married. The economy is a joke. Our political officials are a joke. I say to myself, 'What the hell does it matter if I vote for so-and-so?' When he's in office, I have zero control. I can only sit back and watch him go through the motions, selfishly looking out for his own interests, while we're getting to the point where the Romans were. Our empire is about to crumble."

Barry's pessimistic world view, I see, has remained unchanged since our last meeting. I draw an analogy between his personal experiences with Linda's "absolute selfishness" in their marriage and Amanda's undependability in their current relationship and the behavior of our public officials. How can we expect our leaders to become any less selfish or undependable, I ask him, if we don't put pressure on them to change or remove them from office?

But Barry insists that we're powerless. He cites the manipulation of the public by television advertising and the media and the impossibility of mobilizing individuals who are all "running this way and that" into groups large and cohesive enough for effective civic action. "Besides," he adds, "there are some factors that can inhibit us from doing what we really feel like doing—like gas rationing, for example. If I were a salesman who had to travel quite a bit, I'd have to resort to some tactics that would deprive somebody else of his gas allotment, just so I could have it. There are influences out there that can affect you," he reminds me. "You can't pull yourself into shell."

I realize that we have come back to the selfishness of the individual so dominated by the values of the business ethic and so dehumanized by other-direction that doing "the right thing" has ceased to provide meaning and pleasure in life. I ask Barry whether our vulnerability to outside influences hasn't become a detriment at a time when people will have to learn to live a little more frugally and like it. Isn't he happier living with Amanda in this apartment than he was in the luxurious splendor of the home he shared with Linda? Does the hypothetical salesman who steals someone else's gas allotment have to make *that* many sales in his car? Why can't we resist the media messages pushing the latest fashions that maybe we can't afford and don't want anyway?

"If you resist them, then you're outdated and old-fashioned," Barry tells me. I am reminded once again of Mitscherlich's observation that in a culture where parents have not been able to pass on a dependable value system to their children by directly instructing them in everyday life, conformity is everything: People feel worthless if they are "out of date" or not socially with the trend. While Barry admits that the cultivation of image (at which he is a master) is a superficial value, he justifies his preoccupation with style as a necessity for advancement in his career. "If you're married and have five kids and have a station wagon, all those style-concious values are really not that important," he says. "However, if you're out trying to *get* the house and the station wagon and the five kids and the wonderful wife, it *is* important. In business you have to *look* successful in order to *be* successful. That's what puts the bread and butter on the table and enables you to be self-sufficient and independent."

LISA: A CHILD OF THE DECADE

To look at her, you would never guess that Lisa Sandrone, a successful, never-married television writer in her late twenties (born in 1952), came within a hair of a full-blown nervous breakdown when her first serious relationship ended right after college in the summer of 1974. Pert and vivacious, with a soft mane of chestnut hair and dancing green eyes, she has the shrewd, supple look of a natural-born winner in a tough field.

"He was my knight in shining armor fantasy," Lisa explains of her traumatic first love. "I was eighteen when I met him, and he was ten years older—a cardiologist who'd skipped years of college and medical school, had been through Vietnam, and was well established in his profession—and I thought, 'This will be just fine.' My problem was, I wasn't going to grow through anything, he was going to tell me how it was, and I was going to learn from him."

Remembering my own marriage in the Fifties to an older, established doctor, I sense that Lisa's story, despite the differences in our backgrounds, might have been mine had I been born twenty years later. "I had a very easy childhood and adolescence, very sheltered and secure," she says, speaking of her small-town parochial Catholic girlhood in upstate Pennsylvania. "My brother and I were always very close to my parents. My father wasn't a big figure in the family at all, but my mother was quite a brainwasher. She instilled in my brother and me the idea that we were going to be educated and get married because there was no other way to make it. She said we would get hurt if we didn't go that way." Lisa mimics her mother's earnest tone, running the sentences together like a catechism: " 'I want you to be happy, and I know what will make you happy, and this will make you happy, and I'm not happy unless you're happy.' " She laughs and continues: "She was totally *for* me, like a cheerleader. In fact, when my brother and I would sit at the dinner table and talk about school, she'd practically shout: 'GO, MARK! GO, LISA! YAY KIDS!' " Lisa shakes her head wistfully. "I thought everyone would always love us like that. For a while, that's the way I thought it *should* be."

When Lisa's four-year relationship with the doctor broke up over another woman (commitmentphobic to the end, he still lives with this woman but won't marry *her* either), Lisa went from complete submission to her mother to vengeful hatred. "I blamed her for everything," Lisa says, "and told her I hated her for destroying my life. I said I would never get over it. She tried to placate me with reassurances that she would take care of me and someone else would come along. But that only enraged me more." Guiltily, Lisa admits: "At one point I felt the only way I'd break free of my mother would be if she were dead. I actually told myself, 'You're not going to be a separate individual until she dies.'"

Lisa is both surprised and relieved to learn how common such desperate thoughts are among people who have been suffocated by their parents and are struggling to set their own limits. I remind her of Philip Roth's pungent observation in *Portnoy's Complaint*: "Good Christ, a Jewish man with parents alive is a fifteen-year-old boy, and will remain a fifteen-year-old boy till *they die!*"

"But I was afraid to tell my mother that," Lisa counters, "because even though I said some wild things to her, I know that I love her, too. I always kept a certain perspective on how marvelous she is. Now I know I can't change her—nor do I really want to change her—I just don't want her to try to run my life."

For Lisa, the struggle to become a separate individual capable of thinking and acting for herself was an ordeal by fire. She had gone from an overprotective home life, the togetherness life of the Fifties, where her mother shielded her from unpleasantness and fought all her battles for her, to an overprotective love relationship with an older man while the nuns watched over her in a secluded private Catholic girls' college. And then it was senior year, and graduation came, and the boyfriend left, and now she was faced with the world. "I had no idea that I was capable of frying an egg," Lisa says, "and I ended up living in an apartment alone in a different city from my parents and starting a new job."

Out on her own, with none of the usual support systems around her, Lisa was overwhelmed by anxiety and dread. She was so out of control that her first visit to a psychiatrist was prompted by the fear that she was going to commit suicide by accident: "When I was by myself," says Lisa, "my thoughts kept going off the deep end and terrifying me. I had fears of insanity, fears of passing out, fears of leaving the house, fears of traveling. My deepest, darkest fear about being alone was that I was so crazy and so out of it and had nobody there to help me or tell me what to do that I'd make a mistake and commit suicide." Lisa realizes that she was particularly vulnerable to feelings of helplessness at the time, but she also attributes "that whole fear business" to her family history. Her father, an immigrant engineer from southern Italy who came to this country a few years before the Depression, passed along the folk insecurity common in immigrant families. From her mother, an Italian-American artist who was born here but has always been highly susceptible to anxiety, Lisa learned how to be afraid of everything. "In my earlier years she would wake up in the middle of the night with an anxiety attack, and I would hold her hand. I learned the behavior from her and then realized I was the same way—but I knew I had to do something about it."

Success was one of the major things Lisa's mother told her to fear, which seems like strange advice to give a daughter growing up in "the Decade of Women." Over ten years have passed since Matina Horner's research on the female "fear of success" syndrome became common knowledge, but like many women her age, Lisa has still felt the sting of ambivalence about her achievements. Always ambitious, she has had to contend with her mother's fears and superstitions about success. Says Lisa: "I've had a million wonderful achievements—either handed to me or worked for, I'm not sure—and those were my most frightening times. I had been told so often when success came, 'Don't be too excited because even though you're up now, something is going to come along and you're going to be down again. Don't enjoy.' " Lisa recalls some specific incidents, once when she was the Homecoming Queen in high school and another when she was singled out by *Philadelphia* magazine as one of "76 People to Look for in '76." When she breathlessly told her parents the news, their only reaction was concern that she would get obscene phone calls because her photograph and name had been published. "And wouldn't you know," Lisa says wryly, "that's exactly what happened. Both times I got a lot of calls in the middle of the night, and it frightened me to have them wake me up and use my name. I had the weirdest feeling that it was like my mother saying, 'I told you so. Don't try to achieve fame and fortune because when you do, you're going to have a far greater set of problems.' "

Was there competition on her mother's part? A fear of losing Lisa if she got to be too successful?

"Yes, I think she was afraid of not being able to share my success," Lisa agrees. "In her mind, she would no longer be her part of my life, the part asking for her aid, because I just would have gone so far that I'd have actually left her in the dust and would never come back." Lisa says that her father and brother also fear success. "They get so overwhelmed by whoever else is out there that they're discouraged from even competing. I still have trouble with success, but I don't avoid it. I'm aware that once I get there my mother will tell me why it's a little screwy, but inside I'm driven to want to achieve."

The strength of Lisa's drive to achieve is apparent in her rapid rise in television from research to head of the research department to writer, a rise all the more remarkable considering the precarious emotional state Lisa was in when she first began working. As she describes it now, the period following her breakup with the doctor and her separation from her possessive, overprotective mother was as profoundly traumatic as a second psychological birth. "I was desperately trying to get other people to tell me that I was okay," says Lisa, "but when they would say I was all right, I didn't believe them. I reached out to everything—and I mean *everything*. I went to Gestalt sessions to relieve some of my anxiety, I did TM, I did yoga exercises, I became involved with the Church, I got into astrology, I did *I Ching*, I went to psychics." She stayed away from LSD and marijuana, which she had enjoyed with the doctor, because they brought out her black thoughts. She admits with some chagrin: "I would only date therapists, and when I wasn't getting help from them anymore, then that was the end of the relationship."

Like many other verbal people who have told me that they turned to writing about their emotions to pull together their disintegrating sense of self, Lisa found that the daily journal she kept was the instrument of her self-creation. "There was no real Lisa that I could create by myself," she says. "It was only the Lisa that people were creating around me. People were telling me, 'You are "sweet" and "nice," and I'd say, 'I am? Is that right?' I would rely implicitly on all these people who were telling me what I was, but they weren't satisfying me because I knew they didn't know me. And that night I'd go home and write down exactly what my feelings were: 'I am angry,' 'I am scared,' 'I hate Mother for doing this to me.' I'd write the things the people had said I was and then I'd contradict them one by one: 'I'm not that way; I'm really this way.' Through all the negative images of what I *wasn't*, the positive me began to emerge. And then I was formed. I was the one who formed and shaped myself because it was in my own writing about how I *really* was that the creation of myself occurred."

Lisa's writings provided the mirroring of her True Self that she had never received in her overprotective environment. Through her journal she was able to bounce off the distorted reflections others had of her in order to form a more realistic self-representation. She is embarrassed at having used people so shamelessly to help her come to know herself, but the others, while poorly served by her as "self-objects," were truly indispensable. As sociologist Erving Goffman has explained, the need for one's own identity is inseparably intertwined with the need for intimacy, making genuine self-knowledge impossible except as an outcome of disclosing the self to another. He says, "What the individual is for himself is not something that he invented. It is what his significant others have come to see that he should be, what they have come to treat him as being, and what in consequence he must treat himself as being if he is to deal with their dealings with him."

How could Lisa learn to treat herself as an autonomous human being in charge of her own life when her mother had always treated her as symbiotically dependent? Says Lisa: "Gestalt therapy taught me how to clarify what I wanted to be—I didn't know that before—and to express anger to my mother that I had never been able to express. I couldn't use the harsh Gestalt language—*I want, I am, I need*—because I didn't want to break off communication with my mother or make her think I was nuts. So when I approached her, I used enough politeness and diplomacy to reach an understanding between us."

When Lisa confronted her parents, she began to see them and herself in a new light. "My father and I would take these long walks," Lisa recalls, "and he finally revealed some of the things that he had gone through as an immigrant boy of nineteen who had a mother and two sisters to support and couldn't find work. He told me how much it hurt him when the people here made fun of him and he had to repeat his education all over again because they wouldn't honor his degree. When he said he'd gone to see a psychiatrist, I couldn't believe it! I was sure my parents would think I was crazy for wanting to see one. And then my mother started telling me about her broken heart over her own four-year relationship that didn't work out. She was so afraid she'd never be married, she didn't want to leave her bed. Her parents' divorce had brought shame on the family, and she was worried about that, too. Her fear of death, she said, came from her boarding school days when the nuns kept reminding her that you had to be good because you could die any minute."

Lisa made her parents repeat these stories to her over and over again. "I needed to know where they were coming from," she says. "I'd been acting as if they hadn't lived because they never said anything about their experiences. I didn't feel judgmental toward them, just grateful that I had finally learned about their lives so I could figure out mine."

Out of these conversations, Lisa pieced together the truth: that her mother's desperate pressure on Lisa to get married and her wariness toward Lisa's success were more a function of her mother's idiosyncratic fears than of reality. "I'm still angry at my mother for pushing marriage as the only fulfilling life," says Lisa, "because I know her life is *not* that fulfilling simply as a married person. She's an artist who doesn't paint anymore, and I'm seeing that she's not so happy with my father now because that's the only focus she's got. Her life was most fulfilling when she was *balancing* her art and her marriage."

Her mother still gives art lessons at home, but Lisa feels that's a cop-out. "When she was in New York, she was successful as an artist, but when she moved to Scranton, people ridiculed her. She just went into a shell about it. I think that when my brother and I came along, she decided to raise us, and that was it. Now she's afraid her talent may be stale."

Although Lisa knows *rationally* that she should not feel obligated to get married because that's what her mother wants, Lisa says: "I do feel guilty in the sense of having disappointed her because my life is not going the way she would like it to go. I constantly explain that what I'm doing now is good and if she'd change her thinking a little bit, she'd appreciate it. When my parents come to see me, I bring them to the station and show them tapes, research handbooks that I've written, scripts I've done. I let them know that I'm doing something I really love to do and that I want them to be part of it, even though it's not what they think I should be doing." Lisa laughs ruefully. "Now my mother's dreams are bigger than ever. She had no idea I had talent in this field, so now her goals for me are: marriage, beyond TV to Hollywood, and then you can have everything."

Whether married or not, most of Lisa's contemporaries are going through the same struggle to find the fine balance between dependence and independence, between autonomy and attachment. If they are single and involved with a lover, as Lisa currently is, they worry that they may be sacrificing too much professionally for the sake of the relationship. If all they have is their profession, it doesn't seem to be enough. And if they are married, they're afraid that the traditional role will not be what they want.

"Sooner or later, I think everyone meets their Waterloo," says Lisa. "I have a female friend who was a whiz in law school and won't get a job. She's totally addicted to marijuana and has to have a joint the minute she wakes up. Without some sort of cloud, she can't face the pressures of the day or the questions about herself that she hasn't answered. A male friend of mine went to dental school and doesn't want to be a dentist—he just wants to keep going to school. I have another friend who is a physician and doesn't think she will ever practice medicine. As soon as she became a doctor she went right back to med school and began teaching." Lisa maintains that her friends love school because school is a shelter for them. "They're afraid," she explains. "When I talk to them, their attitude is, 'Don't put me out in that world.' They look at me as odd because they can't believe that I can be happy and survive in a world where there is no structure."

Her married friends from her college days, Lisa feels, are no different. "In college they were a lot more independent than I was," she says, "because their parents didn't protect them. I was very jealous of all the traveling they'd done and the experiences they'd had. Their worldliness and their parents' money gave them a sense of security. But when they got out of college and were worried about being on their own without money, they freaked out. They grabbed for men who were making money in the businesses back home and got married immediately." At Christmastime, when Lisa went home and visited these friends at parties, the constrictiveness of their lives appalled her. "Every family was a carbon copy of the one before," she says. "The men were in the basement talking about hunting and the women were upstairs talking about their babies. *These were people my age.* That scared me. I felt so cramped and shaken by what I saw and their envy of my freedom that I couldn't even think in terms of an alternative, like maybe I'll get married and not have children. I suppose I could do that, but I think part of the fear of commitment stems from the family structure as it is. There's a fear that that's the only way you *can* have a family."

Lisa feels that her friends who ducked into marriage as a shelter as soon as they hit the sunlight after college would have fared much worse than she did had they been forced to be on their own. "I was too close with my mother, but even so, I was *close* with her," she says. "They were not close with their families at all because their parents were off doing what they wanted to do. My friends had nothing to go on except material rewards and a lot of religious absolutes about right and wrong. They weren't independent enough to live with somebody, so it was marriage or nothing."

Lisa's point is that while her mother's possessiveness submerged her own sense of limits, the love she'd received had also armed her to fight back against coercion. Out in the void of an external world where there were no guideposts anymore, that little bit of spine gave her an advantage over her more vulnerable peers who'd been subjected to the permissiveness of negligence. Lisa had suffered from "too good" mothering; her friends had suffered from not enough. As victims of contradictory authorities and that confused and inconsistent style of parenting adopted by adults of the Fifties and Sixties, Lisa's friends lacked her determination to pull herself out of the dependency trap and stay out. "There's a trigger inside me that tells me when to step back from a situation before I lose control and become possessed by it," says Lisa. She still has an interest in Eastern mysticism and is open to exploring new psychologies, but she says she now has the ability to discard the false and the dangerous. "I didn't do est," Lisa explains, "because it is unbelievably coercive. I went to one of their meetings, and they called me and called me and harassed me, but I just refused. I have to walk toward something myself; I can't be pushed into it." Lisa was surprised when people criticized her for constantly experimenting and not sticking to anything. "I'm not upset that I didn't become a follower," she says. "I think an obsession with anything is an escape—it's an escape from yourself and a projection of all of your responsibility and guilt. When you start melting and merging into something and you're not sure of anything else about yourself except for that, then you're in trouble."

Self-preoccupation, Lisa discovered, has its limits too. "After a while, my life had become so centered around myself," she says, "that I began to feel a lack of depth. It bothered me that I wasn't *giving* anything as a human being. I felt I should be leading Girl Scouts or something." Lisa explains that she grew up in a town where charity work was an important part of the community ethic. "I don't subscribe to all that religious dogma that you have to join seven churches and do your good deed one time a week or something," she says, "but somehow I feel that we've gotten a little too far away from that old community standard that we must give back."

Lisa wanted to do something for others, not as a ritualistic palliative for guilt or boredom, but as an act of sharing. She found the answer in friendship. "After I had gone through all of this self-exploration," she says, "I realized that what I can do for other people is to understand them. I can take what I've learned about myself and empathize with their problems. It's so enriching to be able to connect with another human being that way."

If this sounds like a trite solution to the crisis of intimacy versus isolation in an autistic age, consider this passage from *The Women's Room,* in which Mira, the mature student who has returned to college after her divorce, ponders why her classmates at Harvard hold her in such high esteem:

They called her wonderful. Thank you, thank you, Mira. You've helped me so much. I feel so much better. You're wonderful. When she did not know, really, what they were feeling, did not understand their particular pain, their particular need. How then could she help? She had not helped, she had done nothing but listen. Yet they were not lying. She had helped, listening. She had not denied their truths. She had not asked, by flicker or gesture, that they censor themselves. She had not insisted that they be happy people with happy problems, that their problem was that they had not learned how to fit into a rational and comprehensible world. All she had done was, unblinking and uninterrupting, let them be whatever horrible creatures they thought they were. . . .

The idea seemed a great truth when it descended upon her

around four in the morning: a space to be and a witness (flawed as any witness had to be). It was enough, or if not enough, it was all, all that we could do, in the end, for each other.

Slowly, as Lisa assembled the pieces of the mainland of her autonomy—a sense of identity, a sense of purpose, a sense of direction—she began to build her personal world. This was different from the *private* world glorified by the leaders of the cult of self-worship, in whose eyes the basic unit of society was "the individual, who is able financially to live alone and find amiable companionship, sex, and other recreation, without having to provide anything more than that in return." Lisa's personal world included that private interior landscape that so many people in the Seventies seemed content to cultivate endlessly, but it also encompassed connectedness with others. The more autonomous she grew, the more important relationship became to her—not simply the self-serving exchange type of relationship based on a pragmatic trade-off or complement of needs—but deeply emotional relationships with loved ones and friends who shared a common set of concerns, common projects, a common life.

Like many of her contemporaries, Lisa has found her love relationship to be a continuing uphill battle against his fear of commitment and her anxiety about being abandoned. Yet Lisa has been willing to fight for this relationship rather than succumb to her normal pattern of bowing out if another woman is involved. When Lisa started dating Don, a television producer who was then twenty-seven and working at the same TV station, he was still seeing the woman with whom he'd been having a serious relationship for six years. It took seven months of Don's erratic seesawing back and forth before Lisa, debilitated by bouts of jealousy, gave him an ultimatum: her or me. Don gave the other woman up, and he and Lisa began their own volatile seesaw relationship, filled with false endings and fresh starts, that has lasted several years.

"Women's liberation has gotten men to investigate their own feelings," says Lisa, "but it has also made them very defensive. The sensitive, emotionally open men like Don are very protective of their inner nature because they think we might have something over them now. They're afraid of our power." Lisa explains that the assertiveness and independence of women have confused men and made them distrustful. "They don't know what their role is in a relationship anymore except that they can't resort to being openly macho. And they don't know what we're going to come up with because they think we have some key to ourselves and we're going to be the dominant person in the relationship, the one who calls the shots, and they haven't worked that out yet." Lisa laughs abruptly and adds, "I haven't worked that out yet either, and that's the killer."

For Lisa, the most frustrating aspect of the relationship has been Don's ambivalence. While he has adventurously carved out a separate identity in his work, in his attitude toward women he has been less successful in shedding some of the superficial values beamed at him by his social family in Chicago. "His mother is so smooth and subtle in her manipulation of him that Don isn't even aware of it," Lisa says. "After he and I had gotten really close, his mother signaled her disapproval of me by telling him that he should date around because he was too young to get married. Yet, six months earlier, when he was so heavily involved with the socialite, his mother said, 'Marry her.' "

At his mother's suggestion, Don decided that he should "sow his wild oats," as he expressed it to Lisa, and date others. In the Fifties, Don would have been an anomaly. Any twenty-eight-year-old man earning twenty-five thousand dollars a year in a "defiantly aggressive" field like television production would have long since passed the point where he could be told by his mother that he was too young to get married, much less listen to her. The prolonged dependency on their parents by the Coddled Generation in the Seventies was not simply a matter of our degree-happy society's making it impossible for them to earn a living before the age of thirty. Their dependency was also very much an outgrowth of the permissiveness of negligence and, as such, it reflected a desperate longing to remain protected by parents who were a source of money, if not the liberating kind of love that fosters growth. Don, who was reared by governesses and rarely saw his mother when he was little, may be an exaggerated case. But he is still typical of many upper-middle-class children of the decade whose *appearance* of independence, particularly if they did manage to become financially self-sustaining, was only a façade. No matter how well they had gotten it together in their work life, emotionally, they were often still in parental custody.

At first, Don's announcement that he wanted to see other women filled Lisa with panic that she would be abandoned as well as a feeling of indignation. But when she examined the situation more closely, she had a sense of freedom and relief. "I realized that we'd been together too much and that we were bored and stale and getting on each other's nerves. We had both shut out every other part of our lives. I hadn't been aware of it, but I missed my activities and my friends. I stopped being defensive and thought, 'I won't concentrate on what he's doing; I'll just concentrate on what I'd like to do again.'"

Lisa was more in control of her feelings and self than she'd ever been. She had learned from the breakup of her last relationship not to indulge in obsessive thoughts about Don's abandonment of her and jealous fantasies of him with other women. "I just stopped the thoughts," Lisa says. "I knew they were destructive, and I said to myself, *stop it!* Five years ago, when that other relationship was falling apart, nobody could tell me to do that. I didn't even know what they were talking about. But somehow, some survival instinct in me said, 'You're not going to go through this again' because in many ways it was a waste of my time."

Lisa decided that getting dates was Don's issue, not hers, so she studiously avoided the singles scene. "By the time I'd met Don," she explains, "I'd already gone through that rebellious stage of jumping from one intimate relationship to another, sometimes juggling two at once for a couple of weeks, in order to prove that I could do just what a man does. But juggling relationships didn't work because my emotions were tied in with sex. Once I forgave myself for having an emotional tie, I didn't need to be rebellious anymore. Intimacy is a statement of some sort, and if I'm going to be intimate with a lot of people, then it means nothing—I'm not doing justice to myself."

Instead of frantically looking for dates, Lisa joined the racquetball club, started a ballet class, went to New York for a weekend, took a trip to Paris in the spring with a woman friend—and then Don was back.

I wish I could say that the story has a happy ending, but all it has is an ambiguous one. There's a lesson in the ambiguity, though. When I first saw Lisa in January 1978, she was still head of the research department at the station, and she stressed that her work was fundamental to her sense of identity. It was part of her "essence," as she called it, and not merely something to sustain her between relationships. Yet she understood that it was only *part* of her identity rather than the whole thing. As horrified as she was by the automated "eaglets" who were still living in conformity to the "happy housewife heroine" role, she was even more horrified by the driven, dehumanized women careerists she saw around her who lived only for their work. In fact, in her hierarchy of needs, Lisa put career advancement second after Don—even though she was well aware that Don put career advancement before her. Somehow reciprocity eluded her. As autonomous as she'd become in some respects, she still could not overcome her childhood conviction of the superiority of the male and her subsequent need to let her life revolve around his.

The following is a brief excerpt from that interview:

M.S.: What about your long-term career goals?

LISA: That's the difference between the female and the male—I don't have long-term goals. Ten years from now I have no idea where I'll be professionally, and I haven't given it a great deal of thought.

M.S.: What about Don?

LISA: Sure, Don's got that together. He has a five-year plan. From producing he wants to get into executive producing, and then he wants to get into management, where he doesn't have to work as hard, but make a lot of money.

M.S.: How does he propose to implement his plan?

LISA: Well, he makes sure he knows what the other markets want, and when the opportunities come, he applies. Before he got this producer's job, he went out to Los Angeles for interviews—he really moved. Now he's keeping in touch with all the contacts he has across the country to get that executive producer job. He plans to devote two and a half years to that, and then he'll figure out from that level where to go.

M.S.: Your insecurity about him seems to have a basis in reality. We often tend to psychologize everything, but listen, here's a guy who might not be here two years from now. Does his mobility ever cross your mind?

LISA: No.

M.S.: That doesn't bother you? Why?

LISA: I don't know—I guess because I have time to think about that. But I haven't moved up myself, and I probably should be thinking about it because my job is getting to the point where I could be advancing. My next step would be a writer's job, but I'd have to work weekends and nights. That would change our relationship entirely, and that scares me.

Six months later when I met with Lisa again, I learned that Don had moved to Chicago. He'd been out there a while, already hard at work on the next phase of his five-year plan. He came to Philadelphia to see Lisa whenever he could, but weeks would go by when they were not together. Lisa was brave about it, but it was clear that the difficulties of maintaining a commuting relationship were beginning to appear insurmountable to her. She was planning to take some time off from work, at Don's request, so they could vacation together. She seemed vaguely hopeful that the vacation would in some way restore the intensity of the relationship and resolve their problem.

The next time I talked to Lisa, the decade was drawing to a close, and so, she said, was her relationship with Don. They had just returned from a romantic idyll in Aruba, and the failure of her attempt to elicit a firm commitment from him had left her angry and disillusioned. Don was still coming to see her, but her feeling for him had eroded. She had advanced to the writer's job and was pouring herself into her work now—every night and weekend. When I asked her what would happen to her job if Don got over his commitment-phobia and proposed marriage, her ready answer sounded as if she'd lifted a page from Don's five-year plan. "I'm situated now so that I could relocate to Chicago and get the same job there," she said. "But I don't think that's likely to happen," she added wearily. She sounded more and more disgusted by the minute. "I'm not even asking him for an immediate answer—just some assurance of where we'll be six months from now—and he can't even give me that. He's so confused. Each time we talk, I get a hundred different messages from him, and they all add up to the same thing—fear."

And then Lisa said something that I heard so often from women in the Seventies it began to sound like an echo. It was an echo reverberating among women who'd been burned by the male fear of commitment badly enough that they decided it was better to lie alone at night and curse the darkness rather than light the fires of passion again. "Love is nice," she said, "but I don't know if it's necessary."

THE LARGER PICTURE

The cynicism and disillusionment that soured the world of intimate relationships in the Seventies was more than just a by-product of the revolution against traditional sexual roles. Our lack of trust in each other in our private lives was also a reflection of our enormous loss of confidence in the American government at large. When the Vietnam War finally ended in 1973, only to be followed by the fall of South Vietnam and Cambodia to the Communists the next year, the myth of our invincibility as a world power was shattered.

Even more frightening was our apparent inability to govern ourselves at home. The decade was rife with the stench of power gone corrupt. It was enough to make *all* of us feel like a disadvantaged and exploited minority—the spectacle of Richard Nixon resigning from the presidency in disgrace in 1974 and receiving, without having admitted his guilt, a "full, free and absolute pardon" that same year from Gerald Ford; the continuous spillage of wrongdoings that came out of the Watergate trial and other federal investigations; the revelations of the illegal harassment and abuse of unsuspecting U.S. citizens by the CIA and the FBI. Confronted daily with the treachery of the people we had chosen to protect us, we succumbed to a monumental skepticism about the motives of our institutions and authorities. In the face of a steadily worsening economic condition that neither Ford nor the subsequent Carter administration was able to resolve—soaring costs, the shrinking dollar, rising interest rates, sinking energy supplies, more married women working, fewer jobs for graduates—our skepticism hardened into a fixed belief that it was useless to try to do anything except save our own skins.

Frustration, anxiety, and a pessimistic uncertainty about the future, coupled with a profound loss of faith in authority figures of every stripe, triggered an orgy of destructive escapism. At times, the destructive quality of the escapism was frighteningly apparent, as on the night of December 3, 1979, when eleven youthful rock music fans were trampled to death outside Cincinnati's Riverfront Coliseum in a stampede for unreserved seats to a Who concert.

But whether the destructiveness flared openly into violence or crime or burned away quietly at people's insides in self-contained alcoholism, drug abuse, or depression, it was there. It was fueled by the powerlessness and rage we felt at having surrendered control over our lives to authorities who had violated our trust and had deeply disillusioned us. Part of it was our own fault. After the enormous dislocations of the Sixties, we had wearied of social protest and had crawled back into the cave of isolated personal fulfillment. We had never been willing to accept a shift in the balance of control between the leaders of our institutions and ourselves. It was easier to believe that we were cut off from power over the political, economic, and social institutions that shaped our lives than it was to believe that we could make effective choices and bring about change. Like our children, by whom we still oriented ourselves, we preferred simply to change leaders and hope that the next one would fulfill our fantasy of unconditional love by providing unlimited economic abundance, employment, and answers to all of our personal problems in living.

When, by the end of the decade, it began to appear that shortages and limitations would be the shape of things to come in the Eighties, we did not want to hear about austerity and sacrifice. We were still hooked on the greed and envy that had been bred into our natures in a competitive society. And having learned overindulgence and irresponsibility as a result of our youth-direction, we had become unable to deal with scarcity in any other fashion except to trample over everyone else to get there first. We had come to the end of a period of breathtaking technological advancement with our moral and social development back in the Stone Age. What had we learned from civilization and its discontents? This lesson, succinctly phrased by composer-lyricist Stephen Sondheim in *Sweeney Todd*, the cannibalistic musical that was the feast of Broadway in 1979:

> *The history of the world, my sweet, is who*
> *gets eaten, and who gets to eat.*

In its own crooked way, the Seventies were the decade when we struggled to achieve a measure of autonomy and independence, even at the cost of isolation. The enormous popularity of Werner Erhard's est was at once a symptom of the cultural problem of symbiotic dependence on "magical helpers" and an attempt to provide a cure by more of the same. For some people—the blamers, specifically—est was effective in motivating them to wrest the initiative and direction for their actions from parent figures and do things on their own. It was not, however, as effective in helping them to deal with the *consequences* of their actions or to cope realistically with their own or others' limitations.

In keeping with the Seventies search for unconditional love, est offered the infant's archaic fantasy of grandiose omnipotence: Each of us is totally responsible for everything we experience as happening to us in life. This is not much different from the hungry baby's imagining that by crying for milk he has created his mother's breast. As one est graduate explained the philosophy to me: "If you allow yourself to *experience* whatever it is that's hanging you up, then you are in control of it."

While this belief in the captaincy of one's soul may be useful at times to help us ride through attacks of self-doubt, as the only way of organizing reality it is a hopelessly utopian concept. If we hold ourselves out to be the authors of all that we experience, the implication is that we will write only the best outcomes for ourselves. But there is a limit to what we can will, particularly if we ignore the role of judgment in the choices we make. As Erikson has said: "Man must learn to will what can be, to renounce as not worth willing what cannot be, and to believe he willed what is inevitable."

We are always better advised to test "expectable reality" rather than dwell in the realm of fantasy, but not without recognizing that the claims of others and the forces of nature are also at play. In their eagerness to flog people into the more assertive style that our uncertain economic and social times called for, est and the other actualization philosophies revived the old "Invictus" illusion of unlimited free choice. This was the only vision that was salable to people who were under the gun to keep up with everyone else's greed. In an era epitomized by a "new selfishness without guilt," in media expert Frank Mankiewicz's phrase, people had to believe that natural and moral limitations simply did not apply to them as individuals.

Est fed into the already overblown narcissism of the Seventies by making the individual's perception of reality the only one that counted. While the intention may have been to restore the primacy of the self in decision-making, the effect was to defeat the construction of a personal world. The individual became the monarch of his private "space," and anyone who was not of like mind was excluded from the kingdom. In interpersonal relationships the estian deflected differences of opinion away from himself by using his one-sided responsibility like a plastic shield: "I'm responsible for me; how you see it is your own problem."

The futility of trying to overcome communication barriers with this stance was made obvious to me by the experience of a couple I know who went through the est program at different times. The couple was also undergoing marital therapy because the wife, who had serious emotional problems, was unable to listen to her husband when he tried to communicate with her. Although advised by the therapist against taking est, the wife went anyway and was told by the trainer: "If your husband wants to communicate with you, he can." When the husband heard this, he scoffed: "People are encouraged to put the burden of the problem where they *think* the problem is. If I think my wife is selfish, can I say it's *her* problem? There are reasons why I can't communicate with her. But it's not *my* problem—she contributes to it." They were subsequently divorced.

The tragedy of the era was our enormous vulnerability in a world where all the old forms of connectedness had broken down. We had grown up expecting that *someone* would always take care of us—our families, the government, God—and now we were expected to produce, like magicians pulling a rabbit from a hat, a full-fledged autonomous self.

Unfortunately, the self many of us had was still mired in dependency, cursed with feelings of emptiness and insecurity, because few of us had been blessed with the situation that fosters independence in the developing person. That situation, according to child development specialist Urie Bronfenbrenner, involves a relationship between developing children and their important loved ones wherein the adults themselves feel effective in the larger society and communicate to the children a sense that the external world can be understood and controlled. In circumstances that are comfortable, supportive, and fun, the child observes the important loved person perform increasingly complicated activities and then does these activities jointly with the same person. Encouraged to question, learn, and grow, the child gradually assumes the initiative for the activities and the control over them from the adult.

The absurdity of Cow Palaces full of adults pinning their hopes on Werner Erhard to toilet train and harangue them into self-reliance and emotional maturity in sixty hours would have been laughable had it not been so pathetic. In a nation that gobbles Valium like peanuts at a cocktail party, nothing succeeds like a quick cure. Although it strains credulity to believe that the mistakes of generations could be undone in two weekends, conversions have been known to happen. Still, paying steep prices to suffer gladly methods that duplicate the *bad* parenting many of us were subjected to in childhood resembled nothing so much as a repetition compulsion. The avidity with which Americans sought out such drastic miracle "cures" in the Seventies said something about self-impotence as a national disease. So did the alarming increase in alcohol abuse and pill-popping. There was no mistaking the roar of laughter provoked by the Valium scene in *Starting Over,* the popular movie comedy about the difficulties of a newly separated man. It was the roar of recognition that came from the audience when the physician attending Burt Reynolds during his separation anxiety attack in a department store asks, "Does anyone have any Valium?", and the crowd of bystanders comes up with an avalanche of pills. Our dependency on mood-altering pills and alcohol was clear evidence of the country's malaise, as Jimmy Carter called it, and another indication that the Me Decade should more properly have been called the "*Help* Me Decade."

Even the outrageous expenditure of money on designer clothes or other personal extravagances during the worst recession we'd had in forty years was not a simple matter of vanity. Much of it was the kind of self-soothing activity people commonly indulge in as a way of coping with the loss of security—"bingeing out" on food, for example, in order to relieve feelings of anxiety or depression. For others, as Lisa Sandrone explained it to me, the buying of goods was not merely accumulation for its own sake, as it was in the Fifties, but a desperate attempt to stake out an individual identity. Describing her life after she'd moved away from her parents, Lisa said: "I got very involved in possession, but it wasn't a materialistic thing. I didn't know what it was. I was frightened by it and thought I must be selfish to want all these things. And then I realized that I wanted to pick out *my own* things instead of having them picked out for me. I wanted my own tea kettle, my own books. I saw that this was an identity for me. This is my taste in whatever it is—it's *mine.*"

THE CLASS OF '83

The strange apathy that persisted throughout the Seventies was also seen as a hallmark of the cultural narcissism of the decade. College professors claimed that students were so despondent about both the past and the future that they had suffered a diminished capacity for connectedness with others and a pervasive sense of powerlessness concerning social issues. A 1979 survey of 17,000 high school seniors, half of whom were about to enter college—the class of 1983—revealed what appeared to their critics to be very "banal" aspirations. Asked to rate the importance of a list of major life goals, the highest proportion of college-bound students (79 percent) rated "Having a good marriage and family life" as their highest priority, whereas only 23 percent listed "Making a contribution to society" as extremely important. The students considered "Having strong friendships" (69 percent) and "Finding purpose and meaning in life" (66 percent) more important than "Finding steady work" (65 percent) and being successful at it (63 percent). Surprisingly, only 16 percent of the students felt that "Having lots of money" was important. But fewer still—a mere 10 percent—regarded "Being a leader in my community" as a goal of high value.

Compared to the campus activists of the previous decade, students in the Seventies seemed to have retreated to a private rest home where their heroes, causes, and visions were suffused with all the fiery idealism of a warm security blanket. Those who were out of college and working—the former radicals and flower children—appeared to lack a passionate commitment to anything except tennis and jogging. Their curiously dispassionate attitude toward their work, like their phobic noncommitment to relationships, moved Herbert Hendin to complain that "an increasingly high percentage of young adults even in challenging professions regard work as merely the means to money for leisure."

Some argued that this was a good sign. They pointed to the increased importance of leisure as evidence of a shift away from the driven 1950s work ethic to more humanistic work-related values. Money had finally come to be recognized as a means to an end, they said, rather than an end in itself. It was no longer merely an empty symbol of ladder-climbing but a door-opener to activities that brought personal enjoyment. Except for the compulsive women workaholics who represented a throwback to the "organization men" of twenty years ago, "New Breed" people were learning not to define themselves through their work role and, consequently, not to sacrifice their conflicting personal desires.

In all fairness, the changed attitudes toward work expressed by many young married men and women I interviewed in the late 1970s revealed that they were committed to their work, but not with such a demonic passion for success that it left them no time for family, friends, or the pursuit of pleasure.

By ranking a good marriage and family life and strong friendships even higher on their list of priorities than success at work or a contribution to society, the class of '83 would seem to be continuing on the right track. I do not find their ambitions and dreams "hopeless," as one critic called them, because they are limited only to "the kind of things that they can count upon their fingers." Having watched cultural supports for loyalty to one's intimates crumble before their very eyes, leaving people abandoned and afraid, these students have learned only too well that connectedness begins at home. They are seeking to work out a grounding of stability in their personal worlds— a balanced and flexible integration of love and work—out of which will come their contribution to society. Even if they do not envision themselves to be "stars," in Hesse's words, neither do they see themselves as "falling leaves."

These will be the kinds of careerists who will not be "absent" parents to their children, if they have them, or will not subject their intimates to ten relocations to different cities as they climb up the corporate ladder to isolated splendor. In their search for meaning and satisfaction in life, they will also have the advantage over their rebelliously idealistic predecessors in the 1960s. As children, they were witnesses to the culture shock brought about by the fragmentation of marriage and family life, and they know that enduring social ties, far from being a hindrance to overall life satisfaction, have consistently proved central to it. As workers, their contribution to society will be to force the workplace to reorder *its* priorities—a movement that is already under way. "One of the biggest problems corporations will be having throughout the Eighties," says the New York director of transfers for the Colgate-Palmolive Company, "is that a man won't move if his wife doesn't want to."

Mundane as their aspirations strike the high-minded, the priorities of the class of 1983 signify the extent to which the instant gratification concept of personal fulfillment had been tried throughout the Seventies and been found wanting. Much to their surprise, those who had tried to "find themselves" by escaping the pursuit of definite goals or social responsibilities discovered that without these touchstones, there was no self. There was only the same old desperate searching to fill the emptiness. The greedy, exploitative philosophy of personal fulfillment as enunciated by Charles Reich did not "green" America so much as alienate, confuse, and fragment the nation into a jumbled mass of self-interested units pressing single-issue claims.

With the approach of the Eighties, the historians announced that our decade-long scavenger search for self among the ruins of our institutions had led our country to an unfamiliar territory with sharply defined parameters—the new Age of Limits. Inflation and the Arab oil embargo had shown us the limits of our economic power; Three Mile Island had shown us the limits of our nuclear power; Watergate and the Ayatollah Ruhollah Khomeini had shown us the limits of our political power; and the doubled divorce rate between 1970 and 1978 had shown us the limits of love.

In the new age, finding our *inner* limits—and reshaping our cultural standards and institutions to accord with them—is imperative not only for our own personal fulfillment, but as a matter of survival. We have learned that unquestioning conformity to the "rules of the game" is not the answer, but neither is the narcissistic indulgence of the imperial self.

We did not listen when futurologist Alvin Toffler warned us at the outset of the Seventies that "choice may become overchoice, and freedom unfreedom." So eager were we to exercise our long-denied right to choose that we quickly produced an option glut, piling up one alternative after another in family life, work, subcultures, lifestyles, and relationships. We ruled nothing out as long as it promised change, novelty, excitement, and above all, transience. To ease our pangs of conscience—also temporary—we could rely on Toffler's book. We welcomed *Future Shock* as a socially redeeming rationalization for the recklessness with which we broke away from all of our old social ties and tore through new ones. But in the fine print it said:

Unless we are literally prepared to plunge backward into pre-technological primitivism, and accept all the consequences—a shorter, more brutal life, more disease, pain, starvation, fear, superstition, xenophobia, bigotry and so on—we shall move forward to more and more differentiated societies: This raises severe problems of social integration. What bonds of education, politics, culture must we fashion to tie the super-industrial order together into a functioning whole? Can this be accomplished? "This integration," writes Bertram M. Gross of Wayne State University, "must be based upon certain commonly accepted values or some degree of perceived interdependence, if not mutually acceptable objectives."

A society fast fragmenting at the level of values and life styles challenges all the old integrative mechanisms and cries out for a totally new basis for reconstitution. We have by no means yet found this basis. Yet if we shall face disturbing problems of social integration, we shall confront even more agonizing problems of individual integration. For the multiplication of life styles challenges our ability to hold the very self together.

To find that integrative mechanism based on commonly accepted values—our new sense of limits both as individuals and as a social order—is at once our challenge and our salvation.

THREE

GETTING
OUR BEARINGS

←————————————————————→

... the great thing in this world is not so much where we stand,
as in what direction we are moving:
To reach the port of heaven, we must sail sometimes with the wind
and sometimes against it—but we must sail, and not drift,
nor lie at anchor.

OLIVER WENDELL HOLMES

←————————— · —————————→

EIGHT

A NEW
LOOK AT
"PERSONAL FULFILLMENT"

What have we learned about ourselves and our society as we have watched the cultural pendulum swing uncontrollably from one polarity to another over the past five decades? We have seen how successive generations, first by abject compliance with authority, then by total renunciation of it, have struggled toward growth via a twisted route. Each, weakened by the failure of leadership of the previous generation, has tried to escape the responsibilities of freedom by clinging to the fantasy of finding unconditional love. But all of the ideologies that promised to make this impossible dream come true for a particular generation—the idyll of suburban togetherness, the doctrine of permissiveness, the philosophy of personal fulfillment—ended in frustration and disillusionment.

Yet, if we examine the dialectic interplay between our own stages of growth and the life cycle of these generations, we can begin to piece out a common pattern and make sense of it. As Carl Jung said: "Irrespective of our conscious convictions, each one of us, without exception, being a particle of the general mass, is somewhere attached to, colored by, or even undermined by the spirit which goes through the mass. Freedom stretches only as far as the limits of our consciousness."

In view of this interrelationship between the two life cycles—personal and cultural—we can see why we, as individuals and as a society, had to go through stages of growth marked by such violent conflict and disruption: the fragmenting of social bonds and beliefs, the tearing apart of the family, the devaluation of work, the flouting of authority, the narcissistic absorption in the self, the replacement of moral and ethical principles with a new cult of "selfishness without guilt."

Our exploration of the past has shown us that in our competitive, upwardly mobile society with its endlessly rising expectations, we started out in the Depression era with a massive injury to the social and individual self. The exploitation of the "general mass" by authoritarian political, economic, and cultural institutions paralleled the narcissistic use of children by their parents who trained them to forfeit their own identities in order to conform with traditional middle-class values. As stagnation set in, the growth of a separate identity for both parents and children could be accomplished only by challenging all of the old assumptions and violently breaking away.

From self-denial, people rocketed to the opposite extreme of self-gratification, feverishly trying to make up for lost time and experience. Gradually, however, after they had indulged their instinctual life long enough, many began to realize that self-indulgence and self-fulfillment were not the same. They recognized that out of the multiplicity of options confronting them, they would have to surrender those that were untenable for them. Trusting their own inner compass to set a direction for them in life consistent with their skills, they developed a sense of purpose and effectiveness. Self-reliance brought them a giant step closer to personal fulfillment—but not yet there. Only when they felt powerful enough to suspend self-concern and enjoy mutuality with others—a relationship to their intimates and the world based on acting for the common good out of choice rather than the compulsive trade-off of needs—did they experience personal fulfillment in its most complete and satisfying form.

THE NORMAL ROAD TO MATURITY

Several theorists have described a hierarchical sequence of stages all normal human beings go through in order to reach a level of social and moral maturity where unity of the self and genuine personal fulfillment coincide. Erik Erikson, Jean Piaget, and Lawrence Kohlberg have given us theories that deal, respectively, with the individual's psychosocial development, cognitive development, and the development of moral reasoning. Collectively, all of these theories present a similar hierarchy of growth. The early stages of childhood are characterized by egocentrism and unquestioning dependence on adults or external authority. In the intermediate stages, greater interaction with peers brings about more egalitarian, give-and-take relationships with others and a feeling of group solidarity. At the same time, a sense of autonomy develops, and moral absolutism gives way to the ability to think and act on one's own. At the highest, most mature level, unselfish concern for the welfare and rights of others and the conscious values of mutual understanding and sharing emerge as a matter of personal choice apart from the authority of the group.

Piaget's stages, for example, which deal with the progressive development of the understanding of rules and the ability to make moral judgments—*thought* processes that may influence moral *behavior* but are not necessarily closely connected to it—may be summarized as follows:

The first stage, called either "heteronomous morality" or "morality of restraint," describes the thinking of children under the ages of seven or eight. The child regards rules, obligations, and commands as "givens," unchangeable realities that are external to the mind. Justice is whatever authority (adults) or the law commands, and good is obedience. Thinking is characterized by beliefs in *immanent justice* (that Nature will punish transgressions) and in the *absoluteness* of values—everything is totally right or totally wrong. Egocentrism is reflected in the child's belief that everyone shares his or her perceptions. Consequences of acts are evaluated rather than the actor's intentions or motivations.

The second stage, one that might be called "semi-autonomous morality," begins at about the age of seven or eight. As the child interacts more extensively and mutually with peers, a sense of autonomy and egalitarianism becomes prominent. Equality begins to take priority over authority, and beliefs in immanent justice and severe punishments are superseded by ideas of reciprocal punishment (punishment fitting the crime).

The third, most mature stage, called "autonomous morality" or "morality of cooperation," generally evolves at about eleven or twelve years of age. Equity dominates the child's thinking about justice; extenuating circumstances, motivations, and intentions weigh heavily in making moral judgments. Egalitarian concepts of justice prevail; arbitrary punishments, immanent justice, moral absolutism, and blind obedience to authority are all rejected. Rules are considered to be products of social interaction and therefore changeable. Largely as a result of reciprocity and role-taking among peers, the child develops ideas of equality and cooperation, egocentrism diminishes, and concern for the welfare and rights of others increases.

How does this orderly progression from early egocentrism and dependence on external authority to the mature, autonomous "morality of cooperation," in Piaget's term, stack up with our own experience in recent decades? If, as Piaget claims, children generally reach the most mature stage of moral development at *eleven* or *twelve* years of age, is it all downhill after that? How do we account for the fact that so many of us today who *have* children of eleven or twelve or older are nowhere near the state of unselfish concern for other's welfare—even our own children's? Why is it that so many of us who have long since attained physical maturity may be capable of *thinking* at the highest level of autonomous morality, yet live lives marred by wretched confusion and ambivalence about our personal goals and standards?

Considering the zigzag, convoluted trajectory people in our competitive culture have often been forced to travel in order to reach true maturity and personal fulfillment, we can see the need for a new sequence of stages. The stages that exist in the literature describe the *normal* developmental pathway, but ours is a neurotic society--the culture of narcissism. The deep fault running through the strata of our crumbling social structure—the greed creed—has devalued the self into a marketable commodity and transformed the child, in Joseph Adelson's words, "from a creature to be nurtured and protected, to a perplexing problem that a good managerial intelligence will solve." Says Adelson:

> This narcissism (of the parents), whatever else it may produce—
> boredom or drug use or some form of fanaticism—will also produce a
> reactive narcissism in the child, partly because he models his
> parental modes, partly because his self-absorption is the best defense
> he can find to use against theirs. So he ends as one of the insulted
> and injured, and he cries out, in one language or another: "Me! Me!
> Look at me, pay attention to me, love me, admire me, tell me that I
> exist!"

Apart from the parent-child relationship, whether too distant or too close, our flawed cultural surroundings have played even more havoc with the development of a secure self in our society. The failure of our profit-motivated institutions to accommodate change without discarding major values that have become unpopular—like sexual fidelity in marriage, for example, or responsibility to one's children—have deprived people of that "second womb" Erikson calls essential to the formation of a unified personality:

> Defenseless as babies are, they have mothers at their command, families to protect the mothers, societies to support the structure of families, and traditions to give a cultural continuity to systems of tending and training. All of this, however, is necessary for the human infant to evolve humanly, for his environment must provide that outer wholeness and continuity which, like a second womb, permits the child to develop his separate capacities in distinct steps, and to unify them in a series of psychosocial crises.

The maturing adult needs this "second womb" of cultural continuity as much as the infant. Without it, our growth pattern is more likely to resemble the crazy quilt of dissonant extremes and counterreactions patched together by us in recent decades than the neat hierarchy of integrative stages that we find in textbooks.

THE WINDING ROAD TO PERSONAL FULFILLMENT

Those who have negotiated the rough road from False Self to True Self in our narcissistic culture have generally gone through four stages to personal fulfillment that represent a *recovery* of the self from fragmentation to a state of wholeness. For many people, a period of radical self-centeredness and violation of the codes of decent behavior—toward spouses and children or lovers as well as competitors in school and the workplace—was necessary and *was supported by the culture* as a corrective to the original abuse of the self by our social institutions. Lacking the security of a cultural "second womb," many individuals in our society have preferred to snuggle into the intermediate stages of development, where concern with the self is uppermost, rather than make the heroic leap toward transcendence of the self and total fulfillment.

Since growth occurs simultaneously in two dimensions—self and relationship to others—I find it useful to describe the four stages to personal fulfillment in our narcissistic culture by using a parallel diagram: "Self" and "Other(s)." These two tracks characterize the major thrust of one's self at a given stage and the corresponding thrust of interpersonal relationship. Historically, our cultural life cycle, from the Thirties through the Seventies, has developed along the lines indicated by the diagram.

| | Individual's growth | | | |
	Self	Other(s)	Cultural life cycle	Generational divide
Stage one	Denial	Compliance	The Depressing Thirties The Patriotic Forties The Square Fifties	Over-thirty-five generation
Stage two	Indulgence	Rejection	The Revolutionary Sixties	Under-thirty-five generation
Stage three	Reliance	Distrust	The Selfish Seventies	
Stage four	Fulfillment	Concern	The Concerned Eighties	

Stage One: *Self-denial/Compliance with other(s).* Individual forfeits self and complies automatically with standards set by external authority or tradition. Relationship with others is characterized by parasitic or exploitative dependency.

Stage Two: *Self-indulgence/Rejection of other(s).* Individual gratifies pleasure-seeking or aggressive impulses without restraint and rebels against traditional moral and social codes in conformity with standards set by subculture. Relationship with others is characterized by egocentric rejection of their needs.

Stage Three: *Self-reliance/Distrust of other(s).* Individual weans self away from excessive dependency on external authority and sets personal standards of achievement in accordance with skills and interests. Relationship with others is characterized by self-protection and distrust of commitment.

Stage Four: *Self-fulfillment/Concern for other(s).* Individual derives sense of purpose and validation from living up to personal standards and setting new goals. Relationships are characterized by reciprocity, unselfish concern for other's welfare (child, spouse, etc.), and social responsibility.

This schema is not intended in any way as a theory of psychosocial development nor does it represent a universal, invariable pattern. There are now some middle-aged members of the Silent Generation, for instance, who had already achieved Stage Four in the Fifties and managed to remain there throughout the Revolutionary Sixties and the Selfish Seventies. Similarly, there are students in the current generation who, by virtue of their own psychological constitution and exposure to beneficial peer interaction, moral education, home life, and other influences in their particular environment, have attained Stage Four in the early Eighties. They have outdistanced their less advantaged peers as well as many confused over-thirty-fives who are stuck at Stage Two today and are mainly involved in seeking personal gratification without concern for others.

As the chart indicates, I am using the early 1960s as a convenient cutoff time for the sexual revolution. Age thirty-five is a good dividing line between generations, as psychologist Perry London has pointed out, because today's thirty-five-year-old women were sexually impressionable adolescents in 1960, the year of the advent of the Pill. People above that age were generally reared in traditional closed family systems and had instilled in them conventional aspirations for marriage, home, family, and career. The over-thirty-five generation rebelled in the Sixties as a corrective to their earlier self-denial, whereas the under-thirty-five generation rejected others and indulged the self in the Sixties in reaction to their parents' experience. As a consequence of the loss of traditional values in the Sixties and the changed economy in the Seventies, many under thirty-fives are tending to get stuck in Stage Three, concentrating narrowly on their own survival.

The chart merely summarizes our collective cultural experience, as we have seen it unfold over the past five decades, and handily reveals in flow-chart form the zigzag route individuals often tend to take when their institutions have been warped by a militantly competitive ethic. It is hardly an ideal path. Quite the contrary, I know that many of us would have preferred to avoid the pain and wretched disruption of Stage Two self-indulgence and rejection of others to whom we were deeply committed. But our course was set by the injury done to the self in Stage One. This does not mean that our much mythologized "mid-life crisis," or even the turbulent crisis of adolescence, cannot become more peaceable transitions in the future. In a society with a more pro-social, cooperative value system, where the self is not so fragmented by upward mobility and a lunatic chorus of competing options, there is no reason why life's major turning points need be as excruciatingly conflict-ridden as they have been in the past.

A quick glance at the chart shows how closely this pendulum pattern of individual growth follows our cultural rites of passage during the last fifty years. It begins with our "seduction into a compliance" with the social norms and middle-class values of the Forties and Fifties; our eruption into a rebellious questioning and rejection of these norms and values in the Sixties; our struggle to achieve autonomy in the Seventies in an atmosphere of alienated commitmentphobia and distrust of authority; and culminating in the Eighties, as a natural outgrowth of autonomy and the crucial setting of valid limits, in that state of healthy equilibrium between the promotion of our own growth and the enrichment of others that we call personal fulfillment.

Comparing the stages of self-growth with the stages of relational growth is a useful concept but only with the understanding that there is enormous variability. In our lopsided culture, the growth of the self through individual achievement often outstrips our growth in interpersonal relationships. Consequently, unhealthy dependency trends commonly persist, like a thorn in the side of the ego, throughout Stage Three self-reliance. Many competent careerists, for example, who are capable of making independent choices about the direction of their work lives, are still enmeshed in—or searching for—symbiotic relationships with others to whom they cannot relate except as a partial self.

Until recently, this dependency dilemma appeared to be more prevalent among women than men in our society because of the dependency engendered by the prescribed female role. But the change in that role since the women's movement has revealed this apparent sex-related difference to be illusory. Sociology professor Dr. Cynthia Fuchs Epstein, codirector of Columbia University's Program of Sex Roles and Social Changes, feels that psychological dependency is evenly distributed among men and women. Dr. James L. Framo, a psychology professor and a pioneer in family therapy, goes even farther. He believes, on the basis of his clinical practice, that men have the greater psychological dependency on women, starting at birth with the mother-child relationship and reinforced throughout elementary and junior high school, where men have mostly female teachers. From my own experience, I have observed as much of a need on the part of highly successful, seemingly autonomous men—doctors, dentists, business executives—to merge the self in a relationship as I have among successful, career-oriented women. The only difference is that men *mask* the need. As one psychiatrist says about this kind of parasitic dependency: "Women *talk* about it; men *do* it."

Stage Four is, of course, not a permanent state of being that we maintain effortlessly in every sphere of life having once reached it. The harmonious equilibrium between self-growth and the enrichment of others is, by definition, a dynamic process. Although it presupposes a clearly defined value system of ideals and aspirations, it requires the constant resetting of goals within that system as well as, in Diana Trilling's apt phrase, "the endless improvisation of mutuality" in our relationships with others.

MORAL CONSISTENCY

Kramer vs. Kramer, the film event of 1979, movingly depicts both the high human costs and even higher rewards that many of us—men and women—discovered as we traveled the twisted road to personal fulfillment and social and moral maturity in recent years. Based on Avery Corman's novel about an impassioned custody battle over a young boy, the movie provides a lucid illustration of the larger battle that dominated family life in the Seventies—the clash of wills between a traditional Stage One husband and an emerging Stage Two wife.

Ted Kramer (Dustin Hoffman) is an ad executive who, in the beginning of the movie, is in such compulsive compliance with the role of "organization man" that his wife, Joanna, and six-year-old son, Billy, are virtual strangers to him. (The first time he drops Billy off at school, Ted has to ask his son what grade he is in.) Despite the tangible rewards that his talents, charm, and hustle have earned him—promotion to vice-president of the firm, the assignment of an important new account, a salary in the over-thirty-thousand-dollar range—it is obvious that Ted is neither self-reliant nor self-fulfilled. He has no identity apart from his work role—no self to speak of—and his relationships with others fluctuate between the two modes of parasitic dependency on his boss and clients and exploitative dependency on his wife.

When we first meet Joanna (Meryl Streep), she is a distraught, desperate woman who has one foot on the rung above Ted—she, at least, is aware that she has no sense of self—but she is unable to get him to stop talking about his achievements at work long enough to recognize her nonexistence. A Smith graduate who worked after college for two years in the art department of *Mademoiselle,* Joanna feels the walls of their Upper East Side apartment closing in on her like a tomb. Panic, the erosion of her love for Ted, and the dependency addict's reckless impulsiveness at the crossroads are pushing her toward a shocking breach of social responsibility. The audience is as aghast as Ted when Joanna, after lovingly tucking Billy into bed at night, abandons him to Ted and goes off to join the crusade of the Seventies: the search for self.

Since Joanna is only a shadowy figure in the story, her Stage Two phase takes place off-screen. Initially, we are unable to feel anything for her except revulsion. Her heartless abandonment of her own child at such a vulnerable age strikes us, even in an egocentric era, as monumentally selfish. Her behavior seems bizarre; yet, on reconsideration, it is very much in conformity with the standards set by her subculture of radicalized homemakers. We are reminded of the *Life* magazine cover story on the "Dropout Wife: A Striking Current Phenomenon" (March 17, 1972), featuring Wanda Adams, a smiling, middle-aged woman with tousled, wind-blown hair and gold hoop earrings, who, it is said, "left home and family for a new life." We are also reminded of all the "runaway mothers" who published articles or had articles published about them or were the subject of interviews on TV shows from CBS's prestigious "60 Minutes" to every local news and morning show in the country. Nor have we forgotten reports like Catherine Breslin's "Waking Up from the Dream of Women's Lib" (*New York* magazine, February 23, 1973) in which, thrown in with the details of the separations, divorces, affairs, "mucking around with psychotherapy," and other changes some thirty-five women were making since the women's movement had collided with their lives, is this chilling line: "Four of them had left their kids with the father when they split, and one seemed about to do so."

Kramer vs. Kramer is not the story of the woman who seemed about to do so and did, but of the husband and child she left behind and how their relationship develops into a thing of beauty. While we watch delightedly, Ted undergoes a metamorphosis from a mechanical man into a caring, nurturant father who will not sacrifice his child's welfare for anything—ambition, money, even custody of the boy if it means putting Billy on the stand in the courtroom. And Ted acts spontaneously. His love for his son is an act of giving, an end in itself. He protects Billy, plays with him, comforts him in the hospital when he is hurt, teaches him how to ride a bike, takes him to the office and shows him his work environment, sends him to bed when he defies orders not 'to eat ice cream instead of his dinner, leaves an important business meeting to watch Billy perform in the school play. Ted does what he must for his son, not for social approval but for *self*-approval—"for the self-administered rewards arising from doing what is 'right.' "

What saves Ted from ignoring his son's innocent but enormous emotional demands and going on his own rampage of self-indulgence—womanizing every night, for example, while Billy is left in the hands of an indifferent parade of baby-sitters? Ted is able to bypass Stage Two—and *unable* to let his own child go down the tubes—because there are some things that he simply *will not do*. Unlike his career goals, which are adjustable, his essential decency is not. It is the baseline of his inner limits. Unyielding when put to the test, it governs Ted's actions on behalf of his son and demonstrates the power of what I call "moral consistency." In contrast to the moral absolutism that made martyrs out of an earlier generation of parents and the moral relativism that has confused and betrayed so many of us in recent times, moral consistency is rooted in choice but impervious to compromise. While the person with moral consistency is flexible with respect to some goals and aspirations, there are other perdurable ideals of right and wrong that he has internalized and to which he adheres despite current cultural trends or, in Jung's phrase, "the spirit which goes through the mass."

It is in his relationship with the boss of his advertising firm that we can see Ted evolve from a rigidly compliant worker into a genuinely autonomous person. Here we witness another conflict that is becoming a dominant one in contemporary life: the clash of motives between a Stage One employer and a Stage Three employee. While Ted's boss exudes a warm, avuncular manner with Ted, he actually relates to Ted on the basis of sheer exploitative dependency. He cares nothing about his employee as a human being. The boss, when he learns that Ted's wife has left him, is concerned only that Billy's needs might hamper Ted's performance on the new account. By way of pragmatic help, he urges Ted to send the boy away to live with relatives. The boss takes the standard corporate attitude that the company comes first—*uber alles*—and that Ted's obligations to his son must be sacrificed.

Ted, on the other hand, would rather risk losing his job than leave Billy untended when he is home with a 104-degree fever. After just such an incident, the boss fires Ted. He is unmoved by the fact that Ted's being out of work will ruin his chances of winning legal custody of Billy in an upcoming courtroom proceeding initiated by the returned and "recycled" Joanna. Ted mounts a successful one-day invasion of a different ad agency (at Christmastime, no less) and lands a job—paying four thousand dollars less than his previous one. He eagerly accepts a salary far below what he knows his skills and experience are worth in the job market, not only out of necessity, but more importantly, because *he* is now in control of his own goals and standards. Having freed himself from excessive dependency on the corporate code, he no longer values himself solely in terms of his job title and how much money he makes.

When Joanna Kramer returns to the scene after eighteen months, she is like a reincarnation of herself—a dramatic "before" and "after" photographic essay showing a former Stage One woman transformed into a Stage Three. The desperate, confused, panic-stricken woman of before has now become a successful sports clothes designer, earning thirty-one thousand dollars a year and exuding an aura of confidence and purpose. (Joanna's salary is one of the film's most glaring departures from reality.) When she later tries to explain her transformation, brought about with the help of psychotherapy in California, she resorts to the familiar, lame clichés of "finding herself" and becoming a "whole person." What she has done, in fact, is to achieve a sense of separate identity by setting her own limits. She is now ready to be a mother to Billy by *choice* and feels capable of taking care of him without obliterating her self. After a period of wistfully watching the boy from her secret observation point at a coffee shop window, Joanna gathers the courage to ask Ted for custody. His adamant refusal triggers *Kramer vs. Kramer's* famous courtroom scene.

Before the two have their day in court, Joanna is granted visitation rights. She and Billy share a gloriously joyful reunion in a park. Running eagerly toward his mother, Billy demonstrates the indestructible love and loyalty children of divorce have for the absent parent—even one who has abandoned them. As Joanna hugs Billy and affectionately whirls him in the air, we can have no doubt about her capacity for deeply felt "mother's warmth."

During the vicious custody battle in court, the lawyers attempt, by turns, a nothing-sacred character assassination of each other's client. But their methods are so heavy-handed that even Ted and Joanna are appalled at the mistreatment of each other. They can see through the distortions, and beyond that, to the truth. While Joanna's attorney tries to malign Ted for losing his job, the circumstances of the firing emerge and Joanna realizes what an unselfishly devoted and concerned parent Ted has become. Although she is awarded custody of Billy—purely on the basis of the court's traditional bias in favor of the mother—Joanna recognizes that Ted has *earned* it. When she goes to pick up Billy, even before seeing him again, Joanna tearfully returns custody of the boy to Ted.

Will Joanna and Ted make it to Stage Four? That remains to be seen in the sequel. All we can say with certainty is that each has matured into a self-reliant, autonomous human being with a strong sense of parental love and social responsibility. We know, too, that each wants intimacy with a sexual partner, but is still manifesting a Stage Three wariness of commitment. Joanna, we have learned from her courtroom testimony, has a lover—a quasi-committed relationship, perhaps, but not as deeply satisfying generally as the commitment of marriage. Ted, as we have seen, has a dalliance going with a former coworker—someone, he tells Billy, he does not intend to marry. He also tells Billy, emphatically, that he and Joanna will never get back together again—but that was before Joanna's supreme act of generosity and selflessness after the custody hearing. Given the growth of the two central characters, whether they reconcile with each other or seek happiness with new partners, the future looks promising.

STAGE TWO AND THE CURRENT GENERATION

When we observe the current younger generation through the prism of the Four Stages to Personal Fulfillment, it appears that many of them are *starting out* from a position of Stage Two self-indulgence and rejection of the needs and rights of others. *Campus Shock* (1979), Lansing Lamont's book based on his tour of prestigious American universities in the Seventies, is a harrowing account of what one reviewer described as "rampant and systematic cheating, constant sexual exploitation, vicious sabotaging of other students' work, crime, racism, violence, lunatic pressure for grades and above all an individualism utterly devoid of concern for the feelings, aspirations and problems of others."

This unsavory picture of campus life seems, on the basis of my own interviews with college professors and students, to be an overstatement of the case and representative of only a small segment of the college population. Yet there is undoubtedly a mood on the campus of intense insecurity, entitlement, and insulation. As an Ivy League professor describes it: "Many students are incredibly narcissistic and demanding in terms of individual attention and time. There's a real self-centeredness on the part of people who have been raised in an overly permissive environment and are still looking for boundaries, coupled with an anxiety about jobs that comes out of the recession."

The students' self-indulgence, whatever form it takes, is not a continuation of the revolution of the Sixties, as Lamont claims in *Campus Shock*. Although on the surface some of their behavior may look the same as the rebellion against the upper-middle-class values of togetherness, upward mobility, and material acquisition, it is not a rebellion at all. It is self-indulgence as a *substitute* for social order.

The Stage Two we have seen in the past was a temporary backslide from moral and prosocial behavior among people who were trying to liberate themselves from automatic compliance with external authority and become more self-reliant. It represented a necessary questioning of traditional moral and social codes in order to learn how to set one's own personal standards and eventually become socially responsible out of choice. As such, it demonstrates "the paradox of maturity" uncovered by a team of Harvard researchers: "The paradox is that *promoting maturity leads first to a decrease in moral behavior*, as the person moves out of a Stage I [Erikson's] reliance on external authority and becomes more oriented toward making choices on his or her own."

But the self-indulgence and antisocial behavior observed among college students today is not linked with anything except an individualistic survival ethic. There is no challenging of upper-middle-class norms and values because no coherent, consistent body of principles exists. Using or more often abusing people to help win economic security or the admiration necessary to keep self-regard alive is all they know. The permissiveness of negligence and youth-direction practiced by their parents has deprived them of both parental authority and identification with their peers. As David Riesman has explained: "They lack the internalized parental values of the inner-directed types, and they are not as sensitive to peers as were the other-directed people."

Today's narcissistic college students, like the rest of us, are living in a cultural void—a values vacuum. Their uncertainty about the future, as well as their own inner uncertainty, is reflected both academically and in their interpersonal relationships. According to Riesman, many narcissistic students tend to delay or totally fail to complete their doctoral requirements by clinging to their defensive perfectionistic standards. In their personal lives, they are unable to invest themselves in friendship or intimacy and are forced to make do with superficial friendships and "quick intimacy combined with loneliness."

As society increasingly prolongs the length of time before students can become economically self-sufficient and confident of their ability to meet others' needs, we are encouraging them to make a niche for themselves indefinitely in the new Stage Two. To release them from permanent adolescence, we must provide an environment where overchoice and the greed creed are brought into line by the setting of limits, and cooperative give-and-take is encouraged instead of solipsist individualism. Otherwise, the foremost aspiration of the class of 1983—"Having a good marriage and family life"—may become, like the search for unconditional love, merely another unfulfillable fantasy.

When we look back on the past five decades, it becomes apparent that the key to personal fulfillment is the integrity of our choices. They must be choices that arise out of a deep sense of conflict-free commitment. Compulsiveness or a feeling of desperation about the limits we set for ourselves—in love, work, parenting, friendship, or serving the common good—is a sign of conformity without the self's assent and is a barrier to self-fulfillment.

The grim air of martyrdom in this forecast of "The Looming

80's" by Eugene Kennedy, suggests that our rediscovery of "personal guilt," welcome as it is, could turn out to be a *regression* to compliance rather than an advancement to maturity. Kennedy says, "America's gradual and grudging acceptance of a sense of national and individual limits during the 80's may arise not so much from a sense of renewed virtue as from exhaustion and desperation at discovering that, although learning to make sacrifices may be unpleasant, trying to be happy without giving something up for others is impossible."

If the acceptance of our responsibility to others is "grudging" and reflects a desperate lack of choice, then how much different are we, really, from the browbeaten Silent Generation of the Fifties? How long will it be before our feeling of being made to do something we don't want to do catches up with us and starts the extremist cycle all over again?

The overtones of the new decade already have a familiar ring: the renewal of the cold war with Russia since the Soviet invasion of Afghanistan, the talk of "back to basics" in the classroom, the pressures on the young to pair up early, the emergence of the female "organization man." Inflation and the energy crisis give the Age of Limits its own agenda, but it is all too easy for us individually to succumb to a feeling of powerlessness and drift back into compliant self-denial and stagnation.

We need something more than the old guilt and shame controls if we are to find personal fulfillment even as we meet those challenges of the 1980s that will "test our qualities as a people, our toughness and willingness to sacrifice for larger goals, our courage and our vision" (State of the Union message, January 21, 1980, President Carter).

Our success hinges on our ability to accept our inner limits, not as constraints, but as the guideposts for growth. We must understand that without them, we have no control over the tyrannical greed and envy within us that makes austerity unendurable and abundance meaningless. Understanding that, we can then see that our sense of limits is not only necessary for our happiness, but indeed the very basis of it.

What is it like for adolescents who are growing up in our cultural values vacuum today? In the chapter that follows we'll examine some of the devastating ways in which children in our society have been harmed because their parents and the larger culture have been unable to transmit clear and consistent signals to help them guide their inner compass.

NINE

COMING
OF AGE IN THE
VALUES VACUUM

The subject was cults. In broadcast parlance, that made it a "hot" studio, a descriptive term that had nothing to do with the weather on May 26, 1979. The studio was hot, meaning explosively volatile, because the two guests facing off against each other at the microphones on my three-hour call-in radio show (WCAU-CBS) that particular Saturday afternoon were a devout missionary of the Moon church and an ex-Moonie about to tell all.

Alan Inman, the missionary representing Reverend Sun Myung Moon's Unification Church, was a muscular, unsmiling man in his thirties with strange eyes—opaque, impenetrable, and frightening. Although his hostility toward the ex-Moonie was inordinate and almost irrational, on the air he was articulate, if unconvincing, in defense of Moon's church and, much to my relief, totally compliant with my authority as the show's host.

The deprogrammed ex-Moonie was Christopher Edwards, a Yale graduate and author of the book *Crazy for God*, a first-person horror story of life in the Moon cult. The book tells how Chris Edwards was inveigled into the cult under false pretenses and then systematically brainwashed and infantilized as a disciple for seven months until his father, a prominent surgeon, kidnaped him and had him deprogrammed by the controversial Ted Patrick.

Chris, a short, vulnerable-looking academician in his mid-twenties, with a fair complexion, wiry brown hair, and brilliant blue eyes, was accompanied to the studio by a woman friend who hovered near him solicitously. Noticeably uneasy in Inman's presence, Chris refused to be left alone with the missionary at any time for fear of the reprisals that speaking out against Moon's church might bring. Yet

Chris doggedly stuck to his story as he had written it and vehemently repudiated Inman's angry attempts to discredit him.

According to Chris, after receiving his B.A. in psychology and philosophy from Yale in 1975, he was searching for a niche for himself in a society that seemed to have no room for his idealism. He had become increasingly disillusioned with Yale, which he described in his book as simply another mill—shades of the 1950s—for "manufacturing doctors, lawyers, politicians, and businessmen primed to control the offices of Wall Street, Madison Avenue, and the bureaucracies of Washington, the exclusive country clubs, and corporate conglomerates throughout the country."

Determined not to "sell out," Chris ended up in Berkeley, California, still remembered as the mecca of the youth movement in the Sixties, and was wandering about in what writer David Black has called "the twentieth-century middle-class American version of the Grand Tour."

Leaning against a signpost on Shattuck Avenue, Chris was studying a map to find the university—only three blocks away—when a friendly young man approached him and offered directions. Jacob, as the young man introduced himself, chatted with Chris and generously invited him to dinner that night. The free dinner and open house, Jacob explained, were sponsored by a "social group" he belonged to—"very loving, very idealistic"—called Creative Community Projects.

Chris Edwards told me that he never would have gone to dinner that night had he known that Creative Community Projects was the front name for the Moon cult. Even on the bulletin boards at the Student Center on the Berkeley campus, the ad that Chris spotted for Creative Community Projects gave no hint of any affiliation with the Reverend Moon. There were only a few simplistic lines about peace and happiness with a sun and a smiley face penciled in above.

Lured by this seemingly innocent overture and by his own desperate hunger for peer approval and acceptance, Chris showed up for the dinner that night and unknowingly found himself in a cult training camp. Disarmed by an immediate "love-bombing"—a torrent of affectionate pressure from persuasive cult members who followed him everywhere, even into the bathroom—Chris stayed on for over seven months. Gradually, through a combination of coercive psychological and physiological techniques amounting to an insidious form of mind control, Chris became utterly dependent on the will of the group. He lost all capacity to think for himself or to experience his own emotions, regressing to the infantile splitting defense. The social order inside the cult was "all good," and anything forbidden by the cult—hostility or sexuality, for example—was "all bad" and was projected onto Satan, the outside world.

For Chris, the problem of overchoice in a morally permissive yet still narrowly competitive society was solved. His confusion had vanished. But so had Chris—his identity sucked right into the "black hole" of the values vacuum. After repeated exposure to the regimentation and control of the cult—incessant bombardment with rhetoric, removal or reinforcement of peer approval, humiliating manipulation of guilt, censorship of the larger world, compulsory auto-hypnotic chanting, constant activity, improper diet, numbing work regimen, celibacy (for three years until the cult chose a marriage partner), denial of medical attention, and perhaps most important, continuous unrelenting sleep deprivation—Chris was reduced to a bundle of sick submission.

Although he phoned his parents every two weeks, he was merely following cult policy by maintaining contact with his father and mother in order to prepare them for his conversion. When his parents suspected him of joining the Moonies, Chris denied it—using "Heavenly Deception"—and told them he was working for a "grass-roots social work community" in Berkeley. He kept insisting that he was "in good hands." But by the time his father discovered his real whereabouts and came to get him, it was none too soon. Chris had deteriorated to the point of masochistic fanaticism. He would chastise himself for feelings of sexual desire or doubts about the motives of Reverend Moon by chanting hysterically to himself in the prayer room until he collapsed on the floor. Knees tucked into his chest, he would curl up in a corner, sucking his thumb while he stared at the picture of Reverend Moon on the wall, and drift into unconsciousness.

DEITIES REPLACE ROLE MODELS

Christopher Edwards is no different from any of the other bright, idealistic sons and daughters of the white, educated upper-middle-class who grew up in the Sixties and Seventies and are susceptible to the cults' promise of unconditional love. He is, in fact, typical of the two to three million people, mostly eighteen to twenty-five, estimated to belong to as many as 2,500 different cults operating in the United States today. According to Rabbi Maurice Davis, founder of Citizens Engaged in Reuniting Families, one of the largest of the country's parents organizations dedicated to helping children leave cults, the profile of the cult joiner is a "loving and giving person" who has a strong need for peer approval, may have trouble "hacking" a permissive society, and would like to see a better world but often prefers "simplistic answers to complicated questions." Rabbi Davis continues:

They may have had a crisis in their lives. Perhaps they dropped out of school or had an unhappy love affair. Often they will be college freshmen in the first couple of months when the school world seems awfully big. Or college seniors in the last couple of months when the outside world seems awfully big. What these kids are looking for is someone who will take away doubt and give them something to believe in. These kids get recruited on the street. One of the things surprising to so many adults is the openness with which kids will talk to strangers. There's a hunger in kids which sometimes the adult world doesn't see. They go down the street, hoping to talk to somebody.

To which Chris Edwards replies that his generation has been victimized by "tremendous expectations of happiness and success along with the realities of broken homes, fragmented neighborhoods, and depersonalized schooling":

Why is my generation so hungry for love that they can be attracted so easily by saccharine promises? I believe the answer is simply this: we as a people seem to have forgotten how to care about and for each other. We are responsible for the desperation which makes cult promises so attractive. We must relearn how to care and relearn how to listen in a fundamental way. If we don't then I fear that cult terrorism and manipulation will only grow until we actually become the type of One-World Family which the Moonies envision.

Cynics may dismiss this as a tepid plea for coddling by one more overprotected rich kid unprepared to cope with an imperfect world or with people who don't love him—Chris's last girl friend at Yale jilted him for an Iraqi Marxist. Others might see Chris's attempt to escape the rabid competitiveness of many of his peers as a pure case of individual psychopathology—in Freudian terms, unresolved oedipal conflicts and a castration complex. They might contend that because Chris fears to compete against his own father in the field of medicine—and either fail to live up to the standards of perfection demanded by his overidealized god or be destroyed by the god's wrath for succeeding—he has rationalized that all competition is a "sellout."

One can only imagine the tensions that exist in the home of a prominent surgeon whose son has renounced the elite route to success mapped out by his father. In our society, the children of doctors, particularly males, have traditionally been regarded as heirs apparent to the royal occupational throne and black sheep or washouts if they have not chosen to follow in the parental footsteps. But identification with the parent figure and internalization of his or her work role—doctor, lawyer, politician, business entrepreneur, or whatever—has become increasingly difficult in our culture. Since the separation of the home and workplace, most children rarely get an opportunity to see their parents functioning effectively and proudly on the job. Usually, the successful working parent is a remote, powerful figure to the maturing child, a phantom who comes home from engaging in shadowy endeavors, complaining of stress and exhaustion, and wanting nothing so much from the child as to be left alone.

In a *Newsweek* article entitled "Who Can Be A Doctor?" (January 21, 1980), admissions interviewers at the nation's medical schools revealed that "the children of physicians don't necessarily have an edge." Every attempt is made to weed out those who are going into medicine simply to *please* a parent rather than out of a genuine desire to *emulate* one—and that, apparently, considerably narrows the field. Said Billy B. Rankin, Baylor College of Medicine admissions director: "You'd be surprised how little contact such candidates have with their parents' professional life. They don't know the kinds of things a doctor puts up with on a daily basis."

But many do know the kinds of things some doctors engage in on a daily basis that have tarnished the image of the medical profession as a noble calling. When Medicaid fraud by physicians amounts to $100 million a year in Pennsylvania alone, as reported by a special State Senate investigating committee on January 25, 1980, we have to wonder whether Christopher Edwards is only being defensive about his own career choice when he calls entering the professions a "sellout" or whether he is reacting to the state of the professions themselves.

Unfortunately, the person trying to resist the new wave of materialism engulfing the campus today often finds himself at odds with both parental *and* peer pressure to achieve at any cost—even an extortionate one. He thus becomes an easy mark for organizations hawking "ready-made" identities. Lacking idealizable role models in his home and school environment to help him set limits based on the integrity of personal choice rather than external demands for achievement, the individual may see the religious cults as his only hope of heaven. The would-be *mensch* is given a rationale—usually some nebulous "Divine Principle"—for trying to *be good* instead of acceding to parental and cultural pressure to *do well.*

"HURRIED CHILDREN"

Besides supplying dogma as a quick, makeshift replacement for the development of self-reliance and soundly internalized values, the cults perform another dubious function. The "God circuit," as Ann Braden Johnson calls it, now serves as a kind of resistance movement among the achievement-pressured younger generation. It has become the underground of their narcissistic rage.

In an illuminating article on the "hurried child" syndrome, psychologist David Elkind contends that many children are growing up too fast socially and psychologically today because they are being pushed toward early achievement without a comparable level of parental support. Unlike the spoiled Spockian children who were given too much power and tried to divest themselves of it in an extended adolescence, today's hurried children feel powerless and, says Elkind, "are trying to divest themselves of the fear and consequences of failure."

According to Elkind, when the "disequilibrium" in the implied achievement-support contract persists, the hurried child eventually evens the score. As adolescents, these driven overachievers vent their anger and resentment on their parents for dealing them "childhood inequities"—pushing them to excel in school, for example, but never reciprocally supporting their efforts by looking at their work or attending parent conferences or school functions. Despite their academic and social precocity, hurried children often experience a sense of failure. It may not be in their actual performance in school, Elkind says, but they feel they have failed in their ability to impress their parents:

Some young people direct their anger outward and engage in activities that hurt them and that are designed to hurt the parents as well. They may begin to do poorly in school, and may drop out entirely. Others may become delinquent; some girls may become pregnant in a misguided effort to "pay their parents back." Still other young people turn their anger inward and blame themselves for not measuring up, and may seek escape in drugs or in religious movements. Indeed, the great appeal of many of the charismatic religious groups is that when young people join, they are assured that support is *not* contingent upon achievement.

Elkind also feels, not unlike Christopher Edwards, that *society* has violated its part of the achievement-support contract. The implicit agreement was that a higher education guaranteed success: If a person worked hard in school and achieved a college degree, the high achiever was assured the support of a suitably high income. But the job market has failed to yield the promised rewards. There are thirty-year-olds who diligently earned their Ph.D.'s and have yet to work for pay.

The self-centeredness of today's college generation, Elkind feels, is a reaction to this violation of the achievement-support contract. People in this self-involved generation tend to make themselves the focal point of their problems rather than affix the blame on society and its institutions, as did their predecessors in the 1960s. This feeling of the "me" generation, that it is primarily their own fault if they don't get the academic position or the job they want, makes them more akin to their grandparents in the Great Depression, who also tended to individualize social problems. But there is one big difference. The contemporary pessimism about the situation ever getting better—an outgrowth of the deep lack of confidence in government after Vietnam and Watergate—has led to a willingness to delay commitments to a future work role and an unwillingness to delay gratification. "Young people are rebelling against the postponement of immediate gratification for later rewards," says Elkind, "because the later rewards are not forthcoming. But the rebellion has its limits: they are not rebelling against the ethic of self-discipline and self-control; they have simply shifted that ethic from work to play."

LATERAL VS. UPWARD MOBILITY

Whether they are responding to the current achievement madness by escaping into cults, succumbing to manic careerism, or drowning their sorrows in play, the younger generation is stalled, if not going backward, on the road to personal fulfillment. Like the other misled generations before them, they are forfeiting their right to their own identity by letting the traditional standard of upward mobility lead them around by the nose.

The situation is much graver today because the standard of upward mobility is twice as fraudulent as it has been in the past. Not only is it incapable of delivering the psychic rewards expected of it in the Fifties, but now, as Elkind and others have pointed out, it is economically bankrupt, too. As a culture we have arrived at a watershed, socially and economically, where the notion that sons and daughters must do better than their parents is an inflated, outdated standard—one no longer feasible for large numbers of the American upper middle class.

When immigrant shopkeepers and seamstresses assigned their children the mission of bettering themselves and the family status by getting an education and becoming doctors and teachers, the country's economic growth was there to support the American Dream. Whatever the narcissistic injury done to the child charged with the assignment, at least it was not a mission impossible. But today, these second-generation doctors and teachers have produced sons and daughters who are neurosurgeons and Ph.D.'s. How realistic is it, given our devalued dollar and overrated degree, that *their* sons and daughters now in college will surpass or even equal them in earning power, professional status, and prestige?

More significantly, where is it given that children can enjoy the economic and emotional rewards of achievement only in fields that surpass their parents in income and in the traditional hierarchy of status? The fact that many former 1960s "rebels" shied away from the traditional professions, doctoral programs, and family businesses and found success in boutique and cottage industries, the arts, communications, and even in the political bureaucracy they once fought, is proof that the standard of upward mobility is, to use their expression, "irrelevant." If the culture continues to pressure today's "hurried children" to adhere to this false, anachronistic standard, both the overanxious aspirants and the educational institutions geared to serve them are headed for serious trouble.

Paul C. Vitz, associate professor of psychology at New York University, argues cogently in *Psychology as Religion* that the current generation of upwardly mobile careerists, now in their mid-twenties, is destined for a "career crisis of tragic intensity" some time in the Eighties. Vitz cites the obvious discrepancy between this narcissistic generation's grandiose expectations of success and the reality of the economic slowdown. He also points out that many of today's popular careers—teaching, psychology, medicine, and law—are overcrowded and offer severely limited opportunities for future success. And while the large corporations or bureaucracies offer a very high proportion of today's career opportunities, they invariably limit advancement "and destroy chances for effective, gratifying action."

But these pragmatic considerations are the least of it. The narrowly focused hopes of this group of people—in part, the result of the disappearance of other higher ideals, Vitz says—is their biggest problem. The career dissatisfaction that regularly strikes people in their late thirties or early forties will be devastating for them because the psychology of self-realization has trained them to believe in the career as "the ultimate source of fulfillment." As Vitz points out, since the divorce and separation rate is very high among this generation of rising careerists, and even their ties to parents, brothers and sisters are often weak, many of them will have no family to provide an alternative source of meaning and emotional support. "Careers are intrinsically too weak an ideal to carry the huge psychic burden they are now given," Vitz concludes. "Even many in that small group who do succeed find success unsatisfying, even bleak and empty."

What is intriguing about Vitz's analysis of "the coming failure of careerism" is his finding that today's generation of narcissistic strivers, for all their apparent "me-ism," are still as utterly dependent on external authority as the Silent Generation in the Fifties. Claiming that "many have chosen careers because it is the thing to do—not because of any deep interest in the activity involved," Vitz elaborates:

Over the last ten years I have discussed psychology careers with at least two thousand different undergraduates—mostly psychology majors. In recent years, more and more of them choose careers for extrinsic reasons, for example, because of their parents, or of the general social pressure, or because of the need for some kind of goal after college. *Today it is the well-socialized student who goes on to graduate training in some career; it is the unusual, imaginative, and interesting student who does not.*

The hurried child's *under*motivated counterpart—the one who has been reared on the permissiveness of negligence and has only diffuse goals and an unfocused image of what he would like to be— often feels obliged to force himself to catch up with his scurrying, well-socialized peers. He thinks they have an "edge for survival" in today's fast-paced world.

Since only two standards of value exist in our modern times— "being socially with the trend, or popular," as Mitscherlich says, "and being forgotten, out-of-date, worthless"—the student who decides not to join the traditional scramble up the academic ladder is the one who is made to feel like a failure in our culture. But perhaps it is *he* who has the edge for survival in the long run: Those who are encouraged in young adulthood to define their own authentic goals and aspirations, regardless of the status or recognition attached to them, may indeed "find themselves" before they are encumbered with a life they never chose. Uncertain and self-doubting as they are today, they are more likely to avoid the predictable mid-life "career crisis of tragic intensity" awaiting the achievement-programmed frontrunners in the upwardly mobile rat pack.

Although most parents still cling to the notion that a college degree is the only ticket of admission to success, educators themselves are becoming more and more aware of the obsolescence of the standard of upward mobility. Dr. Donald Oliver, a professor at Harvard's Graduate School of Education, has identified parental prejudice against professions that do not require a college degree as "a social-class problem." Discussing the problem in the *New York Times,* Oliver debunked the myth about the monetary value of a college degree with these statistics drawn from his own research: a postdoctoral graduate in the sciences might earn ten thousand dollars, whereas a beautician could earn twenty thousand dollars to forty thousand dollars, and a truck driver could earn forty thousand dollars. But, as Oliver pointed out, "someone in science has more social status than a beautician or a truck driver."

Decrying this status-conscious approach to career goals, Oliver advised parents of children who did not want to be railroaded into college to "search their souls about their prejudices" and to "look around at vocational schools and be supportive of the possibilities." He underscored the fact that many of the available vocations involve having a business, which gives the person the freedom to set hours and other advantages of autonomy, independence, and creativity not generally found in positions that require a bachelor of arts. Suggesting that parents visit some of the vocational schools, Dr. Oliver said: "Many parents would be surprised at how interesting they are."

Dr. Oliver's open-minded endorsement of vocational education is part of a growing recognition among educators that academia will soon be under siege to do something about the disequilibrium in the achievement-support contract. Clark Kerr, former president of the University of California, sounded this theme when he ended his five-year reign in January 1980 as director of the Carnegie Council on Policy Studies in Higher Education. In his lengthy report (155 pages), entitled "Three Thousand Futures—The Next Twenty Years in Higher Education," Kerr predicts that the 3,000 colleges in America will be hard-pressed to survive unless they keep in mind an education that leads to a paying job. He foresees a shift away from the traditional academic emphasis on liberal arts and the humanities and more emphasis on hard-nosed instruction in vocational skills like nursing and accounting. In the words of the report: "Excellence was the theme. Now it's survival."

While no lover of learning wants to see excellence suffer, neither can we continue to permit the inhumane suffering of our hurried children. As David Elkind has warned:

In adolescence the symptoms of hurried children become most
evident, often taking the form of severe anxiety about academic
success. Among the teenagers I have treated, drug use is often
associated with school failure. Even young people who are doing well
academically may be tempted to fall into drug use because of the
great personal toll that their effort to succeed exacts. Many teenage
girls get pregnant partly to prove that they can accomplish

something. To be sure, young adolescents in previous generations have abused drugs and become pregnant. What is different today is not the presence of the phenomena, but their frequency. When a million 12 to 17 year-olds get pregnant each year, and one in five uses drugs more than once a week (and three million teenagers are "problem drinkers")—when increasing numbers of adolescents take the more drastic steps of running away, committing acts of violence, or taking their own lives—we have to look beyond individual families to the social dynamics shaping parenting practices.

What is the single, most consistent social dynamic that has shaped parenting practices for the past five decades, if not the standard of upward mobility? The psychological injury caused by the standard as well as its increasing impracticability make it one that has outlived its use. The time has come to replace it with a healthier ideal integrating the positive aspects of 1960s nontraditionalism with the traditional values of self-reliance and social responsibility: the standard of *lateral* mobility.

By recognizing that it has become untenable to define achievement on the basis of the income and occupational status achieved or aspired to by a parent, the standard of lateral mobility redefines achievement in terms of the individual's own capacities, interests, opportunities, and goals. Thus, the meaning of achievement broadens out to encompass a child's moving into a job that is *different* from a parent's, but not necessarily of a higher or lower status. Success, once strictly a matter of *upward* movement, now becomes a matter of *inward* movement according to one's personal limits.

But lateral mobility means *mobility* all the same. It involves attaining competence in one's field, and competence cannot be acquired without the desire to work hard and to pursue challenging tasks—the two factors, incidentally, that research has shown to be more important links to success than high competitive drive.

And where does education fit into the scheme? James Michener, examining "The Revolution in Middle Class Values" in the late 1960s, insisted that "education is essential to any young person who wants to attain his potential," but he made a nice distinction between *formal* learning and *real* learning. Michener sympathized with the "philosophical dropout who quits college to find his Walden Pond" only if the dropout has temporarily rejected formal learning in order to gain competence—real skills and experience that would qualify him for political or moral leadership or, at the every least, would save him from the doom of mediocrity. Responsibility remains a foundation of civilized society, Michener noted, and it is the responsibility of the best minds of the middle class to be sufficiently educated to address social problems and challenge existing patterns in need of change. Assessing the significance of the rebellion of the Sixties, he wrote: "The test will come in the years ahead when to assert one's responsibility will no longer be exciting, but merely hard work. The easy contests have been won; the flashy victories are in the bag. It is performance over the long haul that will determine the value of the rebellion."

Some of the former revolutionaries, like solar energy advocate Tom Hayden and Sam Brown, director of ACTION, the federal agency that includes VISTA and the Peace Corps, have met the test of performance. By tempering their radical Sixties idealism with reality, they have managed to graduate from professional protester to professional political leader working within the system for progressive social change. But many others in their generation and the succeeding one are making a lifestyle out of avoiding the test of performance altogether. Our culture's incessant demand for upward mobility, coupled with its failure to provide empathetic role models has perverted this generation's grandiose idealism into a fear of failure. These children are the ones who are hiding out in graduate school, or living off welfare, or working at menial jobs like supermarket stock boy or car wash attendant that are far beneath their level of intelligence and potential.

Gifted at rationalization and denial, these cultural narcissists are often able to convince themselves and others that they are acting out of noble motivations. The young men, particularly, are able to mask "a cop-out for not having any masculine strivings," as a psychiatrist I interviewed put it, behind the jargon of the new masculine ideal. When responding to happiness surveys, like the one devised by Gail Sheehy—whose findings were published in *Esquire* magazine—such a young man typically put "being loving" higher on his list of priorities than "being ambitious" and "being able to lead effectively." He talks loosely about "personal growth" and "freedom," but he has no goals for himself except remaining single for at least ten years and leading a life of monied leisure without having to work hard for it. Although, after having completed four years of college, he has found no substantive means of earning a living and no purpose in life other than staying out of the family business, he claims to be one of the survey's most happy fellas.

This profile of a "happy" young man, it turns out, is actually a portrait of a self-deceptive young man who has confused transient pleasure with sustained joy in life. In the *Esquire* article, Sheehy reported that, *overall*, her survey of 1,851 men showed that "a well-satisfied man usually records as one of his three lifetime goals 'family security—taking care of loved ones.' . . . The highest satisfaction indicated on the survey was the experience of having children. . . . The everyday proof that one is needed by others and the interplay with people who are strongly identified with one's hopes and ambitions can become the mainspring of continual motivation."

Sheehy also noted: "A central theme running through the biographies of the least happy men is their self-absorption. . . . Though the least satisfied men usually don't see themselves as loners, the sad echo throughout their self-description is an impaired capacity to reach out and form friendships, to be vulnerable to love." Elsewhere she observed: "It's intriguing to note that of all the men who have answered my questionnaire, the majority are *not* 'devoted to some purpose or cause outside themselves and larger than themselves.' But the minority who *do* have a purpose larger than self are consistently among the happiest."

Perhaps we should pause here and ask ourselves, what is the difference between happiness and joy? I suspect that the person who says he is "happy," even though he lacks the capacity to express and enjoy his actual abilities, is speaking about a fragmentary and fleeting state of pleasure rather than the sustained joy of self-fulfillment. As Heinz Kohut explains it:

Joy is experienced as referring to a more encompassing emotion such as, for example, the emotion evoked by success, whereas pleasure, however intense it may be, refers to a delimited experience, such as, for example, sensual satisfaction. . . . Joy relates to experiences of the total self whereas pleasure (despite the frequently occurring participation of the total self, which then provides an admixture of joy) relates to experiences of parts and constituents of the self.

To arrive at the fullness of joy, according to Kohut, we need "a reliably organized framework" for experiencing the satisfaction of self-expression. This structure consists of a set of firmly internalized ideals of perfection on one side, our grandiose, exhibitionistic ambitions on the other, and a correlated system of abilities and skills to mediate between the two. If our ideals of perfection, instead of being self-chosen goals with some promise of attainment, are the primitive all-or-nothing kind that make every compromise necessarily second best, then we become victims of our grandiose ambitions. And no matter what "happiness" we may know momentarily, joy eludes us. Rather than give up our dream of omnipotence, we inhibit the enjoyment of our self-expression in work and love by overcontrolling ourselves and our environment.

In his description of successful psychoanalysis, Kohut makes the difference between pleasure and joy even clearer:

. . . the principal indicators that a cure has been established will be the disappearance or the amelioration of a patient's hypochondria, lack of initiative, empty depression and lethargy, self-stimulation through sexualized activities, etc., on the one hand, and the patient's comparative freedom from excessive narcissistic vulnerability (the tendency, for example, to respond to narcissistic injuries with empty depression and lethargy, or with an increase of perverse self-soothing activities) on the other. And, on the whole, the positive achievement of a good analysis will here be confirmed by the fact that the patient is now able to experience the joy of existence more keenly, that, *even in the absence of pleasure,* he will consider his life worthwhile— creative, or at least productive.

THE CREDENTIALS RACE

Unless one expects to become a tennis pro, it is unlikely that retiring to Martha's Vineyard at the age of twenty-seven to spend the rest of one's life playing tennis will lead to experiencing the joy of life more keenly. It is more apt to earn one the sentence to mediocrity that Michener called "the penalty for sliding through life without mastering any competence." Mediocrity is the very doom that the younger generation is trying to avoid, but their escape routes are also leading them away from the "personal growth" they so desperately want to achieve.

The basic dilemma of the younger generation in our narcissistic culture is that they know only what they do *not* want to become, not what they do. Their trust in our institutions has been so damaged and their sense of self so malnourished that they have no valid, dependable ideal of perfection toward which to strive. Some, driven by the outmoded standard of upward mobility, want nothing more than to bury the competition. Others, determined to avoid getting entrapped in the roles that claimed their parents, want simply to be "free"—but how personal freedom can be accomplished without economic freedom remains a universal mystery.

Still others insist that survival is all that matters and life should be played like a game, with noncommitment to any particular job or person as the strategy for beating the odds against old age and death. Some notable authorities, including David Elkind, agree that the willingness to delay commitments is an adaptive solution to the uncertainties of our time. Perhaps so, but it is, nonetheless, "a neurotic evasion of growth." Like all attempted resolutions of the conflict between the impulse to grow and the fear of facing the unknown, "noncommitment" and "vicarious living," as Betty Friedan pointed out, "may temporarily lessen the pressure, but they do not actually resolve the problem." Quoting a psychiatrist, she wrote: "Their result, if not their intent, is always an evasion of personal growth."

A better solution would be to engender greater trust in the self and others by creating a less hostile and indifferent social structure. We need to exert pressure on our institutions to serve rather than exploit the individuals who maintain them. How can we blame people for remaining at a Stage Two level of functioning when they are made to feel—in their social relationships, on the job, at school—that they are completely interchangeable with anyone else, have no worth as individuals, make no contribution of any significant purpose, and have no real power or control over the course of their lives?

Regardless of the parenting practices—or lack of them—in the original family environment, the credentials race fostered by the standard of upward mobility has systematically infantilized our late-adolescent generation and inhibited their social and moral growth. By perverting the academic degree from a *recognition* of achievement into a *requirement* for it, we have kept young adults penned up in college for four, six, or eight years, where, by all accounts, they have been mainly educated in the art of getting good grades. Whatever unconscious feelings of powerlessness their permissive upbringing has bred into them, their financial dependence on their parents or on the state for such a protracted length of time is no help.

The inseparable connection between moral maturity and material means can be inferred from the dismal statistics: defaults on low-interest federally insured student loans have totaled $668 million since 1967. Assuming that the students had no intention of repaying the loans, we must conclude that our colleges and universities have become breeding grounds for the moral weakness that arises out of a prolonged state of helplessness. Or, if the students intended to repay the loans but lacked the funds, we must swallow another unpalatable fact—the students' academic training failed to develop the competence they needed to become economically self-sufficient and therefore capable of carrying out their good intentions.

In either case, it is not the individual who is to blame, but our social institutions. Academia and the workplace are guilty of the collusive credentialism that has aborted the formation of valid educational goals and filled in the void with driven narcissistic competitiveness. The academic-corporate combine, in its rigid Stage One adherence to the standard of upward mobility, has made the degree more important than the training of the mind, the acquisition of skills, or the building of character. It has convinced those "well-socialized" individuals in conformity with the combine's rules that the degree is what really counts. As Daniel Yankelovich has drily observed of the degree mystique: "That credential is worth more (supposedly) than almost anything else—including what you may have learned."

But research into success, at least among male executives, has repeatedly shown a person's values—his belief in self-reliance, commitment to social responsibility, nurturance of the bonds of friendship, devotion to family stability—to be the major determinant of his success along with his ability, and not the money mentality that has mythologized the degree into an icon. "Economic success," one researcher reported after studying one hundred male executives over a decade, "was the highest preoccupation of the *least* successful executives":

The most successful men, I discovered, seem to have more social awareness than other executives. More significantly, the highly successful leader adhered to values incorporated early in his career regardless of the changes in his social milieu. On the other hand, the least successful men have a higher degree of disequilibrium between previous goals and aspiration.

To alleviate the fear of failure and feelings of worthlessness so rampant among our younger generation, we need to free achievement from imprisonment behind the Duncan scale bars of income and occupational status and return it to its original meaning of competence. If parents and the academic-corporate combine equated achievement with performance, in James Michener's sense, rather than with some empty stereotype of success, we would have not only more individuals experiencing the joy of life, but a better society.

Learning, it needs to be said, is a *lifelong* process. It is not some enforced labor, like military service for the draftee, to be crammed into an intermission from the real work of the world. Pressure should be brought to bear on the academic-corporate combine to curb credentialism and support the inclusion of work-related experience into the academic program. As the founder and director of a nationally recognized social service agency, I've seen how this *non*traditional system encourages people to grow intellectually even as they are making a contribution to the larger culture. Even more to its credit, perhaps, it promotes the vision of education as a continuing and integral part of life rather than some kind of monastic preparation for it.

The masses of "hurried children" in our society—whether addicted to alcohol, drugs, or upward mobility—are like infants whose parents are so eager for their babies to walk that they force them to stand upright prematurely and thereby impede their progress. Margaret Mahler offers us a perfect description of one such success-oriented mother pushing her infant "Junie" toward physical maturity—and delaying her—in *The Psychological Birth of the Infant*. It can be read almost as a metaphor, I think, for lateral vs. vertical mobility:

One of the mothers harbored unusually high ambitions for her
child in all areas of functioning. Her favorite word was "success."
Her sturdily endowed baby, Junie, had to cope with the stresses of
the mother's narcissistically tinged symbiotic relationship to her.
Junie could stiffly maintain a standing position on mother's lap,

and mother would clap Junie's hands as if she were already at the pat-a-cake stage. Keeping the little body erect on her lap did not leave Junie's hands free to pat or explore her mother; she would undoubtedly have done so if left to her own devices. This pattern of standing Junie erect, of which her mother was inordinately proud, became, of course, greatly libidinized and preferred by the young infant [and] very marked in Junie's first motor patterns. Later, at the beginning of the practicing period, the impulse to stand up seemed to be a most prominent pattern in Junie's locomotor repertoire, *interfering* (that is, competing) for a relatively long time with the desirable, more mature motor pattern of *propelling oneself forward toward a goal.* . . . Junie's inclination to stand up interfered with her ability to move her arms and legs forward, to make them work together to approach the mother, to crawl forward. Crawling was one of the motor achievements that Junie's mother impatiently encouraged and expected her baby to attain.

In our eagerness to help our children, how do we know when motivation becomes seduction into compliance? And even more relevant to our recent history, how do we know when freedom of choice, offered as an inducement to assume initiative and responsibility for the self, becomes merely an invitation to flounder?

Mahler, again, proves illuminating here with these brief descriptions of two other mothers, one with her infant "Jay," the other with her child "Mark."

Jay's mother thought that any limit set on Jay would interfere with his budding personality and independence. She watched in terror while Jay got himself into dangerous situations. She could not remain in contact with him by talking to him, as she did not want to interfere with his "independence." Although his mother watched him anxiously from a distance, Jay felt, and in a way actually *was,* deserted by her, even in her presence. Over and over again he got himself into dangerous situations that he could neither judge nor master; even while he was doing just the ordinary, he was particularly prone to hurting himself. Once he had fallen and was crying, his mother felt free to help him.

Mark was one of those children who had the greatest difficulty establishing workable distance between himself and his mother. His mother became ambivalent toward him as soon as Mark ceased to be part of herself, her symbiotic child. At times she seemed to avoid close body contact; at other times she might interrupt Mark in his autonomous activities to pick him up, hug him, and hold him. She did this when *she* needed it, not when *he* did. This lack of empathy on mother's part may have been what made it difficult for Mark to function at a distance from her.

"Junie," "Jay," and "Mark," all infants in the early 1960s, are members of the college generation today—and culturally we are still struggling, much as their mothers did, to establish that "workable distance" between coercive overcontrol and negligent permissiveness. Having experienced or experimented with both, we know that Mahler is right. In order to promote autonomy, and with it a desire to reach beyond success to personal fulfillment, we must provide our children with empathetic guidance: restraint or affirmation when *they* need it, not when *we* do.

GUIDANCE WITHOUT COERCION

At Harvard University, the curriculum reform instituted in May 1977—not because of student demands, but because the dean of faculty recognized the need for stricter requirements and some common educational standards—is an example of such empathetic guidance. The surprisingly positive response to the reform from the majority of Harvard's undergraduates clearly signaled their need, previously unspoken, for structure, order, and a supportive foundation of goals to go along with the new campus freedom they inherited from the Sixties. As government professor James Q. Wilson, the head of the faculty-student committee appointed by the dean of faculty to draw up the proposal for curriculum reform, put it in his task force report: "No doubt many students could profit substantially from an unfettered opportunity to find their own way through the two thousand or more courses now offered in the Harvard catalogue. Our judgment, however, is that more students are bewildered than stimulated by this cornucopia. Though they cherish their freedom, they also seek guidance."

Following Harvard's lead, hundreds of colleges around the country have reduced their unwieldy "Chinese menu" catalogues to manageable size by requiring a clearly defined core curriculum, and the response of the students has always been the same—relief and gratitude.

But where do we draw the line? When college students are confused about their educational goals and the faculty responds with more structure and control over the curriculum, this clearly meets the Mahler definition of empathetic guidance: The students are given restraints when *they* need them, not when the teachers do. But when the Los Angeles Board of Education votes for a return to corporal punishment in the city schools—spanking with paddles—because the disciplinary problems are intractable, are we talking about guidance or repression? Is control by physical punishment what the students need in order to become more socially responsible, or is the use of force what the school authorities need to relieve their sense of ineffectuality?

Findings from various studies all lead to the same conclusion: Of the different disciplinary techniques in use—corporal punishment, withdrawal of love, and reasoning—corporal punishment and similar "power assertive" techniques are least effective in stimulating prosocial behavior. The user of force communicates that external power and authority, rather than evaluating the consequences of one's behavior, should control the decisions one makes on how to act. According to one pioneering study conducted by the University of Michigan's Martin Hoffman and his colleagues, the use of power assertion like spanking is not conducive to internalizing control because:

. . . it elicits intense hostility in the child and simultaneously
provides him with a model for expressing that hostility outward. . . .
Furthermore, (power assertion) makes the child's need for love less
salient and functions as an obstacle to the arousal of empathy.
Finally, it sensitizes the child to the punitive responses of adult
authorities, thus contributing to an externally focussed moral
orientation.

And what of the motivations of the pro-spankers? I must confess to feelings of intense uneasiness when I saw the widely circulated newspaper photograph of forty-two-year-old Los Angeles school board member Bobbi Fiedler getting spanked before she cast her vote for corporal punishment in January 1980. Smiling for the camera while a male school official administered three swats of the paddle to her behind, Mrs. Fiedler later claimed to the press that she had endured the paddling in order to vote in a responsible manner. In the article I read (*Philadelphia Inquirer*, February 9, 1980), Mrs. Fiedler, a Republican about to announce her congressional aspirations, was identified as the founder of Bustop, "the largest and most powerful antibusing organization in Los Angeles." Kathleen Brown Rice, another member of the school board and sister of California Governor Jerry Brown, was particularly offended by the spanking pictures, which she thought were "a little bit obscene." Although conceding that Mrs. Fiedler was "bright" and "a quick study," Mrs. Rice described the antibusing, pro-spanking extremist as someone who "hits below the belt." Said Mrs. Rice: "She's a reactionary. There's a kind of intransigence about her."

Intransigence about one's system of beliefs, whether reactionary or radical, always seems to signify that one's actions do not arise out of moral choice but out of mortal fear. The moralistic extremist, who has only a "shared identity" with like-minded others, is not motivated by social concern but by a territorial need to defend the self. As Erikson has explained:

. . . the moral proclivity in man does not develop without the
establishment of some chronic self-doubt and some truly terrible—
even if largely submerged—rage against anybody and anything that
reinforces such doubt. The "lowest" in man is thus apt to reappear
in the guise of the "highest." Irrational and prerational
combinations of goodness, doubt, and rage can re-emerge in the
adult in those malignant forms of righteousness and prejudice which
we may call *moralism*. In the name of high moral principles all the
vindictiveness of derision, of torture, and of mass extinction can be
employed.

While it is admittedly a big leap from the school paddle to the crematorium, the trajectory is still the same. The savage conditions that public school teachers find themselves in today need redress—not by a return to corporal punishment, which is a counter productive and dangerous trend, but, again, by a return to standards.

In his book *The Literacy Hoax*, Paul Copperman convincingly marshals the evidence attributing the current crisis in our high schools to the abandonment of academic standards of performance by teachers and principals in the period of rebellion after 1963. Copperman shows that the educational establishment, carried away by fashionable youth-direction like the rest of us, tried to justify their wholesale defection from standards of academic performance on the basis of accommodating social change. Educational policy-makers claimed that adherence to standards was impossible because of the special needs of minorities, yet the major increase in minority enrollments occurred *before* 1963, when performance standards—and the literacy scores of American high school students—were never higher.

Today we are faced with the fact that literacy performance scores have declined as sharply in many suburban upper-middle-class schools as they have in urban school systems. Our failure to set valid educational limits in our secondary schools has produced a mass of adolescents, privileged and minority alike, who are as deficient in rudimentary academic skills as they are in the fundamental moral values of self-discipline and social responsibility. When the Department of Health, Education and Welfare tells us that 13 percent of all seventeen-year-olds are "functionally illiterate" and that violence and vandalism in the nation's public schools cause more than half a billion dollars in damage yearly, we know that something is radically wrong.

Will the return of academic and behavioral standards to the school system mean the stifling of individual initiative and the exclusion of the socially disadvantaged? Not if the return is more than a mere going back to basics and a dusting off of the old school paddle. The remarkable success of experimental schools that combine structure and discipline with deep concern for the students' psychological needs is instructive. One such school, described by *Time* magazine as a "therapeutic bootcamp," has a student body composed mostly of suburban upper-middle-class "incorrigibles"—half of them drug users by the age of twelve, some beaten and abused much of their lives, others rape victims and prostitutes or classified as hopeless schizophrenics. The school's program, devised by founder Mike DeSisto, a teacher and therapist, leans heavily on Gestalt therapy—individual psychological sessions at least once a week, continual group therapy, and week-long sessions of parent-child group therapy. But discipline is strict and enforced mainly by the students themselves: "The use of drugs, alcohol, or any violence or sex results in an instant dorm meeting and, sometimes, a call for a temporary expulsion. The student is sent outside the gates, then allowed back in after agreeing to perform 250 extra work hours for the community. If homework is neglected or a bed left unmade, fines are subtracted from the $10 weekly allowance earned by each student. An honor code requires everyone to report infractions by other students."

Apparently, the DeSisto method brings results. One of the reclaimed is a boy who had previously been expelled from a state mental hospital as uncontrollable. Another had been a seasoned hand at theft-and-burglary whose career goal, until the school shaped him into college material, was to be a bank robber.

For many overprivileged yet psychologically malnourished late adolescents, college may be a last chance to internalize the kinds of goals that will save them from mediocrity or worse. Given the right direction, they can channel their strivings for recognition into productive, gratifying pursuits. Those who are *too* focused, whose intense drive for achievement may be more in the service of enhancing their self-esteem than in carrying out the natural aims of the self, can benefit from empathetic guidance as well.

At Harvard, for example, before the curriculum reform, freshmen advisers found that preprofessional students did not want to "waste" time on any courses outside their major, a single-mindedness that has traditionally produced highly trained technocrats who are basically uneducated. Conversely, social science and humanities majors, who were afraid to risk getting slaughtered in the "grade war" by coming up against the redoubtable premeds in math and science, later found themselves handicapped by an unfamiliarity with those concepts. The required core curriculum was designed to redress these problems. It includes not only basic subjects like expository writing, math, physics, and biology, but also courses aimed at helping students to internalize and integrate a firm set of values: courses dealing with the moral issues raised by Vietnam and Watergate, the influence of modern technology on our lives, and the comparison between Western and non-Western cultures.

Survival and excellence, it seems to me, need not be mutually exclusive considerations. Excellence suffers most when our institutions grow fat and lazy and unresponsive to our needs. Our failure in the past has been not to recognize the lifelong nature of learning and the way our educational needs change as we do. Since the campus rebellion of the Sixties, our colleges have offered us nothing but monolithic diversity. Now we must get them to recognize the differing needs of their constituencies.

Mature students, who are more experienced in self-discipline and have gained some mastery over their environment, may be good candidates for a "nondirected" career or the pursuit of knowledge purely as a feast for the mind. But the younger students are untried—and they have learned something from the excesses of their predecessors in the Sixties. They do not, as Professor Wilson has put it, "value freedom of choice above all other values." They also admit to a need for guidance, control, and structure. And they are hungry for challenging opportunities to prove themselves or exercise their idealism— a hunger that the charismatic religious cults appeal to and manipulate for their own gains. Academic excellence will not suffer by addressing these needs for challenge and opportunity. On the contrary, the quality of life on the campus can only improve—for everyone— with the tailoring of an academic program that both educates the young and trains them to find, in Erikson's phrase, "a home in the actuality of work and love."

PARENTAL SOUNDS OF SILENCE

If the insidious process of youth-direction stemming from the Sixties turned our colleges into student-run supermarkets of higher education and rendered the professors little more than cashiers at the checkout counter, what has it done to the parents? In effect, it has reduced them to the status of their children's playmates. When the parents began to relive their own adolescence, smoking marijuana and indulging in promiscuous sex in conformity with the standard set by the younger generation, they surrendered their authority as competent role models to their children and became quasi-peers. Today, even if they think their junior high school-age children are too young to be using drugs or experimenting sexually, how can the parents stop them when psychologically they themselves belong to the same peer group?

To make matters worse, when the parents in their frustration turn for help to the high priests of the new religion—psychology, or more particularly, the cult of self-worship, as Paul Vitz has called it—

they become only more confused. Like the rest of us, the therapeutic community is split into two camps: the traditionalists and the new-fashioned.

The traditionalists have always insisted—and time has proven them right—that a sense of guilt is a basic component of our capacity to achieve social maturity and personal fulfillment in adult life. The new-fashioned therapists, on the other hand, have no use for guilt. As much victimized by authoritarianism as we were and as much under the sway of youth-direction, they see themselves as being strictly in the business of absolution. No matter what the dereliction of duty or the destructiveness of the behavior—on either the parent's part or the child's—the new-fashioned therapist is always prepared to see the best in the worst. Infidelity becomes "a growth experience," smoking pot "a rite of passage," disturbed sadomasochism "a sexual preference," the abandonment of one's children "a running toward something" rather than running away.

But the repression of guilt has been a failure. The shamanic waving away of the individual's sense of responsibility by the new-fashioned therapist has cured neither the parents' problems nor the children's. For the irresponsibly liberated, anxiety and depression have moved in on the psychic turf once occupied by guilt. And parents in respectable suburban neighborhoods are watching in helpless terror as their alcoholic and pothead children, many in their early teens, are joining the legions of the "wasted." As illustrated by this mother's response to a *Newsweek* article on marijuana use (January 28, 1980), there is now a growing awareness that the laissez-faire attitude has run its course:

In your article "New Look at Marijuana" (LIFE/STYLE, Jan. 7), you reported a suggestion by some psychiatrists that parents simply accept pot use as a rite of passage. This is the very attitude that keeps the problem with us; most parents would love to view it that way. I was one of them; but I need no controlled studies to see marijuana's role in the stagnation of a young mind or to recognize it as a block to emotional growth rather than a rite of a passage. These children need our help with this problem, not our collusion in it. They need our loving control.

"SOFT DRUG" DOUBLE-TALK

In their role of ever-assenting parents to the parents, the new-fashioned therapists are not only guilty of the parents' same permissiveness of negligence, but they are legitimizing it to a dangerous degree. Their refusal to regard the use of "soft drugs"—marijuana, hashish, mescalin, et cetera—as a cause for concern has imposed an unofficial gag rule on parental objections to the practice. A counterreaction in part to the drug hysteria of the late 1960s, the tendency now, as Keith Stroup of NORML (National Organization for the Reform of Marijuana Laws) has observed, is to exaggerate the harmlessness of marijuana the way we used to exaggerate its harm.

During my four-year stint from 1975 to 1979 as a daily radio commentator on women's issues, I followed the developments of research on the effects of marijuana use with keen interest in order to report on them accurately. Because of my passion for credibility, I found myself doing a disconcerting kind of double-talk routine. In one breath I would give the bad news—the sobering results of a study by a group of researchers showing that "marijuana smoke contains more carcinogenic tar than the smoke from ordinary cigarettes," that "5 marijuana cigarettes are the same as 112 regular cigarettes in terms of inflammation of the lungs," that "mental impairment caused by marijuana smoking may not be completely irreversible," that "the accumulation of THC, marijuana's most potent chemical, in the sex organs may cause sterility in women or birth defects," et cetera. But in the next breath I was forced to give the good news: "Disregard all previous reports because another study has just come out showing that the evidence against marijuana is inconclusive." And in the *next* breath it was: "Sorry, folks, but marijuana smoking *is* dangerous."

My personal inclination is to believe the bad news. I became convinced of the psychological and physical damage soft drugs can cause when burn-outs as young as age nine—middle-class children of divorce—began showing up in my counseling center. Their distraught parents had brought them there—the children stoned on marijuana—after the children had become implicated in such incidents as setting fire to a school building and burning it to the ground.

While all of the effects of habitual marijuana use have not been documented as yet, the psychological damage is inarguable. Reliance on soft drugs as a substitute for self-reliance is no different from any of the other methods of growth evasion—it purchases deliverance from anxiety and stress by ransoming autonomy. Youth-direction has promoted a cultural tolerance of soft drug use amounting to the kind of benign indifference induced by marijuana itself. But even parents who readily accept marijuana smoking as their own social norm are willing to concede the danger of abuse to developing adolescents. They realize that if chronically stuporous children are diverted away from the essential tasks of growing up intellectually, emotionally, and socially, they may never reach psychological adulthood.

Yet the same could be said for psychologically immature adults. How is it possible for sophisticated, bright, even talented people to "find themselves" or to become self-fulfilled when they continually foil the aims of the self by doping themselves up? How can they make the decisions that would lead to an autonomous identity when they repeatedly surrender the self's right to choose and escape into mindless euphoria?

A divorced woman in her late thirties, a successful executive, told me that she'd begun smoking marijuana regularly as an aphrodisiac. She had become involved with a man who aroused her sexually but whose compulsive, controlling nature made her feel very ambivalent. She had hoped marijuana would, to use the terminology, "put her in touch with her real feelings." But marijuana *subverted* her real feelings by repeatedly dissolving her hostility toward the man in a wash of sensuality.

A stormy four-year relationship ensued during which the woman's two young sons became very attached to her lover. When marriage was imminent, her misgivings drove her into psychoanalysis, where, for the first time, she confronted her real feelings. After nine months of analysis, she arrived at the decision that she did not want to live in conflict with an obsessional neurotic the rest of her life. But she had become habituated to the man, just as she had to marijuana. Although their constant fighting had extinguished her capacity to enjoy sex with the man—even on marijuana—the woman could not bring herself to separate from him. Self-denial had become such a pattern with her that she felt constrained to go on simulating the chemistry of love with chemical sex—this time on quaaludes. Eventually she married the man, consigning herself to life with an abusive, unstable neurotic.

Aside from their use as relaxants, instant disinhibitors, and aphrodisiacs, soft drugs promised something much more compelling to the many upper-middle-class adults who turned to them in the late Sixties and early Seventies. Marijuana and pills, the straights hoped, would help them break down the False Self defense they had erected over three or four decades to protect the True Self from compliance with traditional moral and social norms. But as soft drug use became the new social norm among upper-middle-class adults, smoking marijuana, sniffing cocaine, or popping Quaaludes at chic parties merely built up the False Self defense and made it impregnable. The True Self was pushed further into hiding by the coercive pressure exerted by the crowd. Today the fascination with faddish drugs has worn off for those who have struggled through self-doubt and have come to rely on the ego to unravel the mysteries of reality rather than a chemical "magical helper."

THE SEXUAL CREDIBILITY GAP

As permissive and contradictory as professional opinion has been on the subject of drugs, the lack of coherent, consistent advice for providing parental guidance to children on sexual matters has been even more disturbing. The resultant cultural confusion, ambivalence, and uncertainty, mirroring and reinforcing the parents' own inner conflict, have imposed another gag rule on parents. What we now have is a *wordless* revolution: The current pattern of radically changed sexual mores is reverberating with a strange—and strained—parental sexual silence.

An extraordinary study released in December 1978 reveals that despite the liberal and open attitudes brought about by the sexual revolution of the Sixties, most parents have not shed their traditional views on every aspect of sex and sexuality—including the double standard. Less than 30 percent of mothers and 40 percent of fathers approve of premarital sex for their daughters, while 60 percent of mothers and 70 percent of fathers approve of it for their sons. While working mothers take a more egalitarian, liberal position both on premarital sex and on masculine and feminine roles, their husbands do not necessarily share their views. Even parents with liberal attitudes about sex are not sure they want to transmit them to their children. Unable to reconcile traditional values concerning sexual intercourse with their altered vision of masculine and feminine roles, parents have been thrown into a turmoil over expressing and discussing sexuality with their children.

Undertaken by the Project on Human Sexual Development, based in Cambridge, Massachusetts, the study gives the results of interviews with 1,400 parents in Cleveland, Ohio, selected to represent a cross section of parents throughout America. Reporting on what these parents tell their three- to eleven-year-old children about sex and sexuality, the researchers write: "It would be comforting to believe that parents are talking through their changing values, adjusting their life-styles, and helping their children understand sexuality. The evidence, however, is not there."

The report attributes the silence of the Reluctant Generation, in Milt Stevens's phrase, to a "fundamental ambiguity about their own attitudes and the applicability of these values for their children's lives." Today's sounds of silence extend beyond the age-old difficulty parents have always had communicating the basic facts of life (menstruation, intercourse, reproduction) to their children. Contemporary parents, who are unsure of their own beliefs about the more emotionally and morally charged aspects of post-Pill sexuality, including contraception, premarital sex, and sex as recreation, simply do not know what to tell their children—and so remain silent.

Less than half the parents of eleven-year-olds, according to the Cleveland study, ever mention intercourse or contraception to their children. Almost 40 percent never even introduce the topic of menstruation among their nine- to eleven-year-old girls, most of whom will be menstruating within a few years. Less than 1 percent of mothers and less than 2 percent of fathers ever discuss ejaculatory dreams. By the time most children reach the age of nine or ten, they are so discouraged by their parents' discomfort about answering initial sex-related questions that they stop asking.

But to today's "hurried children," the sounds of silence are generally interpreted as an invitation to find the answers out on one's own. *Teen-age Sexuality*, by UCLA sex researcher Aaron Hass (Macmillan, 1979), reports that among fifteen- to 16-year-olds, 43 percent of the boys and 31 percent of the girls have had intercourse. About 28 percent of the boys and 7 percent of the girls have had ten or more sexual partners. More than two-thirds of the girls and nine-tenths of the boys approve of oral sex, and among seventeen- to eighteen-year-olds, more than half of each group has performed it. If such precocity dispels fear and ignorance about sex—a doubtful presumption—it unquestionably tends to devalue sexuality for adolescents, perhaps permanently. Asked to rank six activities in order of importance—doing well in school, friendships with boys, friendships with girls, romance, athletics, and having sex—the seventeen- to eighteen-year-olds ranked having sex last.

While our bewildered silence about sexual behavior and sexual morality propels many adolescents into premature sexual activity and exposure to the risk of undesirable social consequences, such as pregnancy and venereal disease, our mute ambivalence also *impedes constructive* changes in sex-related behavior. For example, 90 percent of the fathers in the Cleveland study reported wanting to express emotion openly. But the fathers themselves rarely shed tears, hugged male friends, or displayed affection toward their wives in front of their children. To compound the inconsistency, both parents discouraged their sons from hugging and kissing, yet sanctioned such affectionate behavior in their daughters. When exposed to this discrepancy between what parents want to communicate and what they actually do, the Cleveland study implies, children may grow up clinging to the notion that nurturance and emotional expressiveness are not masculine traits. Ambivalently reared children may be as loath to depart from stereotypical sex roles as they have been quick to embrace the new morality in their sexual behavior.

No parent has had to contend with more inner and outer conflict, ambivalence, and soul-wrenching confusion about sexuality and the children than the single parent. Having lived through the experience of being a single mother entrusted with the daily care of our two adolescent daughters during the last half of the Seventies, I am personally sensitive to the issue as well as professionally familiar with it. I know only too well how the need to be a "sexual person with your own rights," in the assertive (but not aggressive) language of the new-fashioned therapies, often clashes rudely with the need to be a responsible, empathetic role model to one's children.

The resolution of this problem in my own life has convinced me that the only satisfying answer for oneself and one's children is seeing to it that the children are shielded from impermanent sexual partners. As parents with our own and our children's sexuality to consider, we cannot hope to build a reliable and transmissible value system on the quicksand of, in Robert Merton's phrase, "the imperious immediacy of interest."

Pressured by a culture that continually reinforces the concept of our sexual fulfillment as an inalienable right, many single parents have been forced to temporize rather than adhere to basic personal values. Living together, or some other alternative based on pragmatic expediency, is often conveyed to their children as a new value that has replaced the parents' belief in traditional family ties and the institution of marriage. Yet the high remarriage rate among the divorced—five out of six men and three out of four women—shows that their attitudes are lagging behind their behaviors. Regardless of the coping mechanisms they temporarily embrace and the garbled and erroneous messages they often convey to their children, most divorced people still retain a strong commitment to marriage and the family.

An article in *Harper's Bazaar* (July 1978) is a paradigm of the hypocritical flimflam constantly served up to single parents by the practitioners of the new-fashioned school of advice. "Sex and the Single Parent" by Jane Adams, a writer and author of a book by the same name, predictably rationalizes away the single mother's responsibility for setting sexual standards for her children and offers her absolution for her narcissistic behavior. "Some professionals admit there is no evidence to support the theory that a parent's sexual behavior actually does determine how a child will behave," Adams assures us. As proof, she quotes Jessie Potter's line: "Children take their values from their parents, but they *do* what their peers do," and concludes: "That should give some comfort to those of us who wonder what kind of example we're setting for our children."

Adams claims that what we are really trying to shield our children from when we do not make them privy to our sexual lives is the failure of love rather than the active use of their sexuality. But like many women who felt they had to conform to the *feminist* mystique, Adams's view of love and sexuality is strangely masochistic:

For most of us, the root of sexuality is not physical desire but the wish to avoid loneliness. We confuse the reaching out for closeness with sex, and then expect sex to provide real intimacy. And this is the message we give our children. It becomes *their* expectation, the

standard by which they measure their own sexuality, and it is an
expectation not always met, a standard not universally achieved in
every sexual experience. It is the difference between the way things
are and the way we hope they will be. But being alive means you
keep hoping. And so our children enter into relationships that may
give them the same kind of pain we have encountered. Ultimately,
we must acknowledge that we cannot shield them from all
disappointment.

But is this what we really want to communicate to our children
about our sexuality—that we use it merely as bait to hook lovers into
what we keep hoping will become an intimate relationship? Or do
we want to pass on to our children the ideal of sex as an integral part
of intimacy and an affirmation of it?

We need not go back to the rigid, restrictive view that the only
place for sex is in a fixed, monogamous relationship. As the Cleveland study pointed out, even many married parents, to whom marriage and the family are supremely important values, would like their
children to know that other sexual options besides marriage exist.
But there is a big difference between discussing alternatives with the
children and having a lover—a tentatively intimate one—sleep over to
make the point.

Despite facile reassurances to the contrary, there is no way to
avoid the crucial role parental modeling plays in our children's internalization of values and in the whole of their social and moral development. It may be, as one authority has suggested, that it is the
concept of a *value system* that should be passed on rather than the
values themselves. But the single mother who exposes her children to
the catch-as-catch-can exercise of her sexuality in the manner advocated by Jane Adams is displaying only the "imperious immediacy of
interest"—not any coherent system of guiding ideals.

It is this absence of a system for guiding one's decisions—a system
in which one assumes responsibility for the effects of one's actions on
others—that causes problems for the single mother like this one in
Adams's article:

" 'I have worked out a sex life which is suitable for me,' says one.
'But I'm still not certain it's right to pass it on to my sixteen-year-old
daughter. When she wants to bring a boy home from spring vaca-

tion, what can I do? Especially when my lover is clearly spending nights with me?' "

Since the article provided no answer to the question, I posed it to a well-known psychologist in one of my interviews and was told, quite summarily: "What is appropriate sexual behavior for a woman in her thirties or forties is not appropriate for an adolescent girl."

A neat, pat answer—but somehow it left me feeling very disquieted. When I pondered it some more, I realized what the incongruity was. The psychologist's views fell short of being "new-fashioned," but they were very liberal and tolerant. She approved of a woman with young children having a live-in lover, for example, and drew the line only at having a succession of lovers sleeping over within a short period of time because that would give the children the impression that the mother was not capable of caring. Here was a professional who was light-years away in her attitudes from my repressive, Victorian father. And yet, when she answered my question about the single mother and her sixteen-year-old daughter, I could almost hear my father's voice echoing in my ears, saying as he did so often in his peremptory, authoritarian tone: "Do as I tell you, not as I do."

When we fail—either out of restrictive authoritarianism or anarchic permissiveness—to imbue our children with a sense of their own inner limits, sooner or later we are forced to fall back on empty, didactic rules. Our children sense that we are not in control of our own lives, much less able to guide theirs. And we are then left, as Gertrude was with Hamlet, to bear recriminations and rage for which we have no answer:

O Shame! Where is thy blush? Rebellious hell
If thou canst mutine in a matron's bones,
To flaming youth let virtue be as wax
And melt in her own fire: proclaim no shame
When compulsive ardor gives the charge,
Since frost itself as actively doth burn,
And reason panders will.

My own children were twelve and thirteen when I separated from my husband in the mid-Seventies, and I felt they were burdened with enough stresses of their own without having to confront the exercise of my sexuality under their noses. Although I went through the usual "unmarried woman" syndrome that most newly separated people of both sexes go through, I felt it was imperative for my children's sense of security that I not compromise my authority as a parent in any way. Out of respect for their privacy and mine, I shielded them not from the failure of love—which they had already seen in the home—but from the narcissistic use of them for my own convenience. No matter what the new-fashioned social norms, a moral sense kept me from becoming—thank God—the kind of single mother described by Catherine Breslin in "Waking Up from the Dream of Women's Lib":

Then there's Mark, sixteen and stormy. One night recently Georgia decided to drop this pretense she had used for years of having lovers wind up in the extra bed in Mark's room when they stayed over. Unfortunately her bedroom door was slightly ajar and in the morning Mark heard things that upset him terribly. He ran out of the house, and that night, still very uptight, he told Georgia next time tell him in advance and he'd sleep at a friend's house. They had to talk out the fact that Mommy is also a woman and Mommy lives alone, and it was less hypocritical for this man to stay in her room than sleep in Mark's.

The subject of hypocrisy always comes up when people defend the practice of having lovers sleep over, as if discretion and consideration for others were somehow hypocritical. Personally, I find it much more hypocritical for women like Georgia to pretend that their insensitivity to their children's feelings is openness and candor.

Certainly there are situations where a single mother may decide that living together with a man as a family unit is within the value system she would like to pass on to the children. But once more, hypocrisy enters the picture unbidden. Is the decision to live together really a self-chosen one based on personal beliefs or are there murkier motives: an accommodation to one person's fear of commitment, for example, or—one of the grimier moral pollutants created by divorce—financial reasons?

The Jacqueline Jarrett case is filled with such moral ambiguities. Jackie, a thirty-six-year-old single mother in Illinois, lost custody of her three daughters, Kathy, fifteen; Debbie, thirteen; and Susan, ten, when a trial judge ruled that Jackie's living-together arrangement with twenty-nine-year-old Wayne Hammon could threaten "the moral, physical, and emotional well-being" of the girls. After Jackie fought to regain custody of her daughters for two-and-a-half years, the Illinois Supreme Court, while not disputing the children's desire to remain with their mother, upheld the trial judge's ruling.

Jackie's ex-husband Walter Jarrett, a devout Roman Catholic, reportedly was angry at Jackie for flouting his values in the open and was willing to let her have the girls back if she got rid of her "boyfriend." But Jackie, interviewed by *People* magazine (January 28, 1980), claimed that her life with Hammon was more loving than her marriage had ever been and that "our morality is the basis of our relationship to the children." Described as a "liberated" woman whose "outrage has hardened into a matter of principle," Jackie was prepared to take her fight to federal court if necessary: "The state is telling me: 'To keep your children you have to be married.' I'm resisting an attempt to force marriage on me."

Enter the hypocrisy. One motive for not marrying Hammon, Jackie admitted to *People,* was purely financial. Under the terms of her divorce decree she was required to sell her house and give half the proceeds to her ex-husband if she ever remarried. Hammon's scruples were not above question either. Although he tried to project sincerity, worrying about the effects of the court battle on the children and proclaiming that a "piece of paper" didn't make him any less committed, there was something not altogether convincing about his performance. A divorced man with no children of his own, he raised the suspicion that underneath his nurturant, emotionally open exterior there beat the cautious heart of a commitmentphobe.

A court decision depriving a single mother of custody of her children simply because she chooses to live with a man rather than marry him is repugnant to anyone who believes in our constitutionally guaranteed civil rights. Even those most committed to traditional marriage as an institution would find the notion of *compulsory* marriage abhorrent. Yet there is something distinctly dishonest about a woman's cohabitating with a man in a home she owns jointly with her ex-husband and attempting to protect her lover's squatter's rights as a "matter of principle." If, as Jackie and her lover claimed, morality was the basis of their relationship to the children, then their plight underscores an earlier point: Moral freedom without material freedom is an illusion. How much freedom of choice do we have to marry or not to marry when one of our considerations is keeping a roof over our heads? To go one step further, are we acting out of moral choice or the corruption of it when keeping a *particular* roof over our heads is more important to us than keeping our children?

Whether we call it hypocrisy or simply moral confusion, we are trapping ourselves and our children in a perilous vacuum between our professed beliefs and our behavior. Our ambiguity is our own worst enemy. Because we cannot decide what really matters to us most in life—money or family, novelty or constancy, status or excellence—our identity has no anchor. And since we ourselves are only muddling through, we have no system for valuing experience to pass along to our children. We can give them no safe conduct to take with them on their journey through a bewildering, often terrifying world.

But if a consensus has been lost, it can also be regained. As each of us is groping toward a personal set of postliberation ideals, we must break our silence on those moral truths that have not been eroded by time or social change. However unsure we are of how to meld them with the particular circumstances of contemporary life, we must still speak out for the major human values embedded in our collective conscience throughout our history: honesty, responsibility, decency.

"Nothing is more seductive for man than his freedom from conscience," Dostoevski's Grand Inquisitor said, "but nothing is a greater cause of suffering." Our long wandering through the desert of narcissistic regression has confirmed the Grand Inquisitor's wisdom: "For the secret of man's being is not only to live but to have something to live for."

FOUR

FINDING OUR WAY

$\longleftarrow$ $\longrightarrow$

*Order is not pressure which is imposed
on society from without, but an equilibrium
which is set up from within.*

JOSÉ ORTEGA Y GASSET

TEN

RATIONAL
LOVE

In Joan Didion's *The White Album* (1979), I rediscovered an old "friend" from the early Seventies—Jennifer Skolnik. Although I'd never met her personally, Skolnik had become real to me when I avidly read her intimate "Notes of a Recycled Housewife" in *New York* magazine (May 22, 1972). Like Wanda Adams, the "Dropout Wife" who had landed on the cover of *Life* only several months before, Skolnik also gained instant celebrity when she uprooted herself and her four young children and emigrated to New York from the suburbs of Baltimore in search of that fabled "new life."

When I first saw Skolnik on the cover of *New York*, surrounded by her three older children as she purposefully wheeled the youngest in a baby stroller across a busy Manhattan street, I thought she had the aura of an emerging folk heroine. Casually dressed in a skirt and T-shirt, with her sunglasses pushed up on the crown of her head and her long chestnut hair tumbling loosely about her angular face, she came across, remotely, as a homespun Jackie Kennedy look-alike. To those of us who were then hovering on the brink of making drastic changes in our lives, this woman—"The Suburban Housewife Who Bought the Promises of Women's Lib and Came to the City to Live Them"—was, despite all the "guilts, ambitions, memories, regrets, confusion" that spilled out in her article, an inspiration.

Didion's vision of her is a much different one. With acuity that makes us wince, she depicts Skolnik as one of the starry-eyed "perpetual adolescents": those who were more victimized by the myth of *romantic love* than by male oppression. Skolnik, she tells us, was simply another in a long line of childlike romantics who invoked the political theory of women's liberation to excuse themselves from coping with adult life: "women unequipped for reality and grasping at the movement as a rationale for denying that reality . . . women scarred not by their class position as women but by the failure of their childhood expectations and misapprehensions."

Splicing together snippets from Skolnik's article, Didion identifies these childhood expectations and misapprehensions with a discriminating eye. The sexual passion that had long been missing from the thirty-one-year-old Skolnik's "worn out" marriage was found again, we are told, in a postmarital affair involving "lying together and then leaping up to play and sing the entire *Sesame Street Songbook* on the piano." The "college girl's dream" that Skolnik hoped to play out in New York is repeated for us: "I am going to New York to become this famous writer. Or this working writer. Failing that, I will get a job in publishing." The "promises of women's lib" that Skolnik bought are enumerated for us: "The chance to respond to the bright lights and civilization of the Big Apple, yes. The chance to compete, yes. But most of all, the chance to have some fun. Fun is what's been missing."

Didion recounts all this, as well as similar utterances from other radicalized women, and comments: "Eternal love, romance, fun. The Big Apple. These are relatively rare expectations in the arrangements of consenting adults, although not in those of children, and it wrenches the heart to read about these women in their brave new lives. . . . The astral discontent with actual lives, actual men, the denial of the real generative possibilities of adult sexual life, somehow touches beyond words." Then Didion concludes: "These are converts who want not a revolution but 'romance,' who believe not in the oppression of women but in their own chances for a new life in exactly the mold of their old life. *In certain ways they tell us sadder things about what the culture has done to them than the theorists ever did.*"

THE MYTH OF ROMANTIC DIVORCE

Having lived through the isolation and cynicism of the latter half of the Seventies, we can readily see how foolhardy Jennifer Skolnik was. Even then, when she wrote her declaration of independence, it was apparent that she was in for a bad time. Underneath her bravado, she herself worried that she had traded in her old life for a new one exactly in the same mold. About the missing fun she hoped to find, she mused, "I wonder if there will be time for that now, finally, or whether I am stuck with so many responsibilities that it will still be impossible." Romance, too, was a problem. One man summed it up succinctly when he said to her, "Who do you think is going to come around? Anyone who is looking for a lasting relationship doesn't want instant fatherhood with it. And anyone who is looking for an easy lay who is as old as you are usually has a wife and children of his own in Greenwich." And then there were the children. Were they *really* all right, Skolnik wondered, being left in the hands of a care-taker, going to an inner-city school where they could be "knifed in the corridors," growing up without a father.

Those of us who once looked up to Skolnik as a heroic trailblazer now tend to think of her as a casualty of culture shock. We recognize how irresistibly drawn she was by the tidal pull of youth-direction that lured so many married people out of basically good connections toward novelty, change, transience, and immediate pleasure-seeking. We sense that if she hadn't been pushed over the edge into Stage Two rebellion by forces at work in the culture, she might have found a way to negotiate the transition from housewife to working woman without erupting out of her marriage. And we also sense that just as she had been duped by the myth of romantic love and marriage in our culture, she was destined to be duped yet again by the new myth that was replacing it: the myth of romantic divorce.

"When many couples divorce," wrote a team of researchers in 1977, "they expect less stress and conflict, the joys of greater free-dom, and the delights of self-discovery. With this happily-ever-after attitude, few are prepared for the traumas and stresses they will find in reaching for these goals." Although the researchers conceded that "divorce can be a positive solution when a conflict-ridden marriage destroys family harmony and harms family members," they also warned that divorce must be seen realistically:

"We didn't find a single victimless divorce among the (72) fami-lies we studied. At least óne member of each family reported distress or showed a negative change in behavior, particularly during the first year. Most of them were ultimately able to cope with their problems, but the adjustment was often unexpectedly painful."

Jennifer Skolnik was certainly one whose expectations of divorce, like her expectations of marriage, did not match the reality. What I found most pathetic about Skolnik's story, as well as most instructive about the deviant new form of romantic love in our culture, was her humiliating postmarital affair. By her own account, she picked a man she knew was all wrong for her—a charming but emotionally inaccessible womanizer fearful of involvement, particularly with a woman who was not yet divorced and had children. She knew it was only a matter of time before he would walk out on her for another woman. When he did, in what must be one of the meanest exit lines ever, he informed her that he had only been toying with her all along: " 'I believe in recycling,' " he told me at last. 'Women who are leaving their husbands are my reclamation project.' "

And that's when Jennifer Skolnik *really* fell in love. Getting the man back—even though she knew he was all wrong for her—became her obsession. She sent "killing little notes" to his office, thought about him endlessly, and phoned him incessantly, even interrupting him one evening when he was "indulging with the someone else."

Skolnik rationalized her hopeless masochism as a need to punish herself for being the wrongdoer in her marriage. Guilt sounds like a plausible explanation, and it is one that I hear today from many other women—and men—who seem to be stuck with or chasing after partners with whom they are not happy. But when one examines the expectations of these couples, it becomes clear that guilt is not the cause of their predicament so much as the myth of romantic love. One finds the same dissatisfaction with "run-of-the-mill responsible caring," as Skolnik described it in her article, and the yearning for "complete adolescent worship." One also discovers that same perverse tendency of Skolnik's to ignore the signs of a fundamental incompatibility with the partner, obvious right from the beginning, and to fall "madly in love" nonetheless.

In our culture the state of being "madly in love," which researchers have shown lasts anywhere from six to thirty months on the average, has always been glorified while the more difficult achievement of staying in love has not. The myth of romantic divorce has not only made the ideal of permanence in marriage seem like an anachronism, but it has also created the impression that personal growth occurs at a rate inversely proportionate to the duration of a marriage. Partners are no longer chosen with an eye toward the benefits of lasting intimacy—"the real generative possibilities of adult sexual life," in Didion's phrase—so much as they are latched onto for the short-term "growth experience" of being in love.

TENDERNESS: THE NEW TABOO

Although the sexual revolution removed much of the fear, ignorance, and guilt that had previously inhibited many couples from the full enjoyment of love-making, it also nullified the sexual values that had regulated the choice of partners. In the resultant confusion and uncertainty, the false expectations of romantic love have been augmented rather than diminished. The hope still persists that an ideal god or goddess, once possessed, will bring total happiness and security. It is especially strong in today's gloomy atmosphere where individuals feel more powerless than ever because they fear a whole variety of potential catastrophes—economic, social, political, nuclear, and environmental.

But the current emphasis on uninhibited sexual pleasure in a relationship has greatly reduced people's chances of finding partners with whom they might have lasting, mutual fulfillment after the overidealization fades. The elevation of passion to a position of primary importance has caused people to overlook the more significant factors that enter into an enduring relationship: the social and cultural background of the partners and their common interests; their conscious expectations of their own and their partner's roles in the relationship; and their unconscious feelings about the role of the self in relation to a loved one. Research into marital relationships has shown that if there is discord at any one of these levels of connection but harmony at the other two, the couple will stay together, although in chronic conflict. If there is basic disagreement at two or all three of these levels, the marriage will usually end in divorce.

The search for the right sexual connection has sidetracked many people into relationships which they knew, consciously or unconsciously, were wrong from the outset. But, like Skolnik, they have pursued these sexually satisfying but emotionally untenable relationships under the romantic illusion that "love conquers all." Others, to avoid the oppressive loneliness and impersonality of the single world, have settled for "second-best" relationships in which they themselves are emotionally unavailable. Although they enjoy a satisfying sex life in a liaison that has all the earmarks of a committed relationship, they yearn continually to have in actual, everyday life their unfulfilled fantasy of ideal love.

Both the seekers and the settlers remind us that in the tradition of romantic love nothing so stirs the passionate longing for another as the other's unattainability. In breaking down the old taboos and prohibitions, the sexual revolution has somehow left the essentially masochistic nature of romantic love untouched. The *sexual* inaccessibility of the idealized god or goddess has merely been replaced by *emotional* inaccessibility.

Yet there are couples I know who have remained wholly and happily committed to each other for twenty years or more in marital relationships that have mutually enriched as well as stabilized their lives. Despite the onslaught of cultural change and the stresses of their own internal changes related to adult psychological growth, their commitment has deepened year after year. One mother of four, for example, whose husband encouraged and financed her through graduate school in the Sixties, reciprocated by supporting the family throughout most of the Seventies after her husband quit his engineering job in mid-life to become a pediatrician. By resisting the myth of romantic divorce, couples like these have shown that personal growth is not a wild flower unable to survive in the hothouse of marriage.

When I talk to men and women who have achieved in their fields and who also have a stable family life or good intimate relationships, I find that these people are the most personally fulfilled—the ones who feel that life has purpose and meaning. Their relationships are molded by a deep awareness of the self and others rather than by fantasies of unlimited success or ideal love. In a culture barren of heroes, they stand out as models to emulate—not some group of lost adolescents who are spinning around in the values vacuum, grasping at wisps of pleasure from moment to moment.

The people I know who've been happily married a long time still have good sex—and they have *love*, not stifling "togetherness" nor practical "arrangements." Their role functions are flexible and interchangeable to some degree, but their commitment remains constant and eroticized. Theirs is not—and perhaps never was—the crazy, intense, delusional passion that burns itself out in a couple of years. It's a more nurturant kind of love, more sustaining. It's romantic, yet not irrational. In fact, rationality, in the sense of accepting reality, seems to be at the core of it. It's what I call *rational love*—and it is shaping up as the love of the future.

THE GOD/GODDESS SYNDROME

Since part of us remains an infant lifelong, how can we possibly cure our generational *Bacillus neuroticus*—the infantile yearning all of us have to regain the lost bliss of perfect attachment we once knew, or might have known, in the womb? How can we bear the burden of our basic core of dependency needs crying out to be met throughout our lives—our needs for security, love, confirmation, recognition—without our palliative fantasies of finding unconditional love?

It is not our fantasies of unconditional love that we have to give up, only our hope of having them fulfilled. "Ideals are guides," as Kohut says, "not gods." When we are functioning on a mature level, the rational part of our mind (the cerebral cortex) recognizes when our more primitive dependency needs are irrational and modulates them. We can distinguish between the self's normal needs for nurturance and those excessive demands for constant, unqualified approval and attention that correspond to our fantasies of unconditional love. It is only when narcissistic injury has fragmented the self with deep uncertainties about its own power and about the virtue of its values that we keep searching for that "oceanic feeling" of perfect merger. Having made a god out of our romantic ideal, we feel we are "settling" or compromising down—rather than compromising *up* with reality—when our demands for unconditional love have to be modified.

Romantic love, like upward mobility, is another of our antiquated cultural ideals that is highly charged with unhealthy narcissism and needs to be replaced. The inspiration of tortured genius from Dante to Woody Allen, romantic love has been called one of Western civilization's greatest inventions, but it has, more dispassionately, been one of our greatest causes of social disorder.

The assault of romantic love on the family, both from within and without, has been relentlessly destructive. Based on what appear to be preoedipal fantasies involving intense feelings of excitement, longing and pining, and idealization, the state of romantic passion depends on the unavailability of the love object. There must be obstacles to overcome—barriers and taboos. The extreme intensity of romantic love requires that the love object remain a mysterious, fascinating stranger—an impossible partner in a close, sustained monogamous relationship but one of the most alluring ones in an uncommitted affair.

Besides being transient and irreconcilable with commitment, romantic love is infantile and outmoded in its attitudes toward male and female sexuality. Implicit in its construct is a symbiotic merger between a strong, dominant male and a helpless, tender female in need of his protection. Each sees the other as the perfect, inexhaustibly available Love Goddess or God who is going to fulfill all of his/her psychic needs.

When the idealization breaks down within a few years, the more narcissistically inclined are unable to recharge it and develop mature genital sexuality based on mutuality and affection. They must be "in love" again, find someone new with whom they can relive the early childhood fantasies of mother-child oneness before the separation process began. The archenemy of family stability, romantic love, in combination with our aberrant individualism, has given rise to the myth that personal growth can best take place outside the family portals. But strongly committed couples who have resisted the pressure to divorce, as we have seen, can facilitate each other's passage through a personal growth crisis. As Dr. Louise J. Kaplan, author of *Oneness and Separateness: From Infant to Individual,* has said of the "second birth" (the stages of psychological development) as they occur in adulthood today: "A person need not actually leave home and return to have the emotional experiences of the second birth. In fact one could almost say that expansion of selfhood and self-realization can occur only in the mind. Perhaps it is symptomatic of our times that people feel compelled to *act out* themes of their second birth rather than experience them internally."

At a time when we are moving ever closer to sexual equality, romantic love has become an anachronism. The feminist movement and the sexual revolution have removed the artificial barriers, taboos, and risks—the fear of pregnancy, the virginity code, et cetera—that were once the props of grand passion. The need to become intensely emotional over sexual attraction has disappeared, but the need to sustain sexuality in an emotionally close relationship has become imperative. We need a new kind of love, and *rational love* promises to be both more personally fulfilling and kinder to the family. Emphasizing the fusion of tenderness and genital satisfaction and upholding the autonomy of the partners as well as the bonds of attachment, rational love draws its wonder and mystery from a deeper wellspring than sexual passion. Its excitement comes from identification, not with a new partner, but with the newness in the same partner as he or she keeps changing and evolving through the different stages of growth.

In *Women on Love*, French feminist Evelyne Sullerot uses a collage of women's writings to give us a panoramic view of the vicissitudes of love from medieval times up to the present. She begins with the flowering of romantic love in the Middle Ages, describing how the social disorder created by sexual greed made it necessary for the church to declare adultery a sin and marriage a sacrament; she shows us how the "purification" of marriage slowly squeezed the sexuality from it and created the madonna/whore schism that was to plague women for the next three centuries; she demonstrates how the rise of materialistic values in the nineteenth century imprisoned "good" women in chaste marriages to mechanical men and drove them into hysteria from sexual repression; she documents how this development led, as the last century ended and our own began, to an outbreak of lesbianism, which Sullerot sees partly as a narcissistic glorifying in selfhood and partly as a hostile counteraction to the crass insensitivity of men. And finally she brings us to our own time when eroticism has turned pornographic and romanticism has gone the way of *Love Story*.

But Sullerot is obliged to give us the truth, even if it hurts her: "Conjugal life, curiously enough, remains the refuge of love amid a thousand fumbling searches for love, a fact which would have come as a surprise to our medieval women writers." Sullerot, who seems surprised by this herself, falls back on idealization, the staple of romantic love, to explain the phenomenon, conjecturing that "today's young women with powerful imaginations reinvent gods in order to adore them. . . ."

From my observations, that is precisely what women who are rationally in love today are *not* doing. Because the women no longer believe the childhood fantasies of their own powerlessness, they have no need to overidealize, to make gods out of the men they adore. The women need only reciprocity, not invincibility. They have accepted the human imperfections, the individuality of the men they are committed to; and the men, who have outgrown the need for their own childhood defensive fantasies of omnipotence, have done the same.

How important is idealization to a true love relationship? Without inventing gods or goddesses, at least initially, are we leveling the grandeur of love to the dull, boringly familiar terrain of the ordinary? It was Freud who originally noted that a good love relationship is not only possible without any idealization, but that in many cases idealization hinders rather than helps the development of mature genital love. In exploring the barriers to falling and remaining in love, psychoanalyst Otto Kernberg explains why this is so. A primitively idealized relationship—the kind one finds in novels of gothic romance—may be tied in with a need to see the love object as all-good (and perhaps pure and unavailable) and the rest of the world as hostile, cold, selfish, and mean. If the person holds onto this splitting defense and never sees the love relationship and the love object realistically, he or she will never develop "the capacity for mourning, guilt, and concern . . . a deepening awareness of the self and of others, the beginning of the capacity for empathy and for higher level identifications" present in mature love.

Both romantic love and rational love are linked to feelings of sadness, but the roots of this sadness are worlds apart. In romantic love the sadness derives from pining and yearning to recover the lost bliss of infantile merger; in rational love, the sadness comes from accepting the loss of this unfulfillable fantasy in order to enjoy the richness of mature intimacy. As Kernberg explains:

The elements I would stress regarding the mourning processes involved in being in love are those of growing up and becoming independent, the experience of leaving behind the real objects of childhood at a time when the most intimate and fulfilling kind of love relation with another human being is established. In this process of separation from the real objects of the past, there is also a confirmation of the good relations with internalized objects of the past, as the individual becomes confident of his capacity for combining love and sexual gratification in a growth-promoting mutual reinforcement—in contrast to the conflict between love and sex in childhood.

THE SEXUAL SWINDLE

Romantic love in our time deceives and victimizes the innocent by implying that sexual passion guarantees the capacity to love. One of the saddest discoveries of the sexual revolution was that the ability to achieve orgasm during intercourse did not necessarily mean that either the individual or the partner had now reached psychosexual maturity. As Kernberg points out, people suffering from severe narcissistic isolation may be fully capable of orgasm during intercourse while people with only a mild neurosis may not. What appears to be the height of romantic passion in the sexually "free" pathological narcissist is only a "split-off" of a primitive drive—a form of isolated need gratification that the more mature, and possibly more inhibited, person may have left behind.

The sexual revolution taught us that complete genital satisfaction with a partner is not a reliable indication that it is possible to fall and stay in love with this partner. In addition to genital satisfaction, a true love relationship includes what has been called "genital identification," whereby the "interest, wishes, feelings, sensitivity, shortcomings of the partner attain—or are supposed to attain—about the same importance as our own." Contemporary romantic love, in which sex precedes intimacy instead of evolving out of it, has itself become a cultural barrier to falling and staying in love. People in search of love are often misled by immediate genital excitement into longing for or becoming committed to partners whose undisclosed interests, wishes, feelings, et cetera, are so in conflict with their own that absolutely no hope for a "genital identification" exists.

In the course of my interviews with single, sexually experienced women in the current postcollege generation, I was surprised at how often they expressed a wistful desire for "courtship"—a curiously quaint word in our modern times. Very frequently I heard women voice the same complaint: They resented being thought "unliberated" when they tried to turn down the sexual advances of a man they had just met. They wanted to restore the option of chastity, but lacked the confidence to do it. When I consulted psychiatrist Joan Enoch, a divorced woman who had experienced this problem herself, she explained: "A man's defensive disdain at a woman's refusal may make him become punitive, and a woman without a strong sense of self has the fear of not being able to stand up against what she perceives to be a stronger personality."

Besides this irrational fear of the opposite sex as inherently stronger, there are other psychological barriers that both men and women must overcome before developing the capacity for the depth and richness of rational love. Many people are crippled by a deep-seated envy of the opposite sex, which makes them controlling or clinging, and yet at the same time they experience normal dependency on a specific man or woman as frightening. The inability to depend fully on a partner, because one is either certain of frustration or uncertain of the ability to preserve one's autonomy, can be a factor in both sexual promiscuity and sexual inhibition.

Romantic love, despite its glorification of sexual passion, makes it difficult to sustain uninhibited sexuality in a committed relationship because its model of total merger exacerbates these primal fears. But rational love, stressing the partners' self-reliance and independence, gives them the courage to be totally vulnerable to each other—sexually and emotionally—without fearing either the loss of the partner or the loss of identity. People who are rationally in love know their own limits. They look to sex to reaffirm their identity—not to create it. They are spared the current obsessive search for sexual variety promoted by our culture because they know that it is not sex that gives us our sense of self, but our sense of self that readies us for complete human satisfaction in a sexual relationship. Kernberg makes this profoundly important point: "Normal sexual identity is a *consequence* of, rather than a prerequisite for, normal identity formation. It cements ego identity and gives it depth and maturity."

CURING THE *BACILLUS NEUROTICUS*

Contrary to popular mythology, it is the sexual passion in romantic love that becomes dull and boring in time, whereas sexual expression in rational love continually reaches new levels of excitement, communion, even mysticism, in partners who have overcome early emotional injury and resolved the oedipal conflicts of childhood. People who have gone through growth phases, both married people and divorced people who have happily remarried or entered into a stable, committed relationship, say that sex is infinitely better now than it ever was. They also describe being able to relate to the partner in a more complete and multifaceted way, identifying not only with the loved person but with the values for which the person stands—intellectual, esthetic, cultural, and moral. Kernberg attributes this higher level of identification with the loved one to a healing of the old wounds of childhood. With the dissipation of rage and rebelliousness, one is able to reach total fulfillment in rational love and also reach a new bridge to one's previously disowned part. "In this establishment of identifications with the love object involving value systems," Kernberg writes, "a movement from the interrelation of the couple to a relationship with their culture and background is achieved, and past, present, and future are thereby linked in a new way."

Total fulfillment in rational love thus hinges on an indispensable precondition: We must first settle the reciprocal relationship of costs between ourselves and our parents. We must separate from them psychologically, with all the anger and guilt that that implies, while still valuing our connectedness to them on an adult level. All too often we tend to dismiss our parents as hopelessly unchangeable—another mythology that our youth-oriented culture supports. But this attempt to "write off" our parents merely perpetuates the generational virus. Our unconscious anger and guilt binds us to the search for unconditional love; and our distancing of ourselves from our parents becomes a role model for our children who, at some future time, will repeat the "writing off" of the older person.

There can be no effective cure of our generational *Bacillus neuroticus* without our personally working through—behaviorally as well as psychologically, if possible—our rage and guilt at not having our childhood emotional needs responded to appropriately by our parents. (Our guilt, incidentally, may have been reinforced by our parents' blaming *us* for their own shortcomings.) As the rage and guilt subside and we develop a mature forgiveness for parental inadequacies, seeing them as the result, perhaps, of our parents' own childhood experience, we become able to love our parents (and others) rationally. If we can take our parents for what they are at the current time, we will discover that, in the words of an authority on geriatrics, "The aging face of life is a stage of atonement." Given half a chance, most older people are very eager to make things right for themselves before they die and right with their family of younger and older adults.

In my relationship with my own mother—she is now seventy-five—I have seen how this desire for atonement has transformed her later years. Always generous with her possessions, she has begun to *love* as an act of giving. Regardless of her own aspirations for us, she can now accept uncritically the limits her children and grandchildren have chosen for themselves. My mother has suffered greatly because of my particular need to distance myself from her in order to live my own life, but I think she understands. Two summers ago, when I went to see her in the hospital after she'd been viciously mugged, she held me close to her and said, "I thought I'd lost you." There was a time when I thought she had, too—but I know now that she never will.

It is only through the process of reconciliation with our parents that we finally learn how to accept *less* than unconditional love—an unavoidable condition of life—with grace. When we have achieved a solid representation of our parents in our mind, accepting them by incorporating both love and hate, we are finally ready to love others and to work with others as mature adults. We have come to the ultimately liberating realization that while we have a right to expect, as Kohut puts it, "a modicum of empathetic responses" from others who are important to us in adult life, we cannot ask them to make up for the "traumatic failures" of those who loved us first in childhood.

Ingmar Bergman's film *Autumn Sonata* is a powerful study of how a woman divests herself of her childhood rage at her narcissistic mother and, by understanding the context in which it arose, frees herself to love. The film centers on an emotionally charged confrontation between Charlotte, the concert pianist mother (Ingrid Bergman) and her older daughter Eva (Liv Ullman). It has been seven years since they have seen each other, and Eva, now grown and married (to a man whose love she cannot return), invites Charlotte to her home after the death of Leonardo, Charlotte's patient and adoring longtime lover.

Furious at her mother for her supreme indifference to her children, Eva attacks Charlotte: "You're shut inside yourself and always stand in your own light." Recalling the pain of her childhood, Eva flails at her mother for inflicting a terrible feeling of abandonment on her when Charlotte went on tour for months at a time. But when Charlotte was home, things were no better. "You were always kind, but your mind was elsewhere," Eva says accusingly. "I knew instinctively that you didn't mean what you said. I loved you, Mama. It was a matter of life and death, but I didn't trust your words."

Eva complains that when Charlotte was not on tour she used her effusive energy to make up for her neglect, never leaving Eva alone, having her hair cut or dresses made for her without even asking Eva what she wanted. And then comes the bitterest recrimination of all, the one leveled at parents almost universally by children who grew up looking in vain for an affirming reflection of themselves in the parental mirror: *"Not a shred of the real me could be loved and accepted."*

Moved as we are by Eva's outpouring of rage, it is Charlotte's response that touches us even more by revealing the tortured inner emptiness of the narcissist. Charlotte describes how she herself was raised without either caresses or punishment, with no tenderness, contact, warmth, or intimacy. "I wonder whether I've lived at all," she says. "I have never grown up. My face and my body have aged, but inside I haven't even been born." And we come to see the dilemma, if we haven't lived it in our own lives, of the parent who has not become an adult—the terror and ambivalence of a child rearing a child. "I wanted to love you," says Charlotte, "but I was afraid of your demands. I didn't want to be your mother. I wanted you to know that I was as helpless as you were."

But the film ends on a note of hope—and its message is vital to our understanding of the need for limits in our lives. What Bergman tells us finally is that no one can live in the world of liberated feelings as if there were no God, no conscience, without ultimately paying a price. As long as Eva wallows in hatred for her mother and insists that there can be no forgiveness, she must remain an emotional cripple, incapable of loving. And as long as Charlotte ignores the guilt she has been harboring and refuses to make reparations, she must remain hounded by emptiness.

Yet there is a mercy after all. It lies in moving beyond the self-centeredness of narcissistic injury toward mutuality—taking advantage of, as Charlotte says, "an opportunity to know each other and to take care of each other." When Charlotte asks for Eva's forgiveness and is rebuffed, she leaves. But Eva reconsiders and begins the healing process of reconciliation by writing a letter to her mother in which she affirms their primary ties and makes this pledge: "I will never let you vanish out of my sight again. I will persist."

THE PETER PAN HANGUP

What of the individuals in our own narcissistic culture who lack Eva's determination and strength—the ones whose injuries to the self have left them without the capacity for the give-and-take of mutuality or the ability to compromise and resolve conflicts? Many such people in their twenties and thirties, who are among the brightest and best-educated of their contemporaries, have been criticized as "selfish" for not wanting to marry or have children. Must we insist that they marry and have children anyway, knowing full well that without a determination to grow they will perpetuate the generational virus?

A study of contemporary young women in America who chose to remain childless either through contraception or sterilization showed that most of the women felt a child would be an overwhelming responsibility for them. Conducted by physicians Nancy Kaltreider and Alan Margolis, who published their findings in the *American Journal of Psychiatry*, the study of thirty-three women also revealed that many feared they would be bad mothers or emotionally destroyed by their children. Over half the sterilized women claimed they had never pictured themselves as mothers and 60 percent said they couldn't stand babies or children. Some of the women were concerned that they would become like their own mothers, whom they described as cold and unresponsive. The researchers concluded that because the women felt they would not be good mothers, they had made their choices in a responsible manner.

My own attitude is best expressed by one of my "role models," Geraldine Spark, formerly associate director of the family therapy department at Eastern Pennsylvania Psychiatric Institute in Philadelphia, a woman of my generation who has combined a productive career with a long, satisfying marriage and motherhood. Says Spark: "I have tremendous respect for the young women I see who have faced themselves and acknowledged openly that they don't have the capacity for motherhood instead of going ahead with it because they feel they have no other options. It's like divorce. In our generation, narcissistically fixated people who didn't think of divorce and didn't dare to divorce lived in marriages where everyone suffered horrendously. In terms of shading, if the marital or parental state is that bad for some people, then it's progress not to live in such misery." But it is not progress to try to postpone maturation. Rejection of the marital or parental role on the basis of responsible choice is not the same as the prolonging of a Peter Pan-like adolescence through "the cult of self-worship" and the myth of romantic love. Our cultural abhorrence of aging—Timothy Leary once admitted that the Woodstock dream was "to create a new species capable of postponing terminal adulthood"—has created a magnetic pull toward youth. For people in their forties and fifties whose early narcissistic wounds have never healed and who feel increasingly helpless and threatened as they face the waning of their physical powers, the draw of youth— not necessarily real—is health. People in their teens or twenties, the supposition goes, have not had enough time to become as battle-scarred by life as those who have reached middle age. The youth-worshipers join the eternal chase to avoid inevitable change. Instead of pursuing real health by consolidating their inner limits and drawing strength and direction from a stable, nurturant source of commitments and goals, they grab at the straws of illusion.

Two popular films of 1979, Woody Allen's *Manhattan* and Blake Edwards's *"10,"* both explore this golden fantasy of the redemptive power of youth against a background of contemporary cultural decay. While *Manhattan* was by far the greater artistic and critical success, it was *"10,"* curiously enough, that dealt more realistically with the fantasy of all-knowing, all-giving youth as the healer of the wounds of time.

In *Manhattan,* Isaac Davis (Woody Allen) is a divorced, middle-aged comedy writer who is a member of a band of roving cultural narcissists. Committed only to their own neuroses, they are unable to invest themselves fully in work or love, and they move in and out of relationships—sometimes with the same person—with kaleidoscopic fluidity.

Besides Isaac, there is his best friend Yale (Michael Murphy), a charming but weak-willed college teacher of literature, a perennial preppie, who intends to write an important book but can't get around to finishing it and who loves his wife but can't stay faithful to her or make the commitment to having children.

Then there is Mary (Diane Keaton), a stylish, sophisticated critic with a fast-talking façade and a heart of mercury, whose quicksilver sense of self bounces up and down as she darts from lover to lover—in this case, from Yale to Isaac and back to Yale again.

Isaac's ex-wife (Meryl Streep), a bisexual who left him for another woman, publishes a book called *Marriage, Divorce and Selfhood*. An embarrassment to Isaac, the book is one of those strange publishing-industry phenomena in which a woman, once known only as the wife of a celebrity, builds a separate new identity for herself by unsparingly revealing the private man. We know that Isaac's ex-wife is a confirmed "identity-shopper" by this much-quoted description of her that Isaac gives to Mary: "She was a kindergarten teacher, then she got into drugs and moved to San Francisco. She went to est, became a Moonie. She works for the William Morris Agency now." This capsule biography is meant to suggest that in our society the quest for spiritual meaning inevitably ends in materialism. But if it does—if the seeker finds only marketable skills and has not also discovered standards for employing those skills to *confirm* the self rather than feed its insatiable hunger for aggrandizement—then the search for personal fulfillment never ends.

Isaac has yet to learn this lesson in love, but in his professional life he is making strides. Disgusted with the inanity of situation comedy, he quits television and throws away a big income to do what he feels he *should* do with his talent—write a book. With women, he is not so secure. Although he is enjoying a relationship with his seventeen-year-old girl friend Tracy, the only character capable of mature love, he abruptly dumps her to take up with Mary after Yale has given her up. Isaac finds the emotionally inaccessible Mary more challenging than Tracy, but also completely unreliable. When Yale decides to resume his affair with her, it is Isaac's turn to get dumped.

Furious at Yale, Isaac drags him away from the class he is teaching and pulls him into an empty anatomy classroom where, with the skeleton of an ape as a backdrop, he delivers the movie's most important speech. "You're too easy on yourself," Isaac tells Yale. "You're not honest with yourself. You want to write a book—instead you buy a Porsche. You cheat on your wife, lie to your friends." Yale retorts, "You're so self-righteous. Who do you think you are—God?" And Isaac replies, only half-jokingly, one imagines: "I have to model myself after someone."

If anything, Woody Allen is *too* idealistic. He is a visionary who would like to believe that by rearing the young on drugs and sex instead of having them "tucked in by their grandparents" as he had been at their age, we have somehow produced a brave new master race. Having presented these children with no definite values of right and wrong and instilled in them a tentativeness about all relations by making recurrent divorce an aspect of their lives, we have allowed them, Allen supposes, to grow up perfect. In Tracy he has created a young wonder woman. At seventeen, she has none of the psychological problems we find so prevalent among adolescents in real life today. Instead, she is possessed of absolute, unshakable self-trust, an ability to invest herself fully in genital love without inhibition, and the discipline—more so than her middle-aged partner—to handle commitment. When Isaac returns to her at the end of the film like a beaten puppy, she shows no anger or vindictiveness, only compassion. "Not everybody gets corrupted—you have to have a little faith in people," she tells him encouragingly as she goes off to study drama in Europe. One wonders if it is not *Tracy* who is patterning herself, in the absence of any other visible role models, after God.

In Blake Edwards's "*10*" we find a similar overidealization of the sexually uninhibited young by a middle-aged man, but under an opposite set of circumstances that lead to the hero's complete disillusionment with the fantasy rather than its reinforcement. George Webber (Dudley Moore) is a forty-two-year-old music writer of some renown who, as his psychiatrist describes it, is obsessed with the ugliness of old age and the fear of dying ("After forty," George says, "it's all patch-patch-patch"). Although George describes his companion "Sam" (Julie Andrews), a singer and a contemporary of his as "mostly great," he is fixated on staving off old age by falling in love with a beautiful young girl. Accordingly, he has adopted the adolescent practice of rating potential candidates for his romantic ideal on a scale of one to ten, purely on the basis of their physical attributes.

George finds his "10" (Bo Derek), a breathtaking young beauty, when he catches sight of her riding in the family Mercedes to her wedding. In the grip of his obsession, he pursues her to Mexico, where she is honeymooning, and doggedly trails her to her hotel. He fantasizes rhapsodically about her as, unnoticed, he lies near her on the beach. His moment to be alone with "10" finally comes after he has heroically rescued her husband from drowning. While her husband is recuperating in the hospital, George pays a call on his fantasy woman in her honeymoon suite.

To his astonishment, it is "10" who coolly seduces George. In the perfunctory manner of someone shuffling a deck of cards before playing solitaire, she invites him to make love to Ravel's *Bolero*. When the music stops and she insists that George get out of bed and turn the record over in order for her to continue, we suspect that "10" is not so sexually "free" after all. George's sensibilities take their biggest beating when "10" receives a telephone call from her hospitalized husband and chats imperturbably while George is lying at her elbow.

Humiliated at being used so dispassionately by a woman, George angrily asks "10" why she got married. "I wanted to," she answers. She then expounds upon her philosophy of unmitigated self-gratification in what sounds like the brief recorded message of a vacuous Phonemate: "I sleep with someone because it makes me happy. I want to. It pleases me." Numb with disappointment, George tells her, "I thought you were someone special." And "10" insists blandly: "I *am* special. I do what I want."

George Webber's punishing experience, I have found, is more typical of the outcome of this kind of relationship in our time than Isaac Davis's. The common confusion between free choice and narcissistic entitlement—"I do what I want"—has not generally equipped the current generation with the value system and sense of identity necessary for real intimacy or commitment. It is self-deceptive for "10" to think that she does what she wants when she has no concept of who she is or what she stands for. Other than making inconsequential choices of the moment, we cannot know what we want without knowing what we believe. How can we say that we want to marry someone, for example, without having clearly defined what we believe a marital commitment means or what our role as a marriage partner should be? (The young woman in "10" admits, in fact, that she married her husband, after two years of living together, to please her parents—a "free choice," the movie suggests, that was made to secure her financial future.)

When George Webber returns to "Sam" at the end of the film and asks her to marry him, it is not in desperation or defeat. Here is a man who has the quiet strength born of the acceptance of reality—a man rationally in love. He has given up frantically trying to cling to something that is impossible—the dream of an eternally blissful "in love" phase that is appropriate in a fantasy life or at the height of adolescence—and has accepted that life goes on, the new phases come whether one likes it or not, and somewhere one reaches an end of "in love."

THE FIDELITY FACTOR

Romantic love exacerbates our terror of aging and death because it exhorts the partners to remain in adolescence forever, whereas rational love lessens these terrors by inviting the partners to depend on each other as they go through their inevitable growth stages. Sustained by their interdependence, partners who are rationally in love summon the courage not to flee the tasks and responsibilities that are involved in each growth phase. Instead, they move into them, individually and together, fighting for themselves and the relationship and accommodating and adjusting to the changes in each other as they go.

Describing marriage as a "huge huge work, like Michaelangelo and the Sistine Chapel," author Enid Bagnold *(National Velvet, The Chalk Garden)* gives us an exquisite delineation of the difference between romantic love and the ideal of rational love in *Autobiography*. Written when she was in her eighties, the book is a remembrance of her life not only as an author but also as the mother of four children and the wife, for forty-four years until his death, of Sir Roderick Jones, head of Reuters, the British news agency. In her memoirs she tells us:

When I look back on the paint of sex, the love like a wild fox so ready to bite, the antagonism that sits like a twin beside love, and contrast it with affection, so deeply unrepeatable, of two people who have lived a life together (and of whom one must die), it's the affection I find richer. It's that I would have again. Not all those doubtful rainbow colours. (But then she's old, one must say.)

The beauty of rational love is the depth and continuity of the commitment. Fidelity is a given; it resides in the nature of human beings who have done the work of adolescence and have ended the search for unconditional love. The commitment, over repeated "genital identifications" with one person, has become internalized. It has fallen into place in the configuration of permanent values that make up the moral consistency of each partner—regardless of whether the prevailing trends in the culture uphold or oppose those values.

But cultural support for fidelity in a committed relationship, whether married, living together, or whatever new form it may take, is imperative for the stability of a society where personal fulfillment has become a dominant goal. As Kernberg explains, the more self-fulfilling one becomes, the more one's capacity for depth in relation to one's own self as well as to others "opens the deep pathways of the unspoken multiple reactions among human beings." The permanence of love, as well as the deepest fruition of it, thus becomes almost exclusively an act of commitment:

As someone becomes more capable of loving in depth and better able realistically to appreciate someone else over the years as part of his or her personal and social life, he or she may find others who, realistically, could serve as an equally satisfactory or even better partner. Emotional maturity is thus no guarantee of nonconflictual stability for the couple. A deep commitment to one person and the values and experiences of a life lived together will enrich and protect the stability of the relationship, but, if self-knowledge and self-awareness are deep, at the cost of activating from time to time a longing for other relations (the potential of which may be a realistic assessment) and repeated renunciations. But longing and renunciation also may add a dimension of depth to the life of the individual and the couple; the redirection of longings and fantasies and sexual tensions within the couple's relationship may likewise bring an additional, obscure, and complex dimension to it. All human relationships must end, and the threat of loss, abandonment, and, in the last resort, of death is greatest where love has most depth; awareness of this also deepens love.

ELEVEN

PILGRIM'S PROGRESS

When I checked back with some of the people whose stories have appeared in this book, I discovered that each of them, despite frustrating setbacks along the way, is groping toward rational love. Whether they are in relationships or between them, thriving in their careers or holding their own, their experiences have given them a deeper sense of self and of their goals and values. Armed with this knowledge, they are making strides in breaking out of the narcissistic lock of the Seventies and are moving toward a more enlightened and nurturant form of relatedness to others.

One of the significant discoveries for me was that the *father* in our society, often perceived as a "missing person" in people's lives, was starting to be talked about more and more. Forced to be absent from his family by the demands of the competitive ethic, and more recently, by our custody laws, father was the one who was now getting his comeuppance instead of "mom"—that overprotective, domineering, or rejecting villainess of case-history fame.

When I heard people reared in the Fifties begin to shift their attention away from the all-too-familiar "mom" to the father they never knew, I was reminded of an observation Erik Erikson made way back in 1950. "Momism is only misplaced paternalism," he wrote in *Childhood and Society.* "American mothers stepped into the role of the grandfathers as the fathers abdicated their dominant place in the family, in the field of education, and in cultural life."

I was aware that focusing on the "sins" of the fathers was not entirely new. But what intrigued me as I talked again with Lisa Sandrone, Barry Golden and Amanda, and Milt Stevens, was that now it was not the experts who were talking about the "absent father," but the people themselves.

LISA SANDRONE

It is nine o'clock at night, and Lisa Sandrone, the young television writer we met in Chapter Seven, is taking a brief respite from work. For the past several hours she has been at her desk in the station's newsroom, pounding the events of April 16, 1980, into terse copy that she hopes the viewers will find noteworthy but not too disheartening.

And what about Lisa's own "story"? When I last spoke to her some months ago, she was on the verge of ending a long, difficult relationship with Don, a commitmentphobic TV producer who'd moved to Chicago to further his career.

"Don and I broke up," she tells me evenly, "and I went back into therapy two months ago. I was afraid I would fall apart without Don the way I fell apart without my first love when we split up after college," she explains. "But therapy is helping me to break patterns that I just couldn't break by myself."

Remembering Lisa's grueling struggle to achieve autonomy from her overprotective suburban mother of the 1950s, I ask her if she's going through something like that again.

"I always thought it was my mother who was the problem," Lisa replies, "but I was astounded to learn that it's my relationship with my father that's the critical factor in my relationship with men." Her mother's possessiveness and domineering qualities were "all out on the table," as Lisa puts it, but her father was never there. Like most "absent fathers," he was totally immersed in earning a living, but he was also two generations older than Lisa and foreign-born. "I'm finding out in therapy that I didn't know how to handle men because I never learned about men from being with my father," Lisa says. "I never *knew* my father that well. Men were always a mystery to me, just as my father was. I was never at ease with them—always anxious and afraid."

Lisa feels that the lack of emotional closeness with her father during her childhood years affected not only her relationship with men, but also her performance on the job. "I always thought I needed a strong boss over me," she says. "I wanted a substitute father—someone who would encourage me to succeed and understand me if I failed." But when her paternalistic boss left during a change in management at the TV station, Lisa found she could make it completely on her own. "I'm in full force with my job now," she says, "making my own decisions, handling everything on my own." .

Because her work has assumed greater significance in her life, Lisa now knows that her next relationship won't be "a 100 percent or nothing deal," but more of a balance. Having become less desperate and more discerning, she has learned to pick men who are *not* emotionally unavailable. "Before," she admits, "I didn't care if a relationship was good or bad as long as I had someone. Now the quality of a relationship is much more important. I'm listening to what men are saying to me, and I'm totally in tune with their message. I *believe* them."

What Lisa means is that she now resists the temptation to impose a fantasy and block out a man's real qualities, a step toward rational love that she has learned from experience. "You have to constantly hit roadblocks before you change your direction," she says. "A lot of men out there give you the green light with one hand and the red light with the other—they invite a relationship but back away at the same time." She cites one network executive, a very appealing man, who told her that he travels for three months at a time during the year. "When I heard that," says Lisa, "I stopped myself from getting involved. Now I know I can make choices—I don't have to settle."

Lisa is aware of the difference between "settling" for an *inappropriate* partner and "compromising up" with reality to accept an *appropriate* partner who is still not the godlike hero in one's fantasy of ideal love. For Lisa, "settling" means feeling that she constantly has to bend herself out of shape to fit in with someone else's plans. "I know my own power now," she says. "I'm not a chameleon anymore, always being absorbed by the other person. I'm the one who's doing the pushing, and I can pull back if I want to. But I don't feel the need to make anyone over in *my* image either."

Lisa feels that her greatest improvement has been in the area of self-trust. She says: "When you have trust in yourself—when you understand that the enemy is you, and you *stop being* the enemy—you don't need others to protect you or save you from yourself."

Loneliness is Lisa's only problem right now, but she says she needs time "to heal" before investing in a new relationship—one that promises to be much closer to rational love than her desperation-prompted romantic involvements in the past.

BARRY GOLDEN AND AMANDA

It is summertime, but the living for Barry Golden is not easy. Financially wracked by a costly divorce from Linda, he is trying to recoup his losses with a new business venture he has started with a friend—a roller skating rink in Atlantic City. Nattily dressed as ever in a black linen shirt, beige linen slacks, and canvas jazz oxfords, he seems more preoccupied than when I had met him last year in the apartment he is sharing once again with Amanda.

But it is Amanda who shows the most remarkable change. There is a new maturity about her, an almost tangible sense of purpose. Besides pursuing her busy career as a model, she is commuting to Atlantic City on the weekends to help Barry out at the rink.

Sensing my awareness of how her role in the relationship has shifted, Amanda says: "It's funny how life turns you around. When I first met Barry I was looking for a father figure, someone to give me some structure in my life—a sense of what's right, what's wrong. But I was leaning on him too much. When I moved out and experienced independence—paying my own bills, handling my own finances—I learned how to face responsibilities on my own. Now I'm in a position where Barry can lean on me for a while because he knows I can accept responsibility."

Barry says that marriage to Amanda has become a "realistic possibility." Although they still theoretically have an "open" sexual relationship, their interest in bisexuality and in other heterosexual partners is waning. Even if Barry does have sex occasionally with another woman—with Amanda's knowledge—he maintains that he will never leave Amanda.

Barry confides that Amanda is the first woman with whom he has ever wanted to have a child. In both of his marriages—the first was a typical youthful "mistake" that ended in divorce after a year—having children was always "the very last thing" that came up in conversation. But with Amanda he has discussed having children. Says Barry: "Amanda has so many good qualities—she's nurturant, caring, giving, supportive—that I think our relationship would work as a family and we could be together for the rest of our lives. And I've never felt that way before. I *said* my marriage to Linda would last forever, but deep down I knew her selfishness was something she would never change. Amanda is committed to change. She's committed to her therapy, and she's happy that she learned how to become dependable—to depend on herself—so she could come back to me and say, 'Hey, Barry, you probably could depend on me again if you're willing to try.' "

Says Amanda: "Marriage doesn't scare me. I know I could make it work with Barry in an everlasting relationship." She adds quickly, "The only way I'd get married is with the feeling that it would be permanent: 'This is forever.' I've been asked to be married before, but I wouldn't do it just to try it out."

About having children, Amanda says, "That's another aspect of responsibility that I'd have to learn—altering my lifestyle. But I would love to have a child and watch her grow and give her what I didn't have." She stops herself and reminisces wistfully for a moment. "When I was growing up, what I saw in my girl friends' families was that most of the time the fathers were away at work and they'd see their children maybe three hours a night. But it was still, 'Wait until your father comes home.' If there was a decision to be made, there was always a family discussion; and while your mother could put in good words for you, your father was the one who had the final say as to whether you got the new dress or how late you stayed out." Abruptly, she brings herself back to my question about having a child and concludes: "If I could give her a responsible father, everything emotionally and monetarily that a child *needs*—not that she wants, but what she needs—not spoiling her but helping her grow up properly, that would be a great satisfaction in life."

MILT STEVENS

None of the people I know epitomizes more closely the man in search of self in both his business life and in his love relationships than the "absent father" himself, Milt Stevens. When we last met Milt (in the chapter on the Seventies), he was agitatedly trying to stave off the collapse of a mini-conglomerate he had attempted to build; and he was worried about the lack of career direction and diffusion of goals exhibited by his three sons. But in his personal life he seemed to have found, at long last, love.

In the year that has passed, I discover, Milt's fortunes have completely reversed. By dint of the ingenuity and resourcefulness that made him a millionaire for the first time at the age of forty—he is now approaching forty-nine—he narrowly escaped total bankruptcy and started a new computer business that he estimates will make him a millionaire again in two years. But his relationship with Ursula, the woman he described as the embodiment of all that he had ever wanted in a lifetime mate, was over—and now there is Joyce.

"Ursula *Who?*" Milt jokes when I ask him about the relationship that seemed like the culmination of his two-decades-long string of extramarital and postmarital affairs set off by his former wife Charlotte's betrayal of him in the late Fifties. I remember when he first told me about Ursula, a thirty-year-old divorced woman who, according to Milt, was consummately devoted to him. He also revealed that she was an independent, aggressive publicist who had landed Milt through direct mail. She sent him a note at work—a dating *vita*—telling Milt that she would like to meet him. Fascinated and flattered by her bold approach, he began dating her and soon developed an exclusive and committed relationship that lasted for a year and a half and appeared to be heading toward marriage. What went wrong?

"When I met Ursula, I was very depressed and concerned about my business problems," Milt recalls, "and she really seemed to fill my little bucket of needs at the time. She demanded almost nothing, and she was a total giver. She was very considerate. When I'd come home from work, she'd say, 'You sit down and read the paper, and I'll take care of everything,'—and she did. She'd cook a delicious gourmet dinner, and then all she wanted to do was hit the sack. I never met anyone like that before. I thought it was a marvelous and exciting opportunity for me to be *me* because there were no requirements. I didn't burn out fast the way I usually do when *I* try to do everything for someone in a relationship."

But after a while, Milt realized that what he thought was "giving" on Ursula's part was merely manipulation. There were hidden strings attached to her uncompromising generosity. The "marvelous" and "exciting" opportunity Ursula was offering Jerry was not to be himself, but to become what she thought he should be. She was trying to seduce him into a compliance with her fantasy of the ideal partner.

"Although she enjoyed taking care of me," Milt says, "she was very critical of my friends and of my lifestyle. She said that my friends were beneath her—and beneath me. She put down my clothes. When we went out to eat, she always found fault with the restaurant: The food was mediocre or the decor was terrible or she didn't like the people there. Her snobbishness proved to be our undoing. After the first year we broke up for about a month, and then she convinced me to give it another try. I agreed, but I knew it was on its way out. She said that I helped her become more tolerant; I saw that she was so intolerant that there was no future in our relationship. We went together for another six months, and I ended it because I felt she deserved a chance to find someone who would make her happy for a long time."

Milt now characterizes Ursula as a very angry and frustrated woman who will not be ready for genuine give-and-take in a relationship until she achieves more financial success on her own. It was during her seven-year marriage to a Brazilian doctor, the only son of very wealthy parents, that Ursula developed her expensive tastes and her condescension toward anything that did not qualify as upper upper class. But she was the same age as her husband when she married him, and in Milt's words, "she evidently outgrew him."

In a session with his psychiatrist after his relationship with Ursula "fizzled out," Milt expressed his disillusionment with women this way: "They're all the same Oh Henry bar in a different wrapper." To me, the narcissistic overtones in this statement are unmistakable. I think of Kernberg's writings about exploitative men, fearful of their oral dependency on the opposite sex, who approach seemingly perfect women as objects to be torn open and consumed, then quickly discarded because of the unconscious need to devalue them.

When I question Milt about his search for perfection in women and his continual disappointment, he says, "I think I may have been looking for some sort of subconscious illusion of this 'perfect person,' yet not knowing what the attributes of this 'perfect person' should be." Milt claims that it was this ignorance of the actual qualities he was seeking in a partner, together with his need for self-protection, that caused him to become unintentionally exploitative of women during his "revolving door" phase of juggling several relationships simultaneously. He wanted to learn about women without becoming seriously involved. "Each time I entered a relationship that didn't work out," he says, "I learned what I *didn't* like." My problem was to determine what I *did* want—which was much more difficult."

Unaware of how degradingly mechanistic it sounds, Milt resorts to the language of the business world and refers to many of the women in his past as "shelf items." Although he found them appealing at first, in time they revealed certain insuperable incompatibilities; and Milt would relegate them to his "shelf" of standbys to be taken out on occasion strictly for good times without any possibility of a serious involvement. Milt explains: "I'd meet someone and think, 'She's terrific, but she's too young.' When we went out with the people who've been my close friends for most of my adult life, I could see that she had nothing in common with them. Everyone was uncomfortable—and if they were uncomfortable, so was I. Well, then, right on the shelf she'd go. Or I'd meet a disco dancer type—a shallow person who made discoing in clubs her whole life—and when I'm tired I don't want to go out and disco. A lot of items went on the shelf."

Enlightened by his experiences with all of these "shelf items," Milt began to form a clearer image of the essential qualities that he *would* like to find in a woman. When I ask him to describe who his "perfect person" has turned out to be after all these years of searching, his answer comes as a total shock.

"Well, I guess if I had to do some self-analysis," he says slowly, "I would say it's almost like Charlotte. It *is* Charlotte, in a way, with some changes—what I mean is, it's the fantasies that I had of her thirty years ago."

Incredible! Can it be that through all the changes wrought by affluence, sophistication, the pain of divorce, psychotherapy, sexual freedom, liberation from traditional roles, and countless couplings with other women of every description—from shallow disco types to fiercely ambitious careerists—can it be that through all this what Milt still wants is what he thought he found in his "Char," the sweater-knitting Fifties schoolgirl he married three decades ago?

The qualities possessed by Milt's "perfect person" are, it turns out, amazingly basic and uncomplicated. His difficulty in finding them seems incomprehensible except as an illustration of how intimacy has been debased in our culture by the standard of upward mobility and the myth of symbiotic romantic love. "What I've always wanted," Milt tells me, "is somebody who is really sweet, who is really nice—and when I say nice, I mean considerate—and who is also capable." That does not seem like a large order to fill. But Milt goes on, "I thought Charlotte was very sweet, considerate, and capable, but I discovered that in reality she was extremely dogmatic and materialistic, always pushing me to live beyond our means. She was capable socially, but she was certainly *not* capable in the areas of child-rearing and homemaking."

But *this time,* Milt says, he has found somebody who actually meets his criteria. She is Joyce—a forty-year-old California woman who is divorced from a chronically philandering oral surgeon, works as a legal secretary, and is the mother of an eleven-year-old son. Milt enumerates her attributes: "She is very attractive, a good dresser, has a nice figure, has good taste, knows class—she is *all* class. She likes to cook every so often, but not that much; she's not a slave to the kitchen. She seems to be kind and caring and decent all around. She's good to her kid, and she's not doing her ex-husband in. She is not an angry person; she's a warm and happy human being."

To me, Milt represents a phenomenon that I've encountered time and again among divorced middle-aged married men. Because the "fantasy woman" they originally picked for a marital partner has so deeply disillusioned them, they feel constrained to search for *absolute perfection* before allowing themselves to become emotionally involved again. But for some reason—perhaps they have realistic intimations of mortality as they approach the half-century mark and are afraid of living out their last years alone—the age of fifty is an awesome milestone for many unattached men. Their fear of commitment is overshadowed by an even more powerful phobia—the fear of death. Suddenly, perfection is not so important to them as loyalty; glamour pales beside the more enduring quality of devotion. Despite Milt's checkered history with women, I'm inclined to believe that his relationship with Joyce might last—mainly because Milt is ready now as never before.

Ever since they met at a party five months ago, Milt has been taking every other week off from work to be with Joyce in California (Charlotte, who has remarried, also lives in California with her new family and Milt's youngest son.) Although Milt and Joyce dated others for a while, their relationship evolved into an exclusive one that has Milt totally enthralled. "I feel as if I'm running *to* someone for a change," he says, "instead of running from one person to another or just holding my thumbs up in the air and letting myself swing as I've been doing all these years. I have nothing on the shelf now, and I'm sort of walking in and leaving myself wide open. So is she. The only problem is that she lives far away, and it's very difficult."

Milt contends that it's the pull of attraction that often makes us minimize or overlook "secondary effects," such as distance or problems with an ex-spouse or children. Our tendency is not to confront one of these glaring obstacles until, as Milt puts it, "it's like the waves in the ocean coming up to hit you from behind." But I wonder whether we've become so inured to impermanence that we *expect* a relationship not to survive. In a world where lovers can become "shelf items" overnight, we take extraordinary risks with our own and other people's emotions because we have ceased to believe that permanence exists other than as a fantasy in our own minds.

With that knowing caution of someone who is all too familiar with the deflation of hope, Milt speaks about "the future" he sees with Joyce. "During the summer we'll spend more time together and learn a lot about each other," he says, "and either we'll be able to expand the relationship or"—he pauses, searches for words, and ends lamely—"go from there."

In his work life, as he is in his love relationships, Milt seems to be growing ever closer toward defining his own personal values rather than remaining in bondage to some cultural standard of unlimited perfection. He has finally freed himself of the driven workaholism that Charlotte complained so much about in their marriage (and to which she contributed by always pushing him to earn more). "My goal at forty was to be a millionaire," says Milt, "and I made it by two months. It was a great satisfaction, and then I said, 'Well, let's see if I can get to the second million.' So I sold my company to a large corporation, made several million, and went to work for them in management. After seven years, a new executive vice-president came in—and I was out in a month."

Explaining how he got into his ill-fated venture with the mini-conglomerate, Milt says, "I've always had an insecurity about money, dating back to my father's experiences in the Depression; and I panicked. I had the world by the ass and didn't know it. If I had put the proceeds from the sale of my company into income-producing investments, I could have retired. But I wasn't a money manager. I had various investments, but they weren't bringing in big dividends. So I decided that since I knew business, I'd use the money to acquire a number of companies and form a mini-conglomerate."

At one point Milt and his partners owned seven different companies. "It was a good idea and it would have worked," Milt says now in retrospect, "except that I didn't hold the reins tightly enough." Five of the companies that formed the basis of the mini-conglomerate were closed up, declared bankrupt, or sold to somebody else at a loss. But the other two worked out beautifully. "I'll have a very large income from the trucking company that I leased to a major corporation," Milt says, "and the motel I sold made back most of the losses from the fiasco of the other five companies."

What has Milt learned from his brush with defeat and his promising comeback? "I've learned that I don't have to feel guilty if I don't go into work every day at nine o'clock in the morning," Milt says. "I have an embryo business (the computer company) that's growing by itself, bit by bit, and in the interim I'm enjoying myself and taking life a little more slowly. I'm finally smelling the roses, and not only the roses, but the daisies and the mums. I'm working only every other week and finding it very enjoyable. The way I look at it, if I have twenty years to live, that's a gift; if I have less than twenty years, then I won't know about it anyway. But during the rest of my life, I want to do something interesting, enlightening, and rewarding for each of the years that are left. I guess I want to do the things that *motivate me at that time*."

Milt is finding that the more aware he becomes of the aims of his True Self, the less preoccupied he is with the fantasy of attaining unlimited success and money—the competitive ethic's equivalent of unconditional love. He says, "I've learned that there *are* things I would really like to do—charter a yacht and go around the Mediterranean, hit the ports in the Greek Islands, travel to Israel and Egypt. If I marry Joyce, I want to build a close family unit and be a good father to her son. I hardly ever played with my own sons when they were little—I was always busy working or doing things related to the business—and I realize now that we all missed out on something that you just can't buy."

Milt's insecurity about money hounded him for a long period in his life because, as he puts it, he was always "a little ahead in the buying and a little behind in the paying." His elaborate lifestyle was the spur that kept goading him on. "I always had something to be paid off or something else to be acquired," he says, "and now I find that I *have* most of the big things: a house, a boat, a car. Suddenly my immediate needs are very small—maybe a jacket, a pair of shoes, a dinner—and I have more than enough money to take care of them. Anyway, it's not how much I have, it's how much I have coming *in* that gives me my base for living. The goal of going from the first million to the second million is over because I've done it once, and I realize that I tried too hard and sacrificed too much in the process. Now I'm not going to try so hard. Whether I get there or not is immaterial because my needs are being met—or else I've lowered my needs to meet my income."

Still, Milt is worried about his income covering the needs of *everyone* if he should marry again. Although he has the money put aside for his youngest son's college education, his experiences with Charlotte's voracious spending have made him wary of getting in over his head again with another woman and her family. Yet he knows that Joyce is not extravagant. "When I learned how much Joyce is living on and saw how well she's managing," he says, "I was impressed. I said, 'My dear'—not to her, but to myself—'I am making a hell of a lot more than the amount you're able to live on nicely.' She isn't a threat to me because I see her as a person who doesn't want the whole world—and that's something you have to establish from the beginning."

I ask about Charlotte, who is the wife of a Beverly Hills doctor now—a widower she met through friends—and Milt tells me: "As far as her values and attitudes go, she's exactly the same person she was ten years ago. She's still immersed in the country club social whirl— not as happy as she might be, but making the best of it." Milt feels that Charlotte is a capable woman who never achieved an independent identity because she lacked confidence in herself. "She never felt worthwhile," he says. "I don't think she has ever really been totally happy with herself, and therefore it has to rub off in her relationships."

For years, Charlotte deluded herself with the myth of romantic love, believing that if only she could find the "right man," she would then be completely fulfilled. Like so many other women who rushed into marriage in the Fifties, she made her husband the scapegoat for the failure of her expectations and for the cultural and parental pressures that aborted her growth. "She was angry at me because she felt I took her out of college and never gave her a chance to be anything," Milt says. "But when I encouraged her to go back to school, she always made excuses: 'No, it's too late. . . . I don't know what I want.' I even tried to set her up in business with a girl friend, and she wouldn't go through with that. Perhaps she felt that when she remarried and moved away, she would now have that second chance. The problem is, you can have that second chance—the name of the game is to take it."

Milt does not foresee a very happy future for Charlotte. Her mother, he says, is a very tyrannical, "hawkish" woman whom Charlotte resents but is still trying to please. He feels that since Charlotte has never been able to separate from her mother, she is destined to become exactly like her. "Charlotte was always very dictatorial," Milt says, "but now she's exhibiting the same queenlike manner that her mother has."

According to Milt, Charlotte has achieved the ultimate in status: "She's Mrs. *Doctor* now," as he puts it, "and her mother has a son-in-law to brag about." But he wonders about her sense of self-worth. "I feel sorry for her because she took the easy way out and she's still lost," he says. "I look at myself and say, 'You know what, Milt? You're going to do your damnedest to be fulfilled. It's very difficult, it's going to be painful, but you have to be aware—*realistically* aware—of what you want.' I tell my sons the same thing. It's hell on wheels if you want everything because then you're forever running and going nowhere. The key to life is direction. Once you have that, you know what to pursue. You may not achieve it, but you can certainly pursue it—and there's something beautiful in the pursuit."

MYSELF

What can I say about myself? My marriage did not survive through the Seventies. Our connection was not strong enough to weather the many struggles I would have to undergo—the rage I would have to work through, the separation I would have to make from my mother, the "restless testing" I would have to engage in to find my own limits—before I would transform myself from a dependent child into a woman capable of intimacy in the truest sense.

By the time my husband and I separated in January 1975, there was nothing left of our marriage except open wounds. In March

1980, almost twenty-three years to the day of our wedding, we were divorced. Whether I marry again or not is immaterial—my hegira to the Fourth Stage of personal fulfillment has developed a momentum of its own. I have experienced incomparable joy from the full invest- ment of myself in my work, progressively expanding my capabilities and the attendant rewards by achieving goals that I have personally set for myself. In love, I am still learning. Yet I know that I am better able to love as an act of giving than I was in marriage. Finding a compatible partner is not so simple—mainly because of the cultural warp in which we now live.

In bleak times I feel that the values of trustworthiness, depend- ability, loyalty, honesty, decency, and unselfish concern for others have permanently vanished from social relations in our culture. But always I am sustained by the magnificent bonds of attachment that I have with my children and friends. The test is not to let the mis- spending of our trust force us back into cynical or reclusive self- protection. If one can love rationally in the open and generous shar- ing of one's human gifts and qualities, even in the absence of a committed sexual partner, a deep and abiding sense of personal ful- fillment is still possible.

Since my divorce became final, the lacerating wounds that my former husband and I inflicted on each other in cutting loose have healed. As part of my maturing process, I still grieve periodically for the unspeakable pain I caused him as I went through my growth phases in the crazy Sixties and selfish Seventies. And sometimes, after a particularly eviscerating demise of a relationship, when the moral aloneness that afflicts our culture seems overwhelming, I yearn to crawl back into the protective womb that my marriage once pro- vided. But I know that this is only a temporary regression. I do not look upon the dissolution of our marriage as anything other than the culture's way of correcting a mistake.

The mistake was that my former husband and I were mismated on *all three* of the major levels, mentioned earlier, at which marital partners have been found to connect: common cultural or social backgrounds and shared interests; conscious expectations of each other's roles; and unconscious feelings about the role of the self in relation to a loved one. We came from different social backgrounds and did not share the same interests and values (he likes the country club life; I like the life of the mind). There was increasing disagreement about our conscious expectations of our roles as I abandoned all pretense of being a traditional housewife and gravitated toward a career. And at the level of unconscious roles, his paternalism infantilized me and lured me into a state of hateful dependency.

If we *could* remarry today, our chances for making the marriage work would be better, if only because our children are grown and our conscious expectations of our roles would no longer be a problem. But there would still be conflict at the level of our shared interests and, possibly, at the level of our unconscious roles. This last is the critical factor. My hard-won independence and internal security would never allow me to become dependent again—I have become a giver as well as a taker. And as it was pointed out previously, a marriage will usually end in divorce if there is basic disagreement at *two* or all three of the major levels of connection.

I say that my divorce was the *culture's* way of correcting a mistake because it was mainly the cultural milieu at the time—and not an awareness of the deepest motives of the self—that precipitated my marriage in the Fifties and gave me the impetus in the Seventies to break out of it. In the Fifties, I married under the influence of the myth of romantic love and togetherness as an alternative to growth. In the Seventies, I fell under the spell of the myth of romantic divorce: It led me to believe that I had found the final solution to all problems in relationship. I suppose that if I'd been born a decade later, I would not have married so needily; if I'd been born a decade earlier, I would still be married.

Although the myth of romantic divorce deceived the innocent into believing that all they needed for eternal bliss in love was a new partner, divorce also forced many of us to set our own limits in love for the first time. This trial-and-error process, as the stories of Lisa Sandrone, Barry Golden, and Milt Stevens have shown, is slow, difficult, and often filled with the kind of pain that one associates with a medieval ordeal. But personal fulfillment in love is impossible without refining our vague ideal of perfection into specific, attainable standards and goals. We must decide what qualities we most value in a partner and what needs we can realistically satisfy and have satisfied in a relationship. Fulfillment always eludes us when we blindly enter a relationship to redress a lack of trust in the self or to comply with cultural expectations. Only those relationships that reconfirm our faith in the self and in our own value system afford the possibility of finding ultimate personal fulfillment.

The hopeful sign that I see emerging from all the travail that people are undergoing in relationships today is the restoration of the self as the arbiter of one's desires and needs. People are increasingly widening their scope of potential partners to include those who best fit in with their own deepest desires or needs, whether they meet with social approval or not.

The best barometer of a couple's progress toward rational love, alongside which their sexual practices seem almost insignificant, is the strength of their commitment and their capacity to appreciate each other's intrinsic human qualities. My own feeling is that the sexual behavior engaged in by Barry Golden and Amanda, for example—behavior that many of us would consider deviant—will probably phase itself out as the couple's deepening commitment engenders greater trust and security and as each resolves his or her own conflicts between sex and love.

It also seems to me that responsible therapy has become more than a substitute for good parenting in our culture. The need for therapy as a source of reinforcement of the self is symptomatic of the psychological turmoil created by our loss of public and private values. But the fact that so many people today are motivated to avail themselves of help is a positive indication that we are, as a society, moving toward a more rational way of living and loving.

What is discouraging about our search for rational love in these times is the contamination from the cultural atmosphere. The air is too heavy with the remembrance of past rejection and the oppression of current disillusionment. We have still not learned, as Barry Golden made clear, that the values of the marketplace—competition, impermanence, unmitigated self-interest—are not appropriate values in social relationships. As a result, we are in danger of becoming a society of sexual burnouts—abused lovers who are permanently fearful of ever reinvesting their emotions in a new relationship. To prevent this from happening, we ourselves must redress the role of the "absent father" in our society and introduce some structure, some code of ethics, some *responsibility* into our patterns of intimacy again.

From my observations, it's the *way* we end relationships today, not the ending of the relationship itself, that sours people and turns them into narcissists. There is no need for the vicious betrayal of trust; the exploitative deception; the sadistic retaliation against the blameless for old hurts; the complete absence of regard for the feelings of the person one discards, as if, in Kernberg's phrase, "squeezing a lemon and then dropping the remains."

A FINAL WORD

To achieve fulfillment in rational love, the partners must be able to appreciate the real qualities they each possess as human beings—their ability to satisfy their own emotional needs and to respond to the sensual and tender needs of the other, their internal values, their physical attractiveness, their capacity to be independent and to structure their life creatively. Clues of potentially serious problems in a relationship should be taken cognizance of immediately. But partners must be able to distinguish between *real* inadequacies in the other—Amanda's undependability or Linda's absolute selfishness, for example—and those aspects of the person that trouble us only because they do not conform to our perfectionistic fantasies. Ursula's continual fault-finding with Milt's lifestyle is an example of how we typically attempt to infiltrate a partner's limits with standards and values of our own. But this is, of course, the quintessential trait of the narcissistic American social character: the selfish use of others to make up for our own deficiencies or to fulfill aspirations that we ourselves do not feel capable of achieving.

The depth of personal fulfillment in rational love arises from the capacity to love and be loved for nothing less nor other than what one really is. No couple can attain this depth of fulfillment, I believe, without being exclusively and permanently committed to one another. It is the beauty of this commitment—the day in, day out, mutual exchange of interest, caring, support, affection, nurturance—that has been sullied by our cultural quest to possess our perfect sexual fantasy.

For myself, I can say only this. Despite the discrepancy of interests and the discordance of roles, the glue that held my former husband and me together in the good days of our marriage has become almost irreplaceable in our culture as it is today. If I could have that back again with a new partner—that same constancy, that same selfless devotion—I would *never*, not for a galaxy of moments of passion, trade it in again.

←————————— • —————————→

TWELVE

THE
SELF-DIRECTED
SOCIETY

The older I get, the more I come to admire, as Seneca put it, "the good things which belong to adversity." Unlike many who view our prospects in the Age of Limits with gloom, warning that America has become a second-rate economic power and lamenting the end of the American Dream, I see the 1980s as a time of opportunity. What abundance and economic growth could not do for the autonomy of our social character in the Fifties and Sixties, the scarcity and declining productivity of the Eighties may yet accomplish. The 1980s are a decade of decision. What are our choices?

We can continue to follow the path we set for ourselves in the Seventies—blotting out our feelings of frustration, anxiety, and powerlessness through the isolated pursuit of pleasure—and make the predictions of gloom a self-fulfilling prophecy. Or we can begin to transform ourselves from a *selfish* culture, characterized by avaricious distrust of the self and others, into a *self-directed* culture, one in which, by virtue of depending on our own resources and finding satisfaction in them, we find even greater fulfillment by sharing our resources with others and concerning ourselves with the common good.

For many people addicted to the narcissistic way of life, the mere awareness that selfish competitiveness keeps us in a constant state of unsatisfiable greed would not be sufficient motivation to change. But when we know that we are headed for economic and ecological disaster if we continue to put the short-term interest of the individual over the long-term interest of the group, our complacency is hard to maintain. Terror may motivate us to do what is good for us a lot more quickly than logic.

The values revolution that the counterculture attempted in the affluent Sixties could not succeed then because the system, though corrupt, was *working*. Still, the effort to create a more humanistic value system will not succeed in the Eighties only because we are staring scarcity and economic hardship in the face. Adversity is a catalyst, but we need something more. If we are to become a caring rather than a competitive society, with a value system based on individual responsibility and mutual cooperation, we must admit to ourselves that it is impossible to go it alone.

Amanda, who *had to* go it alone temporarily while therapy helped her to become dependable, spoke to me about her generation's inability to rely on others: "All the people I know who still have a head on their shoulders—and aren't totally burned out on drugs or whatever—are striving very hard to make something of themselves. But very few of them are willing to let other people get close to them. Most say they want to do everything on their own. Their reaction to my being in therapy is, 'I wouldn't go to a therapist—I don't need anyone to help me.' I think they don't want to give anyone any ammunition to use against them."

This obsessive individualism is as prevalent among my own generation as it is among Amanda's. Not only is it a major barrier to the community cooperation we now need to meet the challenges of inflation, scarcity of resources, and economic slowdown in the Eighties, but it is also a significant cause of personal unhappiness.

The uncertainty of living at a time when all connections with past traditions have been broken, and the future looks stark, has thrown many people back upon themselves with a vengeance. But the belief that *every* man is an island, entire of itself and *not* a part of the main, has become, rather than an answer to our fear of the unknown, the cause of still more anxiety and self-doubt.

THE TYRANNY OF INDEPENDENCE

Although the threat of eventual loss or abandonment has always been inherent in human relationships, the new norm of transcience has turned the remote threat of loss into an ever-present likelihood. To help people cope with the emotional havoc created by the plague of tentativeness, our culture has responded with the myth of the superindependence of the individual.

Ever conformity-minded, new-fashioned therapists have encouraged us to adapt to a disturbed society by denying the reality of human nature. As they did with guilt, they have tried to talk us out of our basic core of dependency needs—to dismiss them as unnecessary—instead of exploring the conflicts underlying them. They have not made it clear that all of us, even extremely healthy people, have some yearning for a "substitute mother" in the sense of needing companionship, affection, confirmation, and security from others. We have been made to feel that there is something pathological about these needs when, in fact, it is only if we are utterly unable to abide being alone at all that our dependency needs have unhealthy roots. It is then that we need to examine our deep-seated feelings of helplessness or inner emptiness, of not being strong enough to deal with a hostile world, of abandonment and unlovableness—feelings that go back, as Winnicott puts it, to the experience of not being alone, as an infant or a small child, in the presence of the mother who naturally balanced our ego-immaturity with ego-strength.

In a culture where the new norm of transience has severed family bonds and enduring social ties, we have been taught not simply to cope with aloneness but to cherish and revel in it. The constant exaggeration of the positive aspects of aloneness—freedom for self-discovery, time and space to grow, et cetera—have made it appear that it is possible to live totally alone and not feel deprived. But research has shown that very few people can actually manage this, and they are generally very isolated individuals who fear attachment. As William A. Sadler, a sociologist who has done pioneering research into loneliness has put it:

> . . . *personal troubles often come from outside,* even though the individual experiences them as very private and intimately his own. This sociological analysis helps to get us beyond a narrow psychological and everyday notion that somehow an individual is at fault when he is feeling lonely. On the contrary, if an individual has lost a parent, a friend, or child in death, has moved from home, has changed or lost his job, is rejected by his group, and has lost his religious faith, is confused by his ambiguous American heritage and does not feel deep, abiding loneliness, then I suspect that something drastic is lacking within him. Much loneliness that I have examined is a normal response to breaks in an individual's important relationships.

Women in our culture have been liberated from the excessive dependency of their traditional role only to be pushed, as men have always been, too far in the direction of independence. Many successful career-oriented women I have spoken to have confessed feeling guilty or disappointed in themselves for needing a special other person in their lives whom they can depend on as a consistent and reliable source of confirmation. This need seems to them, particularly if they are divorced, like a painful throwback to the childlike helplessness and powerlessness they felt at an earlier time in their lives and have struggled so hard to overcome. Yet sociologist Robert Weiss, a leading authority on loneliness, has maintained that the need for an attachment is part of the biological inheritance of all human beings. The absence of either of our two basic social requirements, an intimate relationship with a spouse or lover and a sense of community provided by a network of friends who share our interests and concerns, can cause loneliness for which the only real cure is replacement.

Single careerists wonder, as they listen to the plethora of self-help advice proclaiming what an ennobling experience aloneness can be, why they are troubled by a painful void. Middle-aged "displaced persons," having read Gail Sheehy's *Passages,* expect the mature years to be a time of "breakthrough to full independence" when people become "quite independent of other people's standards and agenda" and "find themselves beginning to welcome detachment from others." Lonely and more in need than ever of others who support their standards, they feel somehow that they are not measuring up. But they have confused self-sufficiency with not needing anyone, which is a terrible misperception that our culture constantly reinforces.

The tyranny of independence is clearly exhibited by the emotional trouble that many working women, married and single alike, are running into today despite their career or job success. In their determination not to be drawn into the dependent role that claimed their mothers, some have suppressed their normal lifelong dependency needs as signs of weakness. Alexandra Symonds, M.D., a psychoanalyst at the Karen Horney Clinic in New York City and an associate clinical professor of psychiatry at New York College of Medicine, has studied the problems of women conflicted about success and has treated many of them as patients. In a paper Symonds gave at a meeting of the Association for the Advancement of Psycho-analysis, she reported the following dream one of these patients had related.

The woman dreamed that she was hanging out of a high story window, holding onto the ledge by her fingernails to keep from falling to her death. At the same time, her husband, completely unaware of her plight, was walking calmly about the room. The woman struggled to cry out to him for help, but all she could do was whisper inaudibly, "Help me."

Symonds concluded that this woman who appeared on the surface to have it all—success at a satisfying job, a happy marriage, good children—inwardly was overpowered because she felt she had to keep up an unyielding façade of self-sufficiency. She is typical of many others whose rebellion against their mothers' dependent, self-effacing role model, usually accomplished without their mothers' unequivocal blessing, has caused them to become confused about feminine identity. They cannot bring themselves to ask for help because they fear that being vulnerable would destroy their autonomy. Yet, in the end, this failure of contemporary women to recognize that autonomy and independence have their bounds, too, takes its toll in depression and repressed rage.

If we are to cure our generational virus, we must understand how our conflicts about our own limits, whether they cause us to deny our dependency needs or to be overwhelmed by them, are transmitted to our children. Just as the self-sacrificing traditional mother caused guilt and ambivalence in her superindependent daughter by secretly resenting or feeling threatened by her success, the superindependent mother of today silently communicates to her daughter that achievement exacts a forbidding emotional price. "Often it's the daughter of a highly trained, successful, professional woman," Symonds has pointed out, "who doesn't want to go to college, doesn't want to prepare herself for a career, and wants nothing more than to fulfill the traditional role of her grandmother."

But what of the opposite, and far more common, ambivalence of "liberated" women toward full-time motherhood today? What of the women who feel compelled to *renounce* motherhood, or full-time devotion to it during their children's early years, in order to prove themselves in the workplace? These are women who are as conflicted about choosing full-time motherhood, *even if they have the capacity and desire for it,* as their mothers were once conflicted about choosing a career. But their conflict is not a purely personal matter of confusion in feminine identity. They are victims, or "sacrificial lambs," as one young woman accurately called them, of a deadly cultural double bind. As serious competitors in the workplace, they have fallen under the sway of values—accumulation and status rewards—that are in direct conflict with the life and growth of the family.

In his shrewd assessment of the changing psychological motivations of people in the workplace, Daniel Yankelovich, president of the social research firm of Yankelovich, Skelly, and White, Incorporated, observed a marked difference between the attitudes of male and female workers today. Men—not all, but many—have begun to place an increasing importance on leisure and the recognition of the worker as an individual whose thoughts, opinions, and personal needs must be given some consideration. But women, the newer arrivals on the track, are complaisantly following the conservative carrot-and-stick incentive system of money and status rewards (the carrot) dangled in front of them alternatively with the threat of losing their job (the stick). Said Yankelovich: "Unfortunately, many women seem to have accepted unquestioningly the male-dominated values of the old era; instead of bringing men to a greater appreciation of the values of home, family, and child care, women have endorsed the male values associated with paid work."

But women are recognizing now, as men have already discovered, that the sacrifices inherent in playing the game by the traditional workplace rules are not worth the candle—the sacrifice of empathy with the deepest desires of one's own self; the sacrifice of depth and richness in relations with others; the sacrifice of having children of one's own or of being there for them, emotionally and physically, in those early years that we know to be so critical; the sacrifice of the unhurried appreciation of a million daily pleasures.

How can it be worth it to have glued together this mosaic of sacrifices with one's own irretrievable life energy only to find, in the long run, that the total realization of the self cannot be accomplished through work alone? That was the hope of women—that if they abandoned the traditional female values of home, family, and child care and embraced the traditional male values of money and status, they would then achieve their own identity. But our mistake, as it was with the sexual revolution, was in not understanding the normal progression of human development. Like normal sexual identity, to paraphrase Kernberg, career or job identity is a *consequence* of, rather than a prerequisite for, normal identity formation. We can look to our work role to "cement" our ego identity, as Kernberg puts it, but we cannot expect it to be the sole source of our sense of self or of personal fulfillment.

This is the conclusion that women who have achieved in the job market are reaching with increasing frequency. As a young woman news correspondent told me, after having performed brilliantly for four years for a radio station only to be fired when they changed their format: "Somewhere along the line I know I'm going to have to make compromises if I want to get married and have a family, and I'm starting now. My men friends are shocked that I've gone against the trend and have taken a job in local public radio. That's a big drop in status, but I have more creative freedom. The pressure in our business is to go national, to make it big in the networks. But I had exposure to the networks earlier in my career, which disillusioned me completely. I feel their corporate policies are disruptive. The compromise for me is the decision to confine myself to one market, and within that compromise, I could negotiate a family. But that's really the thing—saying, 'No, I'm not going to travel.' Part of it is that it doesn't mean that much to me now, and a lot of it has to do with the development of the ego, too. I'm not sure where I'm going with my work, but I'm constantly being challenged in many ways, and my ego is not involved. I don't have any design to be a great person because, at this point, I feel like a great person. Maybe one day I'll say, 'Hey, I'm ending up to be pretty damn normal.' But that doesn't bother me because I've explored the other possibilities, and I know what really matters and what doesn't."

When I asked her what she wanted out of life, she answered unhesitatingly, "I don't want to be extreme in any way—an extreme careerist—I want to be balanced. The people I admire, the special ones who have lived right, are the ones who have remained flexible in terms of their careers and jobs, who haven't gotten locked into patterns in general. So I spend more time asking myself not where is my job taking me, but what kind of lifestyle am I setting up? Is it one in which I can remain flexible—not accumulating lots of possessions, not piling up huge bills, not giving up my freedom to do other things? There's a big risk in figuring it out for yourself—a fear that you're going to miscalculate and put yourself in a box. But most people are already *in* a box and are just being shoved along by other people's goals."

This determination not to be herded into an isolated boxcar rattling toward empty success is the force that will shape a new work ethic in the Eighties. As economic animals, we have been beaten, tricked, taken from, and controlled too long. The sacrifices that our technology has demanded of us—the dislocation of the family, the alienation of each of us from the other and from our own self—are no longer necessary and have, in fact, become counterproductive. The persistent and unprecedented decline in our economic productivity is an indication that the workplace must become more responsive to our human needs.

Yankelovich, Toffler, and even Betty Friedan have all defined the challenge of the Eighties in terms of restructuring the workplace and our family patterns to allow both sexes to achieve full human identity without having to make the hideous personal sacrifices of the past. Yankelovich speaks of incentives and motivations that pay attention to the "human side" of the organization—the recognition of the worker as a distinctive individual, reorganization of workers into smaller groups, greater involvement of the worker in solving daily problems, more leisure and family time. Toffler emphasizes a system that penalizes workers who show blind obedience and rewards those with minds of their own: "workers who seek meaning, who question authority, who want to exercise discretion or who demand that their work be socially responsible." And Betty Friedan, having come full circle in twenty years, understands the practicalities of what it takes to keep a family *together* when husband and wife both choose to work outside the home: flexible working hours, flexible benefits, quality daycare, co-parenting and shared responsibilities that will liberate men and women—once and for all, let us hope—from the tyranny of independence. In Friedan's words: "None of us can depend throughout our new, long lives on that 'family of Western nostalgia' to meet our needs for nurture and support, but all of us still have those needs. The answer is not to deny them, but to recognize and strengthen new family forms that can sustain us now. . . . The new urge of both women and men for meaning in their work and life, for love, roots and family—even though it may not resemble the ideal family that maybe never was—is a powerful force for change."

IDEALS FOR THE NEW AGE

The thrust toward change is ingrained in each of us as part of our evolutionary drive. But we are also creatures who cannot function without, in Mahler's phrase, "a beacon of constancy"—a lucid inner moon illuminating who *we* are through all our various roles and lighting up our movement through life with our own sense of purpose. It may tell us, for example, when faced with a career decision, to go with the employer who respects our individuality rather than the one who, purportedly, can make us a star; or it may tell us, when faced with a decision in love, to disregard the prevalent attitudes in the culture around us, and make a commitment based on our own needs for love and intimacy as well as shared ideals, values, and goals.

The ability to form this "beacon of constancy" has been badly impaired by the fragmentation of our institutions under the onslaught of moral relativism—the belief that value judgments vary with each new set of circumstances. When our cultural parents fail to support our basic value judgments of right and wrong, the beacon tends to become clouded over by self-doubt. The "demassification of the media," as Toffler calls it in his latest work—our constant bombardment by conflicting, fragmentary messages sent out to small, highly differentiated groups—has also been a factor. He writes:

The demassification of the media today presents a dazzling diversity of role models and life styles for one to measure oneself against. Moreover, the new media do not feed us fully formed chunks but broken chips and blips of imagery. Instead of being handed a selection of coherent identities to choose among, we are required to piece one together: a configurative or modular "me." Building a coherent "self" becomes far more difficult, and it explains why so many millions today are desperately searching for identity.

Toffler seems to envision a "trying on" of different images of self, so that we will somehow develop a heightened awareness of our own unique traits as individuals; and this awareness will, in turn, make us demand that we be treated as individuals. But what we have actually

seen is that this repeated trying on of different selves leads to identify *diffusion:* a terrifying feeling that *no* "real me" exists. And it is
this deep feeling of inner emptiness, of being a nonperson, which
makes us demand not recognition of our true individuality, but entitlement. This expectation that everyone else will grant us special
favors without our having to do anything in return, which often takes
the form of an abrasive, finger-waving insistence, is the hallmark of
our culture today—and it is no basis upon which any civilized society,
now or in the future, can long survive.

A distinction must be made between idiosyncrasy—making love
only to the strains of Ravel's *Bolero,* for example—and genuine individuality. No matter how many quirks or affectations we borrow
from television and assemble into our "modular" self, we can never
have an authentic identity without a framework of guiding ideals
that give us a conscious sense of purpose. To live without purpose is
to live in a peculiar kind of hell. As George Bernard Shaw so aptly
pictured it in *Man and Superman,* it is a hell where the punishment
for sin is the sickening boredom of eternal pleasure. In the third act
of the play, when Don Juan tries to explain to Dona Ana de Ulloa
why perpetual meaninglessness is unbearable, he gives us Shaw's view
that a rational sense of purpose is a universal necessity. It is the
"mind's eye" of evolutionary progress:

. . . Just as Life, after ages of struggle, evolved that wonderful bodily
organ the eye, so that the living organism could see where it was
going and what was coming to help or threaten it, and thus avoid a
thousand dangers that formerly slew it, so it is evolving today a
mind's eye that shall see, not the physical world, but the purpose of
Life and thereby enable the individual to work for the purpose
instead of thwarting and baffling it by setting up shortsighted
personal goals. . . .

. . . as long as I can conceive something better than myself I cannot
be easy unless I am striving to bring it into existence or clearing the
way for it. That is the law of my life. That is the working within me
of Life's incessant aspiration to higher organisation, wider, deeper,
intenser self-consciousness, and clearer self-understanding.

In *Man and Superman,* Shaw urges us to think how, when we do
not know the *why* of what we do, life "wastes and scatters itself in its

ignorance and blindness. It needs a brain, this irresistible force, lest in its ignorance it should resist itself." Having seen the incalculable emotional wreckage and material loss left by the convulsive upheavals of the past two decades, can any of us doubt the truth of Shaw's message? Surely if our "mind's eye" had been more developed, if we ourselves had not been so blind to our own goals when we sprang out of the starting gate after late adolescence, all this waste and scattering of life would not have been necessary.

The hunger for a sense of purpose in people today—and our respect for someone who manifests this trait, even if we don't necessarily share his convictions—was evinced by the extraordinary reaction to Pope John Paul II's visit to this country in October 1979. In city after city during his seven-day visit, the Pope drew millions of Americans to him of all ages and faiths. Every expert commenting on the phenomenon mentioned not only the magnetism of the Pope's personality, but also that we are a rudderless society in need of a strong leader. "We are in a political void and a spiritual void," said one expert, Dr. Nick Roback, a sociologist at St. Joseph's University in Philadelphia. "All religions—not only Catholics—are in trouble, trying to find out what should be what." Roback explained that the Pope projected the image of the kind of leader people in our country were looking for—"firm but loving" . . . "strong and convincing" . . . "enough certainty and authority to command respect" . . . "a man who knows where he is going."

Yet, after the Pope had gone, many Catholics and non-Catholics alike expressed disappointment with his doctrinaire views on celibacy for priests, the ban on the ordination of women, opposition to divorce and to artificial birth control. Despite the immensely appealing warmth of his personality, his hard-line theological rigidity dismayed Americans and left them hoping, as one priest put it, that the Pope "could be melted by human misery."

In affirming the importance of personal fulfillment and growth, Pope John Paul II has advocated goals that are directly in line with our American preoccupation with self-fulfillment. But he would have us reach that goal by a path of abject compliance ("Our surrender to God's will must be total") that most Americans have already rejected. And most of us would find the limits he would propose too narrow and unacceptable because they refuse to acknowledge the positive changes that have come out of the women's movement and the sexual revolution—our new ideals of sexual equality and control of sexuality and conception on the basis of responsible choice.

Having lived through the torturous changes that have evolved in our culture over the past five decades, most of us find it unthinkable to go back to the self-denial of blind obedience to rules. We are horrified when we read headlines in the newspaper about parents who, because of their religious beliefs, let their children die from lack of medical care—or even, as in Guyana, force them to commit suicide. We are alarmed when we hear about the many well-educated, middle-class professionals—even someone as distinguished as psychiatrist-author Elisabeth Kübler-Ross (*On Death and Dying*)—whose search for a higher purpose in life has ended in emotional subjugation to the codes and shibboleths of a bizarre religious cult. Although we understand the deep need of these people to ascribe meaning to life according to some spiritual or moral law, we know that we will never again compromise the integrity of the self in submission to another's will. Our struggle to free the self from bondage to others, without destroying either ourselves or those we were struggling against, has left us convinced of this supremely inviolable truth: "*Immorality*," as Winnicott has said, "*. . . is to comply at the expense of the personal way of life.*"

That is why the limits we set for ourselves must arise out of a *conscious* sense of purpose and not the compulsion to believe, which the person struggling to reach autonomous morality will eventually find insupportable. Walter Kerr, in his review of Brian Friel's play *Faith Healer*, said it perfectly:

The compulsion to believe—in something, anything—can't be shaken off. . . . But the moment a man says "I believe" he is committing himself to a tension that is next to intolerable. What he says he believes may or may not be so. He *may* not even believe what he says he believes. He is impaled now on chance, uncertainty, the damnable odds. Unable to live without belief, and unable to live with it painlessly, he has just one out. Death is certainty. Only death can salve the wounds that are opened by faith. Death is the faith healer.

But this is so only if the faith is blind. If we have internalized our beliefs and given them our rational assent, we are no longer at the mercy of the "damnable odds." Certainty is ours, irrespective of the unforeseeable workings of chance. We have moral consistency: we do what we *know* to be right because, at the highest level of social and moral maturity, what is morally right is also personally fulfilling. Since our cardinal belief is in our own power to confront reality, even the inevitability of death, our beliefs are a source of joy to us, not pain.

The God we believe in is an ideal of ethical perfection—not the anthropomorphic God of our childhood, the towering father figure who will either love us unconditionally or make us suffer and whose message is still fear, prejudice, exclusivity: "I have the answer, and you don't." As Freud wrote over fifty years ago in *The Future of an Illusion*, "If the sole reason why you must not kill your neighbor is because God has forbidden it and will severely punish you for it in this or the next life—then, when you learn that there is no God and that you need not fear His punishment, you will certainly kill your neighbor without hesitation, and you can only be prevented from doing so by mundane force."

Was Freud overemphasizing the importance of the intellect over our instinctive feelings of love and empathy with others when he maintained in *The Future of an Illusion* that "the primacy of the intelligence" is the psychological ideal? The human potential movement and the countercultural proponents of "drug-thought" and the "liberated lifestyle" would say he was. But Freud did not feel that the dominance of our intelligence over our instinctual life would convert us from a tortured race of repressed savages with lust in our loins and larceny in our hearts into a civilization of technological zombies incapable of feeling. He believed that if our civilizing trends could triumph over the human instinct of aggression and self-destruction, the intellect would ultimately set as its aims "the love of man and the decrease of suffering." Curiously enough, these are the very same aims as those advocated by the new-fashioned thinkers who put the senses above rational thought, and orthodox religion which puts doctrine prohibiting rational thought above the senses.

When we have reached the point where reason is in command of the self, orchestrating both our ideals and our instinctual drives, the unity within ourselves will lead us naturally to a sense of our connectedness to others. Having reconciled our standards of perfection with our basic human drives for love and recognition, we will no longer need to abuse or deny any part of the self or to exploit or depend excessively on those around us. Social responsibility and moral freedom will thus exist side by side as integral parts of the self, and our love of man will not demand the sacrifice of our love of *particular* others in submission to God's "inscrutable decree." Our limits will be ours alone, but we alone will be accountable for how we live up to them. In *The Women's Room*, Marilyn French examines this duality between moral responsibility and moral freedom in this insightful discourse:

As I understand it, the medieval view of sin was very personal. Dante placed his murderers in a higher circle of hell than those who committed fraud. A sin is a violation not of a law but of a part of the self; punishment is meted out according to what part of the self has been abused. In the neat hierarchy of Dante's hell, sins of concupiscence are less severe than sins of irascibility, but the worst are those that violate the highest faculty, reason.

. . . I imagine it costs someone something to break and enter, to steal, to murder, costs something quite apart from the fear of discovery or punishment. . . . I think that one's way of perceiving himself and his relation to the world must be jarred, must contain some hurt, some rift, some germ of hopelessness. Of course, lots of people besides those who commit crimes feel that way too, I suppose. . . . So maybe it is impossible to talk about crime. But then the old categories come flaming up again, looking better than ever, although in need of revision: a good life is one in which no part of the self is stifled, denied, or permitted to oppress another part of the self, in which the whole being has room to grow. But room costs something, everything costs something, and no matter what we choose, we are never happy about paying for it.

But in the Seventies we made only part payment. Many of us chose limits that gave the self room to grow, and we paid for this choice with the loss of our security and comfort. When we earned our autonomy we thought we had come out ahead, even though our loneliness and isolation often made us wonder. Now, having entered the Eighties, the sobering new Age of Limits, we find that there is yet another price to be paid. We see that it is impossible for the self to grow in a room of its own at the cost of the life growth of others—spouses, children, friends, lovers, parents, competitors, consumers, the larger society. Concern for others is the final payment each of us must make as we transform our culture of narcissism into a new social order incorporating timeless moral values with postliberation ideals.

We do not need some strong, charismatic leader to tell us "what should be what." We need only listen to our own inner voice. It is telling us that we can create a new climate in which human needs and values can be nurtured one more time: a *parent-oriented* society that supports the family as the mainstay of the community; a *responsible* society that values excellence and the common good over money and power; a *caring* society that promotes decency and reciprocity in our relations with others and balance between the opposing but inseparable aspects of the self; a *communal* society that encourages the individual to make a connection with something larger than one's own life—a social issue, a political movement, a cultural matter—and through one's commitment to it find a sense of purpose.

RESETTING OUR INNER COMPASS

To accomplish this transformation of our society from a narcissistic culture into a socially responsible and caring one, we ourselves must become the leaders of a values revolution that does not aim to disrupt and divide our culture, but to strengthen and unify it. Our moral development, as we have seen, is a continuing, dynamic process that extends beyond adolescence into adulthood. As members of our cultural family, the standards that determine what we should or would like to be—our limits—change as we identify with "significant others" and internalize new roles. In the Eighties our very survival demands that we reverse the tide of conformist other-direction and make a bold new move toward personal fulfillment by becoming *self-directed*, seeking out and identifying with other self-directed people whose lives are lived on the basis of a value system that replaces the competitive ethic with lateral mobility, the lack of commitment with moral consistency, and romantic love with rational love.

We must begin now to build a self-directed society—one that provides the self with empathetic guidance from infancy throughout life—to ensure the unfolding of personal fulfillment not only for ourselves, but for future generations. In a self-directed society the individual's capacity to make moral choices will not be blunted by compliance or overindulgence. It will evolve naturally from our having learned to set healthy inner limits and to organize these limits collectively into a cultural moral code that each of us may be guided by in his or her own way. In such a society the narcissistic use or neglect of children by their parents will cease—and so will our moral aloneness.

Only a narcissistic culture has so little regard for the developing self of others that children are left to fend for themselves or are shuttled back and forth between divorced parents like contraband. In a self-directed society we will have nurturant parents, parents who affirm their children's individuality but also know how and when to say "no" and who, in their own lives, exhibit caring and considerate behavior and maintain high standards. The children of these parents will grow into socially and morally mature adults. Their concern for others and willingness to accept responsibility for their actions will spring spontaneously from their own unity and strength of self. They will not have to be taught courses on moral reasoning or moral judgment in the classroom; nor will they, as they pass through adolescence, become desperate wanderers in search of a learned master to lead them out of the spiritual wilderness. *"Moral education,"* as Winnicott has said, *"is no substitute for love."*

Central to our evolution into a self-directed society is the rebuilding of the family. We must make responsible relatedness to our loved ones our supreme cultural value—a higher priority than materialism, success, status, image, or consumption of experience. Youth-directed parents must now become, once again, youth *directors,* involving themselves in their children's daily lives as competent models, showing them through their own example how to confront the stresses of life with strength and mastery and how to function in the adult world as someone who has integrity of self as well as concern for the rights of others. The rearing of children must become a shared responsibility not only of coparents, but of parents and institutions—a cooperative family-government-business-church-school enterprise—making both "Momism" and the "absent father" anachronisms in our society.

With the continuing influx of women into the work force, the need for more and better quality daycare is obvious. But far more critical is the need for better quality *parenting* and a society that fosters parents' physical and emotional availability to their children by modifying the dehumanizing values of the old competitive ethic. When the financial, emotional, and educational needs of parents are properly addressed in our culture, parenting will be seen not as a sacrifice, but as an opportunity—a chance to share what we have with our children and to get back a thousandfold more from them in terms of their affirmation and enrichment of our lives.

Both the goals of personal fulfillment and the exigencies of physical survival are pushing us inexorably in the direction of reshaping our social and cultural institutions. If we can fashion them into a "second womb" for the self—a structure that provides stability, security, nurturance, and above all, an anchor of guiding ideals—then ours will cease to be a society in search of unconditional love. Tilting quixotically at the windmill of life, hoping to snag our ever-retreating fantasy of unlimited success or perfect love, will have lost its attraction. When we have created a society in which people can act, with faith in the consequences of their actions, there will be no need to barricade the self behind a stockpile of money, possessions, celebrity, status, image, admiration, sexual experience, or cultish dogma. The last stage of personal fulfillment will have been reached: the confirmation of the self through our commitment to a rationally chosen system of beliefs about the purpose of our particular life and how it should be lived.

The past and the present shape us and we in turn shape the future. A self-directed society is the only redress for the alienation of our age. There is no "answer"—there is only relatedness. And this relatedness for which we hunger so fiercely, this ultimate state of personal fulfillment, this transcendence of the self into loving community with others, can never be ours until we have chosen limits that are genuinely our own. Only then, when we proudly accept what we will *not* be as well as what we would, will our deepening sense of self unfold and reveal to us that indelible human fiber, beating with life, that links us all.

NOTES

1 THE GENERATIONAL VIRUS

Pages 4-5: The Erich Fromm extract is from Erich Fromm, *Escape from Freedom* (New York: Holt, Rinehart & Winston, 1941; Avon edition, 1965), p. 44. Italics are mine.

Page 5: Nadine's quote is from Judith Rossner, *Attachments* (New York: Simon and Schuster, 1977; Pocket Books edition, 1978), p. 16.

Page 6: Michelle Triola Marvin is quoted from Knight-Ridder News Service, "And Now, As Then, She Goes Home Crying" (Woman in the News), *Philadelphia Inquirer*, February 17, 1979, 4-B.

Page 8: Lasch's explanation of the "therapeutic ethic" as a replacement for traditional morality appears in Christopher Lasch, *The Culture of Narcissism* (New York: W. W. Norton, 1978), pp. 30, 234.

Pages 8-9: Kohut's metaphor of the "Guilty Man vs. the Tragic Man" appears in Heinz Kohut, *The Restoration of the Self* (New York: International Universities Press, 1977), pp. 132-33, 271-73.

Page 10: For a detailed account of the "rapprochement crisis" that occurs at eighteen months, see Margaret Mahler in collaboration with Fred Pine and Anni Bergman, *The Psychological Birth of the Human Infant* (New York: Basic Books, 1975), pp. 76-108, 120, 129, 132-33, 134, 142-44, 145, 159, 164, 225-30; see also Louise J. Kaplan, Ph.D., *Oneness and Separateness: From Infant to Individual* (New York: Simon and Schuster, 1978), pp. 191-230.

Page 11: Statistics on divorce are from U.S. Department of Health and Human Services, Monthly Vital Statistics Report, Advance Report, *Final Divorce Statistics,* 1978, Publication No. (PHS) 80-1120, vol. 29, no. 4, supplement July 31, 1980, from the National Center for Health Statistics, 3700 East-West Highway, Hyattsville, Maryland 20782.

Page 15: For leading writers on the narcissistic nature of our contemporary culture, see Peter Marin, "The New Narcissism," *Harper's*, October 1975, p. 46; Tom Wolfe, "The 'Me' Decade and the Third Great Awakening," *New York*, August 23, 1976, pp. 26-48; Richard Sennett, *The Fall of Public Man* (New York: Knopf, 1977), pp. 8-12, 220-21, 262-63, 264, 326-36; Lasch, *Culture of Narcissism*, pp. 3-30, 31-33, 50-51, 63-64, 235-36.

Page 16: The origins of clinical narcissistic personality disorder have become the subject of a heated controversy between psychoanalysts Heinz Kohut and Otto Kernberg. Kohut, in a departure from Freudian instinct theory, sees pathological narcissism as an arrest in the development of the self arising out of early childhood frustrations by parental "self-objects" (*The Restoration of the Self*), pp. xiii-xiv, 28, 51, 77, 90, 92, 118-19, 121, 123-25. Kernberg, an object relations theorist, takes the view that narcissism always involves the relationship of the self to love objects and object-images, as well as the struggle between love and aggression, and that pathological narcissism is a defense against unconscious dependency, rage, or envy *(Borderline Conditions and Pathological Narcissism,* New York: Jason Aronson, 1975), pp. 230-37, 283. Although this difference in viewpoints may affect the treatment of the disorder (Kernberg sees dangers in Kohut's emphasis on treatment as a corrective emotional experience), it does not present a problem in a discussion of narcissism as a cultural phenomenon. For the purposes of this book it does not matter whether narcissistic personality traits, such as exploitativeness, entitlement, preoccupation with fantasies of unlimited success or ideal love, etc., are genetic or defensive in origin. What matters is that our social structure, by failing to provide the self with a nurturant and stable public value system, predisposes us to develop these traits. For a complete description of clinical narcissism, see Harold I. Kaplan, Alfred M. Freedman, Benjamin J. Sadock, eds., *Comprehensive Textbook of Psychiatry;* 3 vols. (Baltimore: Williams & Wilkins, 1980), 3, p. 1578.

Page 18: Coles's quote is from Robert Coles, *Privileged Ones:* vol. 5 of *Children of Crisis* (Little, Brown in association with The Atlantic Monthly Press, 1977), reprinted in *Town and Country,* June 1978, p. 86.

Page 19: Alan Ross quote is from Maralyn Lois Polak, "The Man Who Named The Brat the Brat" *(Today Magazine, Philadelphia Inquirer,* March 4, 1979), pp. 11-12.

Pages 19-20: Riesman quotes are in David Riesman in collaboration with Reuel Denney and Nathan Glazer, *The Lonely Crowd* (New Haven and London: Yale University Press, 1950), pp. 16-17.

Page 21: Seligson's description of Sandstone is from Marcia Seligson, *Options* (New York: Random House, 1978), pp. 262-85.

Page 21: The term *fun morality* was originated by Martha Wolfenstein, "Emergence of Fun Morality," *Journal of Social Issues* 7, no. 4 (1951). For a more detailed discussion of the concept, see chapter 4 of *Limits,* The Patriotic Forties.

2 OUR INNER COMPASS

Page 23: The Rollo May definition of purpose (or "intentionality," as he calls it) is from Rollo May, *Love and Will* (New York: W. W. Norton, 1969; Delta Books edition, 1973), pp. 223-45, 308.

Pages 24-25: The Jenny Fields extract is from John Irving, *The World According to Garp* (New York: E. P. Dutton, 1978), p. 5.

Page 26: Sumner and Keller quote is from William Graham Sumner and Albert Galloway Keller, *The Science of Society,* vol. II, *Self-Maintenance: Religion* (New Haven: Yale University Press, 1927), p. 1478.

Page 28: Erikson quote is from Erik H. Erikson, *Insight and Responsibility* (New York: W. W. Norton, 1964), p. 133.

3 THE DEPRESSING THIRTIES

Page 33: The discussion of "penis envy" and female dependency is from Margaret Mahler, in collaboration with Fred Pine and Anni Bergman, *The Psychological Birth of the Human Infant* (New York: Basic Books, 1975), pp. 83-84, 102, 105-6, 130, 147-50, 214, 229.

Page 34: Lifton's observations on cults are from Robert Jay Lifton, "The Appeal of the Death Trap," *New York Times Magazine,* January 7, 1979, p. 27.

Page 34: Roth quote is from Philip Roth, *Portnoy's Complaint* (New York: Random House, 1969), p. 118.

Page 35: Greer extract is from Germaine Greer, *The Female Eunuch* (New York: McGraw-Hill, 1971), p. 146.

Page 38: Reference to techniques used by contemporary cults is from Lifton, "The Appeal of the Death Trap," p. 27.

Page 39: Arieti's views on subservience to a "Dominant Other" or a "Dominant Goal" as a key factor in depression are found in Silvano Arieti and Jules Bemporad, *Severe and Mild Depression* (New York: Basic Books, 1978), quoted in *Psychology Today*, April 1979, pp. 54ff.

Page 40: In a psychobiography of Richard Nixon by psychiatrist David Abrahamsen, *Nixon Vs. Nixon: An Emotional Tragedy* (New York: Farrar, Straus and Giroux, 1977), pp. 29, 136-40, 152, 161-62, 225-26, 248, the author postulates that Nixon was a victim of a compulsive need for failure stemming from unconscious guilt. Relying on orthodox Freudian theory, Abrahamsen attributes this guilt to an unresolved Oedipus complex: Nixon could not desexualize his attachment to his mother and neutralize his omnipotent expectations of himself because he was unable to identify with his hostile, aggressive father. More contemporary theorists would tend to see Nixon's problems in terms of the splitting defense against narcissistic rage engendered by early frustration and deprivation. Nixon's psychic survival depended upon dividing the world into his all-good allies—"My mother was a saint," he said when he left office in disgrace after Watergate—and his all-bad opponents, whom he sought to destroy. It was his need to maintain his illusion of omnipotence that drove Nixon first to the presidency and then to his downfall.

Page 40: Explanation of the structure of the superego is from Paul Mussen and Nancy Eisenberg-Berg, *Roots of Caring, Sharing, and Helping* (San Francisco: W. H. Freeman and Company, 1977), p. 25.

Page 41: Extract from Hennig and Jardim study is from Margaret Hennig and Anne Jardim, *The Managerial Woman* (New York: Doubleday & Company, 1977; Pocket Books edition, 1978), pp. 107-8.

Pages 43-44: Ackerman quotes are found in Studs Terkel, *Hard Times* (New York: Pantheon Books, 1970; Avon edition, 1971), pp. 229-30.

Page 46: For an explanation of the origin and dynamics of the sense of guilt, see D. W. Winnicott, "Psycho-Analysis and the Sense of Guilt," *The Maturational Processes and the Facilitating Environment* (New York: International Universities Press, 1962), pp. 15-28.

Page 47: Rollo May's views on guilt and autonomy and the extract of Ada's case history are from Rollo May, *The Meaning of Anxiety* (New York: Ronald Press, 1950), p. 131.

Pages 48-50: Extracts from *Final Payments* are found in Mary Gordon, *Final Payments* (New York: Random House, 1978; Ballantine edition, 1979), pp. 21, 304-5.

Pages 50-51: Stierlin's findings on the family system are from Helm Stierlin, *Psychoanalysis and Family Therapy: Selected Papers* (New York: Jason Aronson, 1977), pp. 248-51; *Separating Parents and Adolescents: A Perspective on Running Away, Schizophrenia, and Waywardness* (New York: Quadrangle, 1974), pp. 49-51, 59-60, 64-65.

Page 51: Kernberg quote is from Linda Wolfe, "Why Some People Can't Love," *Psychology Today*, June 1978, p. 56.

4 THE PATRIOTIC FORTIES

Pages 53-54: The Purdue University survey findings and the *Seventeen* "Letter to the Editor" are reprinted in *This Fabulous Century* by the Editors of Time-Life Books, vol. 5, 1940-50, *The Forties* (New York: Time-Life Books, 1969), p. 28.

Pages 54-56: The extracts from Winnicott concerning the False Self vs. True Self concept are from D. W. Winnicott, *The Maturational Processes and the Facilitating Environment* (New York: International Universities Press, 1962), pp. 133, 146-47, 144.

Pages 56-57: Prinze's troubles were well documented in "Good Night Sweet Prinze" by Peter S. Greenberg, *Playboy*, June 1977, pp. 102-4, 110, 202, 204-16. Greenberg also produced a television play based on his article, "Can You Hear the Laughter," which was broadcast by CBS-TV on September 11, 1979.

Page 57: Tierney's mental problems are recounted in *Gene Tierney* with Mickey Herskowitz, *Self-Portrait* (New York: Wyden Books, 1978), pp. 3-9, 62-65, 85, 119, 170-82, 191-216, 220-32, 241-45.

Page 57: Winnicott reference is from Winnicott, *The Maturational Processes and the Facilitating Environment*, pp. 141-42.

Page 63: Marcia findings are from J. E. Marcia, "Development and Validation of Ego Identity Status," *Journal of Personality and Social Psychology* 3 (1966), pp. 551-59. For a concise description of the J. E. Marcia paper, see Gail Sheehy, *Passages* (New York: E. P. Dutton, 1976; Bantam edition, 1977), pp. 82-83.

Page 64: Adelson quote is from Joseph Adelson, "Is Women's Lib a Passing Fad?" *New York Times Magazine*, March 19, 1972, p. 94.

Page 69: Wolfenstein findings are from Martha Wolfenstein, "Emergence of Fun Morality," *Journal of Social Issues* 7, no. 4 (1951), pp. 15-25. For a trenchant discussion of the Wolfenstein article, see Eric Larrabee, *The Self-Conscious Society* (New York: Doubleday, 1960), pp. 123-27.

5 THE SQUARE FIFTIES

Pages 71-72: Adlai Stevenson quotes are from Alden Whitman and the *New York Times, Portrait of Adlai E. Stevenson* (New York: Harper & Row, 1965), p. 181. Excerpt of speech is reprinted in *This Fabulous Century* by the Editors of Time-Life Books, vol. 6, 1950-1960, *The Fifties* (New York: Time-Life Books, 1970), p. 50.

Pages 73-74: The statistics on American consumerism in 1956 are quoted in Carl Solberg, *Riding High* (New York: Mason and Lipscomb, 1973), p. 263. The extract is from pp. 264-65. The remarks about the significance of the split-level house are from pp. 378-79.

Page 75: The quote attributed to Arthur Miller appears in Rollo May, *Love and Will* (New York: W. W. Norton, 1973; Dell, 1974), p. 324. The remark attributed to the salesman leaving the theater after seeing *Death of a Salesman* is quoted in Time-Life Books, vol. 5, *The Forties*, p. 273.

Page 82: The students' descriptions of their mothers reported by Hendin are from Herbert Hendin, *The Age of Sensation* (New York: McGraw-Hill, 1977), pp. 49, 28, 108, 156, 40, 214, 208.

Page 83: Ibid., pp. 323, 59, 336.

Pages 83–84: Ibid., pp. 378–79.

Page 84: Fromm quote is from Erich Fromm, *The Art of Loving* (New York: Harper & Row, 1974), pp. 21–22.

Page 85: Lasch's comments about the "mechanical manner" of "the American mother" in the 1950s are from Christopher Lasch, *The Culture of Narcissism* (New York: W. W. Norton, 1978), p. 175. His remarks about the lack of "maternal feelings" in the "narcissistic American mother" are found on p. 170.

Page 85: For a summary of contemporary opinion discounting the existence of a maternal instinct in humans, see Nancy Friday, *My Mother/My Self* (New York: Delacorte, 1978), pp. 15–19.

Page 86: The description of the mother of "more patterned societies" is from Geoffrey Gorer, *The American People: A Study in National Character* (New York: W. W. Norton, 1948), p. 74; quoted in Lasch, *Culture of Narcissism*, p. 170.

Page 88: The extract from Friedan on symbiotic love is from Betty Friedan, *The Feminine Mystique* (New York: W. W. Norton Company, 1963; Dell edition, 1964), p. 286.

Page 89: French's comment on "typical suburban monsters" is from Marilyn French, *The Women's Room* (New York: Summit, 1977), p. 259.

Page 90: Winnicott's observation about compliance is from D. W. Winnicott, *The Maturational Processes and the Facilitating Environment* (New York: International Universities Press, 1962), p. 102.

Page 91: Kohut's observations about the children of psychoanalysts and other psychoanalytically sophisticated parents is from Heinz Kohut, *The Restoration of the Self* (New York: International Universities Press, 1977), p. 146.

Page 91: Winnicott quote from "On Communication" is from Winnicott, *The Maturational Processes and the Facilitating Environment*, p. 187.

Page 95: Solberg quote from Solberg, *Riding High*, p. 259.

Page 99: Kerouac quote is from Jack Kerouac, *On The Road* (New York: The Viking Press, 1957; Signet edition; Penguin edition, 1976), reprinted in *This Fabulous Century* by the Editors of Time-Life Books, vol. 6, *The Fifties*, p. 89.

Page 99: Solberg quote from Solberg, *Riding High*, p. 359.

6 THE REVOLUTIONARY SIXTIES

Page 100: Macdonald quote is from Dwight Macdonald, *Discriminations, Essays & Afterthoughts* (New York: Grossman, 1974), p. 416.

Page 101: For further information on the motivations of "idealistic young political activists" in the 1960s, see David Rosenhan, "Prosocial Behavior of Children," *The Young Child: Reviews of Research*, vol. 2, ed. W. W. Hartrup (Washington, D.C.: National Association for Education of Young Children, 1972), pp. 340–59, reported on in Paul Mussen and Nancy Eisenberg-Berg, *Roots of Caring, Sharing, and Helping* (San Francisco: W. H. Freeman and Company, 1977), pp. 88–90. The Rosenhan study of Freedom Riders differentiated two types of workers who were active in the civil rights movement of the late 1950s and 1960s. The first type, the *fully committed*, were guided by what Rosenhan called "autonomous altruism," remaining active in the movement for a year or longer, often at great personal sacrifice. The second type, the *partially committed*, believed as strongly in the equality of whites and blacks but limited their activities to one or two rides or marches without much sacrifice or inconvenience. Rosenhan attributed the difference to the modeling of the parents and reinforcement of the modeling by parental nurturance. The fully committed Freedom Riders grew up in homes where the parents had worked vigorously for altruistic causes and had always maintained warm, loving, respecting relationships with their children into early adulthood. In contrast, the parents of the partially committed Freedom Riders commonly preached prosocial behavior and practiced a different morality. They provided symbolic but not behavioral modeling and were not as nurturant with their children as the parents of the fully committed Freedom Riders.

Pages 105-6: Johnson quotes and extract are from Ann Braden Johnson, "A Temple of Last Resorts: Youth and Shared Narcissisms," *The Narcissistic Condition,* ed. Marie Coleman Nelson (New York: Human Sciences Press, 1977), pp. 43, 28-29.

Page 106: Statement about the lack of "relevant models of competence" in the hippies' backgrounds is from J. R. Allen and L. J. West, "Flight From Violence: Hippies and the Green Rebellion," *American Journal of Psychiatry* 125 (3), 1968, pp. 364-70, quoted in Johnson, *A Last Temple of Resorts,* p. 45.

Pages 107-8: Expression "loose change" and the sense of self it conveys is from Sara Davidson, *Loose Change: Three Women of the Sixties* (Garden City, New York: Doubleday, 1977), pp. 238-41, 254, 312-13, 346, 349, 351, 357, 359, 366.

Page 108: Slater quote is from Philip Slater, *The Pursuit of Loneliness* (Boston: Beacon Press, 1976), p. 116.

Page 109: Johnson reference to "identity-shopping" is from Johnson, *A Last Temple of Resorts,* p. 54.

Page 110: Extract about dependency trends of "identity-shoppers" is from Edith Jacobson, *The Self and The Object World* (New York: International Universities Press, 1964), p. 201, quoted in Johnson, *A Last Temple of Resorts,* p. 54.

Page 111: Account of TM conference at Squaw Valley is from Special to the *New York Times,* "At Squaw Valley It's the Quiet Hour," *New York Times,* August 18, 1968, 1-78.

Page 111: Quote about TM attributed to *New York Times,* March 1975, is from Denise Denniston and Peter McWilliams, *The TM Book* (Allen Park, Michigan: Three Rivers Press, 1975), p. 1.

Page 112: Joe Namath and Franklin M. Davis quotes, ibid.

Page 113: Eleanor Coppola extract is from Eleanor Coppola, *Notes* (New York: Simon and Schuster, 1979), reprinted in *New York Times Magazine,* August 5, 1979, p. 42.

Pages 114-15: Siddhartha extracts are from Hermann Hesse, *Siddhartha* (New York: New Directions, 1951), pp. 78-79, 145.

Page 115: Quote attributed to Hesse's biographer is from Ralph Freedman, *Hermann Hesse: Pilgrim of Crisis* (New York: Pantheon, 1979), reviewed by Peter Gay, "A Genius of Self-Regard," *New York Times Book Review,* January 21, 1979, pp. 24-45.

Page 116: Extract is from Hesse, *Siddhartha,* p. 125.

Page 117: Hendin quote is from Herbert Hendin, *The Age of Sensation* (New York: McGraw-Hill, 1977), p. 288.

Pages 117-18: Ibid., pp. 288, 289, 301.

Page 119: For a discerning and compassionate examination of how and why the youth movement became radicalized, see Kenneth Kenniston, *Young Radicals* (New York: Harcourt, Brace & World, 1968), quoted in Johnson, *A Last Temple of Resorts*, p. 50.

Pages 120-21: Johnson extracts on student protest are from ibid., pp. 50-51, 52.

Page 122: Hendin's account of young radicals is from Hendin, *The Age of Sensation*, pp. 303-4.

Pages 124-27: Reich's quotes and extracts are from Charles A. Reich, *The Greening of America* (New York: Random, 1970; Bantam edition, 1971), pp. 321, 289-90, 234-35, 394.

Page 130: The essentials of psychological well-being provided by work are from Daniel Yankelovich, "The New Psychological Contracts at Work," *Psychology Today*, May 1978, p. 47.

Page 133: The quotes from the *New York Times* article are from Tony Schwartz, "Decade of Change for 60's Youth Altered Living Styles But Not Some Attitudes," *New York Times*, August 13, 1979, A-15. Italics are mine.

Page 138: Friedan quote and extract are from Betty Friedan, *The Feminine Mystique* (New York: W. W. Norton Company, 1963; Dell edition, 1964), pp. 59, 293.

Page 143: Mitscherlich quote is from A. Mitscherlich, *Society Without The Father*, translated by E. Mosbacher (New York: Harcourt, Brace & World, 1963), p. 150, quoted in Johnson, *A Last Temple of Resorts*, p. 57.

7 THE SELFISH SEVENTIES

Pages 146-48: Tracy Johnston, "Who Else Is Looking for Mr. Goodbar?" *Ms.*, February 1978, pp. 24-26; 26.

Page 149: Extract illustrating the *feminist* mystique is from Jessie Bernard, *The Future of Marriage* (New York: World Publishing Company, 1972; Bantam edition, 1973), p. 318.

Page 150: E. Mavis Hetherington, Martha Cox, and Roger Cox, "Divorced Fathers," *Family Coordinator*, October 1976, reprinted in *Psychology Today*, April 1977, pp. 42-46.

Pages 152-53: Barbara Jacobs interview is from Lindsy Van Gelder, "Having It All— Do We?" *Ms.*, March 1978, p. 49.

Pages 153-54: Rollo May extracts are from *The Meaning of Anxiety* (New York: Ronald Press, 1950), pp. 128, 129. May explains in a footnote that the terms "autonomous" and "responsible" are placed in quotation marks because he does not believe that genuine autonomy is possible without corresponding responsibility.

Page 154: Information about members of the Academy of Women Achievers was quoted in personal communication by Karen Springhorn of the Colgate-Palmolive Company, cosponsor with the YWCA of New York City of the annual "Salute to Women in Business." In 1979, out of twenty-three women selected from those nominated by the participating corporations, sixteen were married (three were divorced and four were single), and all earned over fifty thousand dollars annually.

Page 155: Anonymous "Letter to the Editor" is from "Letters," *Ms.*, April 1979, p. 4.

Page 155: For an illuminating article on pathological confusion of power and love, see Michael Vincent Miller, "Intimate Terrorism," *Psychology Today,* April 1977, pp. 79–82.

Page 156: Recent studies reported by the National Center for Health Statistics show the prevalence of commitmentphobia among men and women of all age groups in the United States. Their data reveal three distinct trends: (1) *the continuing postponement of marriage by the young* (one-third more women aged 20 to 24 did not marry in 1978 as did in 1968, and the increase in the proportion of never-marrieds between 25 to 29 years of age was four-fifths of the 1968 figure); (2) *the continuing rise in the divorce rate* (an increase of 2 percent in 1979 over the rate for 1978); and (3) *the continuing decline in the remarriage rates of divorced men and women* (between 1978 and 1979, declines of 10 percent or more among divorced men and women aged 14 to 24 years, more moderate declines in the age group 25 to 44 years, and declines of over 10 percent for widowed men and women 65 years and over). While the marriage and remarriage rate based on the total population has increased each year since 1976 (this rate was 2 percent higher in 1979 than in 1978), the first-marriage rate for women continued its long decline. Except for 1972, this rate has declined every year since 1969. Between 1977 and 1978 the first-marriage rate declined for single men and women in every age group except for women aged 25 to 29 and for single men aged 30 to 34, and these increases were very small (about 1 percent). These data are from the National Center for Health Statistics' *Monthly Vital Statistics Report* (Advance Report), Final Marriage Statistics, 1978, DHHS Publication no. (PHS) 80-1120, vol. 29, no. 6, supplement (1), September 12, 1980; *Monthly Vital Statistics Report* (Provisional Statistics), Births, Marriages, Divorces, and Deaths for 1979, DHEW Publication no. (PHS) 80-1120, vol. 28, no. 12, March 14, 1980.

Page 158: Extract on narcissistic sexual behavior is from Otto F. Kernberg, *Object-Relations Theory and Clinical Psychoanalysis* (New York: Jason Aronson, 1976), p. 187.

Page 160: Newspaper account of singles bar circuit is from Ann Kolson, "Where Are They, the Dreammates in Singles Land?" *Philadelphia Inquirer,* December 31, 1978, F-1, F-8.

Page 171: Extract on the "cognitive vacuum" caused by the lack of parental expectations or standards is from Caryl Rivers, Rosalind Barnett, and Grace Baruch, *Beyond Sugar and Spice: How Women Grow, Learn and Thrive* (New York: G. P. Putnam, 1979), reprinted in *McCall's,* July 1979, "How Not to Do to Your Daughter What Your Mother Did to You," p. 140.

Page 188: Goffman quote is from Miller, "Intimate Terrorism," p. 80. For a more complete understanding of Goffman's position, see Erving Goffman, *The Presentation of Self in Everyday Life* (University of Edinburgh, Social Sciences Research Centre, Monograph no. 2, 1956, 1958; Anchor edition, 1959), pp. 1–16, 17–76, 208–37, 238–55.

Page 192: Extract from *The Women's Room* is from Marilyn French, *The Women's Room* (New York: Summit, 1977), p. 288.

Page 193: Quote about the individual as the basic unit of society is from Perry London, "The Intimacy Gap," *Psychology Today,* May 1978, p. 40.

Page 200: Erikson quote is from Erik H. Erikson, *Insight and Responsibility* (New York: W. W. Norton, 1964), p. 118.

Page 200: Frank Mankiewicz quoted in *Newsweek,* November 19, 1979, p. 95.

Page 201: Bronfenbrenner's views on fostering independence in the developing person appear in Urie Bronfenbrenner, *The Ecology of Human Development* (Boston: Harvard University Press, 1979), pp. 27-28, 288-89.

Page 203: Findings of 1979 survey of high school seniors is from Jerald G. Bachman and Lloyd D. Johnston, "The Freshman, 1979," *Psychology Today*, September 1979, pp. 79-87, 80.

Page 203: Hendin comment is from Herbert Hendin, *The Age of Sensation* (New York: McGraw-Hill, 1977), p. 331.

Page 204: Quote about ambitions of the class of '83 being limited to "the kind of things that they can count upon their fingers" is from G. Daniel Marino, "Letters," *Psychology Today*, December 1979, p. 9.

Page 206: Extract from *Future Shock* is from Alvin Toffler, *Future Shock* (New York: Random House, 1970; Bantam edition, 1971), pp. 321-22.

8 A NEW LOOK AT PERSONAL FULFILLMENT

Page 209: Jung quote is from Carl Jung, *Psychological Reflections: A Jung Anthology*, vol. 15, *Paracelsus the Physician* (New York: Pantheon, 1942), p. 143.

Pages 210-11: Description of theories of social and moral development is from Mussen and Eisenberg-Berg, *Roots of Caring, Sharing and Helping* (San Francisco: W. H. Freeman and Company, 1977), pp. 113-26; Jean Piaget, *The Moral Judgment of the Child* (Glencoe, Ill.: Free Press, 1965), pp. 1-103, 171-94, 195-325, 325-414; Lawrence Kohlberg, "The Development of Children's Orientations Toward a Moral Order: Sequence in the Development of Moral Thought," *Vita Humana*, 6 (1963), pp. 11-33; Henry W. Maier, *Three Theories of Child Development* (New York: Harper & Row, 1965), pp. 13-157; Erik H. Erikson, *Childhood and Society* (New York: W. W. Norton), pp. 44-92, 182-218, 219-34, 244-83, 359-69.

Page 212: Adelson extract is from Joseph Adelson, "Is Women's Lib a Passing Fad?" *New York Times Magazine*, March 19, 1972, p. 98.

Page 213: Erikson extract is from Erik H. Erikson, *Insight and Responsibility* (New York: W. W. Norton, 1964), p. 114.

Page 218: Catherine Breslin quote is from Catherine Breslin, "Waking up from the Dream of Women's Lib," *New York*, February 26, 1973, p. 31.

Page 219: Explanation of *self*-approval is from R. E. Goranson and L. Berkowitz, "Reciprocity and Responsibility Reactions to Prior Help," *Journal of Personality and Social Psychology*, 3 (1966), pp. 227-32, 228; quoted in Mussen and Eisenberg-Berg, *Roots of Caring, Sharing and Helping*, p. 5.

Page 222: Reference to Lansing Lamont's *Campus Shock* (New York: E. P. Dutton, 1979) is from Andrew M. Greeley, *Chicago Sun-Times*, August 24, 1979, p. 54.

Page 222: Quote about "the paradox of maturity" is from David C. McClelland, Carol A. Constantian, David Regalado, and Carolyn Stone, "Making It to Maturity," *Psychology Today*, June 1978, p. 53.

Page 223: Riesman quote is from Kenneth L. Woodward with Rachel Mark, "The New Narcissism," *Newsweek*, January 30, 1978, p. 9.

Page 224: Kennedy extract is from Eugene Kennedy, "The Looming 80's," *New York Times Magazine*, December 2, 1979, p. 112.

9 COMING OF AGE IN THE VALUES VACUUM

Page 227: Chris Edwards quote is from Christopher Edwards, *Crazy for God* (Englewood Cliffs, New Jersey: Prentice-Hall, 1979), p. 13.

Page 229: Rabbi Davis is quoted in David Black, "The Secrets of the Innocents: Why Kids Join Cults," *Woman's Day*, February 1977, p. 168; statistics on number of cults in the United States and size of membership attributed to William Rambur, president of the Citizens' Freedom Foundation, ibid., p. 166.

Page 229: Chris Edwards extract is from ibid., pp. 231-32.

Page 230: Billy B. Rankin is quoted in Matt Clark, Frank Maier, and Marsha Zalarsky, "Who Can Be a Doctor?" *Newsweek*, January 21, 1980, p. 57.

Pages 231-32: Elkind quotes and extract are from David Elkind, "Growing Up Faster," *Psychology Today*, February 1979, pp. 38, 41-42, 45.

Pages 234-35: Vitz quotes and extract are from Paul C. Vitz, *Psychology as Religion: The Cult of Self-Worship* (Grand Rapids, Michigan: William B. Eerdmans, 1977), pp. 131-33; observation about students who go on to graduate training can be found in the footnote, pp. 132-33. Italics are mine.

Pages 235-36: Dr. Donald Oliver is quoted in Dena Kleiman, "When They Don't Want College Next," *New York Times*, January 6, 1980, EDUC 5.

Page 236: Clark Kerr is quoted in "Clark Kerr's Valedictory," *Time*, January 28, 1980, p. 55.

Page 236: Elkind extract is from Elkind, "Growing Up Faster," p. 38.

Page 237: Michener is quoted from James Michener, "The Revolution in Middle Class Values," *New York Times Magazine*, August 18, 1968, section 8, p. 20ff.

Pages 238-39: The profile of a "happy" young man is from a newspaper reprint of the *Esquire* article: Gail Sheehy, "The New Man: He Tries Hard to Take It Easy," *Philadelphia Inquirer*, February 3, 1980, I-1. Sheehy quotes are from "The Esquire Survey," *Esquire*, October 1979, pp. 26-33; 29-30; 29; 28.

Pages 239-40: Kohut extract on joy is from Heinz Kohut, *The Restoration of the Self* (New York: International Universities Press, 1977), p. 45; extract on the cure of self pathology is found on pp. 284-85.

Page 241: The psychiatrist quoted by Friedan is Andras Angyal, and the quote can be found in Betty Friedan, *The Feminine Mystique* (New York: W. W. Norton Company, 1963; Dell edition, 1964), p. 280.

Page 242: Extract of the study of one hundred male executives is from Henry A. Singer, "Human Values and Leadership," *Human Organization*, Spring, 1976, p. 86. Singer, of the Human Resources Institute in Westport, Connecticut, reported on his findings in "Getting Ahead," *Psychology Today*, October 1979, p. 6.

Page 242: Daniel Yankelovich from *Psychology Today*, July 1979, p. 31. In "Who Gets Ahead in America" Yankelovich claimed that this is one of the "logical but misleading messages" in *Who Gets Ahead?—The Determinance of Economic Success in America* by Christopher Jenks and eleven colleagues at the Harvard Center for Educational Policy Research (New York: Basic Books, 1979).

Pages 243-44: Extract on "Junie" is from Margaret Mahler in collaboration with Fred Pine and Anni Bergman, *The Psychological Birth of the Human Infant* (New York: Basic Books, 1967), p. 50; extract on "Jay" and "Mark" can be found on p. 70.

Page 245: The James Q. Wilson task force report is quoted in Berkeley Rice and James Cramer, "Comes the Counterrevolution," *Psychology Today,* September 1977, p. 59.

Page 246: The Martin Hoffman extract is from Martin Hoffman and H. D. Saltzstein, "Parent Discipline and the Child's Moral Development," *Journal of Personality and Social Psychology,* 5 (1967), p. 558; quoted in Paul Mussen and Nancy Eisenberg-Berg, *Roots of Caring, Sharing, and Helping* (San Francisco: W. H. Freeman and Company, 1970), p. 95.

Page 246: Description of Mrs. Fiedler's school board activities is from Barbara Kantrowitz, "She Put Her Body on the Line Before She Voted for School Spanking," *Philadelphia Inquirer,* February 9, 1980, A-4.

Page 247: Erikson extract is from Erik H. Erikson, *Insight and Responsibility* (New York: W. W. Norton, 1964), pp. 223-24.

Page 247: The Copperman findings are from Paul Copperman, *The Literacy Hoax: The Decline of Reading, Writing & Learning in the Public Schools & What We Can Do About It* (New York: Morrow, 1978), pp. 75-89. The Health, Education and Welfare study is from an agency report issued in April 1979.

Page 248: Description of DeSisto school is from "Getting That DeSisto Glow," *Time,* November 26, 1979, p. 98.

Page 251: Mother's response to *Newsweek* article on marijuana use is from Pat Lowery Collins, "Looking at Pot," *Newsweek,* January 28, 1980, p. 6.

Pages 252-53: An excellent statement of the case against marijuana use by teenagers was made in the NBC-TV documentary "Reading, Writing and Reefer," narrated by Edwin Newman and telecast on April 17, 1979. The Keith Stroup quote is from that documentary.

Pages 254-55: For a thorough report on the Cleveland study, see Natalie Gittelson, "What Should We Tell The Children?" *McCall's,* January 1979, pp. 153-56; *153.*

Page 255: The findings of the Hass study were reported in "Flaming Youth: A Hite Report on Teens," *Time,* October 8, 1979, p. 110.

Page 257: Merton quote from "Unanticipated Consequences of Purposive Social Action," *American Sociological Review* (December 1936), pp. 894-904, quoted in Solberg, *Riding High,* p. 3.

Pages 257-58: Adams extract on love and sexuality is from Jane Adams, "Sex and the Single Parent," *Harper's Bazaar,* July 1978, p. 115; quote attributed to the single mother is also on p. 115.

Page 259: Hamlet quote is from William Shakespeare, *The Tragedy of Hamlet, Prince of Denmark,* III, IV, 82, *The Complete Works of William Shakespeare,* Cambridge edition, William Aldis Wright, ed. (Garden City, New York: Doubleday, 1936), pp. 760-61.

Page 260: Breslin extract is from Catherine Breslin, "Waking Up from the Dream of Women's Lib," *New York,* February 26, 1973, p. 33.

Pages 260-62: Report on Jacqueline Jarrett case is from Barbara Kleban Mills, "It May Be Nice to Have a Man Around the House, But It Cost an Illinois Mother Her Three Kids," *People,* January 28, 1980, p. 93.

Page 262: Dostoevski quotes are from Fyodor Dostoevski, *The Brothers Karamazov, Great Books of the Western World,* 52, trans. by Constance Garnett (Chicago: Encyclopaedia Britannica, 1952), pp. 132, 131.

10 RATIONAL LOVE

Pages 265-66: Didion's observations on Jennifer Skolnik and others similarly affected by the women's movement are from Joan Didion, *The White Album* (New York: Simon and Schuster, 1979), pp. 116-18.

Page 267: Skolnik's musings about her own and her children's future are from Jennifer Skolnik, "Notes of a Recycled Housewife," *New York*, May 22, 1972, pp. 36-40; 40.

Page 267: Findings of researchers on the "myths of romantic divorce" are from E. Mavis Hetherington, Martha Cox, and Roger Cox, "Divorced Fathers," *Family Coordinator*, October 1976, reprinted in *Psychology Today*, April 1977, p. 46.

Page 268: Skolnik's account of her first postmarital affair is from Skolnik, "Notes of a Recycled Housewife," p. 39.

Page 268: Statistic on the duration of the in-love phase is from Dr. Elaine Walster, coauthor with William Walster, *A New Look at Love* (Addison-Wesley, 1978), quoted in Leslie Bennetts, "A Scientist's Love Story: Research on Passion and Beyond," *New York Times*, July 28, 1978, A-12.

Page 269: Analysis of three levels of connection in marital relationships is from H. V. Dicks, *Marital Tensions* (New York: Basic Books, 1967), quoted in Otto Kernberg, *Object-Relations Theory and Clinical Psychoanalysis* (New York: Jason Aronson, 1976), p. 129.

Page 272: Kaplan's observations on contemporary tendency to act out themes of the "second birth" are from Louise J. Kaplan, *Oneness and Separateness: From Infant to Individual* (New York: Simon and Schuster, 1978), p. 254.

Page 273: Sullerot's commentary on romantic love is from Evelyne Sullerot, *Women on Love: Eight Centuries of Feminine Writing*, trans. Helen R. Lane (New York: Doubleday, 1980), quoted in Françoise Giroud, trans. Richard Miller, "The Changing Modes of Love," *New York Times Book Review*, January 20, 1980, p. 24. A paper on the decline of romantic love and the reemergence of conjugal love was presented by Professor G. Marian Kinget at the International Conference on Love and Attraction, Wales, 1977.

Page 274: Kernberg's explanation of idealization as a possible barrier to falling and remaining in love is from Kernberg, *Object-Relations Theory and Clinical Psychoanalysis*, pp. 218, 216, 219-20; extract on the mourning processes involved in being in love can be found on p. 220.

Page 275: Balint's explanation of "genital identification" can be found in M. Balint, "On Genital Love," *Primary Love and Psychoanalytic Technique* (London: Tavistock, 1948), pp. 109-20, 115; quoted in Kernberg, *Object-Relations Theory and Clinical Psychoanalysis*, p. 218. Kernberg's comments on capacity for orgasm appear on pp. 217-18.

Page 277: Kernberg's observations about the relationship between normal sexual identity and normal identity formation are from Kernberg, *Object-Relations Theory and Clinical Psychoanalysis*, p. 220; quote about identifications involving value systems can be found on p. 210.

Page 277: The authority on geriatrics is Robert N. Butler, director of the National Institute on Aging; and the quote attributed to him is from a personal interview with Geraldine Spark, formerly of the family therapy unit at Eastern Pennsylvania Psychiatric Institute.

Page 280: Findings of researchers who studied voluntary childlessness among contemporary young women in America is from Nancy Kaltreider and Alan Margolis, "Childless By Choice: A Clinical Study," *American Journal of Psychiatry,* February 1977, vol. 134(2), 179–82.

Page 281: Timothy Leary, "In the Beginning Was Woodstock, and It Was Good," *Philadelphia Inquirer,* October 28, 1979, p. 14H.

Page 285: Enid Bagnold extract is from Enid Bagnold, *Autobiography* (Boston: Little, Brown, 1969), quoted in Jane O'Reilly, "Why Liberated Women Are Getting Married," *McCall's,* April 1978, p. 235.

Page 286: Kernberg extract on commitment is from Otto Kernberg, *Object-Relations Theory and Clinical Psychoanalysis* (New York: Jason Aronson, 1976), pp. 237–38.

11 PILGRIM'S PROGRESS

Page 287: Erikson's observation about "momism" is from Erik Erikson, *Childhood and Society* (New York: W. W. Norton, 1950, 1963), p. 295.

Page 303: Kernberg quote about "squeezing a lemon" is from Linda Wolfe, "Why Some People Can't Love," *Psychology Today* (June 1978), p. 57.

Page 303: For characteristics needed for mature love, see Otto Kernberg, *Object-Relations Theory and Clinical Psychoanalysis* (New York: Jason Aronson, 1976), pp. 215–39.

12 THE SELF-DIRECTED SOCIETY

Page 307: Winnicott observation on the experience of not being alone in the presence of the "good enough" mother is from D. W. Winnicott, "The Capacity to Be Alone," *The Maturational Processes,* pp. 29–36; 32.

Page 307: Sadler extract is from William A. Sadler, Jr., "The Causes of Loneliness," *Science Digest* (July 1975), pp. 65–66.

Page 308: Weiss viewpoint on loneliness is from Robert Weiss, *Experience of Loneliness: Studies in Emotional and Social Isolation* (Cambridge: M.I.T. Press, 1973), quoted in Zick Rubin, "Seeking a Cure For Loneliness," *Psychology Today,* October 1979, p. 85.

Page 308: Sheehy on independence in mature years is from Gail Sheehy, *Passages* (New York: E. P. Dutton, 1976; Bantam edition, 1977), chapter 25: "quite independent of other people's standards and agenda" (p. 510); "find themselves beginning to welcome detachment from others" (p. 506).

Pages 308-9: The material from the Alexandra Symonds paper is quoted in Elizabeth Elliot, "Are We Still Afraid of Success? Yes," *Working Woman,* May 1978, p. 37ff.

Page 310: Yankelovich observation about women's acceptance of male-dominated values in the workplace are from Daniel Yankelovich, "The New Psychological Contracts at Work," *Psychology Today,* May 1978, p. 49.

Page 312: Toffler quote about workers who have a mind of their own is from the adaptation of *The Third Wave* (New York: Morrow, 1980): "A New Kind of Man in the Making," *New York Times Magazine,* March 9, 1980, p. 26.

Page 312: Friedan quote is from Betty Friedan, "Feminism Takes A New Turn," *New York Times Magazine,* November 18, 1979, pp. 40ff., 102, 106.

Page 313: Toffler extract is from *The Third Wave* adaptation, "A New Kind of Man in the Making," p. 30.

Page 314: Shaw extract is from George Bernard Shaw, *Man and Superman* (Harmondsworth, Middlesex, England: Penguin Books, 1946), Act III, p. 151.

Page 315: Reactions to Pope John Paul II's visit are from John F. Clancy, "Why the World Makes a Leader of John Paul II," *Philadelphia Inquirer,* October 7, 1979, L-1, L-4.

Page 316: A report on Elizabeth Kübler-Ross's association with Jay Barham, founder of the Church of the Facet of Divinity, appeared in "The Conversion of Kübler-Ross," *Time,* November 12, 1979, p. 81.

Page 316: Winnicott statement about immorality is from D. W. Winnicott, *The Maturational Processes and the Facilitating Environment,* p. 102.

Page 316: Kerr extract is from Walter Kerr, " 'Faith Healer'—A Play That Risks All," *New York Times,* April 15, 1979, D-3; D-9.

Page 317: Freud quote about the fear of God's punishment is from Sigmund Freud, *The Future of an Illusion,* translated by W. D. Robson-Scott (New York: Doubleday, Anchor Books, 1957), p. 64; quote about the ultimate aims of the intellect can be found on p. 88.

Page 318: Extract is from *The Women's Room* by Marilyn French (New York: Summit Books, 1977), pp. 210–11.

Page 320: Winnicott comment on moral education is from Winnicott, *The Maturational Processes and the Facilitating Environment,* p. 97.

INDEX

ACKNOWLEDGMENTS

We gratefully acknowledge permission to reprint from the following:

"And Now, As Then, She Goes Home Crying" (Woman in the News) from Knight-Ridder News Service, the *Philadelphia Inquirer*, February 17, 1979. Used with permission.

The Psychological Birth of the Human Infant by Margaret Mahler in collaboration with Fred Pine and Anni Bergman, 1967. Reprinted by permission of Basic Books.

"The Man Who Named The Brat the Brat" by Maralyn Lois Polack from *Today Magazine*, the *Philadelphia Inquirer*, March 4, 1979. Used with permission.

Options: A Personal Expedition Through the Sexual Frontier by Marcia Seligson. Copyright © 1977, 1978 by Marcia Seligson. Reprinted by permission of Random House, Inc.

The World According to Garp by John Irving. Copyright © 1976, 1977, 1978 by John Irving. Reprinted by permission of the publisher, E. P. Dutton.

Insight and Responsibility by Erik Erikson, 1964. Reprinted by permission of W. W. Norton & Company, Inc.

The Female Eunuch by Germaine Greer. Copyright © 1970, 1971 by Germaine Greer. Used with the permission of McGraw-Hill Book Company.

Final Payments by Mary Gordon. Copyright © 1978 by Mary Gordon. Reprinted by permission of Random House, Inc.

The Feminine Mystique by Betty Friedan, 1964. Reprinted by permission of W. W. Norton & Company, Inc.

The Women's Room by Marilyn French. Copyright © 1977 by Marilyn French. Reprinted by permission of Summit Books, a Simon & Schuster division of Gulf & Western Corporation.

"A Temple of Last Resorts: Youth and Shared Narcissisms" by Ann Braden Johnson from *The Narcissistic Condition*, edited by Marie Coleman Nelson. Copyright © 1977 by Human Sciences Press. Reprinted by permission of Human Sciences Press, 72 Fifth Avenue, New York, New York 10011.

Notes by Eleanor Coppola, 1979. Reprinted by permission of Simon & Schuster, a division of Gulf & Western Corporation.

Siddhartha by Hermann Hesse, translated by Hilda Rosner. Copyright 1951 by New Directions Publishing Corporation. Reprinted by permission of New Directions.

The Greening of America by Charles A. Reich. Copyright 1970 © by Charles A. Reich. Reprinted by permission of Random House, Inc.

"Who Else Is Looking for Mr. Goodbar?" by Tracy Johnston from *Ms.* magazine, March 1978. Used with permission.

"Divorced Fathers" by E. Mavis Hetherington, Martha Cox and Roger Cox from *Psychology Today Magazine*, April 1977. Copyright © 1977, Ziff-Davis Publishing Company.

"Having It All—Do We?" by Lindsy Van Gelder from *Ms.* magazine, March 1978. Used with permission.

Anonymous "Letter to the Editor" from *Ms.* magazine, April 1979. Used with permission.

Object Relations Theory and Clinical Psychoanalysis by Otto Kernberg, 1976. Reprinted by permission of Jason Aronson, Inc.

"Where Are They, the Dreammates in Singles Land?" by Ann Kolson from the *Philadelphia Inquirer*, December 31, 1978. Used with permission.

Beyond Sugar and Spice: How Women Grow, Learn and Thrive by Caryl Rivers, Rosalind Barnett and Grace Baruch. Copyright © 1979 by Caryl Rivers, Rosalind Barnett and Grace Baruch. Reprinted by permission of G. P. Putnam's Sons.

"The Freshman, 1979" by Jerald G. Bachman and Lloyd D. Johnston from *Psychology Today Magazine*, September 1979. Copyright © 1979, Ziff-Davis Publishing Company.

Future Shock by Alvin Toffler. Copyright © 1970 by Alvin Toffler. Reprinted by permission of Random House, Inc.

"Waking Up from the Dream of Women's Lib" by Catherine Breslin from *New York* magazine, February 26, 1973. Used with permission.

"The Secrets of the Innocents: Why Kids Join Cults" by David Black from *Woman's Day* magazine, February 1977. Copyright © 1977 by David Black. Used with permission.

"Growing Up Faster" by David Elkind from *Psychology Today Magazine*, February 1979. Copyright © 1979, Ziff-Davis Publishing Company.

Psychology as Religion: The Cult of Self Worship by Paul C. Vitz, 1977. Reprinted by permission of William B. Eerdmans Publishing Company.

"The Esquire Survey" by Gail Sheehy from *Esquire* magazine, October 1979. Used with permission.

"She Put Her Body on the Line Before She Voted for School Spanking" by Barbara Kantrowitz from the *Philadelphia Inquirer*, February 9, 1980. Used with permission.

"Sex and the Single Parent" by Jane Adams from *Harper's Bazaar*, July 1978. Used with permission.

The White Album by Joan Didion, 1979. Reprinted with permission of Simon & Schuster, a division of Gulf & Western Corporation.

"Notes of a Recycled Housewife" by Jennifer Skolnik from *New York* magazine, May 22, 1972. Used with permission.

Autobiography by Enid Bagnold, 1969. Reprinted by permission of Little, Brown and Company.

The New York Times. Copyright © 1968/72/79/80 by The New York Times Company. Reprinted by permission.